SOCIAL CHANGE AND ECONOMIC LIFE INITIATIVE

Series Editor: Duncan Gallie

GENDER SEGREGATION AND SOCIAL CHANGE

THE SOCIAL CHANGE AND ECONOMIC LIFE INITIATIVE

This volume is part of a series arising from the Social Change and Economic Life Initiative—a major interdisciplinary programme of research funded by the Economic and Social Research Council. The programme focused on the impact of the dramatic economic restructuring of the 1980s on employers' labour force strategies, workers' experiences of employment and unemployment, and the changing dynamics of household relations.

ALSO PUBLISHED IN THIS SERIES

GENDER SEGREGATION AND SOCIAL CHANGE

Men and Women in Changing Labour Markets

Edited by

ALISON MacEWEN SCOTT

OXFORD UNIVERSITY PRESS
1994

Oxford University Press, Walton Street, Oxford OX2 6DP
Oxford New York Toronto
Delhi Bombay Calcutta Madras Karachi
Kuala Lumpur Singapore Hong Kong Tokyo
Nairobi Dar es Salaam Cape Town
Melbourne Auckland Madrid
and associated companies in
Berlin Ibadan

Oxford is a trade mark of Oxford University Press

Published in the United States
by Oxford University Press Inc., New York

British Library Cataloguing in Publication Data
Data available

Library of Congress Cataloging in Publication Data
Gender segregation and social change / edited by Alison MacEwen.
(Social change and economic life initiative)
Includes bibliographcal references.
1. Sexual division of labor—Great Britain—Case studies.
2. Sexual division of labor—Great Britain—Surveys.
3. Women—Employment—Great Britain—Surveys.
4. Great Britain—Economic conditions—1945–
I. Scott, Alison MacEwen. II. Series.
HD6060.65.G7G46 1994 306.3'615—dc20 94–2564
ISBN 0–19–827393–2 (cloth)
ISBN 0–19–827944–2 (pbk.)

1 3 5 7 9 10 8 6 4 2

Typeset by Hope Services (Abingdon) Ltd.
Printed in Great Britain
on acid-free paper by
Biddles Ltd.
Guildford & King's Lynn

FOREWORD

This volume is part of a series of publications arising from the
Social Change and Economic Life Initiative—a programme of
research funded by the Economic and Social Research Council.
The major objectives of the programme were to study the nature
and determinants of employer labour force policies, worker experiences of employment and the labour market, the changing
dynamics of household relations and the impact of changes in the
employment structure on social integration and social stratification in the community.

The research programme focused on six local labour markets:
Aberdeen, Coventry, Kirkcaldy, Northampton, Rochdale, and
Swindon. These were selected to provide contrasting patterns of
recent and past economic change. Three of the localities—
Coventry, Kirkcaldy, and Rochdale—had relatively high levels of
unemployment in the early and mid-1980s, whereas the other
three experienced relatively low levels of unemployment.

The data collected by the Initiative give an exceptionally rich
picture of the lives of people and of the operation of the labour
market in the different localities. Three representative surveys
were carried out between 1986 and 1987, providing fully comparable data across the localities. The first—the Work
Attitudes/Histories Survey—was a random survey of the non-
institutional population aged between 20 and 60, involving interviews with about 1,000 people in each locality. It provides
information on work histories, current experiences of employment or unemployment, and attitudes to work. This was taken as
the point of departure for the other two surveys, focusing respectively on the household circumstances of respondents and on the
policies of their employers. In the Household and Community
Survey approximately a third of the original respondents were
reinterviewed to develop a picture of their household strategies,
their organization of domestic work, their leisure activities, their

friendship networks, and their attitudes towards welfare provision. Where people had partners, interviews were carried out both with the original respondents and with their partners. The Employers' Survey was based on telephone interviews with senior management in the establishments for which respondents in the original Work Attitudes/Histories survey worked. A further non-random follow-up survey was carried out involving 180 of the establishments that had taken part in the initial survey. The details of the research design and sampling for the different phases of the programme are provided in an Appendix at the end of this volume.

In addition, related studies were carried out in individual localities, focusing in greater depth on issues that had been covered in the common surveys. These included studies of the historical context of employment practices, current processes of technical change, managerial/employee relations policies, industrial relations, gender segregation, the relationship between employer and employee perceptions of employment conditions, and household strategies with respect to labour market decisions and the organization of work within the household.

The team that implemented the programme consisted of thirty-five researchers drawn from fourteen different institutions. It brought together sociologists, economists, geographers, social historians, and social psychologists. The major common research instruments were collectively constructed through a series of working groups responsible for particular aspects of the study. The programme involved, then, a co-operative interdisciplinary, research effort for which there are few precedents in British social science.

DUNCAN GALLIE
National Co-ordinator and Series Editor

CONTENTS

LIST OF FIGURES

LIST OF TABLES

NOTES ON THE CONTRIBUTORS

BRENDAN BURCHELL is Lecturer in the Social and Political Sciences Faculty and Fellow of Magdalene College, University of Cambridge.

ROSEMARY CROMPTON is Reader in Sociology at the University of Kent at Canterbury.

SARA HORRELL is Assistant Lecturer in Economics and Fellow of New Hall, University of Cambridge.

JOHN LOVERING is Professor of Geography, School of Geography and Earth Resources, University of Hull.

ANN MARTIN works on the statistical modelling of anti-cancer drugs in Belgium.

ROGER PENN is Reader in Economic Sociology at the University of Lancaster.

JILL RUBERY is Senior Lecturer in Industrial Relations at the Manchester School of Management, UMIST, and Co-ordinator of the EC Network of Experts on the situation of women in the labour market.

KAY SANDERSON is Manager of the Women's Employment Enterprise and Training Unit (WEETU), Norwich.

HILDA SCATTERGOOD is Honorary Research Fellow at Lancaster University, engaged in research on ethnicity in the North-West.

ALISON MacEWEN SCOTT is Senior Lecturer in Sociology at the University of Essex, Colchester.

PETER SLOANE is Jaffrey Professor of Political Economy and Head of the Department of Economics, University of Aberdeen.

CAROLYN VOGLER is Lecturer in Sociology at the City University, London.

1

Gender Segregation and the SCELI Research

ALISON MacEWEN SCOTT

During the last decade or so, research on women and employment has increasingly focused on gender segregation, that is, the
fact that women tend to work in jobs and occupations that are
dominated by women and men in ones that are dominated by
men (Reskin and Hartmann 1986, Purcell 1988, Dex 1988, Walby
1988a, Crompton and Sanderson 1990). This segregation has
been shown to be strongly related to inequalities in pay, career
prospects, and employment protection. It has proved to be one
of the most profound dimensions of labour market inequality
(compared with, say, race or class) and the most enduring. Yet
the sex ratio of a job has only recently come to be taken seriously as a labour market variable, and then only in studies of
women and employment. This book shows, however, that it is an
essential datum for the analysis of employment whether or not
the research is specifically concerned with gender.

The Social Change and Economic Life Initiative (SCELI) studied six British labour markets between 1985 and 1988. Gender
was incorporated into this research at the outset.[1] In each of the
three surveys, on individuals, households, and firms, it was
always one of the variables included.[2] Because of this integrated
approach, gender appears as a topic for analysis in many of the
SCELI publications and this volume represents neither the first
nor the last word from SCELI on the relationship between gender and employment.

This book focuses on the gender segregated nature of occupations and jobs (sometimes known as the occupational sex ratio or
job segregation by sex). Each of the topics analysed—work
attitudes, career patterns, pay, employment contracts, employers'
recruitment policies, and so on—is systematically related to

gender segregation. This means that it is treated as a basic aspect of employment, along with other more conventional variables such as pay, skill, or hours of work. The results show that it is relevant not only to the analysis of women's employment but to the operation of the labour market and the structuring of work more generally.

Three concerns run through the chapters presented here. First there is a concern to push forwards our analytical understanding of the phenomenon of gender segregation. Despite the recent burgeoning of work on the subject, much of the literature has been descriptive rather than analytical and even the descriptions are incomplete because of the tendency to focus on women. There are still many unanswered questions, particularly regarding how the links between gender and job characteristics are to be unpacked, how gender segregation is incorporated into payment structures and job contracts, how sex-stereotypes affect managerial practices and employees' behaviour and how these stereotypes themselves are generated and maintained, how gender compares with other forms of differentiation such as occupational class, and how important are differences within gender groups compared with differences between them. Many of the chapters take up these questions in new and interesting ways.

The interdisciplinary nature of this book is of particular interest here. To date, research into gender segregation has been extremely diverse and fragmented by both discipline and theoretical orientation. The SCELI team was interdisciplinary and theoretically eclectic, and this book brings together an unusually rich mixture of approaches and methodologies. The combination is fruitful and provocative and reveals the extraordinary complexity of gender segregation itself.

A second concern in the book is methodological innovation. There are several aspects here: increased precision in the measurement of gender segregation, the inclusion of men (and systematic male–female comparisons) as subjects for investigation, the triangular structure of the three SCELI surveys, and the development of work and life history techniques as a method for incorporating longitudinal elements into the analysis.

The SCELI research has attempted to refine the measurement of perceived gender segregation by using a five-point rather than a three-point scale and by being more precise about whether it is jobs, work, or work-places that are being measured. These measures are outlined in the next section. The inclusion of men might seem obvious to many working in this field today, but we should remember that gender segregation is still popularly perceived as a 'women's problem'. Moreover, early studies of gender segregation were mainly concerned with women, and, perhaps as a consequence of this, there have been few data available for men. Studies of men's employment—which dominated industrial relations and labour market studies for so long—were not specifically concerned with gender segregation. Until recently, the subjective measure of gender segregation, which is now used as the common datum in research, was only available for women. In Britain, the pathbreaking Women and Employment survey of some 5,500 women (1980) was the first national survey to include a question on subjective perceptions of gender segregation at work (Martin and Roberts 1984), but it referred only to women.[3] This meant that the impact of segregation on the largest group in the labour force was ignored, and systematic comparisons between men and women—which are essential to the analysis of relative inequality—could not be made. The SCELI research is one of the first large-scale surveys to investigate men's attitudes and experiences of gender segregation in their jobs (as well as women's), and this book places male–female comparisons at the centre of the analysis.

Gender segregation in employment is the product of complex interrelationships between employers, employees, and households. The triangular structure of the three SCELI surveys (see Methodological Appendix) provides a unique opportunity to examine these linkages. Some of the chapters in this volume have concentrated on the survey of individual work attitudes and work histories, others have used the Employers' survey data, and one has linked up the survey of individuals with the households from which they came. As a collection, therefore, the chapters cover both demand and supply sides of the question and many attempt to link the two directly.

One of the novel aspects of the SCELI data is the development of a sophisticated instrument for the collection and analysis of life and work histories (for a detailed description see Marsh and Gershuny 1991). Longitudinal data are important in the analysis of gender and employment because women's labour-force participation is heavily influenced by the life cycle (Martin and Roberts 1984*a*, Dex 1987, Joshi 1984, Elias 1988). Longitudinal data can also be used for the analysis of movement within the labour market more generally (e.g. career patterns), and can uncover generational changes in employment (e.g. Elias 1988, Main 1988). The SCELI research provides an exceptionally rich source of longitudinal data for analysing these issues, and for the first time provides comparable information for men and women. Several of the chapters in this book have incorporated these data into their analyses (Scott and Burchell, Burchell and Rubery, Penn *et al.*).

The third concern that runs through the book is the relationship between gender segregation and social change. This is one of the most puzzling aspects of the subject, since gender segregation has tended to show more continuity than change. Aggregate segregation indices suggest that there has been little change over the years, despite substantial change in the structure of employment (e.g. shifts in industrial and occupational structure, fluctuating levels of unemployment, rising female participation rates and the introduction of sex discrimination legislation). Small changes have occurred in the sex composition of particular occupations but these have been offset by greater concentration in others, so the aggregate index has remained the same (Siltanen 1990).

The SCELI research was planned and carried out against a background of cyclical and structural change. Britain had moved from a period of low growth and high unemployment during the early 1980s to the 'Lawson mini-boom' of the mid-1980s which saw high growth rates and falling unemployment. However, these processes were unevenly distributed in Britain, being particularly concentrated in the South East. Their impact on the SCELI labour markets was also uneven; therefore comparisons between depressed ones such as Rochdale and buoyant ones such as Swindon provide a useful insight into the effect of these trends. The cyclical changes of the 1980s have also to be situated within longer-run processes of structural change involving, for example, the rising labour-force participation rates of women, the decline of manufacturing and the expansion of the service economy, and the deinstitutionalization of labour markets (the dismantling of internal labour markets within firms and the rise of casual and part-time employment). Most of these changes have occurred in the SCELI labour markets, although they have been more pronounced in some than in others.

The chapters towards the end of the book are particularly concerned with changing patterns of gender segregation: Scott's and Crompton and Sanderson's chapters analyse changes within three industries that have been protagonists in the rising service economy (retailing, banks, and building societies), while Penn *et al.* and Lovering look at the influences of industry and employer changes on gender segregation within particular localities. The common finding in most of these chapters is of a remarkable continuity in patterns of gender segregation despite cyclical and structural change.

Before turning to the chapters in more detail, let us consider the nature of the gender segregation measures provided in the SCELI research and the patterns of segregation which it reveals.

MEASURES OF GENDER SEGREGATION IN THE SCELI DATA

Gender segregation can be measured objectively or subjectively. Objective measures are constructed by calculating the observed sex ratio in an occupation, on the basis of survey or census data. This measure has been used successfully in a number of studies (e.g. Hakim 1979, Reskin and Hartmann 1986); its major advantage is that the degree of gender segregation can be measured very precisely and there is good comparability between studies, provided that the same occupational classification is used.

The major disadvantage is that the unit of measurement is the occupation rather than the job: gender segregation is highly sensitive to the way that occupational data are classified and aggregated. Segregation is most extreme at the most disaggregated level, that is the level of jobs or even job tasks. Occupations are clusters of jobs and most conventional occupational classifications are aggregates of these clusters. The process of aggregation can disguise the extent of segregation; for example, the occupation 'teacher' will aggregate mainly female primary schoolteachers with mainly male secondary teachers. 'Cleaners' will consist of male street sweepers and female office cleaners, and 'sales workers' include female sales assistants working on checkout tills as well as male salesmen selling cars and machinery. Some occupations are more homogeneous than others and suffer less from the effects of aggregation. Objective measures of segregation are best when they are based on highly disaggregated data, but it is often awkward to work with such high levels of disaggregation.

Subjective measures of job segregation can obviate these difficulties by asking about *job* segregation directly. However, much depends on the question wording, for there may be ambiguities about what is meant by a 'job'. This term can easily shade into less precise terms such as 'work' or 'work-place'. Provided that the wording is clear and precise, subjective measures of segregation can give better information than occupational sex ratios because the unit of measurement is more disaggregated. There are problems, however; informants' ability to distinguish degrees of segregation may not be very precise, and individual perceptions may vary even within the same job. Slight variations in the question wording can limit comparability between different studies.

Two subjective measures of gender segregation were used in the SCELI surveys: perceived job and work-place segregation. The perceived job segregation measure was based on a five-point scale: people were asked 'in general, is your type of job done almost exclusively by men, mainly by men, by a fairly equal mixture of men and women, mainly by women, or almost exclusively by women?' This contrasts with the Women and Employment survey which referred to 'work' rather than 'job' and used a three-point scale.[4] The work-place measure had four categories: working mainly with men, with a fairly equal mixture of men and women, mainly with women, and working alone.

In one of the studies (Scott and Burchell this volume) an objective occupational sex ratio measure was constructed, based on observed male–female proportions in the 161 three-digit key occupational unit groups (OUGs) of the Office of Population Censuses and Surveys (OPCS) classified in 1980. This was divided into five categories: almost all men (90–100 per cent men), mainly men (70–89 per cent men), mixed (31–69 per cent men), mainly women (11–30 per cent men), almost all women (0–10 per cent men). These different segregation measures are presented in Table 1.1.

At the level of the 161 OUG groups, there are high correlation coefficients between these three measures (Table 1.2), but at the

TABLE 1.1 *Different measures of gender segregation in SCELI*

	Degree of gender segregation					Total
	Exclusively men (EXM)	Mainly men (M)	Mixed (MF)	Mainly women (F)	Exclusively women (EXF)	
Perceived job segregation						
Men	44	39	15	1	a	99
	‿‿‿ 83 ‿‿‿			‿ 1 ‿		
Women	1	5	27	45	22	100
	‿‿ 6 ‿‿			‿‿ 67 ‿‿		
Perceived work-place segregation						
Men		66	22	8	(4)b	100
Women		13	27	54	(6)b	100
OUG sex ratio						
Men	34	30	23	11	2	100
	‿‿‿ 64 ‿‿‿			‿ 13 ‿		
Women	1	5	17	33	43	99
	‿‿ 6 ‿‿			‿‿ 76 ‿‿		

Note: N = 4,283 (2,492 men, 1,791 women).
a Less than 0.5%.
b Works alone.
Source: SCELI Six Areas Work Attitudes and Work Histories (WAWH) Survey.

level of individuals there are some discrepancies in the distributions. Most striking is the fact that perceived *job* segregation shows higher proportions of men in 'male' jobs and lower proportions of women in 'female' jobs, compared with the OUG sex

TABLE 1.2 *Correlations between three measures of gender segregation based on OUG groups*

	Sex ratio	Work-place segregation
Work-place segregation	0.919	
Job segregation	0.958	0.926

Note: N = 161 OUG groups.
Source: SCELI Six Areas WAWH Survey.

ratio. This may be because of the distinction between occupations and jobs mentioned above. Men's occupations may be less
homogeneous than women's, with some internal segregation
between men's and women's jobs within the occupation, particularly between the top and bottom positions. Women's occupations may have less internal differentiation, and be more mixed
at the level of jobs. Some of the discrepancy may be due to differences in individual perceptions. These perceptions may themselves be gender-biased. For example, men may tend to overstate
their presence in their jobs and women to understate theirs, especially in jobs where women are already a minority.

In comparison with the other two indices, the work-place measure shows less segregation: there are more women in 'male'
work-places and fewer in 'female' work-places. This is to be
expected in view of the fact that many women work with men in
their place of work, even if in 'female' jobs (e.g. secretaries, dental nurses). This variable is the least useful for the analysis of
occupational segregation because of ambiguities about how informants interpret 'work-place' (the office?, the department?, the
enterprise?), and because the anomalous category of 'works
alone' cannot be located on a gendered continuum. The most
useful index is that of perceived job segregation, and with few
exceptions, it is used in most of the analyses presented in this
book.

THE PATTERN OF GENDER SEGREGATION IN THE SCELI LOCALITIES[5]

The data on perceived job segregation in Table 1.1 show a high
degree of polarization of the sexes between 'male' and 'female'
jobs, with men much more highly concentrated in 'male' jobs
than women in 'female' ones, particularly at the extreme ends of
the spectrum: 83 per cent of men are in 'male' jobs and almost
half of these are in 'almost exclusively male jobs'; in comparison,
only about a fifth of women are in 'exclusively female' jobs and a
higher proportion are in 'mainly female' or 'mixed' jobs. This
table can be rearranged to form a comparative index of segregation, so that 'exclusively male' and 'exclusively female' jobs are
classified as high segregation, 'mainly male' and 'mainly female'

classified as moderate segregation and 'mixed' as low segregation, the residual being classified as 'other' or 'cross-sex' (see Tables 1.5 and 1.6). This shows that men are twice as likely as women to work in highly segregated jobs and only half as likely to work in unsegregated jobs.

Gender segregation is strongly related to occupational class, industry, and economic sector. Table 1.3 gives the data for social class according to the Registrar-General's classification and Table 1.4 according to the Goldthorpe classification. Amongst men, segregation is much higher in manual than non-manual work, whereas amongst women, it is as pronounced in low-skilled non-manual work as in manual work. We can see in Table 1.3 that the three manual classes have the highest concentrations of workers in the highly segregated categories, and these concentrations are particularly high for men. In fact, these three classes account for almost three-quarters of all men in exclusively male jobs. Most of them are concentrated in skilled manual work, and this class has a higher proportion of extremely male jobs than any other class.

About a fifth of women are in 'exclusively female' jobs, and most of them are in unskilled work at the bottom of the manual and non-manual hierarchies. Classes IIInm, IV, and V account for 78 per cent of the women in extremely female jobs. Thus there is a tendency for male exclusivity to be associated with highly skilled manual work and female exclusivity with low-skilled manual and non-manual work.

In non-manual work, there are higher proportions of men and women in mixed jobs, particularly in classes II and IIInm. On the whole, however, there are more women in this category than men. Major inroads into 'mainly men's' jobs are limited, and confined to the professional class. This corroborates other research on the increasing entry of women into the professions as a result of greater access to appropriate credentials (Crompton and Sanderson 1986). Thus 37 per cent of professional women work in 'mainly men's' jobs compared with 5–6 per cent in most other classes. However, it should be noted that this is an extremely small group of women (nine cases) and represents only 1 per cent of all working women.

The Goldthorpe classification gives similar results; the main difference between it and the Registrar-General's scale is the

A. M. Scott

TABLE 1.3 *Distribution of men and women by Registrar-General's social class and by perceived job segregation (%)*

Social class		Degree of segregation					Total	Col. %	N
		EXM	M	MF	F	EXF			
I.	*Professionals, and high admin.*								
	Men	35	44	18	3	—	100	7	182
	Women	4	37	26	23	11	101	1	25
II.	*Intermediate and managers*								
	Men	28	41	28	3	a	100	27	668
	Women	2	6	40	41	11	100	25	451
IIInm.	*Skilled non-manual*								
	Men	22	47	28	2	1	100	11	266
	Women	1	6	23	47	23	100	36	646
IIIm.	*Skilled manual*								
	Men	63	33	4	a	—	100	34	843
	Women	—	5	33	38	24	100	7	130
IV.	*Partly skilled*								
	Men	48	43	9	a	—	100	16	399
	Women	1	3	20	47	29	100	22	388
V.	*Unskilled*								
	Men	61	27	10	1	—	99	4	106
	Women	a	a	11	56	33	100	8	135
All men		44	39	15	1	a	99	100	2,464
All women		1	5	27	45	22	100	100	1,776

a = Less than 0.5%. Missing cases = 43.

Source: SCELI Six Areas WAWH Survey.

identification of separate categories for small proprietors and supervisors and technicians, and a more heterogeneous composition in the lowest class (semi- and unskilled manual workers). This class amalgamates classes IV and V of the Registrar-General's scheme, but more importantly, recent versions now include sales workers who were previously placed in class IIInm.[6] This is significant for women because of the large numbers of female sales assistants in this category.

TABLE 1.4 *Distribution of men and women by Goldthorpe social class and by perceived job segregation* (%)

Social class		Degree of segregation					Total	Col. %	N
		EXM	M	MF	F	EXF			
I.	*Service class*								
	Men	36	42	21	1	—	100	16	395
	Women	1	22	47	21	9	100	4	72
II.	*Junior service class*								
	Men	25	44	28	3	—	100	18	456
	Women	3	6	37	43	11	100	20	351
III.	*Routine non-manual*								
	Men	19	39	37	5	a	100	7	165
	Women	a	5	24	48	23	100	28	498
IV.	*Small proprietors*								
	Men	45	41	13	1	—	100	9	224
	Women	—	10	43	25	22	100	4	71
V.	*Supervisors and technicians*								
	Men	51	42	7	—	—	100	7	176
	Women	—	5	30	42	23	100	3	57
VI.	*Skilled manual*								
	Men	68	29	3	a	—	100	1	482
	Women	—	6	33	38	24	101	5	96
VII.	*Semi- and unskilled manual*[b]								
	Men	51	40	9	a	—	100	23	578
	Women	—	2	18	51	29	100	36	631
All men		44	39	15	1	a	99	100	2,476
All women		a	5	27	45	22	100	100	1,776

[a] Less than 0.5%. Missing cases = 31.
[b] Semi- and unskilled workers includes routine sales workers formerly placed in group III.
Source: SCELI Six Areas WAWH Survey.

The Goldthorpe scale shows only small differences in the pattern of gender segregation in the first three classes, except that women in the service class are much less successful in entering 'male' jobs. Women are poorly represented in the two extra classes in the Goldthorpe class scale, being only 25 per cent of both small proprietors and supervisors and technicians. Both of these classes are highly segregated, although women who are small proprietors are more 'mixed' than most. Class VII in this table shows high levels of segregation, as do classes IV and V in the previous table. In short, the two versions of the occupational structure present broadly similar patterns of gender segregation; I have provided both classifications because they are referred to by a number of contributors to this book.

Gender segregation is also strongly related to economic sector and industry. Table 1.5 presents the segregation data in terms of the comparative index, described above. It shows that segregation is much higher in private manufacturing than in private or public services, and this is so because of the predominance of men in 'exclusively male' jobs there (men are three-quarters of the manufacturing work-force and over half of them are in highly segregated jobs). Segregation is less extreme in public and private services; therefore as this sector increases its share of the total work-force, we might expect segregation to decrease. However, these aggregate figures conceal variations within particular industries. A detailed breakdown by industry shows that for men the most highly segregated industries are construction, energy and water, extractive, engineering, and transport industries, and the least segregated are distribution, hotels and catering, banking, and other services. Women are less segregated than men in all industries, most of them being in moderately segregated jobs. Distribution, hotels, and catering is the only industry where significant numbers of women are in mixed jobs. However, as various chapters in this volume will show, even within these industries, there is substantial segregation (see Scott, Crompton and Sanderson, Lovering).

Variations in the pattern of segregation within industries is reflected in the localities. Although the pattern of gender segregation is broadly similar between the SCELI localities, Swindon and Rochdale stand out in having lower proportions of highly segregated jobs than other areas (see Table 1.6). In both cases this is related to the decline in traditional manufacturing and the increase in service sector employment, either in public sector services (Rochdale) or in high-technology or financial services (Swindon). The two locality case-studies in this volume are based on these towns and provide an interesting case for comparison (Penn, Lovering).

We find the usual earnings differentials between men and

TABLE 1.5 *Perceived job segregation by economic sector* (%)

	Degree of gender segregation				Total	N
	High	Medium	Low	Other		
Private manufacturing[a]						
Men	58	35	6	[b]	99	936
Women	25	43	26	6	100	290
Private services						
Men	29	47	22	3	101	625
Women	19	44	31	6	100	717
Public services						
Men	30	39	29	3	101	534
Women	24	49	23	5	101	684

[a] Public manufacturing has not been shown because of small numbers (126 men and 29 women).
[b] Less than 0.5%.
Source: SCELI Six Areas WAWH Survey.

TABLE 1.6 *Perceived job segregation in different SCELI localities* (%)

	Degree of gender segregation				Total	N
	High	Medium	Low	Other		
Men						
Aberdeen	48	36	13	3	100	443
Coventry	49	37	12	1	99	390
Kirkcaldy	47	39	14	[a]	100	373
Northampton	44	40	15	1	100	449
Rochdale	37	44	17	2	100	401
Swindon	42	37	20	1	100	438
Women						
Aberdeen	27	43	24	7	101	339
Coventry	26	43	26	5	100	284
Kirkcaldy	23	53	20	4	100	262
Northampton	23	41	30	6	100	307
Rochdale	18	47	27	9	101	293
Swindon	16	46	34	5	101	299

[a] Less than 0.5%.
Source: SCELI Six Areas WAWH Survey.

women and between social classes. Taking the whole employee sample, women's average hourly earnings are 65 per cent that of men's; taking full-time employees only, the differential is 73 per cent.[7] The detailed breakdown within social classes by perceived job segregation shows that men earn more than women within each social class but their earnings tend to be even higher in more 'male' jobs (Table 1.7). Similarly, women earn less than men within each class, but their earnings are lowered further by

TABLE 1.7 *Average gross hourly earnings by Registrar-General's social class and perceived job segregation (£)*

Social class	Degree of segregation					All
	EXM	M	MF	F	EXF	
Professionals, high admin.						
Men	5.5	5.7	5.6	6.8[a]	—	5.6
Women	6.1[a]	4.3[a]	6.2[a]	5.9[a]	4.8[a]	5.1
Intermediate and managers						
Men	6.7	6.3	5.5	5.6	2.5[a]	6.2
Women	2.5[a]	4.7	4.2	4.1	3.7	4.1
Skilled non-manual						
Men	4.6	4.7	3.7	3.3[a]	2.2[a]	4.4
Women	4.5[a]	3.6	2.7	2.7	2.8	2.8
Skilled manual						
Men	3.9	3.8	3.4	—	—	3.9
Women	—	3.8[a]	2.5	2.5	2.6	2.6
Partly skilled manual						
Men	3.8	3.3	2.7	2.9[a]	—	3.6
Women	5.0[a]	2.9	2.3	2.3	2.2	2.3
Unskilled manual						
Men	3.2	3.0	2.3[a]	—	—	3.0
Women	1.8[a]	—	2.1	2.3	2.1	2.2
All men	4.4	4.6	4.6	5.0	2.3	4.6
All women	3.6	3.8	3.2	2.9	2.7	3.0
All classes	4.4	4.6	3.8	3.0	2.7	3.9

Note: N = 4,283 (includes part-time employees, excludes self-employed and over-time). Missing cases = 903.

[a] Less than 10 cases.

Source: SCELI Six Areas WAWH Survey.

being located in more 'female' jobs. Note that these figures are based on *hourly* earnings and thus control for part-time work. These data suggest that confinement to 'female' jobs has a depressive effect on earnings, and that as individuals move towards more 'male' jobs, even within the same occupational class, they will increase their earnings correspondingly (this hypothesis is examined by Sloane in this volume).

Part-time work is highly feminized and contributes greatly to both segregation and earnings inequality: 44 per cent of women work part time compared with only 1 per cent of men. Both full-time and part-time women are concentrated in moderately segregated jobs (42 and 49 per cent respectively), but part-time women are much more likely to be in highly segregated jobs than full-time women (29 per cent compared with 17 per cent). About 45 per cent of part-time work is in semi- and unskilled work and a third is in clerical and sales work, leaving 15 per cent in intermediate occupations. However, within these categories part-time work is a variable proportion of the work-force. Generally speaking it is a higher proportion where the work is less skilled and where the jobs are most feminized (see Table 1.8). The issue of part-time work is considered in many of the chapters in this volume, and is the special focus of Chapter 6 (Rubery, Horrell, and Burchell).

The SCELI survey asked why informants thought their type of job was exclusively or mainly done by men or women. This was an open question and a coding scheme with sixty possible responses was developed at the pilot stage (thirty-three for 'men's' jobs and twenty-seven for 'women's' jobs). The high degree of detail in this code was in order to capture the full complexity of people's attitudes on this issue and to avoid categorizing the responses into common stereotypes. Theories which have tried to explain gender segregation have generally fallen into two camps: those that stress economic factors (such as skills and qualifications, domestic constraints of women, or employers' discrimination) and those that stress social factors associated with gender roles and norms. The latter group argues that recruitment is not just a process of individual decision-making but is influenced by social expectations governing the gender qualities men and women bring to their work and the types of jobs that are appropriate for them. These are normative influences and are

TABLE 1.8 *Proportion of work-force in part-time work by Registrar-General's social class and perceived job segregation*

Social class	Degree of segregation					All	%N
	EXM	M	MF	F	EXF		
Professionals, high admin.	0	2	0	0	66	2	a
Intermediate and managers	1	2	9	30	45	12	15
Skilled non-manual	0	4	25	44	47	30	34
Skilled manual	0	1	2	37	32	5	5
Partly skilled manual	2	3	41	1	71	31	30
Unskilled manual	5	0	46	85	86	51	15
All men	1	1	2	5	0	1	
All women	7	14	33	50	56	44	
All classes	1	2	19	47	57	20	100

Note: N = 3,818 (excludes self-employed).
a Less than 0.5%.
Source: SCELI Six Areas WAWH Survey.

based on social rather than individual characteristics, although the two are often combined. The influence of gender on work attitudes is a relatively new field of enquiry (cf. Hakim 1991, Scott and Duncombe 1992) and is taken up in a number of contributions to this book, especially the chapters by Vogler and Scott.

Table 1.9 shows the reasons given for why the informant's job is gendered in one way or the other. What is striking about these data is the low emphasis on skill, domestic constraints, or employers' hiring policies (these factors are only 10 per cent of the reasons for 'male' jobs and 17 per cent of those for 'female' jobs). Much more stress is placed on social factors relating to gender roles. As far as 'men's' jobs are concerned, both the 'male' elements of these jobs and men's masculine qualities are given high priority. 44 per cent of the responses are to do with the fact that 'men's' jobs are heavy, dirty, dangerous, or involve outdoor work; heavy work is far and away the most important factor, accounting for 73 per cent of the 'type of work' responses and 32 per cent of all responses regarding 'men's' work.

'Masculine' qualities involve such things as aggressiveness,

TABLE 1.9 *Reasons for gender segregation in 'men's jobs' and 'women's jobs' (multi-response)*

	%	
'Men's jobs'		
Skill	3	
Freedom from domestic constraint	3	10
Employer's policy	4	
Male type of work	44	
Masculine qualities	9	55
Social pressure	2	
Tradition	22	
Other	3	
No reason why women should not do it	10	
Total (N = 3,143 responses)	100	
'Women's jobs'		
Skill	5	
Domestic constraints	10	17
Employer's policy	2	
Low pay	11	21
Poor-quality job	10	
Feminine qualities/type of work	23	31
Social pressure	8	
Tradition	23	
Other	5	
No reason why men should not do it	3	
Total (N = 1,904 responses)	100	

Source: SCELI Six Areas WAWH Survey.

ambition, ability to exercise authority and cope with stress, a natural affinity with machines, and superior intelligence (!). These 'manly' qualities account for 9 per cent of the responses. A further 2 per cent concern social pressure, such as the fact that the work group is male and would not accept women, men would not accept a woman supervisor, and the public would expect a man in the job. These three factors, 'male' job characteristics, men's masculinity, and social pressure are 55 per cent of reasons given for the existence of 'male' jobs. Finally, we have the influence of tradition, which is mentioned in 22 per cent of the responses. This is illustrated by statements such as 'it's always been that way'. Often informants would add that there was no particular reason why it should be that way, for women would be able to do the job.

The reasons given for why a job is mainly or exclusively done by women also stress social factors and tradition, but they differ from the reasons given for 'men's' jobs in some respects. There is slightly more emphasis on conventional economic factors, although at 17 per cent this is still a low figure (surprisingly, domestic constraints are given relatively little importance (10 per cent)). Much more stress is placed on the fact that 'women's jobs' involve low pay and poor quality (boring, low-grade, low-status, subservient work), and hence are not attractive to men. A fifth of the responses mentioned this.

Feminine qualities and social pressures amount to nearly a third of the responses. Women's qualities include their caring abilities, the fact that they are 'better with people', the job resembles their domestic work, it involves dexterity, or it is 'not a masculine job'. Social pressures refer to the fact that the work-group consists of women, the public expects women in the job and the clients or customers are women. Finally, as in the case of men, tradition is cited in almost a quarter of the responses. In sum, 54 per cent of reasons are associated with tradition or gender roles and 38 per cent are directly or indirectly associated with economic factors, including low pay and poor quality jobs.

These data indicate that as far as employee perceptions and attitudes are concerned, gender segregation is strongly associated with social roles and traditional customs. These findings are similar to those reported earlier for women in the Women and Employment survey (Martin and Roberts 1984*a*). The question is, how far do these attitudes influence actual decision-making by employers and employees? Although there is a role for preferences in the theoretical literature, these are usually framed in terms of individual interests rather than social customs and expectations. There is clearly a need for a broader approach to be developed in the future which can show how these two elements interact.

SCELI APPROACHES TO THE EXPLANATION OF
GENDER SEGREGATION

There are many different theoretical approaches to the analysis of gender segregation, and I do not propose to review them here. Comprehensive surveys can be found in Blaxall and Reagan 1976, Amsden 1980, Reskin and Hartmann 1986, Purcell 1988, Dex 1988, Walby 1988*a*, Stromberg and Harkess 1988, Crompton and Sanderson 1990. The main issues concern the following: the characteristics of labour supply to 'male', 'female', and 'mixed' jobs, the job characteristics of these jobs, employers' policies and mechanisms of recruitment, and pay.

All these issues are addressed in this book. It is not easy to classify the chapters in terms of a particular focus, but, broadly speaking, the first three are concerned with labour supply, the last five with job structures, sex-typing and the pattern of demand for labour, and Chapter 5 and parts of Chapter 6 are concerned with pay.

Most of the chapters stress the importance of the domestic division of labour as a major determinant of gender segregation, either through the influence of marital status on pay (Sloane), the negative effect of breaks for full-time housework on long-term prospects (Burchell and Rubery, Scott and Burchell), or the development of 'sexist' attitudes that affect men's and women's orientations to work (Vogler, Burchell and Rubery, Scott).

The role of qualifications is addressed in a number of chapters, but with contradictory findings. Higher qualifications provide entry into less segregated jobs (Vogler, Scott), they are associated with less sexist attitudes (Vogler), and they play an important role in raising women's earnings (Sloane). Qualifications have been associated with the reshaping of firms' internal labour markets, opening up recruitment to women (Crompton and Sanderson, Scott). However, there is evidence of overqualification of women relative to men, which suggests that additional qualifications may not always give them a competitive advantage. Moreover, the use of formal credentials in recruitment does not preclude discrimination in the selection process (Scott, Lovering, cf. Curran 1988, Collinson *et al.* 1990).

Various authors have investigated how employers make use of

a differentiated labour supply as part of their survival strategy in the face of competition, and how this feeds into job structures and payment systems. Technological deskilling and the use of part-time workers are good examples of this (Rubery *et al.*, Scott, Lovering). However, some of the chapters point out that the sex composition of the labour-force is only one element in employers' strategies of labour use, and a change in the sex ratio of the work-force can be a by-product of other factors, such as technological upskilling (Penn *et al.*), the decline in internal labour markets and the movement to tiered entry into white-collar work (Crompton and Sanderson, Scott, Lovering), and the rise of alternative opportunities in the local labour market (Penn *et al.*, Lovering).

Most of the employer- or industry-focused chapters stress the importance of occupational sex-typing in the way jobs are defined and labour recruited into them (Scott, Crompton and Sanderson, Lovering). At this stage, it is not possible to say *why* this occurs, or how it influences economic decision-making exactly. Sometimes it constrains employers, and other times it dovetails with other strategies. Much of it reflects inertia in the labour market. These data complement the reasons given by employees for gender segregation, which also stressed gender roles. Clearly, gender ideology strongly permeates the labour market as well as the family.

GENDER SEGREGATION AND SOCIAL CHANGE

As already indicated, the 1980s saw many processes of cyclical and structural change which might be thought to affect patterns of gender segregation. From the demand side, these include: variations in the tightness of the labour market (as reflected in levels of open unemployment), changes in the sectoral composition of employment, and the associated switch from the rigidified, regulated labour markets of traditional manufacturing industries to the more casualized and flexible forms of employment (including part-time work) typical of many service industries. Also relevant are the continuing concentration within many industries, the professionalization of many white-collar occupations, the increased reliance on formal credentials as mechanisms of recruitment, and the opening up of firms' internal labour markets to external recruits via tiered entry ports. Last but not least, there is increased pressure from equal opportunities legislation to limit discrimination in recruitment, promotion, and pay. The effect of these processes on gender segregation is examined in Chapters 7–10.

From the supply side, we have the increased labour-force participation of married women, the improvement in the quality and quantity of female qualifications, and the increasing commitment of women to long-term careers in the labour market. These processes have been analysed as outcomes in most of the chapters, rather than as changes *per se*, and their impact on labour market structures is analysed in various chapters throughout the volume. Note that changes in household structure and the domestic division of labour which underpin many of these supply factors are the subject of another SCELI volume (Anderson *et al.* 1994). Some brief conclusions on the effects of these changes in demand and supply are presented at the end of this chapter.

THE CHAPTERS

Vogler: what effect do sexist attitudes have on gender segregation?

In Chapter 2, Carolyn Vogler examines the association between gender segregation and 'sexist' attitudes. Sexism is defined by Vogler as a belief in the legitimacy of gender inequality. It is measured in a variety of ways, but mainly focuses on support for primacy of the male breadwinner role and the belief that gender characteristics are relevant to job performance. These attitudes are underpinned by the division of labour within the family and a naturalistic gender ideology which identifies masculinity with physical strength, dirt, and danger, and femininity with caring qualities and drudgery. Sexism is examined in relation to three factors that affect gender segregation: labour market participation, occupational sex-typing, and employer discrimination.

In general, there is a high level of sexism in the SCELI workforce, with women scoring as high if not higher than men on some items. In particular, there is a high level of consensus amongst both sexes about the primacy of the male breadwinning role. There is stronger support for this notion in the context of the home than the work-place; sexist attitudes relating to the work-place are variable by class and qualifications but attitudes towards domestic roles are much less affected by these factors. Furthermore, even where there is some *normative* support for greater equality within the home, actual practices revealed by time budget studies show discrepancies. The association between sexism and segregation is thus underpinned by strong ideological and behavioural divisions within the family.

Vogler shows that sexism is greater amongst men than women. Men are more likely to claim greater entitlement to work in times of high unemployment and a better aptitude for positions of responsibility. They are also more likely to explain gender segregation in terms of sex-role stereotyping, rather than individual abilities. Finally, there is more consistency in men's attitudes towards domestic and work-place roles and in their actual experience of segregation in both places.

Amongst women, while there is also strong support for the traditional domestic division of labour, there is a more energetic defence of women's entitlement to work and their suitability for positions of responsibility. There is also a greater tendency to explain the existence of female-dominated jobs in terms of women's domestic constraints or the poor quality of their jobs rather than inherent female characteristics. While just over a third of them do mention such characteristics as a reason for segregation, this is only half the proportion of men mentioning male characteristics. High degrees of sexism amongst women are associated not just with segregated work *per se* but with part-time work and class; the highest scores are amongst part-time women in the intermediate and working classes.

Vogler shows that sexist attitudes are strongly associated with segregation, although they play a small role as a determinant of occupational segregation when qualifications, industry, and class are controlled for (Tables 2.14 and 2.15). However, sexism is not independent of class and qualifications, since the higher and better educated social classes exhibit less sexism and also work in less segregated environments. Thus even if sexist attitudes only have a small independent effect on segregation, they are clearly intertwined with other variables that do. At the very least, sexism plays an important role in justifying gender inequality in the labour market and in interpreting it as 'natural'. This may explain why there is little pressure for change from either the demand or the supply side.

Burchell and Rubery: identifying segmentation in labour supply

The chapter by Brendan Burchell and Jill Rubery (Chapter 3) provides an analysis of the segmentation of labour supply in Northampton. The method used to distinguish segments is cluster analysis, which sorts individuals with an array of characteristics into meaningful groups. A novel feature of this analysis is that it includes attitudinal and work history data besides the usual individual and job variables.

The analysis finds five main clusters with clearly distinguishable characteristics in terms of advantage and disadvantage in the labour market. These are: 'the primary segment', 'stickers', 'female descenders', 'young and mobile males', and 'labour market descenders'.[8] Burchell and Rubery point out that although each of these clusters has some gender bias, gender does not 'map onto' the clusters directly. Moreover, the fact that there are women in all the clusters means that there are significant differences *amongst* women in terms of labour market disadvantage. The variable distribution of women between clusters hinges particularly on the degree of 'domestic interference', that is breaks in employment for domestic reasons. This shows up the importance of domestic constraints for women, which is emphasized in a number of chapters.

An important aspect of this analysis is the incorporation of a longitudinal element, that is the link between past labour market experiences, current position, and future outcomes. Burchell and Rubery are able to show the legacy effect of breaks from employment for future labour market position (see also Scott and Burchell). They also use these longitudinal data to explain job and pay satisfaction, which, surprisingly, is higher amongst the predominantly female 'stickers' than amongst the predominantly male primary segment. The authors argue that this is more explicable in terms of the work history than in terms of current employment situation. It reflects the fact that individuals adjust their expectations to their past and future constraints. Thus, the relevant job comparison for part-time women may be a previous period of unpaid 'inactivity' at home rather than the pay level of full-time women in the primary segment.

Burchell and Rubery argue that labour supply is segmented through the interaction between the domestic division of labour and personal career trajectories, and attitudes reflect and reinforce this interaction. They suggest that employers respond to these supply variations in terms of differentiated employment contracts, payment systems, and so on (see the analysis of part-time work in Chapter 6). The implication here is that in order to understand the dynamics of labour market segmentation we have to go beyond the current characteristics of employees and firms and look at the long-term interactions between the two.

Scott and Burchell: gender segregation and gendered careers

Longitudinal segmentation is analysed again in Chapter 4, by Brendan Burchell and myself. Here we look at the extent to which men and women are confined to similarly segregated jobs over their lifetimes, thus creating 'gendered careers'.[9] The chapter uses the work history data in two ways; first to look at individuals' career trajectories, and second, to analyse the nature of the job changes, comparing the characteristics of source and destination jobs.

The cross-sectional data on gender segregation by age show that the confinement of men to 'men's jobs' and women to 'women's jobs' is very polarized in all age groups. This might suggest that individual men and women would be confined to similarly segregated jobs for most of their working lives. However, the longitudinal data reveal that this is not so. Only a third of men are confined to 'own-sex' jobs during their working lives and half of women. Moreover, these proportions decline over time. Amongst over-40-year-olds, the figures fall to 27 and 45 per cent respectively.

Further analysis shows that these patterns are variable by sex and class; first, women's careers are more gender-confined than men's. Second, 'male only' careers are concentrated at the top of the manual and non-manual hierarchies, whereas 'female only' careers are at the bottom of these hierarchies. The analysis suggests that patterns of career segregation vary as a result of men's and women's different location in the occupational structure and their different trajectories through it over time. An 'only male' career can be the product of direct entry into skilled 'male' jobs or upwardly mobile movement through 'male' jobs, whereas an 'only female' career is associated with immobility and confinement in low-skilled jobs. 'Mixed' careers are associated with upward mobility, but men have more of these than women.

We look at job transitions in order to see whether a promotion (defined in terms of movement towards a 'better' job and higher pay) is associated with the gender-segregated nature of a job. We find that most promotions are concentrated within similarly segregated jobs (especially if they are 'male' jobs), but of the ones that do occur between jobs with different degrees of segregation, a promotion is more likely to occur when it involves a move towards a more 'male' job. Promotions are also variable by sex and class: men have more promotions than women and more of them take place at the top of occupational hierarchies where women are less well represented.

Finally, we look at the extent to which promotions are affected by the domestic cycle. Not surprisingly, we find that women's promotions are greatest before they take breaks for full-time housework, and fall sharply after they have taken these breaks. There is a strong legacy of 'domestic disruption' on women's careers. There is likely to be a class effect here in so far as professional women are better placed than women in other classes to avoid such 'disruption'. This chapter provides further evidence for the need to analyse labour market processes in longitudinal terms, especially where gender is concerned.

Sloane: gender segregation and the gender–wage differential

Chapter 5 presents an analysis of the gender–wage differential by Peter Sloane. Using multivariate regression techniques, he estimates the contribution of a range of personal and institutional variables to the logarithm of hourly earnings and the extent to which discrimination can be said to exist after controlling for them. The standard Mincer human capital model is applied, with such variables as qualifications, work experience, and training, as well as sex, marital status, and father's socio-economic group. Job variables are also included such as establishment size, public/private sector, unionization, job security, full time/part time, manual/non-manual, whether the job involves shiftwork, merit pay, and the degree of gender segregation in the job.

The full equation including both men and women shows the overwhelming importance of professional qualifications, which raise pay by 30 per cent, other things being held constant. This is followed closely by other educational qualifications; work experience and training are significant but less important. Of the other variables, white-collar employment, establishment size, and full time/part time are the most important, each raising average earnings by around 15–18 per cent. The gender segregation variable is significant even after controlling for sex, but the effect is relatively small: over 70 per cent female concentration in a job depresses pay by about 8 per cent and over 90 per cent female concentration by 10 per cent. These figures are comparable with the effects of unionization, apprenticeships, and on-the-job training. However, holding all these variables constant, gender is the most important contributor to earnings variation after professional qualifications, being male raising pay by 29 per cent. Therefore, while human capital variables are undoubtedly important in explaining variations in earnings, and to a lesser extent so are institutional ones, sex has a significant independent effect on earnings, after controlling for these variables.

Sloane goes on to show that an adequate explanation of the gender–wage differential requires the earnings functions of men and women to be estimated separately because the impact of some of the explanatory variables differs between the two groups. Moreover, there is an interaction between sex and marital status which contributes approximately 40 per cent of the overall sex differential in earnings. The rest of the chapter is dedicated to showing that discrimination rests not just on sex but on the combination between sex and marriage.

Separate earnings equations show some variation in the coefficients for different sex/marital status groups. For example, amongst all groups, the human capital variables are the most important determinants of earnings, but on balance, married women get a higher return to qualifications and less to experience than married men and they benefit more from unionization. Married men, on the other hand, benefit more from employment in large organizations and white-collar employment. Sloane asks whether some of these sex/marital status differences might arise from their different location in the occupational structure. He finds that controlling for occupational attainment the discrimination coefficient between married men and women actually rises. Pay differentials within occupational groups are roughly three times as important as differentials between them. The implication here is that women would benefit more from staying in the same occupational group and earning a married man's wage than from changing occupational group.

Rubery, Horrell, and Burchell: the gendering of part-time work

The chapter by Jill Rubery, Sara Horrell and Brendan Burchell takes up the question of the relationship between job structures and gender with reference to part-time work. The authors ask whether the distinction between part-time and full-time jobs is independent of gender. One way of looking at this is to ask how wide are the differences between male and female full-time jobs compared with the differences between female full-time and part-time work. The methodology involves comparing three categories of job, male full time, female full time, and female part time, and assessing whether the first two categories have more in common than the third (in which case a real difference in job structures can be said to exist) or whether the last two have more in common with the first (in which case gender differences are paramount).

Rubery *et al.* find that the situation is not clear cut either way. On most dimensions, there are clear differences between part-time and full-time work, after controlling for gender. Part-time work is associated with particular occupations and industries; it is less skilled in terms of the formal qualifications and training required for the job and part-timers' perception of the skill content of their job. Part-time jobs score significantly lower on the composite skill index, developed by the authors (see Horrell *et al.* 1990). They also involve little responsibility, have few promotion prospects, and have fewer fringe and welfare benefits. Similar characteristics are described in Scott's chapter on part-time work in retailing.

Two other aspects of part-time work deserve special mention because they contradict notions that it is more casual and flexible than full-time work. First, part-time work is not seen as particularly insecure work: 85 per cent of part-timers see their jobs as very or fairly secure. Second, it is not clear that part-time work is more flexible than full-time work in terms of working time. Rubery *et al.* show that working-time arrangements are extremely varied in terms of the number of hours, the amount of involuntary overtime required, the degree of choice over hours worked, whether work is scheduled for unsocial hours, and so on. Both full- and part-time jobs are extremely heterogeneous in these terms, and different *types* of flexibility are drawn on in both sectors.

However, despite these substantive differences between full- and part-time work, Rubery *et al.* find that part-time pay reflects gender rather than working-time differences. Controlling for skill, there are fewer differences between the hourly earnings of full- and part-time women than between full-time men and women. The authors conclude that part-time work is a distinct segment of the labour market with identifiable characteristics in terms of job content, skill, and market situation, as well as working-time arrangements. However, the levels of pay are depressed by the fact that it is women who are employed in these jobs.

Scott, and Crompton and Sanderson: gender segregation in retailing, banking, and building societies

Chapters 7 by myself and 8 by Rosemary Crompton and Kay Sanderson examine changing patterns of segregation in some of the key growth industries of the 1980s; retailing, banking, and building societies. These industries are significant for the analysis of gender segregation because they are major employers of women. Part-time employment is a feature of one of them (retailing) and is growing fast in the other two.

The industry focus of these chapters enables us to see how gender segregation has been affected by industry-specific factors such as product market conditions, industrial concentration, technological innovation, and changing employment structures. They both show how competition has led to the rationalization of labour use and increasing employment of women.

Both retailing and banking were originally male-dominated industries, with entry regulated by apprenticeships. The employment of women largely occurred as a result of growth in the volume of trade, increasing concentration in industrial structure, and shortages of male labour. In recent years, technological change has been important, producing increasing routinization and deskilling of both sales work and banking. This radically altered the structure of the labour process with an expansion of deskilled (female) jobs. These jobs have lately come to be threatened by the development of self-service shopping and banking.

Both industries originally had internal career structures leading to top management, although this was more highly developed in banking than in retailing. In both cases, internal promotion was largely reserved for men, designed to promote career progression over the lifetime in return for loyalty to the firm. With the expansion of banking in the 1950s and the need for cheap (female) labour to perform routine cashier operations, a low-skilled non-career work-force developed. This produced an internal labour market segmentation between career-track men and non-career women, with a common port of entry at the lowest level.

However, after the equal opportunities lobby was able to show that this discriminated against women, the banks moved towards specialized management development programmes and a system of tiered entry with different entry qualifications required at each level. In retailing too, the concentration of firms led to an increasing centralization of management, the development of specialized management traineeships, and tiered entry. Management trainees are now recruited directly from universities rather than promoted internally from lower levels.

Crompton and Sanderson argue that the switch to impersonal and formal criteria for entry and promotion has opened up opportunities for women in banking, although it has not resulted in desegregation. More women apply for jobs requiring low levels of qualification and more men apply for higher-level jobs, and these differences are reflected in recruitment. The change in the grading structure has created a short career hierarchy for women in clerical grades, but career track jobs are still monopolized by men. However, this situation may be changing as increasing numbers of young women are recruited to career-track positions. In both industries, career progression within management is contingent on mobility between different regional branches, which works against women with family commitments. Thus despite the adoption of more formal and non-discriminatory promotion systems, the odds continue to be stacked against women.

The situation in building societies is slightly different, in that the expansion of the industry during the 1970s and 1980s occurred alongside technological advances which permitted the use of semi-skilled (female) labour within a fragmented, branch network. Internal career structures did not develop to the same extent as in banking and there was multi-tiered entry from the start. In the building societies women are also largely confined to short-span local-based career hierarchies, while the men monopolize the top managerial positions.

In all three industries there is evidence that sex-typing continues to influence the way jobs are defined and this affects recruitment. Saleswomen are considered appropriate for the selling of certain types of products, and are thought to have special skills in dealing with certain types of customer; women in banks and building societies are considered to be especially good at dealing with clients who are unfamiliar with the world of finance. In all three cases, women managers are pushed towards staff management or the 'soft' side of commercial work. In contrast, men are still considered more appropriate for aggressive sales and high-level finance. Thus, even in these new, dynamic industries where access to employment and management is relatively open, segregation and an ideology of sex-typing persist.

Penn, Martin, and Scattergood, and Lovering: gender segregation in a locality context (Rochdale and Swindon)

Locality is an important aspect of labour market structure because in the short run, labour supply is geographically bounded and this brings firms and industries into relationship with one another; for example, rapid growth in one local industry may draw labour away from other sectors and a slump in the dominant industry will depress other sectors of the local economy. Rochdale and Swindon provide some particularly interesting similarities and differences in labour market structure and in traditions of female employment. Historically, both were primarily manufacturing towns, dominated by a single industry—textiles in Rochdale and railways in Swindon. Both suffered a massive reduction in manufacturing employment during the 1970s and 1980s, especially in the dominant industry, and both experienced growth in service sector employment. However, in Rochdale, ser-

vice sector growth was not sufficient to compensate for the collapse of manufacturing, so there were high levels of unemployment. In contrast, Swindon's growth in services was spectacular,
producing high rates of growth in the locality as a whole and low
levels of unemployment. There are important differences in the
nature of service sector growth in the two localities, Rochdale's
being based primarily on public sector services orientated to the
local economy (particularly local government and health)
whereas Swindon's was stimulated by national, private service
companies that had relocated from London (particularly in retailing and financial and business services). These towns exemplify
the different regional trends which accentuated the north–south
divide in Britain during the 1980s.

The two areas had different traditions of women working. In
Rochdale, women had always been involved in textile employment, whereas they were largely excluded from the railway industry in Swindon. As a result Rochdale traditionally had high
female participation rates compared with Swindon. The slump in
manufacturing combined with differential expansion in services
produced much faster growth in female employment in Swindon
than in Rochdale. This is reflected in the growth of part-time
employment, which was twice as high in Swindon as in Rochdale.
By 1987, part-time employment in Rochdale was only about a
third of total female employment, while in Swindon it was
around three-quarters. In summary, Rochdale exemplifies a local
economy that is still orientated towards manufacturing and is
depressed by the slump in this sector but is maintained somewhat
by public sector services. Women's employment there is concentrated in these two sectors and is mostly full time. Swindon, on
the other hand, illustrates the more modern trend towards ser-
vice-led employment, in which part-time jobs play an important
role.

The textile industry in Rochdale, which is the focus of enquiry
for Roger Penn, Ann Martin, and Hilda Scattergood in Chapter
9, has not only declined in real terms, but has become more male
and more full time. It thus provides an interesting contrary case
to the service industries discussed above, and the model of the
'flexible firm' postulated by Atkinson and others (Atkinson 1984,
OECD 1986).

Penn *et al*. argue that the slump produced some rationalization within the industry, with a shift to industrial textiles and incorporation of new technology, both of which favoured male workers. There was an upgrading of the skills of the already skilled labour-force but traditional customs continued to prevent women from entering this type of work. There was also a decline in unskilled, part-time labour, associated with the elimination of evening and night shifts. However, the main reason for the fall in female employment in textiles was the alternative opportunities that were developing in the service sector. There was increased demand for female labour here, and a shift in women's preferences towards these kinds of jobs. Life history data show that fewer and fewer young women were entering textile employment during the 1970s and 1980s.

John Lovering's chapter (Chapter 10) provides an analysis of gender segregation at the level of the enterprise, showing how this reflects shifts in the local economy in Swindon. His case-studies are drawn from manufacturing and services and represent 'traditional' and 'new' types of establishment. Patterns of gender segregation in the manufacturing firms are remarkably conventional, whether it is an old established bakery or engineering firm or the more modern pharmaceuticals or electronics firm. Gender segregation is extreme and women are concentrated in the more routine, less skilled jobs. Sex-labelling, word-of-mouth recruitment and a preference for single-sex work teams are the main factors here. Shiftwork and part-time work are of varying importance, and are as much supply driven as a device to meet fluctuations in demand. Competitive pressure varies between firms, as do the responses. In the bakery, the response was to increase output through technological change, which raised the ratio of skilled to unskilled labour, reducing the demand for women; in the pharmaceuticals firm, the response was to use part-time work as a device to meet short-run changes in demand; and in the electronics firm, it was to maintain product quality, which implied a strategy to develop a stable and skilled (male) labour-force.

The service firms have a variety of employment structures. Some establishments, such as the research institute, are biased towards the professions, others to low-wage, highly routinized jobs such as the fast food and retail firms. Yet others, in the hospital and the local authority have a variety of professions, semi-professions, and clerical work. Patterns of gender segregation vary between these different institutions, but tend to follow conventional lines. Service sector firms also differ greatly in their exposure to market conditions; the private sector firms are under great competitive pressure, but public sector institutions are hampered by a lack of autonomy in responding to local market conditions. In Swindon, the growth in private sector services was creating difficulties for the local authority and the hospital, who were unable to compete in terms of wages. This was producing a strategy to entice married women back into the market via supply-orientated hours of work and retraining schemes. In catering and retailing, competitive pressure was leading to a stress on quality of service and *de*casualization of the work-force.

Lovering's chapter shows that gender segregation can be found in both expanding and contracting industries, in all sectors of the economy and at all levels of the occupational hierarchy. These patterns persist despite changes in employers' practices. Sex-typing is widely prevalent and constrains the recruitment process, so that segregation becomes self-perpetuating. There is some evidence that employers are keen to break with old patterns and wish to promote new opportunities for women, e.g. via the creation of short-span internal career hierarchies. However, as Lovering says, this potential for greater equality will only be realized if women can take advantage of them. Domestic constraints may limit the equalizing impact of these new opportunities.

CONCLUSION

What overall picture of gender segregation can be gleaned from the SCELI research and what have been the effects of social change? There is no SCELI theory of gender segregation as yet. Nevertheless, certain common themes have emerged. As far as supply is concerned, there is an acknowledgement of the importance of individual characteristics (particularly attitudes, skills, and uninterrupted work experience), but this is combined with an emphasis on the way these characteristics are shaped by domestic constraints and gender ideology. There is also a stress on diversity within the male and female work-forces, associated with, for example, class, marital status, and the life cycle. As far as demand is concerned, there is an emphasis on the diversity of strategies used by employers in the face of increasingly competitive market conditions, and the importance of social or normative influences on the recruitment process. Perhaps the most distinctive feature of these chapters—given the tradition of presenting demand and supply theories as competing explanations of gender segregation (e.g. Blau and Jusenius 1976, Walby 1988*b*)— is a common emphasis on the need to analyse these factors in conjunction, with attention being paid to the ways in which each shapes the other.

As far as social change is concerned, the 1980s generated new opportunities for women, although new constraints too. Firms were exposed to increased competitive pressure, locally and internationally, and this led, on the one hand, to increased rationalization of labour use, deskilling, and the growth of low-grade, part-time work, and on the other hand to the opening up of internal labour markets, increased credentialism, and more open recruitment of highly skilled labour.

Some of these changes benefited women. Despite the low levels of pay, the growth in demand for part-time labour clearly suited many women with strong domestic commitments, as is indicated by high job satisfaction amongst this group. In the primary sector, the break-up of internal labour markets and increased reliance on formal qualifications in recruitment undermined traditional exclusionary practices which discriminated against women. The monitoring of this process by the Equal Opportunities Commission was an additional force for change, as Crompton and Sanderson's chapter shows.

The analysis of gender segregation by occupational class shows that women's best chance for access to good jobs was in the professions, especially in the public sector. However, this sector has been subject to deteriorating conditions because of increased financial constraint and work intensity. In the dynamic service industries, increasing scale and centralization had led to a professionalization of management, with increasing opportunities for women graduates. However, linked to this was the requirement for geographical mobility: an important constraint on married women, who found their career ambitions frustrated as a result.

Despite the economic changes of recent years, women's increased labour market participation, and changes in family structure, such as increases in divorce and single parenthood, there appears to be enormous stability in women's and men's domestic roles and the value system that underpins them. This book provides further evidence that women's role as primary childcarers causes severe disruption to their long-term labour market position. This is mirrored in the fact that male breadwinners increase their career opportunities over their lifetime and enjoy a substantial earnings premium in the process. (However, let us remember that this is a constraint for men as well as women; being the main breadwinner is a responsibility and creates it own pressures.)

The primacy of the male breadwinner role continues to structure the labour market in a variety of ways, mainly through the material and ideological differentiation of labour supply. In many cases, this is translated into employment structures and payment systems, which further rigidifies segmentation (e.g. part-time work). However, gender segregation is not based solely on primary or secondary earner status. There is much evidence that naturalistic beliefs about gender, embodied in notions of strength, dexterity, sensitivity, and so on, play a fundamental role in the sex-typing of jobs. These beliefs seem to be much more enduring than economic and family structures. Finally, there is substantial inertia in the labour market; traditional employment practices persist despite pressures for change. Patterns of gender segregation are sustained by 'tradition' as much as by the rational strategies of individual employers and employees. All in all, despite marginal changes within specific occupations, there is much less evidence of desegregation than might have been expected given the extent of social and economic change during the 1980s. The SCELI research suggests that this is mainly due to enduring inequalities in the domestic division of labour and deeply held beliefs about the nature of gender itself.

NOTES

1. In the preliminary formulation of the Initiative, the research agenda included female labour-force participation, occupational segregation, and the employment experience of men and women workers (see Gallie 1985: 518–20).
2. In addition to the three main surveys that formed the core of the

SCELI locality data, there were two free-standing projects on gender segregation conducted by Rosemary Crompton and myself designed to investigate the situation in specific occupations and industries outside the SCELI localities (see Chapters 7 and 8).

3. In addition to the 5,588 women who were interviewed, a small sample of informants' husbands were interviewed (799), but this was not a representative sample of the male labour-force.

4. The wording in the Women and Employment Survey was: 'Do you think of your work as . . . mainly women's work, mainly men's work, or work that either men or women do?' (Martin and Roberts 1984*b*: 54). This wording is directed at ideological definitions of work rather than actual job practices.

5. For parts of the analysis in this section, I have drawn on unpublished work by Carolyn Vogler.

6. This revision was made in 1986 in the light of Goldthorpe's application of his classification to women. See Goldthorpe and Payne 1986, and comments by Marshall in Marshall *et al.* 1988.

7. These figures are based on gross earnings net of overtime earnings, and exclude the self-employed.

8. These clusters are very uneven in size: 'the primary segment' is 40% of the sample, 'stickers' are 31%, 'female descenders' are 13%, 'young and mobile males' are 5%, and 'labour market descenders' are 5%. The remaining 7% fell into very tiny groups.

9. The term 'career' is used here to mean any sequential job trajectory; the popular connotation of vertical mobility is not intended.

REFERENCES

AMSDEN, A. (1980), *The Economics of Women and Work*. Harmondsworth, Penguin.

ANDERSON, M., BECHHOFER, F., and GERSHUNY, J. (1994) (eds.), *The Social and Political Economy of the Household*. Oxford, Oxford University Press.

ATKINSON, J. (1984), 'Manpower Strategies for Flexible Organizations', *Personnel Management*, Aug.

BLAU, F., and JUSENIUS, C. (1976), 'Economists' Approaches to Sex Segregation in the Labour Market', in M. Blaxall and B. Reagan (eds.), *Women and the Workplace*. Chicago, University of Chicago Press.

BLAXALL, M., and REAGAN, B. (1976) (eds.), *Women and the Workplace*. Chicago, University of Chicago Press.

COLLINSON, D., KNIGHTS, D., and COLLINSON, M. (1990), *Managing to Discriminate*. London, Routledge.

CROMPTON, R., and SANDERSON, K. (1986), 'Credentials and Careers: Some Implications of the Increase in Professional Qualifications amongst Women', *Sociology*, 20/1: 25–42.

—— —— (1990), *Gendered Jobs and Social Change*. London, Unwin Hyman.

CURRAN, M. (1988), 'Gender and Recruitment: People and Places in the Labour Market', *Work, Employment and Society*, 2/3: 335–51.

DEX, S. (1987), *Women's Occupational Mobility*. London, Macmillan.

—— (1988), 'Gender and the Labour Market', in D. Gallie (ed.) *Employment in Britain*. Oxford, Blackwell.

ELIAS, P. (1988), 'Family Formation, Occupational Mobility and Part-time Work', in A. Hunt (ed.), *Women and Paid Work*. London, Macmillan.

GALLIE, D. (1985), 'Directions for the Future' in B. Roberts, R. Finnegan, and D. Gallie (eds.), *New Approaches to Economic Life*. Manchester, Manchester University Press.

GOLDTHORPE, J., and PAYNE, C. (1986), 'On the Class Mobility of Women: Results from Different Approaches to the Analysis of Recent British Data', *Sociology*, 20: 531–55.

HAKIM, C. (1979), *Occupational Segregation*. Research Paper No. 9, Department of Employment, London, HMSO.

—— (1991), 'Grateful Slaves and Self-made Women: Fact and Fantasy in Women's Work Orientations', *European Sociological Review*, 7/2: 101–21.

HORRELL, S., RUBERY, J., and BURCHELL, B. (1990), 'Gender and Skills', *Work, Employment and Society*, 4/2, June: 189–216.

JOSHI, H. (1984), *Women's Participation in Paid Work: Further Analysis of the Women and Employment Survey*. Research Paper No. 45. Department of Employment, London, HMSO.

MAIN, B. G. M. (1988), 'The Lifetime Attachment of Women to the Labour Market', in A. Hunt (ed.) *Women and Paid Work*. London, Macmillan.

MARSH, C., and GERSHUNY, J. (1991), 'Handling Work History Data in Standard Statistical Packages', in S. Dex (ed.), *Life and Work History Analysis*. London, Routledge.

MARSHALL, G., ROSE, D., NEWBY, H., and VOGLER, C. (1988), *Social Class in Modern Britain*. London, Unwin Hyman.

MARTIN, J., and ROBERTS, C. (1984*a*), *Women and Employment: A Lifetime Perspective*. London, HMSO.

—— —— (1984*b*), *Women and Employment Technical Report*. London, OPCS.

OECD (1986), *Labour Market Flexibility: Report by a High Level Group of Experts to the Secretary General*. Paris, OECD.

PURCELL, K. (1988), 'Gender and the Experience of Employment', in D. Gallie (ed.), *Employment in Britain*. Oxford, Blackwell.

RESKIN, B., and HARTMANN, H. (1986) (eds.), *Women's Work, Men's Work: Sex Segregation on the Job*. Washington, DC, National Academy Press.

SCOTT, J., and DUNCOMBE, J. (1992), 'Gender-role Attitudes in Britain and the USA', in S. Arber and N. Gilbert (eds.), *Women and Working Lives*. London, Macmillan.

SILTANEN, J. (1990), 'Social Change and the Measurement of Occupational Segregation by Sex: An Assessment of the Sex Ratio Index', *Work, Employment and Society*, 4/1: 1–29.

STROMBERG, A., and HARKESS, S. (1988) (eds.), *Women Working*, 2nd edition. Mountain View, Calif., Mayfield.

WALBY, S. (1988a) (ed.), *Gender Segregation at Work*. Milton Keynes, Open University Press.

—— (1988b), 'Segregation in Employment in Social and Economic Theory', in S. Walby (ed.), *Gender Segregation at Work*. Milton Keynes, Open University Press.

2

Segregation, Sexism, and Labour Supply

CAROLYN VOGLER

This chapter is concerned with a rather neglected aspect of labour market segmentation and segregation: attitudes towards and perceptions of gender inequality. Most theories of gender segregation contain inferences about the role of attitudes in shaping and reflecting gender inequality; they receive most systematic attention in neoclassical consumer preference theory and very sketchy treatment in other theories, but in most cases it is unsatisfactory. In neoclassical theory attitudes are presented as part of the baggage of labour market decision-making accompanying the 'free' choices of workers 'shopping around' for jobs, whereas in structural theories they are seen as the outcome of cultural socialization or capitalist strategies. In both cases, however, attitudes are assumed to be unproblematic—homogeneous, self-evident, consistent, and rational. There has been relatively little systematic analysis of the different attitudes people hold towards gender segregation or the extent to which the components of such attitudes are consistent with each other. There has also been little investigation of the extent to which attitudes vary between different social and occupational groups, or the extent to which they are associated with different job situations. The wider question of how attitudes are formed and whether they affect segregation independently of structural factors cannot be addressed until these more descriptive aspects have been investigated.

This chapter presents an exploration of the relationship between attitudes towards gender inequality and gender segregation. Starting from the definition that attitudes are sexist if they are based on or endorse a belief in the legitimacy of gender

The author is grateful to Alison Scott for invaluable help with conceptual clarification and restructuring of the chapter.

inequality, it measures the degree of sexism expressed in relation to three main areas: labour market participation, occupational sex-typing, and employer discrimination. It then measures the degree of association between these sexist attitudes and perceived occupational segregation, and considers this association in the light of other predictors of segregation in a series of regression equations. We shall see that the Social Change and Economic Life Initiative (SCELI) labour-force shows evidence of considerable sexism and that it is strongly related to occupational segregation. Sexist attitudes are affected by the same variables as segregation itself, namely, class, qualifications, and sex. However, the regressions also show that attitudes have a relatively small *independent* effect when considered in conjunction with structural variables. Sexist attitudes and segregation are thus strongly interrelated with each other.

First, a note on the selection of the three areas mentioned above for the analysis of labour market attitudes. Participation rates, occupational sex-typing, and employer discrimination correspond broadly to the main theoretical focuses of work on gender segregation. While initially the debate was between 'supply' and 'demand' theories, where the former emphasized participation issues (neo-classical and cultural socialization theories)[1] and the latter discrimination (segmentation theory),[2] the current trend is towards examining the interdependence between the two. Occupational sex-typing refers to the process whereby wider sex roles become incorporated into the structure of jobs, thereby affecting both supply and demand (Reskin and Hartmann 1986, Murgatroyd 1982). A parallel and related process is the social construction of skill, whereby men's jobs come to be defined as skilled, while jobs done predominantly by women are regarded as unskilled. Cockburn (1988), for example, argues that male workers actively engage in the sex-typing of occupations, in order to protect their privileges from the encroachments of women. Once jobs have been culturally defined as appropriate to one sex, sexual harassment is used to prevent women crossing the gender boundaries.

More recently, Pringle (1988) has argued that men's dominance in the labour market is maintained with less coercion and more pleasure than is allowed in Cockburn's analysis, since power relations between male bosses and female subordinates mirror traditional familial and sexual relations outside work. Pringle argues that sexuality is central to work-place relations and crucial to definitions of selfhood, and that this meets with the approval of female employees. Far from wanting to remove sexuality and gender difference from the work-place, secretaries regarded it as one of the more pleasurable aspects of their jobs, adding excitement to an otherwise monotonous situation.

Another example of the interaction between supply and demand is the work of Humphries and Rubery (1984), who argue that employers are able to pursue the policies they do because of the division of labour within the household. While the struggle for a family wage, they argue, was initially part of a nineteenth-century working-class defence against an anarchic labour market which provided no floor to wages, the division of labour within the family and women's partial financial dependence on family income in turn not only provide employers with a cheap supply of female labour and a legitimation for pay inequalities, but also play an important role in structuring the attitudes and commitment to paid work of individual family members.

The implication of these latter pieces of work is that part of the reason for the remarkable persistence of gender segregation over time is that it is intimately linked to sexist attitudes. If, as Pringle (1988) suggests, those working in segregated jobs are sexist in their general attitudes to gender roles they are likely to approve of rather than challenge the structure of segregation in the labour market. In this way attitudes may not only play an important role in legitimating and stabilizing segregation in the labour market, but may also inhibit the possibility of shifts to desegregation. Even though processes on the demand side may change, particularly with the emergence of new occupations, the sexist attitudes of male and female employees may lag behind and prevent the potential for desegregation being realized.

MEASURES OF SEXISM

The chapter is based on the six-area core data from two surveys, the Work Attitudes and Work Histories Survey and the Household and Community Survey. Data on respondents' experiences of and attitudes toward gender segregation in the labour market, which was collected as part of the first survey, has been

linked to data on the division of labour within the home which
was collected as part of the second survey. Since the chapter aims
to link sexist attitudes to segregation in the labour market, the
analysis is restricted to those in employment. The economically
inactive and the unemployed are excluded.

The chapter is based on three measures of sexism constructed
from attitudinal questions relating to the three main substantive
areas in gender segregation analysis, namely labour market participation, occupational sex-typing, and employers' discrimination. These were constructed as follows.

Labour market participation

The Work Attitudes and Work Histories Survey contained a
series of questions focusing on the extent to which people
thought that gender differences in the division of labour within
the home—particularly men's responsibility for breadwinning—
should legitimately be associated with inequalities in men's and
women's participation in the labour market. Respondents were
asked how strongly they agreed or disagreed with each of the following statements:

1. Men are more suitable for positions of responsibility at
   work.
2. In times of high unemployment married women should stay
   at home.
3. I'm not against women working, but the man should still be
   the main breadwinner in the family.

Individuals' scores on these items were then aggregated to
form an index of *participatory sexism*, which may be regarded as
a measure of explicit recognition of women's secondary status in
the labour market. However, it was felt that even if people
thought that women should have equality in the labour market
with men, they would still be implicitly sexist on this issue if they
subscribed to traditional notions of the division of labour within
the home which constrained the possibilities of such equality. In
order to examine this possibility an index of *domestic sexism* was
constructed on the basis of items from the Household and
Community Survey.[3] Respondents and partners were asked
whether they thought the husband, the wife, or both equally
should have ultimate responsibility for

1. ensuring that the housework was done properly;
2. ensuring that the family had an adequate income.

These questions are distinct from the previous measures of participatory sexism, in that they focus on gender roles exclusively within the context of the home rather than linking them with gender roles in the labour market. (These data are subsequently compared with subjective perceptions about who *really* carried out these tasks and household time budget studies of what *actually* happened.)

Occupational sex-typing

Occupational sex-typing was measured in two stages. Respondents working in segregated occupations were asked to give up to four reasons why they thought their job was done exclusively or mainly by men or women.[4] Attitudes were considered to be sexist if they referred to biologistic or natural gender characteristics or if they referred to women's role in the domestic division of labour. A rough indication of the extent to which respondents approved of gender segregation was then obtained by analysing their reasons in relation to the indicator of participatory sexism.

Employer discrimination

Obviously it was not possible to ask directly about employers' discrimination in a survey of employees, and employers' responses would be unlikely to shed much light in view of current sex discrimination legislation. (It should be noted in passing, that this legislation refers mainly to discriminatory practices by employers, rather than to other types of sexism more widely exhibited in the work-place, such as occupational sex-typing).[5] However, it was possible to ask about the role of gender (as well as age and race) in recruitment and promotion, and thus obtain some information about *perceived* discrimination. Respondents were asked which of a range of factors they thought would make it difficult to get a job like theirs in their organization, and which were important in determining who was selected for a better job from among those doing their type of work within their organization. Being a man and being a woman were listed alongside a range of apparently gender-neutral factors such as experience, qualifications, age, preferences, experience in the organization, heavy domestic commitments, and personal contacts. These questions were used as subjective measures of direct discrimination in the labour market.

LABOUR MARKET PARTICIPATION

Participatory sexism

What is the pattern of participatory sexism amongst men and women? Is there any direct evidence that those with sexist attitudes to female labour-force participation are more likely to work in segregated occupations? Table 2.1 shows the proportions of men and women agreeing with or being indifferent[6] to each of the Likert statements on labour-force participation. Both men and women were most likely to agree that they were not against women working but the man should still be the main breadwinner in the family and somewhat less likely to agree either that in times of high unemployment married women should stay at home or that men were more suitable for positions of responsibility at work. Men were somewhat more likely than women (and nearly twice as likely as women in full-time employment) to see themselves as more suitable for positions of responsibility at work and to consider that in times of high unemployment they had a greater right than women to jobs. The fact that men appear to be less likely than women to agree that women's employment should not threaten the man's status as breadwinner (40 and 49 per cent respectively) is explained by a large difference between women in full- and part-time work. Men and women in full-time employment had similar attitudes on this issue, while part-time women were much more strongly in favour of women's secondary status in the labour-force. Overall then, women were much more likely to challenge men's dominance in the workplace and their greater right to jobs in times of unemployment, than to contest men's status as the main breadwinner within the family. Finally, there were clear differences between classes.[7] Men and women in the working class were much more likely to agree with each statement than those in the service class, although the same pattern of differences between men and women existed within each class.

TABLE 2.1 *Participatory sexism by class[a] and gender*

Likert statements	% of respondents agreeing with or indifferent to statements					
	Men	Women	Sig.[b]	Women		
				Full-time	Part-time	Sig.[b]
1. *Men are more suitable for positions of responsibility*						
at work	20	14	<0.00	11	18	<0.01
Service class	21	7	<0.00	7	10	n.s.
Intermediate class	17	14	<0.08	11	19	<0.01
Working class	22	18	<0.05	16	19	n.s.
2. *In times of high unemployment married women should stay*						
home	31	23	<0.00	19	28	<0.01
Service class	25	18	<0.00	17	21	n.s.
Intermediate class	31	22	<0.00	16	33	<0.01
Working class	35	26	<0.00	24	26	n.s.
3. *I'm not against women working but the man should still be the main breadwinner in*						
the family	40	49	<0.00	39	61	<0.01
Service class	29	30	n.s.	27	40	<0.01
Intermediate class	41	46	n.s.	40	57	<0.01
Working class	48	62	<0.00	52	67	<0.01

Note: N = 4,277.

[a] For definition of class see n. 7.   [b] Sig. = significance.

Source: SCELI Six Areas Work Attitudes and Work Histories (WAWH) Survey.

An index of participatory sexism was constructed by summing the scores for the three attitudinal items, producing a scale ranging from 3 to 15. This showed that men were significantly more sexist in their attitudes to women's labour market participation than women—the mean score for employed and self-employed men was 7.9 while for women it was 7.1. Sexism was also clearly related to qualifications, age, social class, and area. The lower people's qualifications the more likely they were to be sexist in their beliefs about women's labour market participation (Table 2.2) and those aged over 35 were more sexist than those under 35 years old (Table 2.3). Skilled and semi- and unskilled manual workers showed particularly high levels of sexism as did small proprietors, while the higher service class were markedly less sexist in their attitudes (Table 2.4). Finally the data also show a

TABLE 2.2 *Mean participatory sexism scores[a] by qualifications and gender*

Qualifications	All men	All women	Full-time women	Part-time women
None	8.8	7.9	7.4	8.3
Vocational	8.4	6.8	6.5	7.4
O-level	7.8	7.1	6.6	7.8
A-level	7.5	6.2	5.7	7.4
Non-univ. higher	7.6	6.4	6.0	7.0
Univ. degree	6.2	5.4	5.1	6.5
Significance	0.000	0.000	0.000	0.000

Note: N = 4,277.

[a] The higher the score the more sexist the attitudes.

Source: SCELI Six Areas WAWH Survey.

TABLE 2.3 *Mean participatory sexism scores by age and gender*

Age-group	All men	All women	Full-time women	Part-time women
Under 25	7.5	6.0	5.9	6.6
25–34	7.6	6.4	6.0	7.0
35–44	7.7	7.2	6.6	7.6
45–54	8.6	7.9	6.9	8.9
55+	9.3	8.6	8.0	9.2
Significance	0.000	0.000	0.000	0.000

Note: N = 4,277.

Source: SCELI Six Areas WAWH Survey.

clear Scottish effect (Table 2.5). Those in Kirkcaldy and Aberdeen were more sexist in their attitudes than those in other areas, although it was notable that in the two areas with no historical tradition of married women's employment—Swindon and Coventry—men and women were more sexist in their attitudes than those in Northampton and Rochdale, which did have such a tradition.

TABLE 2.4 *Mean participatory sexism scores by Goldthorpe class position*

Goldthorpe class position	All men	All women	Full-time women	Part-time women
Higher service class	7.4	5.8	5.6	7.2
Lower service class	7.2	6.0	5.8	6.5
Routine non-manual	7.8	6.8	6.3	7.9
Small proprietors	8.0	7.9	7.3	8.5
Lower technicians, supervisors	7.9	7.1	7.0	7.3
Skilled manual workers	8.4	7.7	7.4	8.4
Semi-/unskilled workers	8.5	7.8	7.3	8.1
Significance	0.000	0.000	0.000	0.000

Note: N = 4,277.
Source: SCELI Six Areas WAWH Survey.

TABLE 2.5 *Mean participatory sexism scores by area and gender*

Area	All men	All women	FT women	PT women
Kirkcaldy	8.7	7.7	7.2	8.3
Aberdeen	8.3	7.5	6.7	8.5
Coventry	8.0	7.2	6.7	7.9
Swindon	8.0	7.0	6.3	7.8
Northampton	7.4	6.6	5.9	7.4
Rochdale	7.4	6.5	5.9	7.2
Significance	0.000	0.000	0.000	0.000

Note: N = 4,277.
Source: SCELI Six Areas WAWH Survey.

An indication of the relative influences of qualifications, age, social class, and area can be obtained from the least squares regression reported in Table 2.6. This confirms that higher levels of sexism were associated with low qualifications and with manual work.

TABLE 2.6 *Regression on participatory sexism scores*

Variables	Beta	T	Significance
Men only (R² = 0.09; N = 2,049)			
No qualifications	0.28	7.2	0.0000
Vocational/O-levels	0.19	5.0	0.0000
A-levels/non-univ. higher	0.12	3.8	0.0002
Aged 55+	0.13	5.9	0.0000
Aged 45–54	0.10	4.4	0.0000
Kirkcaldy	0.14	6.0	0.0000
Aberdeen	0.13	5.4	0.0000
Swindon	0.08	3.4	0.0006
Coventry	0.07	2.8	0.0054
Skilled manual workers	0.06	2.7	0.0069
Semi-/unskilled workers	0.06	2.3	0.0209
(Constant)		25.05	0.0000
Women only (R² = 0.14; N = 1,838)			
No qualifications	0.29	6.9	0.0000
Vocational/O-levels	0.21	5.5	0.0000
A-levels/non-univ. higher	0.11	3.3	0.0011
Aged 45–54	0.20	8.1	0.0000
Aged 55+	0.18	7.6	0.0000
Aged 35–44	0.11	4.4	0.0000
Kirkcaldy	0.11	4.7	0.0000
Aberdeen	0.11	4.7	0.0000
Rochdale	−0.05	−2.3	0.0246
Semi-/unskilled workers	0.10	4.1	0.0000
Skilled manual workers	0.08	3.5	0.0006
Small proprietors	0.07	3.1	0.0020
Higher service class	−0.06	−2.6	0.0091
(Constant)		20.3	0.0000

Note: Variables entered into the equations were qualifications, age, social class, and area. For categories see Appendix 2.1.

Source: SCELI Six Areas WAWH Survey.

Participatory sexism and segregation

Chapter 1 has already presented a review of the factors that are associated with gender segregation, namely class, industry, qualifications, age, part-time work, breaks from employment, and locality. Here we shall examine the role of sexist attitudes relative to these other variables. Note that the index of *segregation* used in some of the tables is a four-category variable consisting of highly segregated, moderately segregated, unsegregated, and cross-sex occupations.[8]

Table 2.7 shows that sexism was clearly related to segregation in the labour market amongst both men and women. The mean sexism score for men in highly segregated jobs was 8.2, as compared with 8.0 for men in moderately segregated jobs, and 7.2 for men in unsegregated jobs. Women in highly segregated jobs scored 7.6, as compared with 7.2 among those in moderately segregated jobs, and 6.8 for those in unsegregated jobs.

TABLE 2.7 *Perceived occupational segregation and participatory sexism controlling for class and gender*

Perceived occupational segregation	Participatory sexism scores			
	All	Service class	Intermediate class	Working class
Men (N = 2,494)				
(Mean)	(7.9)	(7.3)	(7.9)	(8.5)
Highly segregated	8.2	7.5	7.9	8.6
Moderately segregated	8.0	7.5	8.1	8.3
Unsegregated	7.2	6.7	7.5	8.2
Significance	0.000	0.01	n.s.	n.s.
Correlation coefficient	0.1			
Women (N = 1,783)				
(Mean)	(7.1)	(6.0)	(7.1)	(7.8)
Highly segregated	7.6	6.3	7.3	8.0
Moderately segregated	7.2	6.1	6.9	7.9
Unsegregated	6.8	5.8	7.2	7.4
Significance	0.000	n.s.	n.s.	n.s.
Correlation coefficient	0.1			

Source: SCELI WAWH Survey.

TABLE 2.8 *OLS regression on the index of occupational segregation*

Variables	Beta	T	Significance
Men (N = 2,049; R^2 = 0.21)			
No quals./vocational/O-levels	0.25	7.7	0.0000
A-levels/non-univ. higher	0.13	4.3	0.0000
Routine non-manual workers	−0.14	−6.9	0.0000
Lower service class	−0.10	−4.6	0.0000
Skilled manual workers	0.09	4.0	0.0001
Construction ind.	0.23	10.2	0.0000
Metal manufacturing ind.	0.20	8.4	0.0000
Energy and water ind.	0.15	7.0	0.0000
Other manufacturing ind.	0.14	6.2	0.0000
Mineral extraction ind.	0.06	2.9	0.0036
Transport ind.	0.07	3.1	0.0020
Agriculture ind.	0.04	2.0	0.0424
Self-employed	−0.07	−3.3	0.0019
Aberdeen	0.06	2.8	0.0051
(Constant)		34.6	0.0000
Women (N = 1,838; R^2 = 0.11)			
Semi-/unskilled workers	0.20	6.8	0.0000
Routine non-manual workers	0.11	4.2	0.0000
Higher service class	−0.04	−1.9	0.0608
Dist. hotels/catering ind.	−0.12	−5.1	0.0000
Part-time work	0.09	3.7	0.0003
Swindon	−0.09	−3.8	0.0001
Rochdale	−0.05	−2.0	0.0407
A-levels/non-univ. higher	0.19	5.4	0.0000
No quals./vocational/O-levels	0.19	5.1	0.0000
Public sector	0.07	2.9	0.0000
Time out of employment	0.05	2.3	0.0223
(Constant)		22.9	0.0000

Notes: Non-significant variables for men were participatory sexism (T = 1.3) and the remaining area, age, class, and industry dummies; non-significant variables for women were participatory sexism (T = 0.07), self-employment, and the remaining age, area, industry, and class dummies.

Variables entered into the equations were qualifications, social class, industry, self-employment, age, and participatory sexism. The women's equation also included part-time work and the time spent out of employment. For categories see Appendix 2.1.

Source: SCELI Six Area WAWH Survey.

The data show that the overall relationship between sexism and segregation resulted from their common dependence on social class and qualifications. While the aggregate relation between sexism and segregation was significant at the 1 per cent level, the net relation between sexism and segregation was not significant at the 5 per cent level, after controlling for social class, qualifications, and other factors related to segregation, namely industry, area, self-employment, part-time work, and the length of breaks from employment. When class and qualifications were omitted from the equation, sexism was significant at the 1 per cent level, after controlling for these other factors (see Tables 2.8 and 2.9).

Why do class and qualifications have this effect? It could be argued that class and qualifications are linked to sexist attitudes and to labour market segregation through class cultures and the class processes that are involved in the structuring of jobs. If the regression on the index of gender segregation in Table 2.8 is compared with that on sexism in Table 2.6, it can be seen that class and qualifications were the main factors affecting both sexist attitudes and the likelihood of working in a segregated job. As qualifications and class position declined, people became more sexist in their attitudes and more likely to work in segregated jobs. Men with no qualifications, for example, and men in the working class (particularly skilled manual workers) were more sexist in their attitudes and more likely to work in segregated jobs. Similarly, women with no qualifications,[9] and women in routine non-manual and semi- and unskilled manual work were more sexist and more job segregated.

The finding that sexism and segregation are linked through class and qualifications is consistent with ethnographic studies showing how gender relations are involved in the structuring of class relations, which in turn strengthen and reproduce sexual divisions. Willis's (1977) study of how working-class boys come voluntarily and enthusiastically to take on the most subordinate and least desirable manual jobs is a graphic illustration of these linkages. He shows how the peer group culture of the working-class male conflates sexuality with class, so as to reverse the usual evaluation of unqualified manual work as undesirable and denigrating and qualified mental work as desirable and self-fulfilling. Masculinity is associated with hard, heavy, unqualified manual

TABLE 2.9   OLS regression on the index of occupational segregation excluding class and qualifications

Variables	Beta	T	Significance
Men (N = 2,049; R² = 0.14)			
Construction ind.	0.31	12.9	0.0000
Metal manufacturing ind.	0.29	11.2	0.0000
Other manufacturing ind.	0.21	9.0	0.0000
Energy and water ind.	0.19	8.2	0.0000
Transport/distribution ind.	0.12	5.0	0.0000
Banking/finance ind.	−0.05	−2.0	0.0422
Mineral extraction ind.	0.08	3.5	0.0004
Distribution, hotels and catering ind.	0.09	3.5	0.0004
Agricultural ind.	0.06	2.5	0.0107
Participatory sexism	0.07	3.2	0.0015
Aberdeen	0.05	2.3	0.0194
Aged 25–34	−0.05	−2.4	0.0171
Self-employed	−0.05	−2.4	0.0159
(Constant)		37.9	0.0000
Women (N = 1,838; R² = 0.05)			
Part-time	0.15	6.2	0.0000
Distribution, hotels and catering ind.	−0.12	−5.2	0.0000
Time out of labour market	0.09	3.6	0.0003
Swindon	−0.08	−3.5	0.0006
Aged under 25	0.07	2.9	0.0034
Participatory sexism	0.05	2.3	0.0216
(Constant)		36.3	0.0000

Notes: Non-significant variables (men) were the remaining area and age dummies; non-significant variables (women) were the remaining area, age, and industry dummies.

Variables entered into the equations were industry, self-employment, age, and participatory sexism. The women's equation also included part-time work and time spent out of employment. For categories see Appendix 2.1.

Source: SCELI Six Areas WAWH Survey.

labour, which is sought after as an arena within which to display masculine toughness and chauvinism, whereas qualifications are equated with femininity and mental work which is disdained and regarded as socially inferior. Sexuality therefore valorizes manual work, which is in turn seen as justifying men's breadwinner role and dominance within the household. As Cockburn (1983, 1988) shows, sexism and segregation are further reinforced in the work-place, as unions construct men's jobs as 'skilled', in order to maintain barriers and pay differentials against other groups of workers, particularly women.[10] As the counterpart to male work-ing-class culture, Willis (1977) describes women's working-class culture as being based on romanticism, collusion in their own domination, and an unquestioned acceptance of their primary role as domestic servicers. The way in which women's sexist atti-tudes are culturally related to segregation is illustrated in Pringle's (1988) work on secretaries, referred to earlier.

Amongst women, sexist attitudes were also related to segrega-tion indirectly, through their effects on two other variables which were in turn directly related to segregation, namely the length of time women had spent out of employment and part-time work. As can be seen in Table 2.10, after controlling for age, class, qualifications, and area, women who were more sexist in their attitudes had taken longer breaks from employment than those who were less sexist in their attitudes. While the main influence on the length of breaks from employment was age, it was notable that women in the non-skilled manual working class had spent more time out of employment than those in the higher service class.

Similarly, Table 2.11 indicates that women who were more sex-

TABLE 2.10 *OLS regression on the time women spent out of employment*

Variables	Beta	T	Significance
Women only (N = 1,838; R^2 = 0.28)			
Aged 45–54	0.52	17.1	0.0000
Aged 55+	0.41	16.1	0.0000
Aged 35–44	0.43	13.5	0.0000
Aged 25–34	0.15	5.0	0.0000
Semi-/unskilled workers	0.15	7.4	0.0000
Higher service class	−0.04	−2.1	0.0366
Lower technicians and supervisors	0.04	2.0	0.0420
(Constant)		−9.0	0.3674

Note: Non-significant variables were qualifications, sector of employment, and the remaining class and area dummies. For categories see Appendix 2.1.

Source: SCELI Six Areas WAWH Survey.

TABLE 2.11 *Logistic regression: parameter estimates for the odds of part-time work*

Variables	Multiplicative estimates
Women only (N = 1,960)	
Semi-/unskilled workers	6.8
Routine non-manual workers	2.1
Time out for employment	3.2
Aged under 25	0.2
Participatory sexism	1.8
Kirkcaldy	0.7
Hotels and catering ind.	1.7
Public sector	1.7
(Constant)	0.006
Minimum significance	0.02

Notes: The multiplicative estimates for time out of employment and participatory sexism were estimated for a move across half the range of these continuous variables (i.e. 201.5 and 6 respectively).

Non-significant variables were qualifications and the remaining class, area, and age dummies. For categories see Appendix 2.1.

Source: SCELI Six Areas WAWH Survey.

ist in their attitudes were also more likely to be in part-time work, after controlling for area, age, industry, social class, and time spent out of employment.[11] It should be noted however that the strongest influence on part-time work was social class. Women in the non-skilled working class, and to a lesser extent those in routine non-manual work, were more likely to be in part-time work than those in other classes. Finally women who had taken longer breaks from employment were also more likely to be in part-time work, as were those in the main child-rearing phase of the life cycle (aged over 25), those working in the public sector, those in the hotel and catering industry, and those who were self-employed.

Overall then, higher levels of participatory sexism were associated with working exclusively with others of the same sex, especially amongst men, manual workers, and the middle-aged. In addition to these variables, women's sexist attitudes were also related to segregation through their association with time spent out of employment and part-time work. Participatory sexism thus had an independent effect on people's chances of working in a segregated job, although the magnitude of the effect was relatively small compared with the effects of other structural variables, particularly industry and, to a lesser extent, locality.

Domestic sexism

Is there any evidence that those with sexist attitudes towards the domestic division of labour were more likely to work in segregated jobs? Table 2.12 shows the proportion of respondents giving traditional or sexist responses to the questions on the

TABLE 2.12 *Domestic sexism by class and gender*

Questions from the	% of respondents claiming that:					
Household and Community Survey	All men	All women	Sig.[a]	Full-time women	Part-time women	Sig.[a]
1. *The female partner should be ultimately responsible for*						
Housework	65	61	n.s.	44	80	<0.01
Service class	58	49	n.s.	44	77	<0.02
Intermediate class	75	61	n.s.	39	94	<0.01
Working class	66	69	n.s.	59	74	n.s.
2. *The male partner should be ultimately responsible for*						
breadwinning	56	44	<0.01	29	60	<0.01
Service class	50	29	<0.01	25	41	n.s.
Intermediate class	66	48	<0.03	27	77	<0.01
Working class	57	51	n.s.	40	55	n.s.

Note: N = 544.   [a] Sig. = Significance.
Source: SCELI Six Areas Household and Community (HC) Survey.

domestic division of labour in the Household and Community Survey. Two points should be noted. First, both men and women were more traditional in their attitudes to responsibilities for housework than to responsibilities for income generation. Approximately two-thirds of men and women thought women should be responsible for housework, while 56 per cent of men and 44 per cent of women thought men should be responsible for income. Secondly, men were much more traditional in their responses to the male breadwinning role in this survey than in the previous one, whereas women were slightly less so. It was also notable that women's relatively progressive views on who should be ultimately responsible for income were not complemented with similar views on who should be ultimately responsible for housework.

A summary index of domestic sexism was constructed by allocating a score of one for each traditional response[12] and then adding them together to produce a scale ranging from 0 to 2. The two indicators of participatory sexism (participatory and domestic) were strongly related to each other, and the correlation was slightly higher for women than for men (0.37 and 0.33 respectively). This was because men with less sexist attitudes on two of the participatory items (namely whether women should give up work in times of high unemployment and whether men should be breadwinners), had relatively high scores on the indicator of domestic sexism. In other words, men were less sexist in their attitudes to women's labour market participation than to gender roles within the home.

A first point to note about the index of domestic sexism is that men were more sexist in their attitudes to gender roles within the home than women (mean scores of 1.21 and 1.05 respectively). A second point is that domestic sexism was more homogeneous than participatory sexism across age and qualification groups, and across social classes and localities. Qualifications, for example, had no effect on domestic sexism until university degree level and age was only significant among those over 55 years (Table 2.13). Men in the intermediate classes (the self-employed and technicians) were more sexist than those in other classes while men living in Rochdale, which has a long historical tradition of married women's employment, were less sexist than men in other areas.

TABLE 2.13 *OLS regression on domestic sexism scores*

Variables	Beta	T	Significance
Men only (N = 281; R² = 0.09)			
Rochdale	−0.19	−3.3	0.0012
Coventry	−0.12	−2.0	0.0500
Univ. degree	−0.18	−3.1	0.0019
Small proprietors and lower technicians	0.13	2.2	0.0303
(Constant)		20.2	0.0000
Women only (N = 194; R² = 0.04)			
Univ. degree	−0.17	−2.4	0.0192
Over 55	0.14	2.0	0.0045
(Constant)		16.7	0.0000

Notes: Non-significant variables for men were age and the remaining class and area dummies. Non-significant variables for women were area, class, and the remaining educational and age dummies. For categories see Appendix 2.1.

Source: SCELI Six Areas HC Survey.

Domestic sexism and segregation

Were those with high domestic sexism scores likely to be working in segregated jobs? Domestic sexism was directly related to segregation amongst men but not amongst women. The mean score for men in highly segregated jobs was 1.4, as compared with 1.1 for men in moderately segregated jobs and 0.8 for those in unsegregated jobs. As can be seen in the regression in Table 2.14, domestic sexism amongst men had an independent effect on their chances of working in a segregated job after controlling for participatory sexism, class, qualifications, age, industry, area, and self-employment.[13]

While women's attitudes to gender roles within the home were not directly related to job segregation, they were strongly related to part-time work, which is in turn related to segregation. Women with traditional attitudes were more likely to work part time, whereas those with less traditional attitudes were likely to work full time (1.4 and 0.7 respectively). Domestic sexism amongst women was also found to have an independent effect on

TABLE 2.14   *OLS regression on the index of occupational segregation including domestic sexism*

Variables	Beta	T	Significance
Men only (N = 276; R² = 0.17)			
No qualifications/voc./O-levels	0.18	3.0	0.0031
Domestic sexism	0.16	2.9	0.0044
Skilled manual workers	0.16	2.8	0.0057
Lower service class	−0.16	−2.6	0.0092
Construction ind.	0.12	2.1	0.0334
(Constant)		19.3	0.0000

Note: Non-significant variables were participatory sexism, age, area, self-employment, and the remaining class and industry dummies. See n. 13. For categories see Appendix 2.1.

Source: SCELI Six Areas HC Survey.

their chances of working part time, after controlling for participatory sexism, social class, time spent out of employment, area, and industry (Table 2.15).[14]

In summary, amongst men there was a strong association between participatory and domestic sexism and being in a 'male'

TABLE 2.15   *Logistic regression: parameter estimates for the odds of part-time work including participatory sexism*

Variables	Multiplicative estimates
Women only (N = 210)	
Semi-/unskilled workers	6.0
Time out of employment	2.7
Participatory sexism	2.3
Domestic sexism	2.2
(Constant)	0.007
Minimum significance	0.05

Note: The multiplicative estimates for time out of employment and participatory sexism have been estimated for a move across half the range of these continuous variables (129 and 6 respectively). For categories see Appendix 2.1.

Source: SCELI Six Areas HC Survey.

working environment. Amongst women, however, the scores on both indices of sexism were lower than men's, and the effect of domestic sexism was mediated through part-time work. The stronger association between domestic sexism and part-time work suggests that attitudes were playing a different role in women's labour market behaviour than men's—more the result of compulsion than choice perhaps? Before turning to the analysis of other forms of sexism, let us briefly consider the role of domestic constraint on women's and men's attitudes towards the labour market.

Sexism and domestic constraint

The preceding analysis has shown that sexist attitudes towards women's status in the labour market and the home were related to job segregation and part-time work. It could be argued, however, that these attitudes simply reflect the constraints of a more traditional division of labour within the home and that the latter may play a more fundamental role in explaining both segregation and part-time work. Constraints resulting from an unequal division of labour within the home may force people into highly segregated or part-time work regardless of their attitudes. Dex (1988) for example, found that the presence of children, the lack of adequate childcare facilities, and inequalities in the domestic division of labour had a greater impact on the decision to work part-time than normative attitudes. It is therefore important to ask how far those working in segregated or part-time jobs were also living in households characterized by a traditional domestic division of labour and how attitudes mediated this linkage.

We have three measures of the domestic division of labour: first, subjective perceptions of who had ultimate responsibility for ensuring that broad areas of household work were undertaken adequately; secondly, subjective perceptions of who 'usually' undertook various tasks; and thirdly, time budget data for the week following the survey showing who actually did what. Respondents and their partners were asked (separately) about the distribution of responsibility regarding three broad areas of domestic life: ensuring that the family had an adequate income, ensuring the housework was done properly, and looking after children. Actual task performance was measured by asking who usually did the housework, the washing-up, the cooking, and washing clothes. Finally, the time budget data were analysed by calculating the proportion of the total housework, washing-up, cooking, and washing clothes undertaken by the man.

Turning first to perceptions of ultimate responsibilities, the data show that responsibilities for housework were related to men's but not women's chances of working in a segregated occupation. Men living in traditional households (in which wives were ultimately responsible for housework) were much more likely to be working in highly segregated occupations than those living in less traditional households (50 and 28 per cent respectively). Amongst women, ultimate responsibilities were unrelated to their chances of working in a segregated job, although they were related to part-time work. Women living in households with a traditional division of responsibilities for income were much more likely to be in part-time work than others.

The reality of who carried out specific tasks within the household was unrelated to job segregation amongst men and women, although, again, it was significantly related to part-time work. Women living in households where they were almost entirely responsible for washing-up, hoovering, washing clothes, and cooking were somewhat more likely to work part time.[15] The time budget data indicated that men who did a smaller proportion of the total washing-up, housework, and cooking in their households during the week following the survey were more likely to be working in highly segregated jobs than men undertaking a larger share, even after controlling for the wife's employment status (Table 2.16). However, amongst women, the proportion of the total household washing-up, hoovering, washing clothes, and cleaning undertaken during the week following the survey was unrelated to either job segregation or part-time work. The apparent contradiction between the subjective and time budget data may result from the fact that perceptions of who does what have a normative component related to women's employment status. It may be thought that when women are in full-time employment, they should do a smaller proportion of the total than when they are in part-time work, yet in reality, as the time budget data show, there is very little difference.

Finally, the impact of domestic constraint on job choice was measured directly. Respondents were asked how far they felt their personal choice of a job was influenced by a range of

TABLE 2.16 *Time budget data: proportion of the total household washing-up, housework, washing clothes, and cooking undertaken by men in partnership households*

Occupational segregation	% of the total undertaken by the man			
	Washing-up	Housework	Washing clothes	Cooking
Men only (N = 276)				
Highly segregated	32	27	8	35
Moderately segregated	48	31	15	39
Unsegregated	57	53	0	58
Significance	0.04	n.s.	n.s.	n.s.

Source: SCELI Six Areas HC Survey.

domestic constraints, namely their household's need for income, having to look after children, having to look after elderly or sick adults, their partner's job, possible loss of welfare benefits, their tax position, their partner's views about what they should do, and wanting to stay in the area. In the case of women, household constraints were unrelated to gender segregation, although they were related to part-time work. Those who felt their choice of a job was less constrained by the household's need for income than by having to look after children and wanting to stay in the area, were more likely to be in part-time work (53, 66, and 57 per cent respectively). Women with no household constraints on their choice of a job were most likely to be in full-time work (67 per cent).

Overall then the data show that men living in households with a more traditional division of labour were more likely to be working in segregated jobs, whereas women's domestic tasks and responsibilities were related to gender segregation indirectly through their effects on part-time work.

In order to assess the relative importance of sexist attitudes and domestic constraint in explaining people's chances of working in a segregated job, all the attitudinal and domestic constraint variables, together with class, qualifications, age, industry, area, part-time work, and the length of breaks from employment were regressed on the index of occupational segregation.

Amongst men, the domestic constraint variables were all insignificant, but their domestic sexism had an independent effect on job segregation, as shown in Table 2.14. This shows that men's domestic sexism was unconstrained by domestic factors, and that their attitudes were mutually reinforced by segregation in the work-place and in the home.

Among women domestic constraint and sexist attitudes were indirectly related to segregation through their effects on the length of breaks from employment and on part-time work. As can be seen in Table 2.17, domestic constraint, in the form of the presence of children and a husband's domestic sexism, were directly related to the time women spent out of employment, whereas their own attitudes were insignificant. Part-time work, however, was affected both by women's attitudes and by domestic constraint. Women who experienced childcare as a constraint on their choice of a job were more likely to work part time, as were women with higher participatory and domestic sexism (Table 2.18).[16]

TABLE 2.17 *OLS regression on the time women spent out of employment including sexism and domestic constraint variables*

Variables	Beta	T	Significance
Women only (N = 210; R^2 = 0.35)			
Aged 55+	0.47	7.1	0.0000
Aged 45–55	0.30	4.3	0.0000
Youngest child 5–15	0.44	5.6	0.0000
Youngest child aged 16+	0.32	4.4	0.0000
Youngest child under 5	0.20	2.9	0.0045
Hotels and catering ind.	0.18	2.9	0.0042
Husband's domestic sexism	0.13	2.2	0.0327
(Constant)		–0.155	0.8773

Note: Non-significant variables were qualifications, social class, area, industry, participatory sexism, domestic sexism, and the remaining domestic constraint variables (household's need for income, having to look after children, having to look after sick or elderly adults, partner's job, possible loss of welfare benefits, tax position, partner's views about what the respondent should do, wanting to stay in the area, partner's domestic sexism). For categories see Appendix 2.1.

Source: SCELI Six Areas HC Survey.

TABLE 2.18 *Logistic regression: parameter estimates for the odds of part-time work including attitudes and domestic constraint variables*

Variables	Multiplicative estimates
Women only (N = 210)	
Semi-/unskilled workers	7.1
Childcare constraint	5.2
Time out of employment	3.2
Participatory sexism	2.9
Domestic sexism	1.9
Household need for income constraint	0.5
(Constant)	0.003
Minimum significance	0.05

Note: The multiplicative estimates for time out of employment and participatory sexism have been estimated for a move across half the range of these continuous variables (129 and 6 respectively).

Source: SCELI Six Areas HC Survey.

These data show that a partner's attitudes and the presence of children were as important in explaining the pattern of women's labour market participation as their own attitudes, if not more so. These findings are consistent with the hypothesis that women's sexist attitudes are likely to be constrained by inequalities in the division of labour within the home. It cannot therefore be assumed, as human capital and cultural theorists have tended to do, that households are egalitarian consensual units within which both partners are equally free to realize their 'choices' on the labour market. Moreover, men's sexist attitudes had implications for women. By influencing the length of time women had spent out of employment, husbands were able to impose their sexism on women within the household as well as in the labour market, and this in turn affected the latter's chances of working in a segregated job.

OCCUPATIONAL SEX-TYPING

Another way in which sexist attitudes may be related to gender segregation is through sex-role stereotyping, in which jobs are thought to require specific male or female characteristics rather than 'gender-neutral' skills and training. The most common of these are physical strength, an ability to endure dirty or dangerous working conditions (men) and dexterity, caring qualities, and physical beauty (women).

As can be seen in Table 2.19, over half of all men thought their jobs were done exclusively or mainly by men because of the masculine nature of the job itself, the most frequently cited quali-

TABLE 2.19   *Sex-role stereotyping: reasons for gender segregation and mean participatory sexism scores*

Reasons for segregation	% of those in sex-segregated jobs giving reason			Mean participatory sexism score
	Highly segregated jobs	Moderately segregated jobs	Total	
Men only (N = 2,076)				
1. Masculine nature of job	66	46	57	8.4[a]
(a) Heavy work	55	39	40	8.5[a]
(b) Dirty work	15	8	10	8.5[a]
2. Male qualities	9	10	9	8.2
3. Training qualifications	9	9	9	7.3
4. Does not fit with domestic role	6	14	10	8.3
5. Male social environment	3	4	3	8.1
6. Employer's policy	6	4	5	7.4
7. Tradition	14	20	17	7.7
8. Women do not apply	15	15	15	7.7
9. No reason	9	9	9	7.6
10. Changing now	3	8	5	7.6

Reasons for segregation	% of those in sex-segregated jobs giving reason			Mean participatory sexism score
	Highly segregated jobs	Moderately segregated jobs	Total	
Women only (N = 1,199)				
1. Inferior quality of job	25	32	29	6.9
(*a*) Low-paid	15	18	12	7.0
(*b*) Boring	6	7	4	7.1
2. Training qualifications	9	7	8	6.8
3. Fits with domestic role	16	13	14	7.8[a]
4. Female qualities	31	25	27	7.4
(*a*) Like domestic work	9	8	6	8.4[a]
5. Not a very masculine job	13	10	11	7.7
6. Female social environment	10	11	11	6.9
7. Employer's policy	6	2	4	7.9
8. Tradition	17	24	22	7.1
9. Men do not apply	14	11	12	7.3

[a] Score above aggregate mean.

Source: SCELI Six Areas WAWH Survey.

ties of men's jobs being heavy and dirty work. If the 9 per cent who mentioned other male qualities are added in, we have two-thirds of all men who attributed gender segregation to specific male characteristics. A further 27 per cent gave traditional answers either by invoking 'tradition' itself or by mentioning domestic roles. Relatively few men gave contingent and potentially changeable reasons such as training, qualifications, or women not applying.

Women doing women's jobs were less likely to see their jobs as requiring inherently gendered characteristics and more likely to emphasize the inferior quality of their jobs, the fact that the job fitted in with women's domestic role and tradition. The most frequently cited inferior qualities of women's jobs were low pay, followed by subservient work, while the most frequently cited qualities of women were their ability to do domestic work and their dexterity. It was notable that men in jobs done mainly by women were more than twice as likely as women to mention low pay, marginally more likely to mention tradition, and far less likely to mention the inherent qualities of women themselves. Overall, the data support Cockburn's (1988) argument that men's jobs are seen as inherently or naturally masculine because they involve heavy work, whereas women's jobs are seen as more suitable for women because of their inferior quality, because of women's so-called natural skills and abilities and because they fit in with women's domestic roles.

The association between participatory sexism and occupational sex-typing was examined as follows: Table 2.19 shows the average participatory sexism scores for each reason given for segregation. Scores above the overall sample mean are noted. In the case of men's jobs, heavy and dirty work clearly had the highest participatory sexism scores whereas training, employer's policies, tradition, and women not applying all had below average scores. Turning to women's jobs, women's ability to do domestic work, the job fitting in with women's domestic role, and, somewhat surprisingly, employer's policies had relatively high participatory sexism scores, while the inferior nature of women's jobs, training, female social environment, and tradition had lower scores. Overall then, there was a high correlation between participatory sexism and occupational sex-typing, and the scores on both were higher for men than for women.

Occupational sex-typing and segregation

How far was occupational sex-typing related to segregation in the labour market? If we sum the total number of times respondents gave 'sexist' reasons for segregation we find that men were more likely to use sex-role stereotypes than women (66 and 38 per cent respectively) and that men giving sexist reasons were more likely than those giving non-sexist reasons to be working exclusively with other men (Table 2.19). While women's sex-role stereotypes were not related to the extent of segregation experienced in the labour market, women mentioning that the job fitted in with women's domestic role were more likely to be working part-time (88 per cent). Both men and women who explained gender segregation in terms of tradition and the inferior characteristics of jobs (which are in principle more open to change) were more likely to be working in moderately than highly segregated jobs.

Since men's work-based culture and peer groups are likely to have a particularly strong association with the gendering of jobs, regression equations were run on a subsample of men in highly and moderately segregated jobs to see how far male sex-role stereotypes had an independent effect on their chances of working in a segregated job after controlling for class, qualifications, industry, and area. As can be seen in Table 2.20, heavy and dirty work both had independent effects on the chances of working in a highly segregated job, after controlling for other factors. If we compare Table 2.20 with a second equation for the same

TABLE 2.20 *OLS regression on the index of occupational segregation including men's sex-role stereotypes*

	Beta	T	Significance
Men in highly and moderately			
segregated jobs only (N = 1,731; R² = 0.11)			
Heavy work	0.10	3.9	0.0001
Dirty work	0.06	2.5	0.0111
Skilled manual workers	0.08	3.3	0.0009
Lower service class	−0.05	−2.3	0.0229
Construction ind.	0.16	6.4	0.0000
Finance ind.	−0.07	−3.0	0.0027
Energy and water ind.	0.11	4.9	0.0000
Metal manufacturing ind.	0.09	3.7	0.0003
Other manufacturing ind.	0.09	3.8	0.0002
Mineral extraction ind.	0.05	2.0	0.0436
Rochdale	−0.07	−3.0	0.0030
No quals./vocational/O-levels	0.05	2.0	0.0499
(Constant)		80.0	0.0000

Note: Non-significant variables were participatory sexism, age, and the remaining qualifications, area, industry, and class dummies. For categories see Appendix 2.1.
Source: SCELI Six Areas WAWH Survey.

subgroup of respondents that omitted heavy and dirty work, we find that 'heavy' and 'dirty' work knocked out class VII (semi- and unskilled manual work), and reduced the coefficient for class VI (skilled manual work) from 5.5 to 3.9 (Table 2.21). This implies that, in effect, heavy and dirty work are mediating the relationship between social class and gender segregation, particularly among male manual workers.

TABLE 2.21   *OLS regression on the index of occupational segregation excluding men's sex-role stereotypes*

	Beta	T	Significance
Men in highly and moderately segregated jobs only (N = 1,731; R^2 = 0.10)			
Skilled manual workers	0.15	5.5	0.0000
Semi-/unskilled workers	0.09	3.2	0.0013
Lower technicians	0.05	2.1	0.0319
Construction ind.	0.19	7.5	0.0000
Finance ind.	−0.08	−3.1	0.0018
Energy and water ind.	0.12	4.9	0.0000
Other manufacturing ind.	0.10	3.9	0.0001
Metal manufacturing ind.	0.10	3.7	0.0002
Mineral extraction ind.	0.05	2.1	0.0372
Rochdale	−0.06	−2.6	0.0091
No quals./vocational/O-levels	0.05	2.1	0.0369
(Constant)		86.0	0.0000

Note: Non-significant variables were participatory sexism, age, and the remaining qualifications, area, industry, and class dummies. For categories see Appendix 2.1.

Source: SCELI Six Areas WAWH Survey.

Overall, then, sex-role stereotyping was more prevalent among men than among women and was independently related to segregation after controlling for class, qualifications, industry, and area. This was much less the case for women.

PERCEIVED EMPLOYER DISCRIMINATION

The reasons given by respondents for gender segregation (Table 2.19) indicate that discrimination by employers was generally perceived as being much less important than the inherent qualities of jobs and genders. Did this mean that respondents were generally unaware of discrimination in the labour market?

Both men and women were more aware of discrimination as a barrier to their own current jobs than to promotion in the internal labour market[17] but perceptions were strongly related to whether they worked in segregated jobs (Table 2.22). In the case of barriers to the respondent's own current job, almost half of all men and women working in highly segregated jobs were aware of gender as barrier compared with just under a quarter of those in moderately segregated jobs and only a twentieth of those in unsegregated jobs.[18] While those in unsegregated jobs were more likely to mention lack of qualifications, bad references, and being too young rather than gender, those in highly segregated jobs were more likely to mention gender than any of these factors.

A very similar pattern emerged in relation to perceptions of the main criteria for promotion in the internal labour market. Those in highly segregated jobs were more aware of discrimination than those in unsegregated jobs (Table 2.22). Those in highly segregated jobs also mentioned gender as often as seniority, whereas those in unsegregated jobs mentioned seniority much more frequently than gender. The implication is that as far as promotion is concerned, gender and seniority alternate in importance according to the degree of segregation.

A striking finding is that those who were aware of direct discrimination in relation to their personal position in the labour market did not necessarily disapprove of it. Even after controlling for the extent of segregation experienced in the labour market, those in highly and moderately segregated jobs who were aware of gender as a barrier to their personal position, were more sexist in terms of participation than those who were not aware of it, and thus may have regarded it as legitimate.[19] This relates to the finding that gender segregation is generally explained in terms of the inherent qualities of jobs and genders, which may also legitimate employer discrimination. Men who were aware of direct discrimination in relation to their current jobs, for example, were much more likely to explain segregation in terms of the inherently masculine qualities of their jobs than other men (74 and 48 per cent respectively), and women who were similarly aware of direct discrimination were marginally

TABLE 2.22 *Sexism and perceptions of employer discrimination by job segregation*

	Highly segregated jobs		Moderately segregated jobs		Significant differences in sexism score
	% giving response	Mean participatory sexism score	% giving response	Mean participatory sexism score	
Barriers to current job					
Men mentioning being a woman	48	8.4	24	8.4	0.006
Women mentioning being a man	40	7.8	22	7.9	0.000
Factors affecting promotion in the internal labour market					
Men mentioning being a man	22	8.5	15	8.4	n.s.
Women mentioning being a woman	15	7.7	10	8.3	0.001

Note: N = 3,265.

Source: SCELI Six Areas WAWH Survey.

more likely to explain segregation in terms of the special qualities of women (34 and 29 per cent respectively). Those who were not aware of direct discrimination in relation to their current jobs were much more likely to explain segregation in terms of tradition, which is more contingent and potentially changeable.[20]

Finally, respondents were asked about their perception of discrimination in a way that was less tied to their personal situation. They were asked how strongly they agreed or disagreed with the statement that 'If a man and a woman have the same qualifications, the employer will always choose the man.' This showed that respondents were much more aware of discrimination at the general societal level than in their own personal circumstances. Once again, however, perceptions of discrimination were strongly related to the extent of segregation in the labour market, particularly amongst men. In aggregate, 55 per cent of men and 48 per cent of women agreed that employers would always choose the man, but those in highly segregated jobs were much more likely to take this view than those in unsegregated jobs. Just over half (54 per cent) of men and nearly two-thirds (63 per cent) of women in highly segregated jobs thought employers discriminated on grounds of sex compared with 45 per cent of men and 53 per cent of women in moderately segregated jobs and 40 per cent of men and 50 per cent of women in unsegregated jobs.

Again, there is some evidence that such discrimination was regarded as legitimate. Those who strongly disagreed with the statement that employers always choose the man, had much lower scores on the index of participatory sexism than others, even after controlling for the extent of segregation experienced in the labour market (Table 2.23). In short, while there were large differences in the perception of discrimination, it was very much higher among those working exclusively with others of the same sex as themselves, who were also the most sexist in their attitudes and by implication most likely to have approved of both segregation and discrimination by employers.

CONCLUSION

The preceding analysis shows that sexist attitudes are clearly related to segregation in the labour market, particularly amongst

TABLE 2.23 *Participatory sexism and perceptions of discrimination by job segregation*

	Highly segregated jobs	Moderately segregated jobs	Unsegregated jobs	Cross sex jobs	Significance
If a man and a woman have the same qualifications the employer will always choose the man					
Men					
Disagree strongly	6.2	6.6	6.2	5.5	
Agree strongly, agree somewhat, or disagree somewhat	8.4	8.2	7.4	7.0	0.000
Women					
Disagree strongly	6.8	6.2	5.8	4.6	
Agree strongly, agree somewhat, or disagree somewhat	7.6	7.3	7.0	5.8	0.000

Note: N = 4,277.

Source: SCELI Six Areas WAWH Survey.

men. Men were more sexist than women on each of the three measures of sexism and their attitudes were also related to segregation in the labour market. The data show further that while men's participatory sexism was linked to segregation through social class and qualifications, their domestic sexism and tendency to use occupational sex-typing had independent effects on segregation, after controlling for class and qualifications.

While women's participatory sexism was linked to segregation in a similar way to men's, namely through class and qualifications, their domestic sexism showed a different pattern. Women's domestic sexism was linked to segregation only indirectly through part-time work and the length of breaks from employment—and domestic constraints appeared to have a stronger effect on these mediating variables than attitudes.

Finally, the data also show that those working in segregated jobs tended to explain segregation in terms of the inherent qualities of jobs and genders and in so far as they were aware of discrimination in the labour market they were unlikely to disapprove of it. Overall then, the data point to a relationship between different types of sexism and job segregation which would support the conclusion that sexist attitudes play a crucial role in stabilizing and legitimizing segregation in the labour market and may also inhibit possibilities for change arising on the demand side. Sexist attitudes may lag behind demand-led changes and prevent the potential for desegregation being realized.

APPENDIX 2.1: VARIABLES USED IN REGRESSIONS

1. QUALIFICATIONS (DUMMIES)

None.
Vocational/O-level.
A-level/non-university higher education.
University higher education.

2. AGE (DUMMIES)

Under 25 years.
25 to 34 years.
35 to 44 years.

45 to 54 years.
Over 55 years.

3. AREA (DUMMIES)

Kirkcaldy
Aberdeen
Coventry
Swindon
Northampton
Rochdale

4. SOCIAL CLASS (GOLDTHORPE SCHEMA) (DUMMIES)

Class I: higher service class.
Class II: lower service class.
Class III: routine non-manual.
Class IV: small proprietors.
Class V: lower technicians and supervisors.
Class VI: skilled manual workers.
Class VII: semi- and unskilled manual workers.

5. OCCUPATIONAL SEGREGATION (SCALE)

Highly segregated.
Moderately segregated.
Unsegregated.

6. INDUSTRY (STANDARD INDUSTRIAL CLASSIFICA-TION) (DUMMIES)

Agriculture.
Energy and water.
Extraction of minerals.
Metal manufacturing.
Other manufacturing.
Construction.
Distribution, hotels, catering.
Transport and communication.
Banking and financial services.
Other services.

7. SELF-EMPLOYMENT (DUMMY)

Self-employed = 1.

8. PART-TIME WORK (DUMMY)

In part-time work = 1.

9. PUBLIC SECTOR (DUMMY)

Public sector = 1.

10. TIME OUT OF EMPLOYMENT

Months spent economically inactive.

11. PARTICIPATORY SEXISM

Scale from 3 to 15 in which high scores indicate sexist attitudes.

12. RESPONDENT'S DOMESTIC SEXISM

Scale from 0 to 2 in which high scores indicate sexist attitudes.

13. PARTNER'S DOMESTIC SEXISM (AS ABOVE)

14. CHILDREN (DUMMIES)

None.
Youngest child aged under 5.
Youngest child aged 5 to 15.
Youngest child aged over 16.

15. DOMESTIC CONSTRAINTS ON JOB CHOICE (DUMMIES) (= 1 IF RESPONDENT SAYS ANY OF THE FOLLOWING ARE A CONSTRAINT)

Household's need for income.
Having to look after children.
Having to look after elderly or sick adults.
Partner's job.
Possible loss of welfare benefits.
Tax position.
Partner's views about what the respondent should do.
Wanting to stay in the area.

16. SEX-ROLE STEREOTYPES (DUMMIES)

Heavy work = 1.
Dirty work = 1.

NOTES

1. Human capital theory (Mincer 1962, 1966; Mincer and Polachek 1974) argues that gender segregation results from differences in human capital (skills, qualifications, and labour market experience), which in turn result from the division of labour within the home. Women who anticipate breaks in their labour market participation for child-rearing are thought to limit their investment in qualifications and training and then to select female occupations which they believe will provide the best rewards for their more limited human capital. Cultural theories, however, focus on the socialization of men and women into different social and cultural values. The main argument is that people choose jobs which are in line with their beliefs about appropriate masculine or feminine behaviour, and which sustain their conceptions of their own masculine and feminine identities. Girls and boys are not thought to be interested in jobs which contradict traditional gender identities or traditional gender roles within the home (Matthaei 1932).

2. In these theories gender segregation is explained as a by-product of employer's strategies to maximize profitability (often with the collusion of male trade unionists and male employees). Employers are thought to discriminate against women in recruitment, training, and promotion, in their attempts to use women as a reserve army to fill low-paying, part-time, deskilled, and secondary sector jobs (Beechey 1987).

3. The analysis of domestic sexism is based on a small subsample of 544 original respondents, interviewed in the second survey, who were still in the same jobs as in the first survey and in exactly the same household circumstances.

4. Since the data show exactly the same pattern of results regardless of whether we take the first reason or all reasons, the analysis is based on all reasons given.

5. The Equal Opportunities Legislation enacted during the 1970s attempted to improve women's formal position in the labour market by outlawing sex discrimination. Sexism was defined as unjustified sex discrimination in the public sphere of jobs, education, goods and services, resulting either from individual acts of prejudice by employers or from the unequal impact of apparently neutral institutional practices such as age limits to entry or promotion. The aim was to establish equality of opportunity and equal treatment for women by removing barriers to access. This has been described as the assimilationist ideal: men are taken as the normative category and simply asked to move over to make a little more room for

women who can conform to the male norm (O'Donovan and Szyszczak 1988).

6. The Likert scales consisted of 5 points: 'strongly agree', 'agree somewhat', 'no strong feelings either way', 'disagree somewhat', and 'disagree strongly'. These were collapsed into agreement versus disagreement with no strong feelings being interpreted as tacit agreement and thus included in the agree category.

7. All class analysis in this chapter is based on the collapsed seven- or three-class versions of Goldthorpe's original (1980) eleven-class schema, in which Personal Service Workers (Class IIIB) have been classified as part of class VII:

Goldthorpe's 1980 11-category class schema		Collapsed 7-class schema		Collapsed 3-class schema
I	Higher service class	I	Higher service class	Service class
II	Lower service class	II	Lower service class	
IIIA	Routine non-manual	III	Routine non-manual	
IIIB	Personal service workers		(to class VII)	
IVA	Small proprietors without employees			
IVB	Small proprietors with employees	IV	Small proprietors	Intermediate class
IVC	Farmers			
V	Lower technicians and supervisors	V	Lower technicians and supervisors	
VI	Skilled manual workers	VI	Skilled manual workers	
VIIA	Semi- and unskilled manual workers	VII	Semi- and unskilled manual workers (inc. class IIIB)	Working class
VIIB	Agricultural workers			

8. This index was constructed on the basis of the perceived job segregation variable. The category 'highly segregated' includes jobs that were defined as 'almost exclusively male' and 'almost exclusively female'; the category 'moderately segregated' includes those defined as 'mainly male' and 'mainly female'; and the category 'unsegregated' includes those that were defined as a 'fairly equal mixture of men and women'. 'Cross-sex' occupations are those where a man was working in a 'mainly or exclusively female' job or a woman in a 'mainly or exclusively male' job. Note that since these categories combine jobs with similar degrees of segregation, but very different gender characteristics, the variable is always disaggregated by sex.

9. It should be noted that while women with A-levels were as likely to be in segregated jobs as those with no qualifications or only O-levels, they were significantly less likely to be sexist in their attitudes than women with no qualifications. This confirms the previous finding that qualifications below degree level play a smaller role amongst women than amongst men in determining segregation.

10. The validity of Cockburn's analysis is supported by the finding that class VI was the only class in which men in highly segregated jobs were significantly more likely to have trade unions at their workplace than men in unsegregated jobs (66 and 53 per cent respectively).

11. Logistic regression is used in Table 2.11 because the dependent variable (part-time work) is a dichotomous categorical variable.

12. The traditional response to each question was that the female partner should be ultimately responsible for housework and that the male partner should be ultimately responsible for breadwinning.

13. Since this equation is based on 276 cases it does not give as detailed a picture of the main structural influences on gender segregation as that in Table 2.8, which is based on 2,049 cases. It nevertheless confirms the importance of qualifications, class, and industry.

14. Logistic regression is used in Table 2.15 because the dependent variable (part-time work) is a dichotomous categorical variable.

15. 64% of women living in households where they were almost entirely responsible for washing-up worked part-time, as did 60% of those entirely responsible for hoovering, 53% of those entirely responsible for washing clothes, and 59% of those entirely responsible for cooking.

16. See n. 13 above. Since the equations in Tables 2.17 and 2.18 are based on only 210 cases they do not give as detailed a picture of the structural influences over time out of employment and part-time work as those in Tables 2.10 and 2.11 which are based on approximately 1,900 cases.

17. 32% of men and 20% of women were aware of discrimination as a barrier to their own current jobs while 17% of men and 9% of women were aware of discrimination as a barrier to promotion in the internal labour market.

18. The same pattern emerged amongst both full- and part-time female workers.

19. Men and full-time women in segregated jobs who mentioned gender as a criterion for promotion in the internal labour market were less sexist in their attitudes than those in unsegregated jobs but not mentioning gender (5.2 and 7.2 respectively for men and 5.3 and 6.2 for full-time women). While there were very few of them, they were

thus likely to have disapproved of discrimination in the internal labour market.
20. For men the relation held after controlling for the extent of segregation in the labour market whereas for women it was only significant among those in segregated jobs.

REFERENCES

BEECHEY, V. (1987), *Unequal Work*.London, Verso.

COCKBURN, C. (1983), *Brothers*. London, Pluto.

—— (1988), 'The Gendering of Jobs: Workplace Relations and the Reproduction of Sex Segregation', in S. Walby (ed.), *Gender Segregation at Work*. Milton Keynes, Open University Press.

DEX, S. (1988), *Women's Attitudes towards Work*. Basingstoke, Macmillan.

GOLDTHORPE, J. H. (1980), *Social Mobility and Class Structure in Modern Britain*. Oxford, Clarendon Press.

HUMPHRIES, J., and RUBERY, J. (1984), 'The Reconstitution of the Supply Side of the Labour Market: The Relative Autonomy of Social Reproduction', *Cambridge Journal of Economics*, 8: 331–46.

MATTHAEI, J. A. (1982), *An Economic History of Women in America*. Brighton, Harvester.

MINCER, J. (1962), 'Labour Force Participation of Married Women: A Study of Labour Supply', in National Bureau of Economic Research, *Aspects of Labour Economics*, Princeton, NJ, Princeton University Press.

—— (1966) 'Labour Force Participation and Unemployment', in R. A. Gordon and M. Gordon (eds.), *Prosperity and Unemployment*. New York, Wiley.

—— and POLACHECK, S. (1974), 'Family Investment in Human Capital: Earnings of Women', *Journal of Political Economy*, 82/2: 76–108.

MURGATROYD, L. (1982), 'Gender and Occupational Stratification', *Sociological Review*, 30/4: 574–602.

O'DONOVAN, K. (1985), *Sexual Divisions in Law*. London, Weidenfeld and Nicolson.

—— and SZYSZCZAK, E. (1988), *Equality and Sex Discrimination in Law*. Oxford, Blackwell.

PRINGLE, R. (1988), *Secretaries Talk*. London, Verso.

RESKIN, B., and HARTMANN, H. (1986) (eds.), *Women's Work, Men's Work*. Washington, DC, National Academy Press.

WILLIS, P. (1977), *Learning to Labour*. Farnborough, Saxon House.

3

Divided Women: Labour Market Segmentation and Gender Segregation

BRENDAN BURCHELL AND JILL RUBERY

INTRODUCTION

This chapter explores the empirical evidence for segmentation of the labour supply with particular reference to gender. Segmentation involves the cumulative development of advantage and disadvantage in the labour market, and divergences in attitudes and expectations between labour-force groups, often related to these objective experiences. Segmentation on the supply side is both the outcome of labour market processes on the demand side and a direct influence on firms' employment and pay policies. For example, systematic discrimination in hiring policies by employers serves to create and reinforce the existence of disadvantaged groups in the labour market (Osterman 1988, Ashton and Maguire 1986). On the other hand, the availability of groups with different attitudes and expectations allows firms greater discretion in their structuring of pay and employment patterns and reduces the link between the content of a job (e.g. technical and skill aspects) and the pay and status of a job (Craig et al. 1985). However, although some recognition exists in the literature of the importance of supply-side segmentation, particularly between women and men, there has been little empirical investigation of the differential effects of experience in and out of the labour market on individuals' expectations, perceptions, and current attitudes, and whether these differences result in the development of distinct clusters or segments, as is implied by both segmentation theory and by employers' views of the labour market. One particular focus in this chapter will be on the differences *within* gender groups that are revealed when a more complex set of supply-side variables are investigated.

The theoretical basis for the hypothesis of supply-side segmentation and its relationship to the structuring of employment is explored further in the following section of the chapter. The third section then outlines the exploratory statistical modelling of labour market segments or clusters, using the Social Change and Economic Life Initiative (SCELI) work attitudes and work history survey for Northampton. The fourth section looks at the characteristics of the segments identified and in the fifth section the characteristics of these segments are analysed with respect to gender segregation.

SEGMENTATION OF THE LABOUR SUPPLY

Segmentation theory has been used to break the assumed direct relationship between the quality of jobs and skills and the distribution of the productivities and abilities of the population implicit in the neoclassical and human capital versions of labour market theory. Industrial organization, product market and technological conditions, systems of labour market regulation, and managerial control strategies are all recognized to have an influence on the structure of jobs, which is relatively independent of short-term conditions in the labour market. Firms are identified as the main agents structuring the system of employment. Competition requires firms to pursue a complex set of objectives so that labour market variables do not provide a deterministic explanation of employment structures. Thus segmentation theory has emphasized the 'relative autonomy' of the demand side of the labour market.

However, further research within the segmentation tradition has persistently revealed the importance of the segmentation of the labour supply in firms' employment policies. This segmentation on the supply side, by which we mean divisions in labour market opportunities between labour-force groups that cannot be accounted for entirely or mainly by differences in labour quality, impacts on and interacts with 'demand-side' segmentation in two distinct ways. First, the characteristics of jobs and the structure of pay are not independent of the type of labour employed; to provide the most obvious example, women's jobs may be low paid because they are feminized and not feminized because they are low paid (Craig *et al.* 1982, 1985, Crompton and Jones 1984, Armstrong 1982). Secondly, firms may be able to utilize this supply-side segmentation to fill, for example, relatively demanding but low-paid jobs with employees drawn from a disadvantaged labour-force segment. Firms have been found to have distinct notions of segmentation in the labour supply; particular groups are favoured to occupy particular job slots as they are seen to be more reliable, stable, or satisfied than other groups at the particular ranges of pay, types of work or supervision systems on offer. Thus the existence of a segmented labour supply has increasingly been incorporated into segmentation theory as a factor which provides firms with considerably more freedom or discretion in structuring their employment systems to meet their competitive objectives.

Moreover, the structuring or segmentation of the labour supply has been recognized to be in part the outcome of the policies of recruitment, pay, and promotion adopted by firms; women are available at low wages and relatively high efficiency because of their exclusion from large areas of the employment system. Thus the breaking of the direct link between current labour market demand and current labour market supply still allows for recognition of interdependency in a historical or long period sense. The expectations and attitudes of the labour-force will be structured by their perceptions and experience of job opportunities. The more the labour market operates so as to provide cumulative opportunities for advancement for some groups rather than others[1] the more there will be a process of cumulative divergence of expectations and attitudes between labour-force groups, affecting in turn the sorts of jobs which individuals will consider applying to; that is a process of labour supply segmentation.

The concept of segmentation on the supply side has tended to be inferred from the practices, policies, and attitudes of employers, or from the observed outcome of labour market processes in longitudinal data sets of individuals' work histories. There has been little direct empirical research of segmentation hypotheses which allow individuals' attitudes and perceptions as well as their behaviour in the labour market to be taken into account. The SCELI work attitudes and work histories data set provides a relatively unique opportunity to meld together information on the individual's past, present, and perceived future, on in-market and out-market influences on employment opportunities, and more general information on their attitudes and employment expectations. This empirical investigation of the characteristics of labour-force segments will be a particularly useful antidote to the more common tradition in segmentation research on the labour supply where attributes of workers are assumed but not investigated. For example the original dual labour market theory of Doeringer and Piore (1971) assumed that individuals in the secondary sector would eventually internalize the casual employment habits associated with secondary sector jobs, thereby over time becoming objectively unacceptable workers for the primary sector. Others, such as Barron and Norris (1976) equated the secondary employment sector with female workers, without allowing for the existence of potential differences within the female and male labour supplies. These approaches have been discredited but have not been replaced by more detailed and sophisticated analyses of employees' attitudes and behaviour.

The SCELI data set also makes it possible to take account of the fact that the processes of segmentation in the labour supply cannot be adequately captured by simple cross-sectional analyses of individuals' current employment position. One of the main hypotheses of recent segmentation theory is that individuals' current opportunities in the labour market will be influenced by their past experience within and outside the labour market. These influences may not be apparent in their current levels of productivity or skill, as is assumed in human capital theory, for the labour market does not function so as to reward workers simply according to their current productivities. For example, events in past work histories such as periods of unemployment, quits for family reasons, redundancy, and dismissal are likely to have cumulative effects on employment opportunities as individuals are excluded from stable employment sectors with promotion prospects. Moreover, individuals' attitudes to particular jobs and the role of that job slot in an individual's 'career' path cannot be understood simply by reference to the characteristics of the job alone. Stewart *et al.* (1980) have pointed to the difference between a permanent clerical job and a clerical job that is a trainee slot for management; these differences occur not so much in the job descriptions but in the occupational trajectories of the individuals employed in the job. Thus employment patterns of individuals should be studied not cross-sectionally as independent events but rather as relatively continuous processes with the past affecting the present and the future. However, this continuity of the employment relationship should not be taken as equivalent to the steady accumulation or erosion of human capital; this model may appear to fit some individuals as they are operating within a stable and continuous career or labour market system which offers progressive opportunities for advancement, however this accumulation of skill and experience is critically dependent on retaining access to the jobs provided by employers. Those who lose such access may be subject to rapid downgrading of employment opportunities, which exceeds any deterioration of skill and has a major impact on their future life chances. As not all individuals experience the same random events or life chances, the influence of such variables on individuals will be discontinuous and not general to all labour-force groups.

Another important issue to be explored is the extent to which differences in attitudes, expectations, and job satisfaction in different labour-force groups are revealed by the SCELI data. If employees' responses to objectively similar job situations are markedly different then labour market segmentation may persist without necessarily generating forces towards convergence. Thus, for example, groups who appear more satisfied with lower-paid jobs relative to job quality may remain relatively permanently in the so-called secondary sector of employment, whereas those who express dissatisfaction may be either 'displaced' workers from higher status 'primary-type' labour markets or those actively seeking mobility into the 'primary' sector. Thus the incorporation of attitudinal alongside more objective data on individuals' employment position should allow for a more complete understanding of the interactions between experience, behaviour, and opportunities.

This approach to the construction of labour supply segments allows us to explore differences between groups of women and differences between women at various stages of their life cycle while at the same time recognizing that these differences may exist within a more general process of segmentation by gender to which all women are subject. While there is unassailable evidence that women face disadvantage in the labour market at all stages of their life cycle, it is also the case that this disadvantage increases significantly for most women after childbirth. However, women are becoming more heterogeneous in their labour market behaviour and in their qualifications and occupational attainment. By looking at labour supply from the perspective of past and current experience and future expectations we can begin to investigate the extent to which there may be differences opening up within the female labour-force in their labour market positions and in their attitudes towards the downgrading and low-skilled work to which they are confined. Such divisions might require firms in the future to adopt a more sophisticated employment policy than that of using gender as an indicator of the type of pay, benefits, and employment opportunities to which the employee aspires.

THE STATISTICAL INVESTIGATION OF SUPPLY-SIDE SEGMENTATION

The most striking feature of initial attempts to analyse the SCELI data was the very weak power of standard cross-sectional variables on current employment conditions in predicting attitudes towards and satisfaction with current employment. Pay, occupation, discretion, promotion prospects, and so on explained little of the variation in current levels of satisfaction, desire to change jobs, or expectations of advancement. Demographic factors such as sex and age were more useful but these were likely to be proxies for other related issues, such as taking time out of the labour market to have children; thus a simple gender variable could be hiding important differences between women. Indeed, amongst labour-force groups with different experiences, attitudes towards jobs, pay, and employment prospects seemed unlikely to be explained by the same variables; for example, amongst the young dissatisfaction seemed to be associated with awareness of potential chances for advancement, while for married women it was related to comparisons with their past experiences. Thus it seemed essential to use some method of statistical analysis which would allow us to take into account the individual's past, their present position, their in-market and out-market experiences, and their expectations and attitudes; variables which cumulatively and interactively generate distinct labour-force segments. It also appeared important to have an empirical and not a theoretical approach to the identification of segments for two reasons. First, since the processes of supply-side segmentation are relatively unknown, one of the purposes of this chapter must be to identify the important differences between segments, and to see how far they support or are compatible with theories drawn from firms' employment practices. Secondly, if we were to allow for more than two labour-force segments, the most significant variables dividing the groups might differ. For example, one segment may be primarily distinguished by the impact of leaving the labour market to have children, but there may also be significant differences, say between male workers, where this variable will not be relevant. Furthermore, the hypotheses put forward by segmentation theorists have generally had a weak empirical base, so an exploratory approach to the data is more suitable.

The usual multivariate techniques for analysing survey data (e.g. multiple regressions) assume that the same processes underlie the interrelationships between variables for the whole of the sample; for instance, assuming that being in an advantaged position in an internal labour market will be a benefit to all individuals. If, however, we accept the basic premiss that different individuals are in labour markets that operate differently then this assumption may well be false. Segmentation theory started off with the notion of primary and secondary labour markets, with the former operated by bureaucratic rules, including seniority, and the latter operating as a casual market subject to the dictates of supply and demand. The result of subsequent research has been to show that there is a very wide range of employee management models, used both within individual firms for different types of employees and also wide differences in practices between firms. No one common labour market model can thus be assumed. To give another example, lack of job security may be of little consequence in a labour market where individuals have a high expectation of moving to a better job with a different employer in the near future but will be the major cause of concern to individuals in a labour market where they would not be able to find another job if they lost their current job.

Rather than being treated as quirks in the data set, such complex interactions should be one of the main concerns of segmentation theorists. One way that they have been dealt with before is to compare regression weights of labour market variables for different groups; for instance males and females or blacks and whites (see Rosenberg 1989 for a review of empirical investigations of differences between segments). The problem with this approach is that one has to start by dividing the sample into two or more groups depending on their hypothesized labour market segment and then see whether there are differences between those groups on, say, the effect of their 'human capital' on their pay. While we accept that this approach has demonstrated convincingly that women do not receive equal rewards compared to men, when all other labour market criteria are controlled for, what is lacking is a clear rationale of the criteria for membership of each of these different groups. It is also true that for a minority of women their relationship to the labour market would, on all objective criteria of skill, productivity, and reward, be indistinguishable from men in the primary segment. Furthermore, even those women with labour market participation patterns very unlike that of any comparable group of men may be a very heterogeneous group. What is needed is an empirical, rather than theory-led, division of labour market participants into their different segments. Until workers can be classified into groups by a constellation of labour market characteristics,[2] questions about the mechanisms by which these differences arise and persist cannot be fully answered.

Cluster analysis

A statistical technique ideally suited to unravelling these complexities is cluster analysis. Cluster analysis groups cases (in this instance, employees) into relatively homogeneous subgroups using similarity on a number of variables as the criterion for the clustering. It is suitable whenever it is hypothesized that a sample consists of a number of different 'types' but the nature of these types is not known, or is not so straightforward that these types can be identified by their scores on one or two known variables.

Cluster analysis serves a number of different purposes (Everitt 1974). In this instance it is being used primarily as a method of data exploration, not so much to subject specific hypotheses to statistical tests but rather to acquire a preliminary understanding of the factors differentiating the positions of individuals in the labour market. However, depending upon the outcome of the clustering, many hypotheses and assumptions about dual labour market and segmentation theories may become testable. Thus no attempt will be made to argue, for instance, that there were necessarily five, and not four or six, main types of individuals in the Northampton local labour market, but that certain characteristics (e.g. job security and skill) are more important in understanding the position of an individual in that labour market than others (e.g. work-force size of current employer). It should also be noted that there is no presumption that a similar analysis of data drawn from a different labour market would give rise to the same types or same numbers of segments.

The data

The empirical findings presented here relate to the 616 employees included in the work attitudes and work histories survey for Northampton (44 per cent of whom were women).[3] These analyses use a combination of core questions (which were also included in the schedules administered in the other five local labour markets) and team-specific questions which reflected the Cambridge team's special interest in labour market processes.

The Northampton 'Travel To Work Area' was typical of many British local labour markets in 1986. It had been going through a restructuring phase for some considerable period while its traditional footwear industry was in decline. Service industries were on the increase during this time; according to the 1984 and 1987 Censuses of Employment there had been an increase of 17 per cent overall in service sector employment, but with rises of 39 per cent in the financial services and 17 per cent and 21 per cent in other services and transport and communication respectively. Much of this growth was in part-time female employment, where there was a 26 per cent rise compared to a rise of 14 per cent in total employment.

In order to divide the sample up into a number of relatively homogeneous groups, a cluster analysis was performed using all of the variables listed in Appendix 3.1. As there were no objective criteria that could inform on the choice of the fifty-one variables, the main criteria for inclusion was that they either reflected some degree of relative advantage in the labour market or were important in the debates about labour market segmentation. This selection seems to have worked well both in a statistical and a substantive sense. Exploratory analyses revealed that the cluster structure was relatively unaffected by the adding or subtracting of a small number of variables, and the clusters that were produced were interpretable, comprehensible, and meaningful.

Appendix 3.1 has been divided up into six sections in order to clarify the description the variables included; all variables were standardized and weighted equally in the clustering. The first group of variables were concerned with the attributes of the respondent's job, such as the skill level. The second group consisted of attributes of the employer, such as size of establishment. The third group was concerned with the manifest rewards of the job, primarily hourly pay. The fourth group were derived from the work histories, to map the trajectory in the respondent's work history. The fifth group incorporated attitudinal items to measure employees' assessment of their current job and future position in the labour market. The sixth and final section included the pre- and extra-labour market variables such as qualifications and household situation.[4]

After a number of exploratory analyses 5 clusters emerged as the cleanest way to divide the sample. These 5 clusters ranged in size from 252 (40 per cent of the total sample) to 23 (4 per cent). A further 26 cases were excluded from the analyses because they formed into exceedingly small clusters (ranging from 1 to 7 cases).

THE CHARACTERISTICS OF THE SEGMENTS OR CLUSTERS

A brief description of the clusters

Group 1: 'The Primary Segment'. This was the largest group (40 per cent of the total sample), and by almost all objective criteria, the most advantaged. They were predominantly male (78 per cent), well paid, in high social-class jobs, and most of their previous job quits had been to get better jobs and had resulted in pay promotions.

Group 2: 'Stickers'. This group (31 per cent of the sample) was a little older than the other groups (43 years compared to a sample mean of 38), and predominantly female (62 per cent). They were the most satisfied group with respect to all aspects of their jobs, even though their pay, fringe benefits, and skill levels were considerably lower than group 1. They were the least likely to state that they would like to change jobs, and saw the internal labour market[5] as being more advantageous than all of the other groups.

Group 3: 'Female Descenders'. Of the 13 per cent of the sample in this group, 96 per cent were women. This group had the highest amount of domestic interference in labour market activity (as measured by working part time, past job quits for domestic reasons, past periods of full-time housework, having to look after children, etc.). They received the lowest pay, and had the highest proportion of job changes to same or worse paid jobs. For half of them their last change of job had been to a worse paid job than the one that they had held previously.

Group 4: 'Young and Mobile'. This small group (5 per cent) was 80 per cent male. They were, on average, a few years younger than the other groups (mean age = 30 years). Their perceived chances of getting better jobs were the highest of all the groups. They were most likely to see those jobs as being with other employers, and saw the advantage of being an insider within a firm as being minimal. They were most likely to have moved to better paid jobs when they changed jobs in the past, but were not the most likely to say that they liked their current jobs better than all previous jobs.

Group 5: 'Labour Market Descenders'. This group was only 4 per cent of the sample and 83 per cent were men. They seemed to have nothing going for them. They had all had a job change in the past that involved a drop in the social-class rating of their job, and most had at some time been sacked or made redundant. They were also the most likely to have been unemployed in the past. They stand out most in their current jobs because of their lack of perceived job security. They were particularly dissatisfied with their job security, as well as being the most dissatisfied group with their jobs overall. Most of them had been looking for jobs in the last year, and almost all said they would be keen to change jobs if plenty of jobs were available.[6]

We have used the term 'primary' to describe one of the clusters as it stands out in clear distinction from the range of less advantaged labour-force segments identified in the remaining four clusters. This terminology does not imply an acceptance of the primary and secondary labour market divisions of Doeringer and Piore, although it may suggest that one of the major dividing lines in the labour market is indeed between those with reasonably stable and full-time jobs (that is those conforming to the standard labour contract) and those that fall outside this sector.

It should be noted that while these descriptions are of types of people in the labour market, it is not being argued that the processes of segmentation are, at root, founded on enduring individual differences. Our argument is, rather, that these people's lives have been shaped and scarred by their labour market experiences, which in turn are a function of the actions and policies of firms and the social reproduction of labour through the family. For instance, being pushed out of an internal labour market, whether by domestic forces or employer forces, seems to have been one of the main determinants of labour market position. As these life events can hardly be seen as arising from free choices, the words 'stuck' and 'pushed' may be better than 'stickers' and 'descenders', emphasizing the way in which the supply side is acted upon by the demand side.

Main differences between clusters

One way of looking at the differences between the groups is by selecting out the variables that best separated cases between clusters, as measured by contingency tables for discrete variables (Table 3.1) or one-way analysis of variance between clusters for continuous variables (Table 3.2). Of the dichotomous variables, gender was a very strong feature in differentiating the groups, the extremes being 4 per cent male in the 'female descenders' and 83 per cent in the 'labour market descenders'. As expected, as soon as one starts dividing up the supply side of the labour market, gender presents itself as an overriding attribute in allocating workers to clusters. In fact, of the dichotomous variables, only one discriminated between the clusters as strongly as gender, and that was the subjective item which asked individuals whether they had a career, with 82 per cent of the 'primary segment' answering affirmatively compared to between 41 and 20 per cent for the

TABLE 3.1 *Percentage breakdowns in each cluster of the seven most discriminating dichotomous variables*

	Cluster					
	Primary segment	Stickers	Female descenders	Young and mobile	Labour market descenders	All
Male? (46)[a]	78	38	4	80	83	56
See yourself as having a career? (31)	82	26	21	41	20	52
Had training for current job? (7)	80	32	28	17	44	53
Skilled (self-definition)? (30)	95	59	38	58	25	72
Promotion prospects in current job? (5)	77	34	22	57	11	53
Employer sees job as permanent? (2)	95	97	86	94	39	92
Want to change jobs if plenty available? (23)	35	17	65	89	84	38
Last quit to worse paid? (20)	2	12	50	11	38	13

Note: N = 580.

[a] Numbers in brackets in Tables 3.1 and 3.2 refer to variable numbers from Appendix 3.1.

Source: SCELI Northampton Work Attitudes and Work Histories (WAWH) Survey.

TABLE 3.2 *Mean scores of each cluster on the six most discriminating continuous variables*

	Cluster						
	Primary segment	Stickers	Female descenders	Young and mobile	Labour market descenders	All	SD
Skill index (1)	7.5	4.0	3.5	3.5	3.0	5.5	2.9
'Female' domestic interference (50)	−1.6	1.4	4.3	−1.4	−0.6	0.1	3.3
Overall job satisfaction[a] (40)	7.8	9.3	7.4	5.5	4.3	7.9	2.1
Hourly pay[b] (10)	4.58	2.99	2.27	3.02	2.63	3.49	1.61
Benefits (11)	8.9	5.7	2.9	6.4	3.8	6.8	3.9
Cambridge Scale Score (4)	151	80	90	90	51	114	81

Note: N = 580.

[a] The job satisfaction scores often tended to be highly skewed towards the positive end of the scale. For this reason they were all 'normalized' before parametric tests were performed, but the means presented here are calculated from the actual scores.

[b] These are geometric means as the pay data was logged to normalize it. These differences do not simply reflect the different sex-ratios in each of the groups; even when the pay for males and females was looked at separately, it still showed large differences between clusters.

Source: SCELI Northampton WAWH Survey.

others. Training for current job varied from 80 per cent in the 'primary segment' to only 17 per cent in the 'young and mobiles' (interestingly, the 'labour market descenders' members claimed the second highest level of training (44 per cent), even though they were very disadvantaged in other ways). Promotion prospects of jobs showed continuing advantage of the 'primary segment' members (77 per cent) compared to the 'labour market descenders' (11 per cent). The 'labour market descenders' were very far away from the others in terms of security of tenure; only

39 per cent reported that their employers saw the jobs as permanent compared to 85–95 per cent for the other groups. Loyalty to the employer was highest in the 'stickers', with only 17 per cent reporting that they would want to change jobs if there were plenty available, contrasting markedly with the 89 per cent in the 'young and mobiles'. The proportion taking a pay cut in their last job move was also very revealing; only 2 per cent of the 'primary segment' had suffered this fate compared to 50 per cent of the 'female descenders'.

The single continuous variable that best differentiated the clusters was the skill index; the 'primary segment' scored much higher than any of the other clusters on the skill content of their jobs. The 'female domestic interference' variable showed that the 'female descenders' were very different from all of the others, but this variable was also important in distinguishing the 'stickers' from the rest of the sample. The 'stickers' also had a very high mean level of overall job satisfaction, whereas the 'labour market descenders' were very dissatisfied with their jobs. The next three variables (hourly pay, fringe benefits, and Cambridge Scale Score) also showed a large gap between the 'primary segment' and the other four clusters, with the two most disadvantaged groups being 3 and 5.

Industry

An important question, but one that can only be speculated on at present, is whether other local labour markets have a similar structure to the one revealed here. To what extent does Northampton have a unique labour market as a result of its industries, geographical position, history, patterns of social reproduction of the labour-force, migration, and so on? It is likely, for instance, that areas of higher unemployment would have larger 'descender' segments.

One way of addressing this problem is to look at the distribution of workers from each segment in each of the industrial classifications recorded. This suggests how Northampton's particular industrial structure has influenced the labour supply, and it also highlights the interrelationship between women's labour market position and industrial sector.

The industry of each of the employers was categorized into

thirteen groups, roughly corresponding to Standard Industrial Classification (SIC) broad groups but with certain industries of local or theoretical interest (i.e. footwear, hotels, pubs, and catering, and public administration) disaggregated into separate categories.

Group 1 ('Primary segment') was over-represented in public administration. This pattern was even more striking when one looks at males and females separately: 65 per cent of the women in group 1 were in public administration, compared to 43 per cent of women overall (the figures for men were 27 and 20 per cent).

Group 2 ('Stickers') was over-represented in the footwear industry. All six of the females in the footwear industry were in this group, as were half of the twelve men in footwear. This is particularly interesting in light of the fact that footwear firms in Northampton were worried that their jobs were perceived by employees (both inside and outside the industry and amongst school-leavers) as being 'dead-end' jobs.

Group 3 ('Female descenders') was slightly over-represented in the hotels, pubs, and catering and 'other services' industrial classifications.

Group 4 ('Young and mobile') was very over-represented in engineering (31 per cent compared to 15 per cent for the sample) and distribution (33 per cent compared to 14 per cent). Only 7 per cent of them were in public administration (30 per cent overall).

Group 5 ('Labour market descenders') were found in engineering (28 per cent) and 'other manufacturing' (17 per cent compared to 9 per cent overall) but noticeably absent from financial services (3–9 per cent) and distribution (0–14 per cent).

Thus there is strong evidence that the supply side of the labour market is used differently by different industries. Whether this means that an area with, say, a higher proportion of the workforce in manufacture than in public administration would lead to a smaller 'primary segment' and more descenders is an interesting question for future research.[7]

Registrar-General's social class

One of the ways in which the labour market is commonly disaggregated is with the Registrar-General's classification of social classes. This was not used in constructing the clusters although a correlated classification, the Cambridge Scale Score (CSS), was. There was a strong but complex relationship between the clusters and the R.-G. classifications. Cross-tabulations of the clusters by social classes (disaggregated by sex) are given in Tables 3.3*a* and 3.3*b*. Among the men, the 'primary segment' was over-represented in all of the non-manual classes while the 'labour market descenders' and (to a lesser extent) the 'stickers' were over-represented in all of the manual classes; the 'young and mobile' were over-represented at both extremes, i.e. the professional and the

TABLE 3.3 *Clusters by Registrar-General's social class for current job*
(*a*) *Men* (N = 282)

	Primary segment	Stickers	Young and mobile	Labour market descenders	Class as percentage of total
Professional	85	0	15	0	6
	7	0	11	0	
Intermediate and managers	85	9	5	0	30
	39	13	20	0	
Skilled non-manual	88	4	4	2	11
	15	2	6	4	
Skilled manual	53	30	7	9	33
	26	47	28	55	
Partly skilled manual	35	39	13	12	18
	9	33	28	36	
Unskilled manual	42	26	21	10	2
	1	2	4	3	
Cluster as percentage of total	65.4	20.7	8.1	5.8	100.0

TABLE 3.3 *Cont.*
(*b*) *Women* (N = 282)

	Primary segment	Stickers	Female descenders	Class as percentage of total
Professional	71	0	28	1
	4	0	1	
Intermediate and managers	55	25	19	30
	66	16	19	
Skilled non-manual	16	56	27	37
	25	45	34	
Skilled manual	11	59	29	7
	3	9	7	
Partly skilled manual	1	54	44	19
	0.8	22	28	
Unskilled manual	0	51	48	6
	0	6	9	
Cluster as percentage of total	24.6	45.9	29.5	100.0

Note: First figures in each category are row percentages (i.e. percentages of each social class), second figures are column percentages (i.e. percentages of each cluster).

Source: SCELI Northampton WAWH Survey.

lower-skilled manual classes. Among the women, the 'primary segment' was over-represented in the professional and intermediate classes, the 'stickers' in the clerical and all manual classes and the 'female descenders' in the semi- and unskilled manual classes. Thus whilst there is a strong relationship between segmentation and class, the association is neither straightforward nor linear.

If the R.-G. categories are taken to indicate the types of jobs on offer, it can be seen that men and women, even from the same labour market segments, have very different job opportunities open to them. For instance, men seem able to attain the 'primary segment' through both non-manual and manual routes, whereas there are no equivalent routes for women to achieve 'primary segment' membership through manual work. This point is clear from Table 3.4, showing the percentage of non-manual employees in each cluster. Non-manual men were just under two-thirds of 'primary segment' men, and were under-represented in all other male segments. However, fully 96 per cent of the women in the 'primary segment' were in non-manual work. This restricting feature of women's manual work is another way in which women's access to the primary segment is curtailed.

TABLE 3.4 *Percentage of each gender by cluster cell who are currently employed in non-manual jobs*

	Primary segment	Stickers	Female descenders	Young and mobile	Labour market descenders	All sample
Men	63	16	—[a]	38	4	47
Women	96	62	55	—	—	68
All sample	70	45	53	48	13	57

Note: N = 580.

[a] In three of the cells there are too few cases to make reliable estimates.

Source: SCELI Northampton WAWH Survey.

Past, present, and future

It is interesting to note that the outlooks of these groups are as easily, and sometimes more easily, distinguished by their pasts and aspirations for the future than by their present situations. For instance, there is no direct relationship between present hourly pay and pay satisfaction at all. The 'primary sector' group were easily the highest paid, but were also far less satisfied with their pay than the 'stickers'. The 'labour market descenders' were not as badly paid as the 'female descenders', but were far less satisfied. In order to understand the individual's interpretation of the present, one must know their position now relative to their situation in the past and their expectations for the future, as well as the reasons for any changes over time. In this case males had higher expectations of pay and were affected more severely by drops in pay because they were imposed externally by redundancies and unemployment, whereas women could at least see their descent as being under their control and part of a long-term strategy (even though, as Marshall (1989) argues, the voluntary nature of such decisions may be questionable). This pattern of only being able to interpret the present through an understanding of the past was repeated throughout the data. It underlines the need to view the labour market as a dynamic process in which individuals are continually trying to interpret and change their situation, rather than being a precise rule-governed system where they are simple reward-optimizers.

Stable or unstable segments?

One of the main questions which must be asked before assessing the significance of these findings is whether we are uncovering systematic processes which confine individuals to particular segments over the medium or long term, or relatively random events and processes, such that if we were to repeat the survey with the same individuals a few months later one would find a high level of mobility between clusters. This question can be answered in two ways; either by making inferences from the nature of the clusters (for example, the stability of the employees' labour market histories) or by a repeated analysis of the same employees at a later point in time. These separate sets of evidence will be examined in turn.

In so far as the 'primary sector' and the 'stickers' had relatively stable job tenure, good chances of internal advancement, and a low desire to change jobs then it might be expected that most of the men here would remain in their current jobs, either because of the relatively high rewards amongst the first group or because of the high levels of personal satisfaction amongst the second. A very small number of men in these groups might be displaced from their relatively secure positions by employer closure, redundancy, or dismissal and thus run the risk of falling into one of the 'descender' categories. This risk is probably much higher for the women in these two groups, particularly those in the 'primary segment' as they were less likely than the women 'stickers' yet to have experienced interruptions to their careers associated with domestic responsibilities.

Those in the 'descender clusters' were anxious to change their employment position but there must be considerable doubt over their actual ability to effect such a change. The histories of unemployment and unstable employment amongst the 'labour market descenders', and the heavy domestic commitments of the 'female descenders' must reduce their chances of being able to move into a better job in the future. Indeed their keenness to change jobs was not reflected in confidence in their ability to secure a better job in the future. The 'female descenders' might be considered more able to secure a better job in the future as their domestic responsibilities decline. Moreover, the difference between female 'stickers' and 'female descenders' was partly one of age so that the latter group may become more stable employees and more satisfied over time. However, an alternative interpretation is that younger women have higher expectations so that they would remain permanently more dissatisfied with the low-paid jobs that the labour market offers them compared with older female cohorts.

Finally, the 'young and mobile' group were the most likely to have had both the desire and the ability to achieve a better job in the future; many of them could be expected to join the 'primary segment' or the 'stickers' in the future, although some may have their expectations dashed and join the 'descenders'. The absence of older men in this group is perhaps evidence of life-cycle effects among males as well as females; perhaps domestic responsibilities lure men away from more mobile labour market strategies to jobs with more stability but fewer prospects (such as those possessed by the men in the 'stickers' group).

Whatever the opportunities for individuals to move between segments it does appear that from the point of view of employers these types of groups can be expected to persist in the labour market and firms thus will have opportunities to target recruitment to workers who respond very differently to jobs with similar skill and pay levels.

The Household and Community Survey took place approximately eight months after the Work Attitudes and Work Histories Survey and provided the potential for following up some of these questions, but unfortunately it is of only limited use for present purposes. This is primarily because of the small numbers in some of the clusters, e.g. 'labour market descenders'. As there were already only twenty-three employees in the 'labour market descenders' group, the 26 per cent resampling fraction for employees in the sample reduced this number to a mere seven. Could any conclusions be drawn about their continued labour market participation from such a small number? Surprisingly the answer is yes. The evidence suggests that the labour market position of the 'labour market descenders' group was still more precarious than the other groups. For instance, while only twelve out of the 121 employees who were still employed at the second survey (10 per cent) felt that they might lose their jobs and become unemployed in the next twelve months, three of the five employees from the 'labour market descenders' who answered the question felt so threatened. Furthermore, while none of the 139 employees from clusters 1 to 4 was unemployed at the time of the second survey, one of the seven employees from the 'labour market descenders' was unemployed.[8]

Reasons for working

One of the reasons often given for labour heterogeneity is that identifiable categories of employees have different motives for working. In order to tap this, each respondent was asked to choose their two most important reasons for having a paid job from nine different options, listed in Tables 3.5a–c. While it must be borne in mind that these self-reports are probably in part *post hoc* rationalizations, they are nevertheless important accounts of the actors' own behaviour. There were no significant differences in the proportions saying that they worked because 'working is the normal thing to do' or because they 'enjoy working', but there were differences between the clusters on the other seven possible responses.

Table 3.5a shows the percentage of each group who claimed to work for each of the nine items (ordered by magnitude of the differences between clusters according to the Chi square statistic).

TABLE 3.5 *Reasons for working by cluster (% giving each reason for working, multiresponse)*
(*a*) *Men and women*

	Primary segment	Stickers	Female descenders	Young and mobile	Labour market descenders	All sample
Working is the normal thing to do	12	14	4	11	7	11
Need money for basics such as food, rent, and mortgage	73	52	39	81	77	63
To earn money to buy extras	20	38	48	60	49	33
For the company of other people	1	7	17	0	6	5
Enjoy working	30	29	21	16	9	27
To use my abilities to the full	19	9	4	12	0	13
To feel I'm doing something worthwhile	23	12	12	7	13	17
To give me a sense of independence	20	30	41	10	25	25
To get out of the house	0	10	12	4	11	5
N	252	192	82	31	23	580

Group 1 ('Primary segment') were the least likely to say that they work 'to earn money to buy extras' or 'to get out of the house', but were most likely to work 'to use my abilities to the full' or 'to feel that I'm doing something worthwhile'. This pattern showed a high commitment to the content of the work itself rather than simply its material rewards.

TABLE 3.5 *Cont.*
(*b*) *Women*

	Primary segment	Stickers	Female descenders	All sample
Working is the normal thing to do	4	8	4	6
Need money for basics such as food, rent, and mortgage	52	39	36	42
To earn money to buy extras	16	45	47	38
For the company of other people	2	11	18	11
Enjoy working	35	28	22	28
To use my abilities to the full	30	8	4	12
To feel I'm doing something worthwhile	27	18	12	18
To give me a sense of independence	32	30	41	34
To get out of the house	0	14	13	10
N	68	134	80	282

Cont. over/

Group 2 ('Stickers') were fairly close to the average on all of the items.

Group 3 ('Female descenders') were the least likely to work because they 'need money for basic essentials such as food, rent, and mortgage', but most likely to work 'for the company of other people' or 'to give me a sense of independence'. This emphasis on the latent and social rather than the manifest rewards of work probably reflected their high domestic commitments and reliance on another salary coming into the household, and their need for a break from menial domestic chores and the isolation associated with housework and childcare.

Group 4 ('Young and mobile') were clearly instrumental in their outlook. They were the most likely to state that they

TABLE 3.5 *Cont.*

(c) *Men*

	Primary segment	Stickers	Young and mobile	Labour market descenders	All sample
Working is the normal thing to do	14	23	11	7	15
Need money for basics such as food, rent, and mortgage	79	72	83	76	78
To earn money to buy extras	21	27	60	50	28
For the company of other people	1	0	0	7	1
Enjoy working	28	29	18	11	27
To use my abilities to the full	17	9	9	0	13
To feel I'm doing something worthwhile	22	3	9	13	16
To give me a sense of independence	16	30	6	20	18
To get out of the house	0	3	4	13	2
N	184	58	23	17	282

Note: Individuals chose up to two reasons, so column percentages sum to more than 100.

Source: SCELI Northampton WAWH Survey.

worked for money (both for essentials and extras) and least likely to say that they worked 'for a sense of independence' or 'to feel that I'm doing something worthwhile'.

Group 5 ('Labour market descenders') were unanimous in *not* declaring the desire to use their abilities to the full as being a reason for working, presumably as a result of their typically unfulfilling jobs. They were fairly instrumentally minded (for instance in their high ratings on the items concerned with purchasing essentials and extras) but not to such an extent as group 4.

Repeating the above analysis for the females in the sample

produced a clear picture of the diversity in their outlooks on work. Differences between the three groups containing significant numbers of women (see Table 3.5*b*) reached statistical significance on four of the nine items: 30 per cent of the women in the 'primary segment' gave 'to use my abilities to the full' as one of their reasons, compared to only 8 per cent of 'stickers' and 4 per cent of 'female descenders'; 'female descenders' and 'stickers' were much more likely to report 'working to earn money to buy extras' (47 and 45 per cent respectively) than 'primary segment' women (16 per cent). Not one of the 68 women in the 'primary segment' reported working 'to get out of the house', compared to 14 and 13 per cent of the 'stickers' and 'descenders' respectively. Finally, only 2 per cent of the 'primary segment' women gave 'the company of others' as a reason for working compared to 11 and 18 per cent of the 'stickers' and 'descenders'. The picture is clear: the 'primary segment' work for intrinsic reasons, whereas other women work more for benefits extrinsic to the content of their jobs (i.e. money and company) and as a way of avoiding staying at home.

Table 3.5*c*, showing the results for the men, revealed less pronounced differences between clusters than for the women, and less of an overall pattern. Only three variables reached statistical significance, 'to earn money to buy extras', 'to feel I'm doing something worthwhile', and 'to get out of the house'.

LABOUR SUPPLY SEGMENTATION AND GENDER

Much of the work on gender in the labour market has emphasized the difference between male and female labour markets and has not investigated divisions within the gender groups (a notable exception to this trend being the work by Dex on different patterns of female participation over the childbirth period (1987)). The female labour market has thus been treated either directly, or by omission, as relatively homogeneous and at times as synonymous with the secondary sector of the labour market (Barron and Norris 1976). This analysis shows that dichotomization of the labour market, whether by industrial or occupational criteria or by gender is much too simplistic. Of the five segments that have been described, women were represented in three of them;

24 per cent were in the 'primary segment', 43 per cent in the 'stickers', and 29 per cent in the 'female descenders' group (the other two groups contained less than 5 per cent of the women between them).

So, in what important ways did the women in these three groups differ? First, we shall consider the differences between the first group and the other two, taken together, and then go on to explore the differences in the latter two groups. Most of these differences were sizeable and predictable, and revealed the greater advantage of women in the primary sector. The eleven largest differences were: (1) the skill content of their jobs was higher, (2) they were better educated, (3) they had less domestic interference with their labour market activity, (4) their Cambridge Scale Scores were higher, (5) they were paid more, (6) they received more fringe benefits, (7) they were more likely to see themselves as having a career and (8) to describe their job as skilled, (9) more likely to have had training for their current job, (10) to be in a trade union, and (11) to say that they had promotion prospects. All of these differences were extremely large (many of the other variables used in the clustering also attained statistical significance). The principal exceptions to this were the job satisfaction items, where there was little difference between 'primary segment' women and the other two groups.

By unpacking the individual variables that constituted the 'domestic interference' compound variables it could be seen just how different the 'primary segment' was from the other two groups of women. For instance, 76 per cent of the other groups had at some point in the past done full-time housework, compared to 35 per cent of the 'primary segment'; 54 per cent of the women in the other two groups had at some point given up a job for domestic reasons, compared to only 15 per cent of the 'primary segment' women. 48 per cent of the other two groups of women stated that their choice of jobs were limited by looking after children, compared to only 17 per cent of the 'primary segment'. Presumably because of these different backgrounds, 60 per cent of the other two groups of women were currently working part time, and 81 per cent had at some time worked part time, compared to only 10 per cent of the 'primary segment' women who were working part time at the time of the survey, or 40 per cent who had ever worked part time.

The differences between the women in the other two groups ('stickers' and 'female descenders') were smaller and were revealed on different items. In general, the former tended to be more advantaged than the latter; the main exception to this being the slightly better education and father's social class of the women in the 'female descenders' group. The main differences between these two groups were their responses to the job satisfaction items. The 'stickers' were easily the most satisfied with their jobs of all the groups, especially with their job overall, their opportunity to use their own initiative and their pay. They were markedly more likely than the 'female descenders' to state that their current job paid as well or better than their previous job and that their jobs were secure and to have access to fringe benefits at work. They were also less likely to think that given their experience and skill they should have been in a better job. On most items the 'female descenders' were the least satisfied group, except for the item about the ability and efficiency of management and the pay where the 'primary segment' had a slightly lower mean score. These women were five times as likely as the 'stickers' to want to change jobs if plenty were available and over twice as likely to have applied for one or more jobs over the last year. They were only a third as likely to see their best chances of promotion internally to the firm and less than half as likely to see their present job as being the one that they liked better than all the others that they had had.

So, although these two groups of women seemed to be doing fairly similar jobs, with little difference in their skill levels, one group was far more satisfied with their lot and less willing to change it than the other. The reason for this is probably to be found in their career trajectories over the recent past. The 'female descenders' seemed to have been going down over recent years to worse paid jobs, which they considered below them—often a major factor in low job satisfaction. The 'stickers' seemed to have started with slightly lower expectations (going by their educational attainments and father's social class) but they had been more successful in minimizing the damage to their labour market position of domestic disruption. It is perhaps because of these differences that the 'stickers' felt very secure and looked to the internal labour market as the way forward while the 'female descenders' were keener to better their position by making a move between firms.

This explanation is supported by the differences in the current domestic interference variables for the 'stickers' and 'female descenders': 35 per cent of the 'stickers' reported being restricted by looking after children compared to 68 per cent of the 'female descenders'; 53 per cent of the 'stickers' worked part time compared to 69 per cent of the 'female descenders'. But there was little difference between the two groups in the way in which their domestic circumstances had interfered with their previous labour market behaviour, as measured by variables such as whether they had ever worked part time, left jobs for domestic reasons, or done full-time housework.

This division between women in secondary labour markets perhaps corresponds to the distinctions that Joshi (1982) found when examining the stability in segments in the labour market through the examination of insurance card records. She found an age effect whereby older women formed a particularly stable work-force, the size of which was particularly resistant to cyclical trends in the economy. The age differences between women in the clusters were in the same direction as this with a higher mean age of women in the 'stickers' cluster (the most stable part of the work-force) (42 years old) than women in the less stable clusters containing significant proportions of female employees, i.e. the 'female descenders' (37 years) or the 'primary segment' (34 years).

A related question to these is whether the analyses presented here disaggregated by clusters give more homogeneous groups than a more traditional analysis by gender. Put another way, are the women in the 'primary segment' more similar to the men in the 'primary segment' or to the women in the 'stickers' cluster? This question was addressed by performing an analysis of variance using both gender and cluster membership as the two independent variables, with each of the fifty-one clustering variables (see Appendix 3.1) as dependent variables in separate analyses. This analysis permits a direct comparison of the predictive power of the clusters with that of gender. Only the cases in the 'primary segment' and 'stickers' clusters were used, as they were the only two with sufficient numbers of men and women to make the analyses viable.

In the vast majority of those fifty-one analyses where there were significant results the 'cluster' independent variable proved to account for more of the variance than gender. There was only one obvious exception to this, the female domestic interference variable; the women in the 'primary segment' had levels of domestic interference nearer to the female 'stickers' than either of the male groups. This suggests that those women are relatively successful in the labour market *despite* their domestic roles, not because they have avoided domestic interference.

There were also a small number of statistically significant two-way interactions between gender and cluster. For instance, the men in the 'stickers' were more likely to be trade union members than the men in the 'primary segment', but that pattern was reversed for women who had higher rates in the 'primary segment'. It was also the case that women in the 'primary segment' were more likely to be married than women in the 'stickers', but there was no difference in marital status between clusters for the men. However, excepting these few variables, it was overwhelmingly the case that cluster membership was a more powerful indicator of an individual's position in the labour market than their gender. With the partial exception of women's domestic interference to their labour market participation, there is little evidence that gender can be treated as a meaningful unifying category of experiences. Advantaged women have more in common with advantaged men than with less advantaged women; some less advantaged women have more in common with men (i.e. the 'stickers' cluster), but other disadvantaged women (i.e. the 'female descenders') do have positions in the labour market unique to women.

Gender segregation and the clusters

As outlined in Chapter 1, four variables in the SCELI data explicitly addressed the issue of gender segregation at work: first, work-place segregation, second, perceived job segregation, third, an objective sex-ratio measure derived by calculating the proportion of women within each occupational unit group, and, finally, the reasons given for why the jobs were segregated. These data were analysed separately for the three clusters of women (1, 2, 3) and four clusters of men (1, 2, 4, 5) where there were enough women or men to make the analysis viable.

There were no statistically significant differences between the clusters for either the men or the women on the first of these items, work-place segregation. However, for women there were large differences in the perceived job segregation between the clusters. Women in the 'primary segment' were much more likely to state that they were doing 'men's jobs' than the other two groups of women; 13 per cent of the women in this cluster were doing jobs done either exclusively or mainly by men, compared to less than 3 per cent in the other two clusters. Conversely, only 12 per cent of the women in the 'primary segment' were doing jobs done exclusively by women, compared to 30 per cent in each of the other two groups (see Table 3.6a). The men's data on gender segregation did not attain statistical significance (Table 3.6b).

These figures closely matched the results given by the objective sex-ratio measure. For instance, 39 per cent of women in the 'primary segment' were in the mixed-job category, compared to only 8 per cent of the 'stickers' and 10 per cent of the 'female descenders'. 'Primary segment' women were only half as likely to be in the exclusively female OUG groups; 28 per cent of them were in this group compared to 54 per cent of the 'stickers' and 50 per cent of the 'female descenders'.

Evidence from the work histories suggests that these differences are enduring features of labour market participation (see next Chapter). If one looks at the proportion of all previous jobs each woman had done that fell into this mixed category, there was still a marked difference between clusters. An average of 23 per cent of the primary segment's previous jobs were mixed, compared to only 10 per cent for the 'stickers' and 17 per cent for the 'female descenders' group. The patterns for the men were broadly similar, with less segregation in the 'primary segment' than in the less advantaged clusters, but the differences were less marked.

In some ways these results confirm previous findings relating to occupation and gender segregation (e.g. Martin and Roberts's (1984), which are also repeated in the SCELI data). However, differences in gender segregation between clusters, rather than between occupations, gives a stronger sense of the way segregation is not just linked to the current labour market position, but to the whole pattern of women's participation in the labour market over a lifetime.

Up to four reasons were recorded for the open-ended question

TABLE 3.6 *Perceived gender segregation of jobs by cluster and by sex*
(a) *Women*

	Primary segment	Stickers	Female descenders	All women in these three clusters
Exclusively by men	2	0	1	1
Mainly by men	11	3	1	5
By an equal mixture of men and women	37	29	20	28
Mainly by women	38	39	48	41
Exclusively by women	12	30	29	25
Total	100	101	99	100
N	68	134	80	282

(b) *Men*

	Primary segment	Stickers	Young and mobile	Labour market descenders	All men in these four clusters
Exclusively by men	43	47	33	49	43
Mainly by men	39	44	35	48	40
By an equal mixture of men and women	17	9	33	3	16
Mainly by women	1	0	0	0	1
Exclusively by women	0	0	0	0	0
Total	100	100	101	100	100
N	184	58	23	17	282

Source: SCELI Northampton WAWH Survey.

probing for explanations of why their job was a man's or a woman's job. These were coded using a frame of 29 and 26 categories for men's and women's jobs separately.[9]

In the Northampton data there were only four men who professed to doing jobs done mainly by women, and none who did jobs done almost exclusively by women. The cluster breakdown of the lay explanations of job sex-typing given by the other three groups, men doing men's jobs, women doing women's jobs, and women doing men's jobs, revealed the following.

The most common reason given by men doing men's jobs referred to the heavy or physical nature of the job (45 per cent of cases), followed by general references to tradition (19 per cent); 13 per cent explicitly stated that there was no reason why women should not do the work, 12 per cent said women did not apply, and 12 per cent said that the work was dirty. All other reasons were given by 9 per cent or less of the sample.

There were marked differences between clusters in the reasons given for perceived sex segregation. The 'primary segment' was much less likely to use the 'heavy work' reason (35 per cent) compared to 59–65 per cent for the other three clusters with men. The similar item about dirty work was only given by 10 per cent of the men in the 'primary segment' compared to 17–25 per cent in the other clusters. Conversely references to tradition were much more likely in the 'primary segment' (26 per cent) than the other three groups (0–7 per cent). The differences between clusters on the frequency of the 'women don't apply' and 'no reason' items were small.

The conclusion that can be drawn from this is that the jobs in the 'primary sector' that women were excluded from are ones where the reason for exclusion has little to do with job content (tradition or women not applying). Jobs that women are excluded from for reasons to do with job content are often physically strenuous or dirty, and, while probably paying better than many women's jobs, would offer little more in the way of status, prestige or skill than the ones that women currently do.

The sixteen women who claimed to be doing jobs done mainly by men formed too small a sample to analyse in any detail, but interestingly the modal answer here was in agreement with the men; four of the sixteen claimed that it was the heavy physical demands of the job that put women in a minority in their jobs.

The six most commonly reported categories of reasons given by Northampton women as to why their jobs were done mainly or exclusively by women were: the low pay (20 per cent), tradition (18 per cent), the caring qualities of women (15 per cent), the short hours or hours more suitable for women with domestic responsibilities (15 per cent), men do not apply (13 per cent), and the skills, qualifications, or experience needed are only found in women (9 per cent).

Women in the 'stickers' cluster were much less likely to say that it was the low pay that made their jobs women's jobs (10 per cent) than the 'primary segment' or 'female descenders' (33 per cent and 26 per cent) (see Table 3.7). They were also less likely to refer to the caring qualities of women (10 per cent compared to 16 and 26 per cent respectively). There was a complete absence of reference to part time or hours by the 'primary segment' women (presumably because 91 per cent of the 'primary segment' women worked full time). The 'female descenders' were much less likely to use tradition as a reason (9 per cent compared to 18 and 26 per cent for the other two groups) but more likely to say that it was because men do not apply (21 per cent compared to 9 and 10 per cent). One other item gave rise to apparently large differences between clusters; 'primary segment' women were more likely to say that public expectations were important (25 per cent compared to 5 and 3 per cent).

These differences in explanations for gender segregation between the clusters certainly suggest that individual perceptions of how gender segregation comes about are influenced by different labour market processes and situations. While management may be able to provide a rationale for every new pattern of gender segregation it is perhaps comforting to note the much greater emphasis placed by these women on the terms and conditions of employment compared to the skills required for the job as the main factors perpetuating segregation.

CONCLUSION

The empirical investigation of labour market segmentation in the Northampton labour market has revealed a structuring of the labour supply which is associated with quite marked and interactive relationships between individuals' past work history, their current labour market position, and their attitudes towards their current jobs and expectations of the future. Gender differences in labour market position arise out of an interaction of all of these features. These findings suggest that attitudes and behaviour in the labour market cannot be inferred either from the individual's

TABLE 3.7 *Reasons for gender segregation by cluster (% giving each reason, multiresponse)*

(a) *Women doing exclusively or mainly women's jobs*

	Primary segment	Stickers	Female descenders	All women in these three clusters
Low pay	33	10	26	20
Tradition	18	26	9	18
Part-time, hours, domestic responsibility, etc.	0	18	19	15
Caring qualities of women	16	10	20	15
Men don't apply	9	10	21	13
Skills, qualifications, experience unique to women	11	9	9	9
Public expectations	25	5	3	8
N[a]	31	73	56	161

(b) *Men doing exclusively or mainly men's jobs*

	Primary segment	Stickers	Young and mobile	Labour market descenders	All men in these four clusters
Heavy work	35	59	61	65	45
Tradition	26	7	5	0	18
No reason—women could do the job	12	18	0	15	13
Women don't apply	13	13	0	15	12
Dirty work	10	10	26	17	12
N[a]	138	49	16	13	216

[a] Excludes men and women working in jobs with other degrees of gender segregation.

Source: SCELI Northampton WAWH Survey.

current job situation or from their stage in the life cycle or family circumstances in isolation. Nevertheless the complexity of the process of labour market structuring does not appear to give rise simply to individualized or seemingly random outcomes. The five clusters that this statistical investigation revealed bear close relationship to labour market segments that have been identified by social researchers and by management in their recruitment policies. Alongside the more career-orientated, higher-paid primary segment we identified several types of secondary-segment workers; from the stable and satisfied female 'stickers', to the temporarily less advantaged young and mobile and the more permanently disadvantaged 'labour market descenders', whose chances of moving out of temporary and insecure work into permanent employment seemed very slim. These categories are similar to the groups often identified by employers as available for secondary jobs—stable female part-timers, young mobile workers, and the long-term or frequently unemployed 'no-hopers'. Perhaps the segment which fits least well with established views of how the labour supply is structured is that of the relatively dissatisfied 'female descenders'. This segment may be indicative of future labour market trends as women, particularly those with more qualifications, become more dissatisfied with their confinement to low-paid and low-status jobs. Further research will be necessary to establish whether we are identifying a minority response by women to their position in the labour market or the first hints of a more fundamental change in the ways in which women interpret and react to their labour market position. In the meantime, these results clearly demonstrate the need to develop a more sensitive and sophisticated approach towards the analysis of the structuring of the labour supply than has been evident in labour market segmentation theory to date.

APPENDIX 3.1: A SUMMARY OF THE VARIABLES USED IN THE CLUSTERING

JOB ATTRIBUTES AND CONTENT

1 Index of skill needed/used in job.[10]
2 Employment contract (permanent, fixed contract, or temporary).
3 Perceived security of current job.

4 Social-class rating of job (Cambridge Scale Score[11]).
5 Whether the job is seen to have promotion prospects.
6 Whether currently a member of a trade union.
7 Whether the individual has received training for this job since leaving full-time education.

EMPLOYER ATTRIBUTES

8 Size of establishment.
9 Public or private sector.

REWARDS

10 Gross hourly pay (logged).
11 Weighted index of fringe benefits (e.g. company car).[12]

WORK HISTORY ATTRIBUTES

12 Whether the individual has ever been unemployed.
13 Whether one has ever been dismissed or made redundant.
14 Proportion of time in jobs that were better paid than the previous job.
15 Proportion of time in jobs from which they moved to a job that was paid the same or worse than the previous job.
16 Proportion of time in jobs taken because they were better jobs.
17 Proportion of time in jobs that one left to go to lower social class (CSS) jobs.
18 Proportion of time in jobs with the same social class (CSS) as the previous job.
19 Mean closeness of supervision in current and all previous jobs.
20 Whether current job paid more or less than last job.
21 Amount of choice respondent reported having when looking for current job.

EMPLOYMENT PERCEPTIONS, ATTITUDES, EXPECTATIONS, AND SATISFACTION

22 Whether respondent has applied for any jobs in the last year.
23 Whether respondent would want to change jobs if plenty were available.
24 Respondents' perception of whether, given their qualifications and experience, they should be in better, similar, or worse job.
25 Their perception of how likely they are to get a better job in the next two years.

26 How easy they think it would be to get another job as good as their current one if they were looking for work today.

27 How likely they would be to find another job in the Northampton area using the same skills.

28 Whether their best chance of a better job would be with the same or a different employer.

29 Whether it is an advantage or not to already be working in their current organization when a better job comes up in the organization.

30 Whether they consider their current job to be skilled.

31 Whether they consider themselves to have a career.

How satisfied they rate themselves as on a scale from 0 to 10 for each of the following attributes of their job:

32 Promotion prospects

33 Total pay

34 Relations with supervisor or manager

35 Job security

36 Use of initiative

37 Ability and efficiency of management

38 The actual work itself

39 Hours worked

40 The job overall.

41 Whether, of all the jobs that they have ever done, their current job is the one that they like best.[13]

EXTRA-LABOUR MARKET VARIABLES

42 Social class of father's job when respondent was 14.

43 Social class of mother's job before she had children.

44 Proportion of time mother worked when respondent was a child.

45 A combined education variable constructed from years of schooling, highest school qualification, and highest post-school qualification.

46 Gender.

47 Age.

48 Marital status.

49 Whether their choice of jobs is restricted by their household's income needs.

50 Female domestic interference (constructed from variables which seem to affect almost exclusively women):

(*a*) part time/full time for current job.

(*b*) the proportion of their working lives that have been part time.

(*c*) whether they have had any spells of full-time housework.

and

(*d*) proportion of time in jobs that they left for domestic reasons.
51 General Domestic Interference (applying to men and women more equally):
(*a*) Total number of dependent children in the household.
(*b*) The amount which choice of jobs is restricted by partner's job, having to look after elderly or sick adults, and having to look after children.[14]

NOTES

1. For example, those who gain entry to a primary segment job also enjoy chances of promotion, while those who experience unemployment are less likely to be hired by a primary firm in the future (Osterman 1988).
2. i.e. variables measuring achieved position, pay, security, satisfaction, perception of future moves, trends in their past work history, education, and so on.
3. The self-employed, unemployed, and economically inactive respondents were excluded from all analyses presented here.
4. A more complete discussion of these variables is contained in Burchell and Rubery (1990). All variables (some being dichotomous, some continuous) were standardized before entry, and all missing values were replaced with the mean scores on each variable.
5. Employees' perceptions of the internal labour market were measured by asking them whether they saw the best opportunities of advancement as being with their current employer or with another employer.
6. The other 7% of the sample were excluded because they formed clusters of less than 6 individuals (i.e. less than 1% of the sample). In the cases that were inspected closely this was because either they had very unusual patterns of responses on the variables, or they had clearly been flippant in their responses.
7. There are other more complex ways in which the clusters may reasonably be expected to change between different local labour markets. For instance, one or more of the five clusters discussed here may be differentiated into two separate groups, while others may become more similar and be formed into one cluster.
8. $p < 0.025$ (1 tailed) for both of these results using Fisher's Exact Test (Siegel 1956).
9. Because of the large number of categories used and the problems with subjecting questions of this sort to rigorous empirical analysis (Belson 1988), the treatment of results here will be straightforward and descriptive.

10. See Horrell, Rubery, and Burchell (1989*a*, 1989*b*) for a detailed description of this scale, which contains items both about the person (e.g. qualifications needed) and about the job requirements (e.g. specialist knowledge).
11. A continuous scale of 'relative advantage' derived from friendship patterns; see Stewart, Prandy, and Blackburn (1980).
12. See Horrell, Rubery, and Burchell (1989*a*, 1989*b*) for a detailed description of this scale.
13. This variable was derived from a question asked directly after the respondents had listed all the jobs that they had ever done in the work history.
14. An exploratory factor analysis suggested this division of these six variables into two groups. Otherwise the problem of multicollinearity may have overemphasized these variables in the formation of the clusters.

REFERENCES

ARMSTRONG, P. (1982), 'If it's only Women it Doesn't Matter so much', in J. West (ed.), *Women, Work and the Labour Market*. London, Routledge & Kegan Paul.

ASHTON, D. C., and MAGUIRE, M. J. (1986), *Young Adults in the Labour Market*. Research Paper No. 55, Department of Employment, London, HMSO.

BARRON, R. D., and NORRIS, G. M. (1976), 'Sexual Divisions and the Dual Labour Market', in D. L. Barker and S. Allen (eds.), *Dependence and Exploitation in Work and Marriage*. London, Longman.

BELSON, W. A. (1988), 'Major Error from Two Commonly Used Methods of Market and Social Research', *Psychologist*, 1: 229–230.

BURCHELL, B. J., and RUBERY, J. (1990), *Segmented Jobs and Segmented Workers: An Empirical Investigation*. Social Change and Economic Life Working Paper No. 13, Nuffield College, Oxford.

CRAIG, C., GARNSEY, E., and RUBERY, J. (1985), *Payment Structures and Smaller Firms: Women's Employment in Segmented Labour Markets*. Research Paper No. 48, Department of Employment, London, HMSO.

—— RUBERY, J., TARLING, R., and WILKINSON, F. (1982), *Labour Market Structure, Industrial Organisation and Low Pay*. Cambridge, Cambridge University Press.

CROMPTON, R., and JONES, G. (1984), *White-Collar Proletariat: Deskilling and Gender in Clerical Work*. London, Macmillan.

DEX, S. (1987), *Women's Occupational Mobility*. London, Macmillan.

DOERINGER, P., and PIORE, M. (1971), *Internal Labour Markets and Manpower Analysis*. Lexington, Mass., D. C. Heath & Co.

EVERITT, B. (1974), *Cluster Analysis*. London, Heinemann Educational.

HORRELL, S., RUBERY, J., and BURCHELL, B. (1989*a*), 'Unequal Jobs or Unequal Pay?', *Industrial Relations Journal*, 20: 176–92. (Also SCELI Working Paper No. 6.)

—— —— —— (1989*b*), 'Gender and Skills', *Work, Employment and Society*, 4/2, June: 189–216.

JOSHI, H. (1982), 'Secondary Workers in the Cycle', *Econometrica*, 48: 29–44.

MARSHALL, A. (1989), 'The Sequel of Unemployment: The Changing Role of Part-Time and Temporary Work in Western Europe', in G. Rodgers and J. Rodgers (eds.), *Precarious Jobs in Labour Market Regulation: The Growth of Atypical Employment in Western Europe*. Geneva, IILS.

MARTIN, J., and ROBERTS, C. (1984), *Women in Employment: A Lifetime Perspective*. London, HMSO.

OSTERMAN, P. (1988), *Employment Futures*. New York, OUP.

ROSENBERG, S. (1989), 'From Segmentation to Flexibility', *Labour and Society*, 14/4, Oct: 363–407.

SIEGEL, S. (1956), *Non-parametric Statistics for the Social Scientist*. Tokyo, McGraw Hill.

STEWART, A., PRANDY, K., and BLACKBURN, R. M. (1980), *Social Stratification and Occupations*. London, Macmillan.

4

'And never the twain shall meet'? Gender Segregation and Work Histories

ALISON MacEWEN SCOTT AND BRENDAN BURCHELL

INTRODUCTION

This chapter looks at the effect of gender segregation on women's and men's work histories, particularly their chances of job promotion and occupational mobility. There has been much interest recently in using work history analysis to reveal the specificity of women's working patterns. As is well known, the structure of most women's labour-force participation is strongly affected by their domestic roles and these roles have different effects at different points in the life cycle. Therefore a longitudinal analysis is necessary to see how women's work histories or 'careers' interweave with their domestic cycle. (Careers are defined here as any sequence of jobs held over the lifetime, horizontal as well as vertical.) Various people have used work histories to trace the changing patterns of women's labour-force participation during their lifetimes, the movement in and out of part-time work, and the increase and decrease in earnings and mobility opportunities. Many authors have pointed to the non-linear trends in these patterns, particularly during the phase of child-rearing (e.g. Martin and Roberts 1984, Joshi 1984, 1987, Dex 1987, Elias and Main in Hunt 1988, Payne and Abbott 1990, Walby 1991).

A similar call for longitudinal analysis has also come from two other bodies of literature, both of which focus on patterns of

This research was partly financed by the ESRC as part of SCELI and partly by the Fuller Bequest of the Department of Sociology, University of Essex. We are grateful to Angela Dale, Shirley Dex, and Peter Elias for comments.

movement between jobs over the lifetime, especially career patterns. First, there is labour market segmentation theory, which emphasizes as evidence of segmentation contrasting patterns of upward mobility through internal career structures in the primary sector and frequent job changing between low-paid jobs in the secondary sector (e.g. Edwards *et al*. 1975). Second, there is the analysis of intra-generational mobility and class structure, which has frequently called for the analysis of sequential patterns of movement rather than comparisons of two points in time (Sørenson 1970, Stewart *et al*. 1980, Bertaux 1991).

It has been an obvious step to bring these concerns together. Dex, for example (1987, 1990), has shown how women's patterns of movement in the labour market produced particular 'career' structures which have implications for their class position and the general process of labour market segmentation. The collection edited by Payne and Abbott (1990) further develops these links in a number of ways.

However, much of this work has focused on movement between broad occupational categories, and although many authors mention the importance of gender segregation in structuring women's opportunities and preferences, there has been little systematic investigation of its effect on career patterns at a more micro-level. Yet its relevance is obvious for at least two reasons. First, gender segregation is strongly linked to job and occupational hierarchies. 'Women's' jobs are clustered at the bottom of these hierarchies, therefore so long as women are confined to such jobs, their potential for upward mobility is clearly limited. This applies most obviously to mobility between broad occupational classes, but it is also relevant within them where gender segregation can impede promotion within short-span career structures. Second, a 'gendering' of careers, that is a lifetime confinement of men to 'male' jobs and women to 'female' jobs would be an important indicator of labour market segmentation. This is suggested by one early British version of dual labour market theory, which argued that gender divisions mapped on to labour market segments directly; men were mainly in the primary sector, which was the one where career progression was concentrated, and women were in the secondary sector, where there was none (Barron and Norris 1976). This implied that men's careers developed by movement between 'male' jobs, while women were confined to job changing between casual low-paid female jobs.[1]

Although it is now known that women do have a presence in the primary sector (Dex 1987, Burchell and Rubery 1990, and this volume), there is some suggestion that they do not have access to internal career structures in the same way as men, and gender segregation may play a role in this. Studies of white-collar employees, for example, argue that men and women are located on different career tracks even though they may for a time be employed in similar jobs (Crompton and Jones 1984). This would imply that men pass through mixed-sex jobs on their way up to the more 'male' jobs at the top; women, on the other hand, increasingly move towards more 'female' ones as they turn to part-time work during their child-rearing phase (Elias and Main 1982, Martin and Roberts 1984, Dex 1987).

In fact, we know relatively little about how *men's* work history patterns link with occupational segregation. Recent explorations of these issues have mainly focused on women, not only because the rich longitudinal data in the Women and Employment survey were only available for women. Are men's mobility patterns confined to 'male' jobs, as was implied by early dual labour market theory? Or do men pass through mixed-sex jobs at the early stages of their careers, as suggested above? Is this 'white-collar' pattern applicable to manual men? Does gender segregation facilitate men's career mobility by limiting the degree of competition for top jobs as these authors have suggested? Do 'female' occupations provide a source of promotion for men who might not make it in 'male' occupations? These questions indicate that mobility analysis needs to take into account the segregated nature of the occupational structure within which people move, and look at the consequences of this for the career patterns of both women and men.

This chapter provides a preliminary exploration of these issues. It examines the effect of gender segregation on mobility at a more disaggregated level than has been done hitherto—at the level of changes between jobs and occupations (defined at the level of 3-digit occupational unit groups). Using these measures, we ask to what extent men and women are confined to 'male' or 'female' jobs throughout their working lives? What effect does such confinement have on career progression? Does movement from a 'female' to a 'male' job involve upward mobility and the reverse direction, downward mobility? How far does the experience of gender segmentation over the lifetime vary by social class? The role of the domestic cycle is important for women. We know that there is an immediate downgrading of occupational status and pay on first return to work, but how far do breaks for full-time housework affect promotion chances later? And how do these kinds of breaks compare with the more typical 'male' breaks such as redundancy and dismissal?

METHODOLOGICAL PRELIMINARIES

The SCELI data set offers a unique opportunity to examine the questions outlined above, first because it contains extremely detailed data on work and life histories, and second because the segregation data include both men and women. We can compare men's and women's experience of the labour market over their lifetimes with a much more complex range of variables for each job held than has been possible to date. For a description of the work and life history technique used in the SCELI research see Marsh and Gershuny 1991, Burchell 1993.

Unfortunately the measure of gender segregation attached to each job in the work history was that of *work-place* segregation, which is inappropriate for the analysis of occupational segregation (see discussion of the various measures in Chapter 1).[2] Therefore we developed an occupational sex ratio index as an alternative measure of segregation, classifying each job in the work histories according to this index. Using current jobs in the work histories, the ratio of men to women in each occupational unit group (OUG) was calculated and this was used to assign each of the 161 OUGs to a point on a scale, from occupations held exclusively by women at one extreme to ones held exclusively by men at the other. (OUG categories that occurred less than ten times in these 4,283 jobs were instead classified on the basis of the 1981 decennial census to enhance accuracy; this involved 7 per cent of the cases). This is referred to as the SEXRATIO variable in this chapter.

This method of measuring occupational segregation was compared with a classification based on the perceived segregation of each current job, contained in the Work Attitudes questionnaire. A subjective segregation scale was calculated by aggregating the perceived segregation of each current holder of jobs within each OUG category. With less data to classify each OUG category, particularly for the infrequently occurring OUGs, this scale may have been less accurate; but it was nevertheless very highly correlated at the level of OUGs with the observed SEXRATIO variable ($r = 0.96$), see also Table 1.2, Chapter 1.

There are three potential drawbacks with a scale computed in this manner. First, it ignores any changes in the gendering of OUG categories over the timescale of the work histories, although the evidence suggests that there has been little change in the majority of jobs (Siltanen 1990). Secondly, it ignores any finer subdivisions between jobs within OUG categories; respondents may classify their jobs at a finer level than the OUG categories and the gendering of those finer categories may be lost in the aggregation.[3] Thirdly, by classifying at the level of the OUG category rather than by taking each individual's perception of their own job, a considerable amount of variability between individual perceptions has been lost. The net effect of all these considerations has produced a greater concentration of the population in 'female' occupations and less in 'male' ones, than that given by the subjectively based scale; see discussion in Chapter 1, pp. 7–8.

In our analysis the information contained in individual work histories is used in two ways. First, taking the individual as the unit of analysis we constructed a 'gender history' variable (GEN-HIST), which identified the ways in which jobs with different occupational sex ratios had been combined over individuals' lifetimes. Because of the large number of possible combinations in individual work histories of jobs with differing occupational sex ratios, we collapsed the SEXRATIO variable into a three-point scale; 'male' occupations were those where men were over 70 per cent, 'female' one were those where women were over 70 per cent, and 'mixed' ones were those where men and women were between 31 and 69 per cent. (In order to compare longitudinal and cross-sectional measures of gender segregation, the three-point measure of the SEXRATIO variable has also been used for the analysis of current jobs in this paper). The GENHIST variable produced seven categories: at the extremes were those who had only ever been in 'male' or 'female' jobs, and in between, those who had combined 'male', 'female', and 'mixed' jobs in various ways. Note that the GENHIST variable is not weighted by the *proportion* of jobs in different segments over the individual career. Thus, for example, a man who appears in a 'male and female' career may have only had one 'female' job and four 'male' jobs. This may have underestimated the degree of concentration in exclusively 'male' or 'female' occupations.

Second, using *job changes* as the unit of analysis we investigated the degree to which movement from one job to another involved 'promotions' or 'demotions' and how far each type of transition was associated with a move to a more or less gender-segregated job. The analysis here built on work already commenced by the Cambridge team on the relationship between job changing and promotions (see Burchell 1993 for a detailed description of this method). This variable permits an analysis of vertical movement between *jobs* rather than *occupations* and hence enables us to assess the influence of gender segregation on careers at a more micro-level.

Finally, a word about the use of class analysis in this chapter. As many have observed (Martin and Roberts 1984, Dale *et al.* 1985), it is difficult to find an occupational classification that suits both men and women. For a number of reasons to do with the small number of categories, the inclusion of manual/ non-manual criteria and comparability with international research, we used the Registrar-General's 'social class' grouping of occupations.[4] In parts of the analysis, we have cross-tabulated work history variables with *current* social class. Care should be taken not to interpret these data as a representation of movement between class categories during the lifetime, but rather as the past profile of movement of those currently occupying a particular class situation.

GENDER SEGREGATION AND GENDERED CAREERS

The results presented in this section use the respondent as the unit of analysis. Although we are using information from their life histories, it is being aggregated to describe and explain their status and employment experiences at the point of the survey in

1986. The total sample size was 6,111 respondents, although most of the following section only applies to those who were employed or in self-employment at the time of the survey (4,283).

The Introduction to this book has given an overview of the structure of gender segregation in current jobs, based on the perceived job segregation measure. This shows a high degree of vertical and horizontal gender segregation; men are concentrated in 'male' jobs, and women in 'female' jobs. Gender segregation is variable between and within occupational classes, the upper echelons of both manual and non-manual work being more dominated by 'male' occupations and the lower ones by 'female' occupations. Overall, manual occupations are much more sex segregated than non-manual ones. Gender segregation is strongly related to earnings inequality because of its association with occupation and gender, and even controlling for both of these, it has a small independent effect on earnings (see Sloane, this volume). Therefore, not only do women earn less than men because of their unequal distribution between occupational classes, but their earnings are lowered further by being located in more 'female' jobs within them. These data suggest that confinement to a 'female' set of occupations over the lifetime would constrain women's chances for promotion, increased earnings and occupational mobility, while men would largely benefit from confinement to 'men's' jobs.

Table 4.1 gives the aggregate distribution of the SCELI sample according to the sex ratio variable. Two-thirds of men are in occupations that are over 70 per cent male, while three-quarters of women are in ones that are over 70 per cent female. Controlling for age shows little change in this situation (Table 4.2). There is some evidence of a decrease in segregation amongst men with age, but not amongst women. The proportions in 'female' jobs are slightly lower in the 30–9 age group than in the previous one, but they revert to their former level amongst the over-40s. Overall, the major pattern is the remarkable stability in the distributions between age groups. This might suggest that men and women remain in highly gender segregated jobs throughout their lifetimes, and that their respective career patterns are largely structured by movement within clusters of 'female' and 'male' occupations.

However, the GENHIST variable does not confirm this. In all, only two-fifths of the sample have worked exclusively in

TABLE 4.1 *Distribution of men and women by occupational sex ratios (current job 1986)* (%)[a]

Occupational sex ratios	Men	Women	Total	% female
>90% men	34	1	20	1
70–89% men	30	5	20	11
Mixed	23	17	20	36
70–89% women	11	33	20	69
>90% women	2	43	19	93
Total	100	99	99	42
N	2,492	1,791	4,283	

[a] Includes self-employed, excludes unemployed.

Source: SCELI Six Areas Work Attitudes and Work Histories (WAWH) Survey.

TABLE 4.2 *Distribution of men and women by occupational sex ratios and age group* (%)

Age group	Male[a]	Mixed[a]	Female[a]	Total	%	N
20–9 years						
Men	68	16	16	100	28	702
Women	7	15	78	100	28	500
30–9 years						
Men	65	25	10	100	32	795
Women	6	21	73	100	30	538
40+ years						
Men	61	25	14	100	40	995
Women	6	16	78	100	42	753
Total						
Men	64	22	14	100	100	2,492
Women	6	17	76	99	100	1,791

[a] Male = >70% men; female = >70% women; mixed = 31–69% men or women.

Source: SCELI Six Areas WAWH Survey.

occupations dominated by their own sex. However, there are marked differences between men and women. Table 4.3 shows that only a third of men have been confined to 'male' occupations throughout their lifetimes, while half of women have been confined to 'female' ones. The distribution of the sample between

GENHIST categories by current age shows a decline in 'male' and 'female' occupational confinement with age (Table 4.4). The proportions of men in 'only male' careers falls from 43 per cent in the 20–9 age group to 27 per cent in the 40+ group, and similarly, the proportion of women in 'only female' careers falls from

TABLE 4.3 *Distribution of men and women in 'gender careers'* (%)

Career	Men	Women	% female	N
Only male	33	—a	1	808
Male and mixed	18	1	4	474
Only mixed	4	4	42	183
Male, mixed, and female	18	9	27	612
Male and female	19	13	34	692
Female and mixed	4	22	78	500
Only female	4	50	90	987
Total	100	100	42	4,256

Note: Missing cases = 27.

a Less than 0.5%.

Source: SCELI Six Areas WAWH Survey.

TABLE 4.4 *Gender careers by current age (grouped) and sex* (%)

Gender careers	20–9 years		30–9 years		40+ years	
	M	F	M	F	M	F
Only male	43	—a	30	—a	27	—a
Male and mixed	13	2	19	1	21	1
Only mixed	5	4	5	6	3	3
Male, mixed, female	9	4	19	9	25	12
Male and female	18	11	17	12	20	15
Female and mixed	3	15	7	26	3	23
Only female	9	64	3	45	1	45
Total	100	100	100	100	100	100
N	695	497	786	535	991	752

Note: Missing cases = 27.

a Less than 0.5%.

Source: SCELI Six Areas WAWH Survey.

64 to 45 per cent in the same age groups. Correspondingly, the proportions of men in 'male and mixed' and of women in 'female and mixed' careers rise with age. Note, however, that the proportions of men and women in 'only mixed' careers are extremely small and decline with age. Therefore even though there is some mixing of experience between occupations with different degrees of segregation over time, most of the work-force has worked in moderately or extremely segregated occupations at some time or other. These data do provide some evidence for the existence of gender segregated careers, and it is much more pronounced amongst women than men, but it is considerably less than might have been expected from the cross-sectional data.

It is not clear from this table whether the age effect is due to a life cycle or a cohort effect. In other words, is it the case that individuals come to experience a greater variety of occupational segregation patterns as they grow older, or is it that those cohorts that entered the work-force, say, in the 1950s and 1960s had less segregated careers than those who entered the work-force in the 1970s and 1980s?

In order to answer this question, it is necessary to reconstruct the age variable such that life cycle and cohort are no longer confounded. This was done by calculating GENHIST only for the jobs held by the respondent up to the age of 30. The age of respondents in 1986, for all those respondents over the age of 30, now becomes a cohort measure, not confounded with life cycle. Those aged 30–9 attained the age of 30 in the years 1977–86, those aged 40–9 attained it in the years 1967–76, and so on. Table 4.5 shows patterns of career segregation up to the age of 30 for respondents now in their thirties, forties, and fifties.

The most striking feature of Table 4.5 is that the distributions across GENHIST by cohort are very similar and, with a sample size of 4,261, highly significant (Chi square (12) = 67, p <0.001). Furthermore, what small differences there are suggest that it is the youngest cohort that has experienced greatest mobility between occupation segregation types before the age of 30, and the least likely to have been restricted to 'female' or 'male' jobs. Two conclusions may be drawn from this. First, the strong effects seen in Table 4.4 are genuinely a life-cycle effect. Second, the confounding but weak effect of cohort will, if anything, have led to an underestimate of the life-cycle effect in Table 4.4.

TABLE 4.5 *Gender careers up to age 30 by cohort (men and women)* (%)

Gender careers	Age in 1986			
	30–9 years	40–59 years	50+ years	Total
Only male	17	21	21	19
Male and mixed	10	11	10	10
Only mixed	6	4	4	5
Male, mixed, female	11	8	11	9
Male and female	15	16	17	16
Female and mixed	14	8	8	11
Only female	27	31	29	30
Total	100	100	100	100
N	1,828	1,269	1,164	4,261

Note: Missing cases = 22.
Source: SCELI Six Areas WAWH Survey.

We must remember that the GENHIST variable merely tells us that older people are more likely to have had some experience of employment in jobs with different degrees of segregation. This is still compatible with the possibility that the majority of their experiences have been in similarly segregated occupations. Without expanding the GENHIST variable to incorporate weights for the number of segregated jobs in the work history, we are unable to say whether this is the case, although the data presented below in the section on job changes are suggestive.

What is interesting about the data provided here is the difference in the degree of segregation in men's and women's careers. It is striking that women face greater long-run concentration in segregated occupations than men. Comparing the percentage of women in 'only female' occupations with the percentage of men in 'only male' occupations, women in the youngest age group are 48 per cent more career segregated than men, and although the level of segregation falls with age, the female–male differential rises to 67 per cent in the 40+ age group.

This could well be associated with differences in promotion and mobility opportunities for the two groups. It would be consistent with the 'white-collar career hypothesis', mentioned above, that is that men's career patterns take them through mixed-sex jobs on their way up to the top, while women are more confined to 'female' jobs at lower levels. (The movement between mixed-sex occupations could also be associated with downward mobility, particularly at lower occupational levels.)

Different mobility trajectories would explain the difference between the cross-sectional and the longitudinal data; the men and women who end up in heavily segregated occupations towards the end of their working lives may have passed through mixed ones on the way, resulting in an overall decline in *career* segregation. However, this pattern would be offset by direct entry into a particular class and career development within it (such as amongst professionals and skilled workers, or alternatively, non-mobile job-changing at low-skilled levels). The 'gendering of careers' could therefore depend on patterns of intra-occupational mobility. Differences in the *degree* of career segregation between men and women would reflect their different mobility trajectories. The next section provides a preliminary exploration of this hypothesis.

GENDERED CAREERS AND SOCIAL CLASS

Table 4.6 shows the pattern of gender segregation in current jobs, as measured by the sex ratio variable, by R.-G. social class, and Table 4.7 gives the distributions of the GENHIST variable by class. Let us take the cross-sectional data first, and assume that manual and non-manual occupations form two separate hierarchies within which most career mobility is structured. As far as manual work is concerned, Table 4.6 shows a high degree of segregation for men and women at all occupational levels. Skilled manual men are the most segregated of any group in the entire class structure, but at partly skilled and unskilled levels, there is a significant number of men working in 'female' occupations. This is not the case for women, amongst whom it is the partly and unskilled workers who are the most segregated, while skilled manual women are to be found in both male and mixed occupations.

We might expect, therefore, that work histories within manual employment would be quite highly segregated at all levels, but with a different pattern of association with skill for men and

TABLE 4.6 *Distribution of men and women by Registrar-General's social class and by occupational sex ratio* (current job) (%)

Social class	Occupational sex ratio			Total	%	N
	Male[a]	Mixed[a]	Female[a]			
Professionals, high admin.						
Men	77	21	2	100	7	182
Women	35	57	8	100	1	25
Intermediate and managers						
Men	36	56	8	100	27	673
Women	7	45	48	100	26	455
Skilled non-manual						
Men	26	21	53	100	11	266
Women	1	5	94	100	36	647
Skilled manual						
Men	89	7	4	100	34	844
Women	21	22	57	100	7	132
Partly skilled manual						
Men	73	8	19	100	16	399
Women	7	7	87	101	22	389
Unskilled manual						
Men	80	—	20	100	4	108
Women	6	—	94	100	8	136
Total						
Men	64	23	13	100	99	2,472
Women	6	17	76	99	100	1,784

Note: Missing cases = 27.

[a] Male = >70% men, female = >70% women, mixed = 31–69% men/women.

Source: SCELI Six Areas WAWH Survey.

women. This in turn will have implications for the pattern of vertical movement between occupational classes and for the development of gender-segregated careers. Skilled men would have been able to make their way up within 'male' occupations or to have achieved direct entry at that level, perhaps through apprenticeship schemes; they would still be relatively segregated towards the end of their careers. However, partly skilled and unskilled men might have been in both 'male' and 'female' occupations. The careers of manual women, on the other hand, would show the opposite pattern; the lower-skilled occupations having higher degrees of career segregation over the lifetime and skilled women showing more movement between mixed-sex occupations as they got older.

Tables 4.7–4.9 confirm these processes. Table 4.7 shows that manual workers had some of the most gender-segregated careers, the highest figures being concentrated amongst skilled men and unskilled and partly skilled women. Table 4.8 shows that skilled men did show a greater propensity to retain their career segregation over their lifetimes, while unskilled and partly skilled men

TABLE 4.7 *Gender careers (GENHIST) by current Registrar-General's social class, by sex* (%)

Social class	Only male	Male and mixed	Only mixed	Male, mixed, female	Male and female	Female and mixed	Only female	Total	N
Professionals									
Men	40	23	10	10	10	6	1	100	182
Women	3	4	34	10	30	17	2	100	25
Intermediate									
Men	14	27	10	24	13	11	1	100	673
Women	—[a]	3	13	10	7	34	33	100	455
Skilled non-manual									
Men	14	12	1	22	24	5	22	100	266
Women	—[a]	—[a]	—[a]	6	12	16	65	99	647
Skilled manual									
Men	52	15	2	12	17	1	2	101	844
Women	—[a]	3	6	12	19	27	33	100	132
Partly skilled manual									
Men	32	14	—[a]	22	28	—[a]	3	99	399
Women	—[a]	—[a]	—[a]	11	16	20	52	99	389
Unskilled manual									
Men	30	16	—	23	30	—	1	100	108
Women	—	—	—	11	24	13	53	101	136
Total									
Men	33	18	4	18	19	4	4	100	2,472
Women	—[a]	1	4	9	13	22	50	100	1,784

Note: Missing cases = 27.

[a] Less than 0.5%.

Source: SCELI Six Areas WAWH Survey.

TABLE 4.8 *Gender careers (GENHIST) by current Registrar-General's social class and age group (men) (%)*

Social class	Only male	Male and mixed	Only mixed	Male, mixed, female	Male and female	Female and mixed	Only female	Total
Professionals								
20–9	56	1	12	4	18	8	—	99
30–9	48	23	8	7	7	6	—	99
40+	25	33	10	15	9	5	2	99
Intermediate								
20–9	25	22	14	10	18	8	4	101
30–9	13	22	13	22	12	16	2	100
40+	9	33	7	32	11	8	—[a]	100
Skilled non-manual								
20–9	12	11	4	12	17	6	38	100
30–9	19	17	—	25	20	3	16	100
40+	12	8	—	30	35	6	9	100
Skilled manual								
20–9	61	11	3	6	15	1	3	100
30–9	46	19	2	12	19	1	1	100
40+	50	14	1	16	18	—[a]	—[a]	99
Partly skilled manual								
20–9	43	14	—[a]	11	25	—	6	99
30–9	30	12	—	26	31	1	—	100
40+	25	15	—	28	29	—[a]	2	99
Unskilled manual								
20–9	46	12	—	14	26	—	2	100
30–9	27	22	—	36	15	—	—	100
40+	15	16	—	26	42	—	1	100

Note: N = 2,472.

[a] Less than 0.5%.

Source: SCELI Six Areas WAWH Survey.

had a greater tendency to move between male and female occupations. Table 4.9 shows that unskilled and party skilled women had a tendency to remain in female occupations throughout their lifetimes, while skilled women were more likely to move between ones with differing degrees of segregation. Thus there is an opposite trend for manual men and women. For men, a highly

TABLE 4.9 *Gender careers (GENHIST) by current Registrar-General's social class and age group (women) (%)*

Social class	Only male	Male and mixed	Only mixed	Male, mixed, female	Male and female	Female and mixed	Only female	Total
Professionals								
20–9	9	—	24	—	50	18	—	101
30–9	—	—	42	22	12	25	—	101
40+	—	14	37	7	27	9	7	101
Intermediate								
20–9	—	5	12	3	8	27	45	100
30–9	1	3	16	10	4	36	30	100
40+	1	1	10	14	8	37	29	101
Skilled non-manual								
20–9	—[a]	—[a]	1	4	8	10	77	100
30–9	—	—	—	6	14	22	58	100
40+	—	—	—	10	14	17	59	100
Skilled manual								
20–9	—	7	12	4	15	16	46	100
30–9	—	2	10	19	22	35	12	100
40+	1	2	—	12	19	29	37	100
Partly skilled manual								
20–9	1	—	—	5	11	15	68	100
30–9	—	—	—	10	17	20	53	100
40+	—[a]	1	—[a]	15	18	22	44	100
Unskilled manual								
20–9	—	—	—	13	32	7	48	100
30–9	—	—	—	7	15	20	58	100
40+	—	—	—	11	25	12	52	100

Note: N = 1,784
[a] Less than 0.5%.
Source: SCELI Six Areas WAWH Survey.

segregated career is to be found amongst skilled workers rather than unskilled or partly skilled ones, but for women it is the reverse. Conversely, less segregated careers are more prevalent amongst skilled women and partly and unskilled men.

Analysis of non-manual occupations shows similar contrasting trends for men and women, although there are some differences because the pattern of segregation in non-manual occupations is slightly different. In particular, men are much less segregated at the lower levels of non-manual work and women are less segregated at the higher levels (Table 4.6). As far as men are concerned, the highest degree of segregation is amongst professionals and top administrators; men in intermediate and lower-grade clerical jobs are more likely to be in mixed-sex or even female jobs. If men are entering the top occupational class by movement through these lower levels, they are unlikely to have highly gender-segregated careers. However, we know that the professions have highly developed internal career structures and recruit directly on to the bottom rungs of these from educational institutions. Therefore, to the extent that these recruitment practices are themselves segregated (or have been in the recent past), it will be possible for some men to reach the top without passing through mixed-sex occupations. Women on the other hand, are most highly segregated at the bottom of the non-manual hierarchy while higher up they are increasingly in mixed-sex or male occupations (especially amongst the professions). In order to reach the top in non-manual employment, they must therefore move out of 'female' jobs at the bottom of the hierarchy and into 'male' or 'mixed' ones at the top.

Tables 4.7–4.9 again confirm these trends. Table 4.7 shows that the most highly segregated careers are indeed polarized at the top and bottom of the non-manual hierarchy, 'only male' careers at the top and 'only female' ones at the bottom. Table 4.8 shows that 'only male' careers are a very small proportion of clerical and intermediate careers for men, even amongst the younger age groups. On the other hand, there is a high degree of segregation amongst the youngest professional group, which implies that some men at the top of the occupational hierarchy will spend their entire career working mainly with men. The sharp decline in 'only male' careers in the 40+ age group, however, suggests that other men are reaching the top by upward movement through mixed-sex occupations.

Career segregation amongst clerical women is the highest of any occupational class (Table 4.7), and the decrease with age is not as greater as in other classes (Table 4.9). Of the women over 40 in this class, well over half had been in 'only female' careers. Amongst professional women career segregation is almost negligible, most of them making their way up through mixed occupations. However, we should be cautious about placing too much weight on these figures because of small cell sizes; although the tendencies are consistent with other evidence of the increased entry of women into the top 'male' professions (see Crompton and Sanderson 1990).

In summary, it appears that patterns of career segregation vary greatly between men and women as a result of the different location in 'male' and 'female' jobs in the occupational hierarchy and their different mobility trajectories through these jobs over their working lives. For men, a 'male' career may be associated with direct entry into top occupations or upward movement through 'male' jobs, while for women a 'female' career is associated with concentration in low-skilled jobs. However, we must remember that gender-segregated careers are actually the minority, especially by the time people have reached their forties. On the whole, 'mixed' careers appear to be associated with occupational mobility (upward and downward) although they have different significance for men and women and in different parts of the occupational hierarchy. However, since women appear to be less occupationally mobile than men, their career patterns are more gender segregated overall.

At this stage of the analysis we are unable to say when in their careers people pass through mixed-sex occupations, or how much time they spend in these occupations compared within the more segregated ones. However, the analysis of job changing presented below suggests that the GENHIST variable actually overestimates the amount of movement between occupations with different degrees of segregation.

So far, we have concentrated on mobility between occupations at a fairly low degree of aggregation (three-digit), but this is only a small proportion of all *job* movement defined in terms of changes in employment contracts. Upward mobility can occur at this level in the form of promotions within grading structures. We now move to an analysis of the effect of gender segregation on job change at this more micro-level.

GENDER SEGREGATION AND PROMOTION

For this analysis we focus on *job changes*, comparing the characteristics of each job with the one previously held, to see whether
this constituted a 'promotion' or 'demotion' and whether or not
there was a shift in the degree of gender segregation. This analysis presents a rather different operationalization of upward and
downward mobility in the labour market than that in the previous section. The main outcome measures we will be using here
have been constructed from respondents' own accounts of job
moves, rather than shifts between more aggregated occupational
categories. For each transition between jobs,[5] respondents were
asked why they left their previous jobs and whether the jobs they
went to were better paid, paid the same, or worse paid than their
previous jobs. Three relatively unambiguous types of job changes
emerged out of the coding scheme, which are used as dependent
measures in the following analyses. First, 'promotions' were
defined as jobs which were left in order to get a better job and
were followed by a better-paid job.[6] Second, 'domestic demotions' were when a job was left for 'family or domestic reasons'
and was followed by a worse-paid job (whether or not there was
a break for full-time housework in between). Finally, 'employer
demotions' were involuntary dismissals or redundancies which
were followed by worse-paid jobs. Table 4.10 shows a full cross-
tabulation of reasons for leaving jobs and the effect on pay for
men and women.

As we can see, there are marked differences between men and
women in the reasons for changing job. A far greater proportion
of men change jobs to get a better job than women (57 per cent
compared with 38 per cent), although they are more vulnerable
to involuntary quits. Only a tiny minority (10 per cent) state that
they changed job for family reasons whereas this category
accounts for 34 per cent of all women's job changes. In all, 58
per cent of destination jobs involve better pay, and this figure is
higher for men (65 per cent) than for women (52 per cent).
Almost a quarter of all job changes are at the same level of pay,
with 21 per cent for men and 27 per cent for women. Less than a
fifth involve a lower level of pay and this category accounted for
14 per cent of men's job changes but 21 per cent of women's.

TABLE 4.10　*Reasons for changing jobs by pay level of next job, by sex* (%)

Pay level of next job	Reasons for leaving previous job			Other	Total
	To get a better job	For family reasons	Made redundant		
Men					
Better	43[a]	5	13	4	65
Same	10	2	7	2	21
Worse	4	3[b]	5[c]	2	14
Total	57	10	25	8	100
Women					
Better	27[a]	13	7	5	52
Same	7	10	5	4	27
Worse	4	11[b]	3[c]	3	21
Total	38	34	15	13	100

Note: N = 16,499 job changes.
[a] 'Promotions'.
[b] 'Domestic demotions'.
[c] 'Employer demotions'.
Source: SCELI Six Areas WAWH Survey.

Thus, although many women do manage to improve their prospects in the process of changing jobs, they are less successful than men on both variables. Combining the two variables, as outlined above, approximately 35 per cent of all job changes are 'promotions', 4 per cent are 'employer demotions', and 7 per cent are 'domestic demotions'.[7] Women have far fewer 'promotions' than men and also less 'employer demotions', but they have more 'domestic demotions'.

We also classified job changes according to the direction of movement between jobs with differing degrees of occupational segregation, either towards a job with a greater concentration of men (a 'more male' shift), towards one with a greater concentration of women (a 'more female' shift), or a move between jobs with the same degree of sex segregation (a 'same segregation' shift).[8] Note that the analysis here was based on the original five categories of the SEXRATIO variable.

In the first part of this analysis we shall be aggregating job changes within each respondent's life history and comparing it to their current position in the labour market. (The data exclude respondents who were unemployed or non-employed at the time of the survey.) For simplification, all job changes which were not 'promotions' on the above definition are treated as 'non-promotions'. On average, the number of job changes per individual is 4.9, with 1.8 promotions and 3.1 non-promotions. Women have fewer job changes than men, 4.5 per person compared with 5.1 (Table 4.11). They also have far fewer promotions than men—1.3 compared with 2.2. These data show a low degree of movement between jobs with different degrees of segregation. Over half of all moves are between similarly segregated jobs, the rest being distributed almost equally between moves towards more 'female' and more 'male' jobs.

In aggregate, there is little association between shifts in gender segregation and vertical job moves. Promotion is as likely to come about through moves between similarly segregated

TABLE 4.11 *Gender segregation shifts and promotions/non-promotions, by sex* (average per person)

| | Gender segregation shift | | | |
	More male	Same segregation	More female	Total
Men				
Promotion	0.5	1.3	0.4	2.2
Non-promotion	0.6	1.7	0.6	2.9
Total	1.1	3.0	1.0	5.1
Women				
Promotion	0.3	0.8	0.2	1.3
Non-promotion	0.6	1.9	0.7	3.2
Total	0.9	2.7	0.9	4.5
Total				
Promotion	0.4	1.1	0.3	1.8
Non-promotion	0.6	1.8	0.7	3.1
Total	1.0	2.9	1.0	4.9

Note: N = 4,283.
Source: SCELI Six Areas WAWH Survey.

occupations as through movement towards a more male or more female one, and in view of the fact that most job changes occur between similarly segregated jobs, promotions are also concentrated there. Bearing in mind that 66 per cent of all men's jobs in the work history data file are 'male' and 78 per cent of all women's are 'female', this means that both job changing and promotions are concentrated in heavily gendered occupations. However, looking at the moves that do occur between jobs with different degrees of segregation, we can see a slight association between promotional and gender shifts; a move towards a more male job being accompanied by a promotion and a move towards a more female job by a non-promotion. The association between promotion and more male moves is stronger for men than for women, while that between non-promotion and more female moves is stronger for women.

The distribution of promotions and gender shifts by current R.-G. social class is shown in Table 4.12. This table is based on the same data as Table 4.11, but each type of job change is expressed as a percentage of the total occurring to those currently in each social class; for instance, 14 per cent of the job changes that occurred to those who are now professionals were promotions to more 'male' jobs.

In all classes except the professions, most job changes are non-promotions. As might be expected, the proportion of promotions increases as we move up the class hierarchy. Thus amongst unskilled manual workers they only represent 21 per cent of total job changes compared with 41 per cent amongst skilled manual workers and 53 per cent amongst professionals. As for clerical and office workers (skilled non-manual), on whom much of the debate on careers has centred, the majority of the job changes of this group have been non-promotions and only a third promotions.

Table 4.12 shows the extraordinary concentration of job changes between similarly segregated jobs in all classes; this type of job change includes promotions and non-promotions although the proportion of promotions increases towards the top of the occupational hierarchy. Shifts towards more male jobs also increase slightly in the upper regions and in doing so they are more likely to constitute a promotion. On the other hand shifts towards more female jobs increase towards the bottom of the hierarchy and they are more likely to be non-promotions.

TABLE 4.12   *Job changes by promotions and gender segregation shift within each current Registrar-General's social class (%)*[a]

Social class	Gender segregation shift			
	More male	Same segregation	More female	Total
Professional				
Promotion	14	35	4	
Non-promotion	12	29	5	99
Intermediate				
Promotion	9	27	6	
Non-promotion	12	34	12	100
Skilled non-manual				
Promotion	7	22	7	
Non-promotion	10	38	16	100
Skilled manual				
Promotion	10	26	5	
Non-promotion	13	37	9	100
Partly skilled manual				
Promotion	9	16	5	
Non-promotion	15	35	20	100
Unskilled manual				
Promotion	6	11	4	
Non-promotion	15	41	23	100
All classes				
Promotion	8	23	6	
Non-promotion	13	35	15	100

[a] Job changes are calculated on the basis of the average per person with an N of 4,148 persons. Each type of job change is expressed here as a proportion of the total for each class.

Source: SCELI Six Areas WAWH Survey.

Table 4.13 shows promotions as a proportion of average job changes by current social class and sex. Within each social class women experienced significantly fewer promotional job changes than men. The discrepancy is especially pronounced amongst the top two social classes. For men, the chances of promotion are similar in these two classes and are almost equally well achieved by a job move between similarly segregated jobs (which effectively means staying in a mainly or exclusively male job) as by a

TABLE 4.13 *Promotions as a percentage of the total job changes within cell by gender segregation shift, current Registrar-General's social class and sex*

Social class	Gender segregation shift			All job changes
	More male	Same segregation	More female	
Professional				
Men	54	53	45	52
Women	56	29	27	35
Intermediate				
Men	48	54	45	51
Women	35	31	25	31
Skilled non-manual				
Men	43	44	40	43
Women	37	33	24	32
Skilled manual				
Men	42	41	33	40
Women	33	28	16	27
Partly skilled manual				
Men	42	39	36	39
Women	35	23	16	24
Unskilled manual				
Men	31	31	34	32
Women	35	19	10	20

Note: N = 4,148.

Source: SCELI Six Areas WAWH Survey.

move towards a more male job or even a more female job. For women, however, there is a different pattern. The chances for promotion are not markedly higher in the top two classes than amongst clerical workers, but they are more strongly linked to moves towards more male jobs. This is particularly the case in the professions where the small number of women who move into more male jobs have slightly higher chances of promotion than men.

We cannot say, without further analysis, how many of these job changes were between occupational classes, rather than within them. However, these data do show that at the level of *job* change, as opposed to *occupational* change, women experience less promotion than men and promotion opportunities for them are more strongly linked to class and changing towards more male jobs, than men's are.

We now turn to the results of a Logistic Regression which was carried out to establish the extent to which gender segregation affected the chances of experiencing a 'promotion', an 'employer demotion' or a 'domestic demotion'. This analysis was performed on the data set of job changes rather than that of individuals, and for greater statistical accuracy some adjustments to these data were made. In order to eliminate a bias toward younger workers and more recent periods in the work histories, only job changes that occurred between 1966 and 1986 and to individuals who were less than 40 years old at the time were included. This reduced the total of 28,448 job changes in the 6,111 work histories to approximately 17,500 job changes.[9] Burchell (1993) gives fuller details concerning the construction of this data set and the reasons for limiting it in this way. Of primary interest in this section will be the SEXRATIO category of the jobs that respondents were moving from and to. We will also consider the ages and life-cycle stages of women's job changes.

First, we examined the influence of the gender segregation of the job they were leaving and the job they were going to on the probability of that job being a 'promotion', a 'domestic demotion', or an 'employer demotion'. Table 4.14 gives the increase or decrease in odds of each type of job change with both source and destination jobs entered into the model.[10] (A figure of <1.00 here means that a particular outcome is less likely to occur than average, a figure of >1.00 means it is more likely and a figure of 2.00 indicates that it is twice as likely as the average for that group).

For 'promotions', there is a significant effect of segregation in both source and destination jobs for both men and women. Men are particularly likely to experience a promotion on leaving a 'mainly female' job or on entering a 'mixed' job. Conversely, they are less likely to experience promotions on leaving 'extremely male' jobs or entering 'mainly female' jobs. For women, promotions are associated with leaving 'female' jobs and going to 'male' ones.

'Employer demotions' are much more likely to be inflicted on men in more 'male' jobs and men having an employer demotion are more likely to end up in mainly 'female' jobs. Controlling for

TABLE 4.14 *Logistic regression results of men's and women's types of job change, by occupational sex-ratio* (job changes per type of change expressed as odds ratios)

	Promotion		Employer demotion		Domestic demotion	
	Men	Women	Men	Women	Men	Women
Proportion of total job changes (%)	42	26	5	3	3	11
Previous job						
>90% men	0.76	—[a]	1.61	—[a]	1.15	—[a]
70–89% men	0.95	0.85	1.24	1.81	1.18	1.16
Mixed	1.06	0.77	0.85	1.27	1.28	1.28
70–89% women	1.32	1.21	0.59	0.72	0.58	0.78
>90% women	—[a]	1.26	—[a]	0.61	—[a]	0.86
New job						
>90% men	1.11	—[a]	0.74	—[a]	0.86	—[a]
70–89% men	0.91	1.26	1.12	0.37	1.92	0.80
Mixed	1.27	1.19	0.69	0.99	0.74	0.73
70–89% women	0.77	0.73	1.73	1.68	1.74	1.60
>90% women	—[a]	0.91	—[a]	1.63	—[a]	1.08

Note: N = 17,949 job changes (9,939 men's, 8,010 women's).

[a] For the men's data the 'mainly' and 'exclusively' female categories were collapsed together, and for the women's data the 'mainly' and 'exclusively' male categories were collapsed together.

Source: SCELI Six Areas WAWH Survey.

women's destination jobs, there is no statistically significant effect of the segregation levels of jobs women are leaving. However, women entering 'exclusively female' jobs are twice as likely to have experienced employer demotions as average, whereas those entering mainly male jobs are only 40 per cent as likely to have experienced this type of demotion.

'Domestic demotions' are associated with both source and destination jobs for women. Women are more likely to experience domestic demotions on leaving 'mixed' jobs and women entering 'mainly female' jobs are much more likely to have suffered a domestic demotion than average. Interestingly, men are also more likely to experience domestic demotion if they are leaving mixed jobs and entering a 'mainly female' job, although men are also likely to experience 'domestic demotions' when they enter 'mainly male' jobs.

In all three groups, segregation in both the source and destination job has a significant effect on the probability of experiencing promotion or demotion, the effects being larger for women than for men. The highest probability of achieving a promotion for both men and women is if they move from a 'female' job into a 'male' one. For men the chances are least likely if they move out of 'male' jobs and into 'female' ones, whereas for women it is both the 'extremely and mainly female' jobs they should move out of and the 'mainly male' ones they should move into. The domestic and employer demotion cases provide reverse evidence of this same trend; there are more chances of experiencing a demotion if one moves from a 'male' job into a 'female' one. Again the trend is the same for men and women although the effect is stronger for women.

THE ROLE OF THE DOMESTIC CYCLE

A substantial literature has shown that women's chances of promotion are affected by their stage in the domestic cycle, particularly taking breaks from employment for full-time housework (e.g. Martin and Roberts 1984, Dex 1987, Joshi 1984, 1987). In order to incorporate this into our analysis, women's job changes were also classified relative to these breaks. There were four categories:

1. job changes happening to women who had not (at the time of the survey) had any breaks for full-time housework;
2. those happening before the first break for full-time housework;
3. those happening to women between their first and last break for full-time housework;
4. those happening to women after the last break for full-time housework.

Transitions between jobs were also classified according to the age of the women on starting the new job (<25, 25–30, 30–5, 35–40).

The analysis here was based on women between the ages of 30 and 40. Women over 40 and job changes occurring prior to 1966 were excluded for reasons already mentioned. Women who were still under the age of 30 at the time of the survey were also excluded because of problems in defining their life-cycle stage.[11] Subsequently, analyses were performed separately with women over 40, and the results were broadly similar to those presented here.

Separate logistic regressions were performed on these data for each of the three dependent variables, promotions, domestic demotions, and employer demotions, by life-cycle position and age. The analysis of promotions and domestic demotions showed very large effects for life-cycle stage and age. Table 4.15 gives the proportionate increase or decrease in the odds of each outcome for each group. Overall, 28 per cent of these job changes are promotions but the odds of promotions are almost twice as high for job changes that took place before the first break for full-time housework, while job changes that occurred between breaks for

TABLE 4.15 *Women's probability of promotions, employer demotions, and domestic demotions, by domestic cycle and age, expressed as odds ratios*

	Promotions	Employer demotions	Domestic demotions
Proportion of women's job changes (%)	28	3	11
Domestic cycle[a]			
No FTHW	1.45	n.s.	0.56
Before FTHW	1.96	n.s.	0.42
During FTHW	0.48	n.s.	1.89
After FTHW	0.73	n.s.	2.24
Age starting job			
<25 years	1.00	0.44	1.19
25–30	0.71	1.08	1.49
30–5	1.09	1.09	1.10
35–40	1.29	1.90	0.51

Note: N = 4,407 job changes of women aged 30–40.
[a] FTHW = breaks for full-time housework.
Source: SCELI Six Areas WAWH Survey.

full-time housework are less than half as likely to be promotions. There is also a sizeable legacy of full-time housework, such that even after returning to work following their last periods of full-time housework, women are still considerably less likely to obtain a promotion than they were before their breaks started. Controlling for life-cycle position, there is also a small positive age effect, such that women are slightly less likely to obtain promotions between the ages of 25 and 30, but more likely to do so after the age of 35.

These changes are mirrored closely by the analysis of domestic demotions: 11 per cent of the job changes fall into this category, but this increases more than twofold between periods of full-time housework. Again, there is a strong legacy effect, with job changes occurring after women's final break still being almost twice as likely to be domestic demotions. There is also a negative age effect, with domestic demotions being more likely in the age-band 25–30 and less likely in that of 35–40, controlling for life-cycle stage.

There is no statistically significant life-cycle stage effect on the rates of employer demotions, only an age effect, with the probability increasing with age. However, this may be due to the confounding of age and calendar time in these analyses and the increased rates of employer demotions that accompanied the increase in unemployment since the late 1970s (Burchell 1993). Note, however, that employer demotions were only 3 per cent of job changes amongst this group of women.

The data for the over-40s were inspected to see if there were differences in the pattern of results from the data in the 'cut down' sample of under-40s. As we only have data on those older groups in the more recent (i.e. higher unemployment) labour markets, such a comparison is necessarily limited. Other analyses of the SCELI data have shown that the dramatic increase in unemployment that started in 1979 was accompanied by an equally dramatic threefold increase in 'employer demotions' (Burchell 1994). Excluding the pre-1979 data to control for this sudden change in labour market conditions thus reduced this observed difference between the over-40s and the younger women. The most marked difference among the over-40s was a twofold increase in employer demotions. However, this difference was similar for both men's and women's jobs: there was little evidence that the gender-specific pattern of results were different for older employees.

The results show the marked disadvantage of women during that period of their lives when they are having to take breaks from employment for full-time housework, most usually, presumably, for childbirth and child-rearing. However, perhaps more surprising is clear evidence of a legacy effect of these breaks. Women who have had breaks for employment for full-time housework do not, on average, revert to the rate of promotion that they attained before taking breaks from employment, perhaps being still restrained by their domestic circumstances or having re-entered jobs with fewer possibilities for advancement.

However, there are deficiencies in these analyses which should be confronted before too much credence is placed on the interpretation of the results. The life-cycle variable is strongly confounded with calendar time and age. Whilst age has been controlled for in this analysis, the same cannot be done for calendar time. With work history data, information about jobs held by older incumbents will only be available for the recent past, whereas information for younger individuals is available over a much wider age band. As the British labour market has undergone such change in this period, this could have a sizeable influence on the results. It should also be remembered that these analyses are based on women who entered the labour market some 15–45 years before 1986, the year of the survey. It is possible that women's careers have changed since then due to such factors as better childcare facilities, structural changes in the labour market, or different expectations of women.

CONCLUSIONS

In this chapter we have investigated the relationship between gender segregation and work histories in terms of movement between jobs and occupations rather than between broad occupational classes. We have looked at the work history data in terms of *individual careers*, i.e. sequences of jobs held up to the time of the survey, and as a set of *job transitions* occurring between 1966 and 1986 to respondents up to the age of 40 years. These different techniques have enabled us to take different 'tacks' on the phenomenon of job changing, career formation, and occupational mobility. It must be stressed that these analyses are only preliminary and both techniques need further development. In particular, it would be desirable to measure the effect of class on each job change within the work history and to focus in more detail on patterns of job changing and subsequent career development amongst the over-40s.

However, from the analysis undertaken so far, several results stand out. First, despite the fact that in any one age group the majority of men and women are concentrated into mainly or extremely segregated jobs, neither men nor women are permanently confined to these types of jobs. At some stage in their lifetimes, most of them will have passed through jobs or occupations with different degrees of segregation. However, the analysis of job changes reveals that over half of job changes occur between similarly segregated occupations. This suggests that although the chances of experiencing different degrees of segregation increase over the lifetime, it is likely that these more mixed experiences will actually be a minority in the final completed career. In other words, in terms of the types of jobs experienced over the life history, career segregation may decline, but in terms of the number of jobs held with differing degrees of segregation, or even the duration of such jobs, it is possible that careers are still strongly segregated. This is an important hypothesis to be tested in future work.

The second point is that the pattern of career segregation over the lifetime indicated both by GENHIST and the job change data, is highly variable by sex and class. For men, career segregation is more accentuated at the top of the occupational hierarchies, both manual and non-manual, whereas for women it is more accentuated at the bottom of these hierarchies. The GENHIST analysis shows that while career segregation does decline with age, it does so less amongst men at the top and amongst women at the bottom, occupationally speaking. Similarly, the job change data show that job changes amongst similarly segregated jobs or towards more 'male' jobs increase towards the top of the class structure while moves towards more female ones increase towards the bottom. Therefore, not only are men's and women's patterns of movement between 'male', 'mixed', and 'female' jobs very different, but they vary at different points in the occupational hierarchy. One implication of this is that many men in positions of power and influence, as in the professions and top administrative posts, will have had little experience of working with women in the same occupations, but women cannot reach such positions without working with men. This situation is reversed at the bottom of the occupational hierarchy where the men are more likely to have worked with women but the women are more likely to have only worked with other women.

The data on promotions reinforce these findings in a different way. Promotions are more frequent in the top occupational classes, the jobs are also more 'male' there, and the men get more promotions in any case. They can achieve promotion either by moving between 'male' jobs or by moving towards more 'male' jobs if they are not already in them. Moving towards a 'more female' job is more likely to constitute a 'non-promotion'. Some women could achieve promotion by staying in a similarly segregated job, but given the cross-sectional structure of gender segregation, this is more likely in 'mixed' jobs than in 'female' ones. Women's best chances of promotion are if they move out of mainly or exclusively female job into a mixed or a male one.

Of course these results are only about tendencies, and there is enough heterogeneity in the data to confirm the fact that some women can achieve promotion within 'female' jobs (e.g. by moving into supervisory grades) and that some men also do this (e.g. by moving into nursing management or becoming heads of primary schools). However, our evidence suggests that these are minority trends and that the more important pattern is the association between good positions and male jobs and between promotion and movement amongst or into more 'male' jobs.

Another minor trend is the upward movement of individuals in 'mixed' jobs. This probably refers to movement within grading structures and occurs to a certain extent within all occupational classes. Thus it is certainly possible for some men and women to achieve promotion lower down the occupational structure and at such levels, this is likely to be in 'mixed' jobs. To the extent that this pattern of upward movement within classes eventually feeds into cross-class mobility, it would confirm the 'white-collar career' hypothesis (Crompton and Jones 1984) that men move through mixed-sex jobs on their way up to the top, producing a long-run decline in career segregation with time.

The final point refers to the strong influence of the domestic cycle on women's careers as measured in terms of breaks for full-time housework. Our analysis shows that such breaks negatively affect women's chances of promotion, not only while working in between breaks, but for some time after returning to work permanently. This is only partially offset by a slight increase in the chances of promotion with age. It would be interesting in future work to see how this domestic cycle effect is related to class and the pattern of segregation in source and destination jobs. Existing research tells us that the typical move after breaks for full-time housework is into part-time jobs, which are highly 'female' and have poor pay and skill levels (Martin and Roberts 1984, Dex 1987, Rubery *et al.*, this volume). The women who are best placed to offset these domestic cycle effects are in the top professional and administrative jobs where provision for maternity leave and childcare is better and part-time jobs are less disadvantageous. Therefore it is likely that the domestic cycle has its most negative impact on women in low occupational classes and 'female' jobs. Again, this is an interesting hypothesis to test in future work.

In conclusion, this analysis has shown the importance of longitudinal analysis for revealing the way in which gender segregation structures men's and women's careers at the level of jobs and occupations. It is clear that the simple form of the dual labour market model, in which men move exclusively between 'men's' jobs and women between 'women's' jobs did not apply to British labour markets in the mid-1980s. Nevertheless there is some evidence for both tendencies at opposite ends of the occupational hierarchy. There is also evidence that within primary labour markets (in which most white-collar work is located), men and women chart different career trajectories and that this is constrained by gender segregation. This constraining effect may well have implications for the broader pattern of cross-class mobility. However, to explore more fully the connections between the analyses reported in this chapter and the broader picture of labour market segmentation and class mobility would require another paper.

NOTES

1. This version of dual labour market theory places major emphasis on gender as the main form of segmentation; US versions paid more attention to race and immigration. Therefore the secondary sector included persons with a variety of social characteristics and, since many of them were men, this sector was less segregated than envisaged by Barron and Norris.

2. Work-place segregation is inappropriate for theoretical reasons, since it may include a number of different occupations, as well as some people working alone. For example, dental nurses would be classified as 'mainly male', because they tend to work with male dentists even though most of them are women.

3. For example, sales representatives of cosmetics may consider themselves to be 'mainly or exclusively female' and salesmen of double glazing 'mainly or exclusively male' even though the general category of sales representatives is actually two-thirds 'male' and would thus classify as 'mixed'.

4. An optimal occupational classification for women is likely to be one that combines some sectoral specificities as well as skill, but employment status (emphasized in the Goldthorpe scale) is probably less important. Most analyses of women's employment in Britain have worked with a modified version of socio-economic group (SEG) but this is not necessarily the most relevant for men and has too many categories for some multivariate analyses. The major problem with the Goldthorpe scale, aside from that already mentioned, is that it lacks a fine grading of manual employment and lumps too many women into the unskilled category (37 per cent compared with 30 per cent in the R.-G. scale). The latter was considered preferable because it is based on a more consistent hierarchical criterion (skill) and permits an easy aggregation into manual and non-manual employment. However, we recognize that it too has many faults. Strictly speaking, the R.-G. scale is a classification of occupational classes; however, since it carries the label 'social class' we have used this term throughout the chapter.

5. A job change is defined by a change of employer, job description, supervisory responsibility, or hours between full and part time.

6. This definition of job 'promotion' may under-represent jobs that were considered 'better' because of criteria unrelated to pay, such as convenient hours, location, etc.,—which may have been important for women.

7. The rest of the job changes were combinations of the two variables

that could not be clearly identified in terms of vertical movement, up or down.

8. This measure focuses on direction rather than location, thus it is possible for a job move to become 'more male' even while still being a 'female' job, as in a move from the FF to the F category.

9. Approximately 3,000 job changes were rejected because the incumbents were 40 years old or more at the time of the transition, and 8,000 were lost because they took place before 1966 (Burchell 1993).

10. All effects entered into the model were significant at the 0.01 level, except where indicated.

11. Women under 30 at the time of the survey who had not had a break from employment for full-time housework would have been a mixture of those who would never have such a break and those who were still to have one. It would be similarly difficult to differentiate between those still between breaks for full-time housework and those who had now finished this stage.

REFERENCES

BARRON, R. D., and NORRIS, G. M. (1976), 'Sexual Divisions and the Dual Labour Market', in D. L. Barker and S. Allen (eds.), *Dependence and Exploitation in Work and Marriage*. London, Longman.

BERTAUX, D. C. (1991), 'From Methodological Monopoly to Pluralism in the Sociology of Social Mobility', in S. Dex (ed.), *Life and Work History Analysis*. London, Routledge.

BURCHELL, B. (1993), 'A New Way of Analysing Labour Market Flows using Work History Data', *Work, Employment and Society*, 7/2, May.

—— (1994), 'The Effects of Labour Market Position, Job Insecurity and Unemployment on Psychological Health', in D. Gallie *et al.* (eds.), *Social Change and the Experience of Unemployment*. Oxford, Oxford University Press.

—— and RUBERY, J. (1990), 'An Empirical Investigation into the Segmentation of the Labour Supply', *Work, Employment and Society*, 4/4: 551–73.

CROMPTON, R., and JONES, G. (1984), *White-Collar Proletariat*. London, Macmillan.

—— and Sanderson, K. (1990), *Gendered Jobs and Social Change*. London, Unwin Hyman.

DALE, A., GILBERT, N., and ARBER, S. (1985), 'Integrating Women into Class Theory', *Sociology*, 19: 384–408.

DEX, S. (1987), *Women's Occupational Mobility*. Basingstoke, Macmillan.

156 *A. M. Scott and B. Burchell*

DEX, S. (1990), 'Occupational Mobility over Women's Lifetime', in G. Payne and P. Abbott (eds.), *The Social Mobility of Women*. London, Falmer Press: 121–38.

EDWARDS, R. C., REICH, M., and GORDON, D. M. (1975) (eds.), *Labour Market Segmentation*. Lexington, Mass., D. C. Heath & Co.

ELIAS, P., and MAIN, B. (1982), *Women's Working Lives: Evidence from the National Training Survey*. Coventry, Institute for Employment Research, University of Warwick.

HUNT, A. (1988) (ed.), *Women and Paid Work*. London, Macmillan.

JOSHI, H. (1984), *Women's Participation in Paid Work: Further Analysis of the Women and Employment Survey*. Research Paper No. 45. Department of Employment, London, HMSO.

—— (1987), 'The Cost of Caring', in C. Glendinning and J. Millar (eds.), *Women and Poverty in Britain*. Brighton, Wheatsheaf.

MARSH, C., and GERSHUNY, J. (1991), 'Handling Work History Data in Standard Statistical Packages', in S. Dex (ed.), *Life and Work History Analysis*. London, Routledge.

MARTIN, J., and ROBERTS, C. (1984), *Women and Employment: A Lifetime Perspective*. London, HMSO.

PAYNE, G., and ABBOTT, P. (1990) (eds.), *The Social Mobility of Women*. London, Falmer Press.

SILTANEN, J. (1990), 'Social Change and the Measurement of Occupational Segregation by Sex: An Assessment of the Sex Ratio Index', *Work, Employment and Society*, 4/1: 1–29.

SØRENSON, A. B. (1970), *The Occupational Mobility Process: An Analysis of Occupational Careers*. Baltimore, Johns Hopkins Press.

STEWART, A., PRANDY, K., and BLACKBURN R. M. (1980), *Social Stratification and Occupations*. London, Macmillan.

WALBY, S. (1991), 'Labour Markets and Industrial Structures in Women's Working Lives', in S. Dex (ed.), *Life and Work History Analysis*. London, Routledge.

5

The Gender Wage Differential and Discrimination in the Six SCELI Local Labour Markets

PETER J. SLOANE

INTRODUCTION

The difference in earnings between women and men can be decomposed analytically into three elements: that which arises from different personal characteristics (e.g. levels of qualification, work experience, preferences), that which arises from variations in employment (e.g. type of job, firm, industry), and a residual element of discrimination, which means that women are paid less than men even after all other supply and demand factors have been controlled for. In this chapter, all three elements are examined in a modified earnings function analysis.

The multiple regression procedures used in this approach allow us to examine the different components of the gender wage differential and the relative contribution of different variables to it. The advantage of this type of analysis is that it provides a precise and rigorous way of measuring the relationship between variables, but technical problems can arise—from the way variables are constructed, assumptions about sampling, and the specification of the regression equations—which can affect the results. In this chapter, the earnings function equations have been modified in certain ways to take account of sample selection bias, variable occupational attainment, and differential qualifications for given levels of pay (through reverse regression), details of which are provided in the methodological section and Appendix 5.2.

I am grateful to Hector Williams for his very efficient computing assistance and to Bob Sandy for helpful comments.

Estimates of the gender wage differential, especially the discrimination component (which is treated as the residual that is left when all other variables have been controlled for), are particularly reliant on as many relevant variables as possible being included in the model. One major advantage of the SCELI data set is that it includes a richer set of variables than most studies. Earlier work on the estimation of wage discrimination by sex and marital status in the UK has utilized a range of data sets. One group of these includes nationally representative data sets such as the General Household Survey (e.g. Greenhalgh 1980), the New Earnings Survey (e.g. Zabalza and Tzannatos 1985, and Miller 1987), the Medical Research Council National Survey of Health and Development (Joshi and Newell 1987), the 1980 Women and Employment Survey, (Wright and Ermisch 1991). Another group consists of data sets relating to particular occupations such as teachers (Turnbull and Williams 1974), librarians (Siebert and Young 1983), and graduates (Dolton and Makepeace 1986 and 1987). A third group consists of attempts to estimate discrimination within particular firms and establishments (Chiplin and Sloane 1976 and Siebert and Sloane 1981).

Three items are of particular interest in the SCELI data set which are not usually available, the work experience, job segregation, and locality variables. Research has shown that differences in work experience contribute significantly to the gender wage differential. However, because this variable is not directly available in most data sets, analysis has had to rely on proxies or crude estimates (the usual proxy is potential total working life, constructed as a variable by deducting pre-school years and years of education from present age). This is inappropriate where labour-force participation is not continuous, particularly for women because of their breaks from employment for child-rearing. The SCELI work history data allow us to measure work experience in terms of months actually worked rather than relying on a proxy or estimated measure.[1]

Recent work on the discrimination component of the gender wage differential has focused on variations in occupational attainment between men and women (e.g. Miller 1987). This takes cognizance of the fact that men and women are distributed very differently between occupations and considers whether this might be due to discriminatory hiring decisions by employers. It is possible to identify that part of the wage differential which arises from different interoccupational distributions and compare it with the differential within occupations. Research has shown that the latter has usually been greater than the former, suggesting that discrimination in occupational recruitment may be less important than other forms of discrimination (e.g. Chiplin and Sloane 1982 and Sloane 1990[2]). However, it is still possible that differential occupational attainment plays a role *within* occupational groups. Vertical segregation (the assignment of more men than women to promoted posts) or horizontal segregation (job segregation by sex within occupational groups across or within firms) may play an important role here. Gender segregation may influence earnings in other ways, but these have not yet been specified clearly enough to be tested quantitatively. For example, it has been suggested that levels of pay in some jobs are affected by the sex-labelling of the job rather than the gender of the occupant. Thus jobs targeted for women are labelled as unskilled and the level of pay set at an appropriate level for women (which is unattractive to men), rather than the skill level being technologically determined and the wage rate being established through the market. A similar argument has been made with respect to female part-time work (cf. Chapter 6). As a first step, however, it is important to assess the degree to which domination by one sex or the other in a job affects pay independently of the gender of particular individuals in those jobs. The SCELI data provide us with the first opportunity to examine the role of this variable within the earnings function, for men as well as women.

Finally, the notion that women act as some kind of labour reserve has led to the hypothesis that the gender wage differential varies with the level of unemployment, being greater in slack labour markets and narrower in tight ones (Masters 1975, Lloyd and Niemi 1979). National level data are not particularly good at capturing this effect, since there are often local variations in unemployment rates. Since the SCELI localities did have strong variations in unemployment rates,[3] it is possible to compare for the first time the gender wage differential across individual local labour markets with varying degrees of labour market slackness and tightness.

THE GENDER WAGE DIFFERENTIAL DESCRIBED

Chapter 1 has already provided a summary outline of the pattern of male–female earnings differentials in the six SCELI localities.

On average, women's full-time earnings excluding overtime were 73.2 per cent of men's, which is comparable with a 1986 New Earnings Survey figure of 74.3 per cent. This differential varied slightly by locality, being higher in Aberdeen, Coventry, Northampton, and Rochdale, and lower in Kirkcaldy and particularly Swindon. Wage differentials also varied by industry and establishment size. As Table 5.1 indicates, for females pay was lowest in Other Manufacturing and Distribution etc. and highest in Energy and Water. The pattern was similar for men, but none the less there were significant variations across industry in the earnings ratio by sex—from 69 per cent in Other Manufacturing and Banking, Insurance, etc. to 81 per cent in Transport and Communications. The percentage earnings gap was higher for non-manual than for manual workers in every industry for which a valid comparison could be made. There is a clear tendency for earnings to increase with establishment size (Table 5.2) for all groups. The extent to which earnings increase by establishment size is greater for men as a whole than for women (but not for manual men in relation to manual women). Men are also employed more than in proportion to their numbers in larger establishments. Though not shown in the table there is not much difference in the distribution of single men and women by establishment size, but married women are much less likely to be found in larger establishments.[4]

The SCELI data show a relationship between occupational group and earnings, the level of earnings being highest amongst the most skilled occupational groups. In the manual groups the earnings differential is inversely related to the level of skill (Table 5.3), but for non-manual groups female professionals have the highest level of earnings and the narrowest earnings differential. We can also compare earnings by degree of job segregation by sex (Table 5.4). This indicates that while women earn most in jobs held mainly by men, men earn most in jobs held mainly by women, though the practice is more confused when the sample is split into manual and non-manual categories. As a consequence the earnings differential is widest in jobs held mainly by women.

Dividing occupational classes into two broad groups—manual and non-manual—reveals that the earnings differential is significantly wider in non-manual occupations in which the majority of female employees are found. There is also more variability in the non-manual differential across localities with non-manual women earning only 56–8 per cent of their male comparators in Swindon and Kirkcaldy compared to 73–5 per cent in Coventry and Rochdale. As far as part-time employees are concerned there are only sixteen male part-timers in the sample, but a comparison of part-time and full-time females reveals that earnings of the former amount to 75 per cent of those of the latter and are fairly uniform across localities.

Turning to job-related characteristics, union membership is more important to female than to male pay, female union members earning on average 23.5 per cent more than unorganized women, while for men the crude mark-up is only 7.5 per cent. There is a tendency for those who regard their jobs as secure to earn more than those who regard them as insecure and this applies equally to men and women. However, it is possible that higher pay is interpreted as a sign of greater job security rather than being independent of it. While those on shiftwork are more highly paid in the case of part-time workers, for full-time workers the reverse is the case. However, when the sample is split into manual and non-manual categories, manual shiftworkers are found to earn 15 per cent more than their non-shiftworking counterparts. However, non-manual shiftworkers earn 10 per cent less than their counterparts, suggesting perhaps that it is the less skilled or junior staff who are called upon to work at irregular hours. Finally, while those on merit pay earn more, the effect is less marked for women than men (raising pay by 6 and 16 per cent respectively for full-time employees) and proportionally fewer women than men benefit from this form of payment.

Concerning personal characteristics, there were only minor differences in the distribution of formal educational qualifications amongst women and men and the data show no significant difference overall in returns to educational qualifications between women and men. Women had slightly less on-the-job training in their current job than men and the return to this was lower than men's particularly for single women. The work experience variable, measured in terms of months actually worked in all jobs, shows that on average, women had less total work experience than men, by nearly seven years in the case of married women relative to married men, but less than a year for single women relative to single men, with the return to experience being lower

TABLE 5.1 *Hourly earnings (net of overtime) by industry division*

Industry division	Full-time employees		Full-time men		Full-time women		Female/male earnings ratio (%)	Male manual		Female manual	
	No. empl.	Earnings (£)	No. empl.	Earnings (£)	No. empl.	Earnings (£)		No. empl.	Earnings (£)	No. empl.	Earnings (£)
Agriculture, forestry, and fishing	12	2.77	10	2.69	2	3.13	116.4	8	2.32	—	—
Energy and water	99	5.05	80	5.26	19	4.18	79.5	42	4.53	—	—
Minerals, metals, chemical	58	3.82	42	4.22	16	2.97	70.4	22	3.53	6	2.83
Engineering	413	3.82	328	4.10	85	2.89	70.5	221	3.78	45	2.77
Other manufacturing	264	3.29	162	3.78	102	2.61	69.1	118	3.42	73	2.48
Construction	101	3.78	92	3.86	9	2.86	74.1	75	3.67	—	—
Distribution, catering, etc.	281	3.13	153	3.63	128	2.61	72.0	78	3.16	14	2.18
Transport and communication	129	3.86	103	4.01	26	3.25	81.1	75	3.60	6	2.86
Banking, insurance, etc.	174	3.94	102	4.62	72	3.19	69.1	21	3.22	3	2.34
Other services	557	3.94	25	4.66	304	3.42	73.4	54	3.00	27	2.34

TABLE 5.1 Cont.

	F/M earnings ratio	Male non-manual		Female non-manual		F/M earnings ratio	Male part-time		Female part-time	
		No. empl.	Earnings (£)	No. empl.	Earnings (£)		No. empl.	Earnings (£)	No. empl.	Earnings (£)
Agriculture, forestry, and fishing	—	2	5.10	2	3.13	61.4	1	2.14	2	1.46
Energy and water	—	38	6.23	19	4.18	67.1	1	5.31	—	—
Minerals, metals, chemical	80.2	20	5.21	10	3.03	58.2	—	—	7	2.23
Engineering	73.2	107	4.85	40	3.03	62.5	2	4.14	20	2.20
Other manufacturing	72.5	44	5.00	29	2.92	58.4	1	5.81	31	2.14
Construction	—	17	4.90	9	3.16	64.5	—	—	5	1.42
Distribution, catering, etc.	69.0	75	4.22	114	2.66	63.0	4	1.86	191	2.08
Transport and communication	79.4	28	5.42	20	3.39	62.5	1	4.06	16	2.32
Banking, insurance, etc.	72.8	81	5.05	69	3.22	63.8	1	12.10	—	—
Other services	78.0	199	5.26	277	3.56	67.7	5	5.87	304	2.41

Note: N = 2,680
Source: SCELI Six Areas Work Attitudes and Work Histories Survey.

TABLE 5.2 *Hourly earnings (net of overtime) by size of establishment* (number of employees)

	1–24 employees		25–99 employees		100–499 employees		500+ employees	
	No. empl.	Earnings (£)	No. empl.	Earnings (£)	No. empl.	Earnings (£)	No. empl.	Earnings (£)
Full time								
Employees	549	3.25	457	3.71	521	3.82	561	4.81
Women	223	2.86	170	3.13	196	3.10	174	3.25
Men	326	3.56	287	4.14	325	4.35	387	4.66
Non-manual employees	339	3.46	260	4.18	301	4.31	300	4.53
Manual employees	210	2.94	197	3.19	220	3.25	261	3.82
Non-manual women	190	3.00	126	3.39	140	3.35	133	3.42
Non-manual men	149	4.10	134	5.05	161	5.37	167	5.70
Manual women	33	2.14	44	2.48	56	2.59	41	2.86
Manual men	177	3.13	153	3.46	164	3.53	220	4.01
Part-time								
Non-manual employees	273	2.20	88	2.66	64	2.41	29	3.29
Manual employees	94	2.01	42	2.05	29	2.25	16	2.36
Non-manual women	267	2.18	85	2.59	63	2.39	29	3.29
Non-manual men	6	3.71	3	7.03	1	4.06	—	—
Manual women	92	1.99	42	2.05	27	2.23	14	2.23
Manual men	2	3.56	—	—	2	2.61	2	3.82

Note: N = 2,723.

Source: SCELI Six Areas WAWH Survey.

TABLE 5.3 *Hourly earnings (net of overtime) by socio-economic group*[a]

Socio-economic group	Full-time women		Full-time men		Female/male earnings ratio	All full-time employees		All part-time employees	
	No. empl.	Earnings (£)	No. empl.	Earnings (£)		No. empl.	Earnings (£)	No. empl.	Earnings (£)
Managers/employers	67	3.53	198	5.70	61.9	265	5.00	14	2.27
Professionals	15	4.06	98	5.21	77.9	113	5.05	3	5.31
Intermediate non-manual	192	3.90	176	5.53	70.5	368	4.75	75	3.78
Junior non-manual	315	2.86	139	3.71	77.1	454	3.10	362	2.16
Foremen and supervisors	13	2.46	54	4.18	58.9	67	3.78	2	1.88
Skilled manual	49	2.69	379	3.67	73.3	428	3.53	16	2.53
Semi-skilled manual	95	2.51	227	3.39	74.0	322	3.10	56	2.34
Unskilled manual	17	2.25	54	2.89	77.9	71	2.72	107	1.92

Note: N = 2,723.

[a] Classification of socio-economic group taken from Gregory and Thomson 1990 (app. B).

Source: SCELI Six Areas WAWH Survey.

TABLE 5.4 *Hourly earnings (net of overtime) by degree of perceived job segregation*

Perceived job segregation	Full-time women		Full-time men		Female/male earnings ratio	All full-time employees		All part-time employees	
	No. empl.	Earnings (£)	No. empl.	Earnings (£)		No. empl.	Earnings (£)	No. empl.	Earnings (£)
Almost exclusively by men	9	3.32	616	4.06	81.8	625	4.06	6	3.63
Mainly by men	59	3.63	499	4.22	86.0	558	4.18	16	2.94
Equally by men and women	213	3.25	189	4.44	73.2	402	3.78	112	2.36
Mainly by women	334	3.00	15	4.90	61.2	349	3.06	316	2.34
Almost exclusively by women	146	2.80	2	2.36	118.6	148	2.77	183	2.10

METHODOLOGICAL ISSUES

The analysis in this chapter is based on the SCELI Six Areas Work Attitudes and Work Histories Survey, with a total of 2,715 employees.[5] The earnings data are based on gross hourly earnings excluding overtime. Respondents were asked what was their gross weekly wage or salary before deductions for tax, national insurance, or superannuation, and how many hours per week they worked during this period, excluding meal intervals and unpaid overtime, but including *paid* overtime. They were also asked how many of these hours were overtime hours.[6] Thus, we have reasonably accurate information on gross hourly pay, including overtime, but overtime earnings can only be estimated by assuming that overtime hours are paid at an arbitrary overtime rate (i.e. time and a half).[7] The argument for excluding overtime in gender earnings comparisons is that overtime working may reflect workers' preferences for income rather than a means by which employers may favour particular groups. For married women in particular family duties may make overtime working unpopular. Further, women in general are employed more than proportionately in non-manual jobs for which overtime working is less common. The implicit assumption in this analysis is, therefore, that there are relatively few women who both wish to work overtime and who are deprived of the opportunity to a greater degree than men.

The conventional method of estimating discrimination is residual in the sense that it analyses what is left after all other variables have been controlled for (see Chiplin and Sloane 1982, ch. 5). This method is particularly susceptible to omitted variable bias—arising from the fact that not all relevant variables may be included in the model. If some of the omitted variables are relevant to earnings then clearly the estimates of discrimination will be inaccurate. However, the particularly rich range of variables in the SCELI data and the improved measurement of variables such as work experience means that omitted variable bias may be less of a problem here.

Another problem which has only recently been addressed in econometric work is sample selection bias. It is possible that women who are participating in the labour-force at any one time

are a non-random subset of all potential labour-force participants, in which case ordinary least squares estimates may be
biased and inconsistent. If there is significant sample selection
bias, estimates of the extent of wage discrimination may well be
inaccurate. Sample selection bias has been found to be significant
by Dolton and Makepeace (1986 and 1987), Wright and Ermisch
(1991), and (for Australia) by Kidd and Viney (1989), but not for
the UK by Joshi and Newell (1987). In order to correct for sample selection bias it is necessary to utilize the Heckman two-step
procedure which requires the explicit modelling of the labour-
force participation decision of women by probit analysis. This
produces a correction term which is added to the earnings equations. This procedure was incorporated in equation (5) below.
Details of the Heckman correction for sample selection bias are
provided in Appendix 5.2.

The standard residual procedure also treats occupational
attainment as given, which ignores the possibility that occupational segregation may be in part the consequence of hiring discrimination. Following Miller (1987) this was corrected for by
estimating an ordered probit model for occupational attainment,
which allowed us to estimate the extent to which female pay is
reduced by a failure to be hired on the same basis as men. (See
Appendix 5.2 for details.)

Finally, the standard residual procedure effectively asks the
question, 'Are members of the different sex and marital status
groups equally rewarded for particular personal characteristics
such as qualifications?' It is possible to change this question
round and ask, 'Are members of the various groups earning the
same rate of pay differentially qualified?' This procedure known
as reverse regression involves putting pay on the right-hand side
of the equation along with the other variables and having education or other personal characteristics as the dependent variable.
Surprisingly, the US evidence shows that it is possible for the
standard residual procedure to suggest the presence of discrimination against a minority group, yet for members of that minority group to be less well qualified than members of the majority
when receiving the same rate of pay (Hashimoto and Kochin
1980). However, it has also been shown that reverse regression
itself may be subject to various biases and fail to yield a
valid estimator. But with this caveat in mind one of the first

attempts to apply reverse regression to a British data set is made below.

THE MODEL

As a starting-point for the analysis of the gender wage differential one can estimate for a sample of individuals an augmented Mincer human capital equation (1974) of the form

$$ln\ E_i = a + bS_i + cX_i + dX_i^2 + eZ_i + f\text{MAR}_i + h\text{SEX}_i + \varepsilon_i \quad (1)$$

where E = earnings of individual i
 $a \ldots h$ = coefficients of variables
 S = years of schooling or educational dummies
 X, X^2 = experience in the labour market (months or years)
 Z = a vector of other characteristics hypothesized to determine earnings
 MAR = dummy for marriage
 SEX = dummy for sex
 ε_i = stochastic error

Additional variables are added as available (in this case whether on shiftwork, on a merit payment system, a union member, in the public or private sector, in a segregated job, in white-collar job, father's socio-economic group, the degree of job security and establishment size). In this equation discrimination is measured by the single dummy variable sex, and focuses on differences in the constant (intercept) term created by the dummy. However, this specification of the earnings function is highly restrictive, since it forces all the slope coefficients (i.e. b, c, d, e, and f) to be the same for men and women, which may not be correct. For example, if women invested less each year in enhancing their labour market productivity, because they expected to spend less time in paid work than men, there would be every reason to expect that the slopes of the male and female earnings/experience profiles would differ for reasons that have little to do with discrimination.

In order to test whether the slope coefficients are in fact significantly different between men and women the above equation can be modified by including the full complement of interaction terms between the sex dummy variable and the other variables.

$$ln\ E_i = a_3 + a_4\text{SEX}_i + b_3S_i + b_4S_i\text{SEX}_i + c_3X_i + c_4X_i\text{SEX}_i + d_3X_i^2$$
$$+ d_4X_i^2\text{SEX}_i + e_3Z_i + e_4Z_i\text{SEX}_i + f_3\text{MAR}_i$$
$$+ f_4\text{MAR}_i\text{SEX}_i + \varepsilon_{3i} \tag{2}$$

It is then possible to decompose the earnings differential into that resulting from varying characteristics (S, X, Z, etc.), that from different slope coefficients (the interaction terms), and the unexplained differential arising in the constant term.

The conventional alternative is to estimate separate earnings functions for each sex (or other comparator groups) and then compare the intercepts and coefficients in the two equations. Distinguishing by sex we have

$$ln\ E_{iM} = a_1 + b_1S_i + c_1X_i + d_1X_i^2 + e_1Z_i + f_1\text{MAR}_i + \varepsilon_{1i} \tag{3a}$$

$$ln\ E_{iF} = a_2 + b_2S_i + c_2X_i + d_2X_i^2 + e_2Z^i + f_2\text{MAR}_i + \varepsilon_{2i} \tag{3b}$$

where M and F represent males and females respectively.

Simplifying the example to males (M), females (F), and personal characteristics (X) the average earnings differential can be decomposed as follows:

$$ln\ E_M - ln\ E_F = (a_M - a_F) + X_F(b_M - b_F) + (X_M - X_F)b_M \tag{4}$$

Discrimination is normally taken to consist of the first two terms on the right-hand side (i.e. the difference in intercepts and slopes). However, attributing the whole of the intercept difference to discrimination is dubious, since part of it may reflect the influence of omitted variables. For this reason measures of discrimination both including and excluding the constant term are provided in Table 5.12 below.

One way of measuring discrimination is by calculating the amount by which pay would have to change for one sex group to reach the level of pay of the other (see Chiplin and Sloane 1982: 65–8). However, different measures of discrimination may be obtained according to whether the earnings function of females or of males is taken as the basis for estimation.[8] Cotton (1988) argues that we must take into account the fact that not only are women undervalued but also that males are overvalued, so that neither earnings function would prevail in the absence of discrimination. He suggests that the male and female wage structures should be weighted by the respective proportions of males and females in the employed labour-force. Yet, this would seem to be arbitrary. What is clear, however, is that the difference between what females currently earn and what they 'would' earn if paid according to the male earnings function is likely to exceed the amount of the potential wage gain to women arising from the measured disparities in the two earnings functions. Output and costs are likely to be influenced negatively by attempts to narrow differentials though this might be offset to some extent by efficiency gains arising from the removal of discrimination. But we cannot necessarily conclude that the actual outcome will be determined by the ratio of males and females in the employed labour-force.

THE RESULTS

Single restricted equations (equation 1)

Initially a single ordinary least squares regression (1) was run with dummies for sex, marriage, and whether full or part time (FT/PT) in order to determine whether the earnings functions were significantly different in each of the six labour markets. As can be seen in Table 5.6 in no case is the *t*-statistic significantly different from zero in relation to the labour market locality dummies, which indicates that variations in the tightness of local labour markets had little effect on the gross wage differential. Over 40 per cent of the variance in earnings can be explained by the model, which is not unsatisfactory given the high proportion of dummies among the independent variables.

Different versions of this equation were run with two segregation variables, MOSTLYWM in equation (1a) with a value of one where the respondent said the job was done either mainly or almost exclusively by women and EXCLUSWM in equation (1b) with a value of 1 where the respondent said that the job was almost exclusively done by women. 36.1 per cent of the respondents said they were employed in mainly female jobs and 12.2 per cent in almost exclusively female jobs. This variable is attempting to pick up the extent to which job segregation depresses pay. In the former case pay was reduced by 7.8 per cent and in the latter by 10.3 per cent, holding other things constant. Table 5.7 presents the results on this variable in equations fitted for separate

TABLE 5.6 *Single equations OLS basic hourly earnings functions (1)*

Variable		(1a) Including MOSTLYWM segregation variable			(1b) Including EXCLUSWM segregation variable	
		Mean	Coefficient	t-stat.	Coefficient	t-stat.
Basic hourly earnings		3.333				
CONSTANT		—	0.531**	(10.73)	0.501**	(10.74)
FT/PT		0.767	0.155**	(6.63)	0.159**	(6.90)
SEX		0.492	0.286**	(11.74)	0.314**	(15.65)
MARRIED		0.716	0.051**	(2.72)	0.052**	(2.75)
EXPER[a]		220.726	0.002**	(8.13)	0.002**	(8.18)
EXPER^2		65,944.338	−0.000003**	(−7.11)	−0.000003**	(−7.17)
OTHERQUAL	⎫	0.166	0.084**	(3.26)	0.083**	(3.22)
APPQUAL	⎪	0.152	0.088**	(3.46)	0.090**	(3.56)
OLVQUAL[b]	⎬ education dummies	0.220	0.194**	(8.11)	0.196**	(8.10)
ALVQUAL[b]	⎪	0.050	0.173**	(4.21)	0.175**	(4.25)
PROFQUAL	⎭	0.110	0.301**	(9.43)	0.301**	(9.43)
SHIFT		0.196	−0.029	(−1.45)	−0.032	(−1.60)
MERIT		0.226	0.103**	(5.33)	0.105**	(5.44)
TRAIN		0.471	0.102**	(5.97)	0.101**	(5.92)
UNION		0.469	0.095**	(5.16)	0.094**	(5.11)
PUBLIC		0.374	0.028	(1.54)	0.026	(1.42)
MOSTLYWM		0.367	−0.078**	—	—	—

	Mean	Coefficient	(t)	Coefficient	(t)
EXCLUSWM	—	—		-0.103**	(-4.07)
FRSEG80	7.252	-0.005*	(-2.47)	-0.005*	(-2.54)
JOBSEC	1.674	-0.017	(-1.75)	-0.016	(-1.69)
COLLAR (1 = MANUAL)	0.393	-0.182**	(-9.80)	-0.182**	(-9.83)
MEDEST	0.215	0.111**	(5.15)	0.107**	(4.96)
LARGEST $\}$ establishment	0.225	0.112**	(5.14)	0.108**	(4.97)
VLARGEST $\}$ size dummies	0.222	0.174**	(7.49)	0.172**	(7.41)
COV	0.151	-0.042	(-1.51)	-0.041	(-1.47)
KIRK	0.172	0.005	(0.18)	0.003	(0.09)
NORTH	0.172	0.014	(0.48)	0.014	(0.51)
ROCH	0.162	-0.032	(-1.13)	-0.034	(-1.20)
SWIND	0.154	0.037	(1.29)	0.035	(1.20)

$R^2 = 0.414$	$R^2 = 0.415$
$\bar{R}^2 = 0.408$	$\bar{R}^2 = 0.409$
Standard error of the equation (SEE) = 0.399	SEE = 0.398
$F = 70.320$	$F = 70.647$

Notes: N = 2,715. Significance levels: * = 5%; ** = 1%.

a This variable is measured in months, so that, although the coefficient may appear small, experience does have a substantial effect on earnings. This includes experience on all jobs, not just tenure on current job.

b The return to O-levels is surprisingly consistently higher than the return to A-levels. Perhaps this reflects the fact that those who complete their education at the A-level stage are those who have failed to gain entry into higher education, whilst those who leave school at 16 have a clear job in mind.

Source: SCELI Six Areas WAWH Survey.

comparator groups. It shows that there is no significant depressing effect of these variables on male pay for the small proportion of men who are found in these jobs. For single women and for part-time women it is only almost exclusively female jobs that have a significant depressing effect on pay. All full-time women have hourly pay that is some 30 per cent less than that of married men, so that the above estimates suggest that job segregation is not responsible for the major component of the difference between male and female earnings.[9]

Regressions (not reported here) were also run with alternative specifications of job segregation—substituting in turn 'jobs held mostly or almost exclusively by men' for 'jobs held mostly or almost exclusively by women' etc., a five-point hierarchical variable (almost exclusively female jobs ranked one and almost exclusively male jobs ranked 5) and dummy variables for each category. These showed that the depressing effect of female-dominated segregation outweighed any positive effect of male-dominated segregation. In the case of the hierarchical variable, the overall impact of segregation in favour of men was to raise earnings by 6 per cent. Yet exclusively male jobs had no significant impact on earnings generally, whilst in the case of jobs done almost exclusively or mainly by men, though earnings were significantly higher for all employees by some 18 per cent, men earned 10 per cent *less* (significant at the 10 per cent level). Married women earned substantially more in jobs held almost exclusively or mainly by men, but substantially less in almost exclusively male jobs. Thus it would appear overall that the percentage loss in earnings for women as a consequence of job segregation is greater than the percentage gain to men resulting from this phenomenon.

As far as the other explanatory variables are concerned educational qualifications and experience raise pay in conformity with the human capital model. The rate of return to qualifications is highly significant with a return of 30 per cent to professional/degree qualifications compared to no qualifications. However, the return to A-level qualifications is slightly lower than that for O-level qualifications. This may reflect the fact that those who complete their education at this stage are those who fail to get a place in higher education. Workers who receive on-the-job training obtain 10 per cent extra pay, as do those subject to merit

TABLE 5.7 *OLS equations for separate comparator groups: impact of job segregation variable on hourly earnings*

Subgroup	Mean base hourly earnings (£)	Jobs mainly done by women			Jobs almost exclusively done by women			
		Mean	Coefficient on MOSTLYWM	t-stat.	Mean	Coefficient on EXCLUSWM	t-stat.	N
FTM men (1e)	4.464	0.012	0.115	(0.96)	0.001	−0.404	(−1.04)	937
FTS men (1d)	3.550	0.015	−0.033	(−0.21)	0.003	−0.243	(−0.64)	388
FTM women (1e)	3.047	0.644	−0.105**	(−2.89)	0.204	−0.094*	(−2.18)	466
FTS women (1f)	3.114	0.610	−0.069	(−1.58)	0.173	−0.123*	(−2.24)	297
All FT women (1g)	3.074	0.631	−0.094**	(−3.39)	0.192	−0.100**	(−2.96)	763
All PT women (1h)	2.264	0.507	−0.057	(−1.8)	0.297	−0.104*	(−2.53)	619

Notes: FTM = full-time married; FTS = full-time single; PT = part-time.
Significance levels: * = 5%; ** = 1%.
These are the results of running equations as in Table 5.1 separately for each sex/marital status group.

Source: SCELI Six Areas WAWH Survey.

related pay. Similarly, union members receive 9.5 per cent more than non-unionists. Manual workers receive approximately 18 per cent less than non-manual workers for given characteristics, and father's membership of a higher socio-economic group has a significant if small effect on an individual's earnings. The sector, shiftwork, and job security variables are the only ones not to be significant by conventional standards and the last two have signs opposite to those anticipated. This is particularly surprising in the case of shiftwork, which is generally subject to premium pay arrangements.[10] Finally, establishment size has a strong independent effect on pay, despite the large number of controls for personal characteristics of individual employees, a finding consistent with that on other studies (e.g. Brown and Medoff 1989). It should be noted that the legislation relates to discrimination within establishments or firms and not across them. Therefore part of the difference in earnings between men and women is due to factors not subject to alteration through the legislation.

To conclude this section, the average earnings of women differ from those of men for a variety of reasons—differences in the degree of human capital, in employment structure, and in the extent of job segregation. Locality of employment does not, however, appear to exert an independent influence.

Single unrestricted equations (equation 2)

The above formulation constrains male and female slope coefficients to be the same. It is possible to overcome this restriction by the use of interaction terms in which each independent variable is interacted with the sex dummy to determine whether there are significant differences between the male and female coefficients. This provides some interesting results (see Table 5.8). Marital status is by itself insignificant, but the interaction of sex with marital status shows that married men earn approximately 14 per cent more than single workers, *ceteris paribus*, a finding again consistent with that of many other studies. Union membership raised the pay of women relative to men by 9.3 per cent. The public sector dummy becomes significant with an 8.4 per cent premium to employment in the public sector and women fare relatively better than men with an 11.3 per cent premium. Thus the public sector does appear to be less discriminatory than

TABLE 5.8 *OLS single hourly earnings equation with sex interaction terms* (2)

Variable	Mean	Coefficient	*t*-stat.
Basic hourly earnings	3.333		
CONSTANT		0.603**	(9.80)
SEX	0.492	0.355**	(2.77)
FT/PT	0.767	0.152**	(6.00)
FT/PTSEX	0.487	−0.188	(−1.81)
MARRIED	0.716	−0.028	(1.07)
MARRIEDSEX	0.346	0.142**	(3.86)
EXP	220.726	0.002**	(8.12)
EXPSEX	112.338	—	
EXP^2	65,944.338	−0.000004**	(−7.35)
EXP^{2}SEX	40,456.735	−0.0000009**	(3.15)
OTHQUAL	0.166	0.066	(1.88)
OTHQUALSEX	0.084	0.036	(0.70)
APPQUAL	0.152	0.119**	(3.12)
APPQUALSEX	0.094	−0.037	(0.72)
OLVQUAL	0.220	0.175**	(5.53)
OLVQUALSEX	0.111	0.037	(0.77)
ALVQUAL	0.050	0.187**	(3.17)
ALVQUALSEX	0.027	−0.039	(−0.48)
PROFQUAL	0.110	0.333**	(7.71)
PROFQUALSEX	0.054	−0.081	(−1.27)
SHIFT	0.196	−0.051	(−1.72)
SHIFTSEX	0.112	0.033	(0.82)
MERIT	0.226	0.073**	(2.33)
MERITSEX	0.150	0.046	(1.18)
TRAIN	0.471	0.069**	(2.82)
TRAINSEX	0.282	0.056	(1.65)
UNION	0.469	0.142**	(5.49)
UNIONSEX	0.270	−0.093*	(−2.54)
PUBLIC	0.374	0.084**	(3.29)
PUBLICSEX	0.160	−0.113**	(−3.08)
MOSTLYWM	0.367	−0.087**	(−3.58)
MOSTLYWMSEX	0.007	0.144	(1.46)
FRSEG80	7.252	−0.004	(−1.66)
FRSEG80SEX	3.569	0.001	(0.29)
JOBSEC	1.674	−0.081*	(−2.30)
JOBSECSEX	0.827	0.023	(1.22)
COLLAR	0.393	−0.098**	(−3.60)

Cont./

TABLE 5.8 *Cont.*

Variable	Mean	Coefficient	*t*-stat.
COLLARSEX	0.264	−0.134**	(−3.57)
MEDEST	0.215	0.097**	(3.38)
MEDESTSEX	0.106	0.018	(0.42)
LARGEST	0.225	0.084**	(2.78)
LARGESTSEX	0.120	0.066	(1.52)
VLARGEST	0.222	0.120**	(3.46)
VLARGESTSEX	0.143	0.083	(1.78)
COV	0.151	−0.052	(−1.31)
COVSEX	0.083	0.014	(0.25)
KIRK	0.172	−0.0003	(−0.07)
KIRKSEX	0.083	0.004	(0.07)
NORTH	0.172	0.036	(0.94)
NORTHSEX	0.084	−0.057	(−1.02)
ROCH	0.162	0.044	(1.11)
ROCHSEX	0.078	−0.151**	(−2.66)
SWIN	0.154	0.034	(0.86)
SWINSEX	0.074	0.002	(0.04)
		R2 = 0.434	
		$\bar{R}^2$ = 0.423	
		SEE = 0.394	
		F = 39.287	

Notes: N = 2,715. Significance levels: * = 5%; ** = 1%.

The sex interaction variables allow us to test whether the coefficients on each of the independent variables are significantly different for women than for men. A positive sign indicates an attribute is rewarded more in the case of men and a negative sign more in the case of women.

Source: SCELI Six Areas WAWH Survey.

the private sector. Similarly the non-manual/manual status inter-action dummy suggests that the differential between male and female pay is narrower for manual workers than for non-manual workers. Finally the sex differential is significantly smaller by 15 per cent in Rochdale compared to Aberdeen.[11]

Overall the shift coefficient (SEX) suggests a wage advantage to men of 35.5 per cent. Including the effects of differences in slope coefficients (interaction terms) raises this to 37.1 per cent. Thus the major part of this wage advantage resides in the shift coeffi-cient which could be subject to omitted variable bias although we have controlled for more variables than in many empirical studies.

Ignoring the shift coefficient the wage advantage to men is only 5.6 per cent. If the decomposition exercise is carried out only for those interaction terms which are significant at the 95 per cent level, the total effect falls from 37.1 per cent to 27.2 per cent, or −8.3 per cent compared with 5.6 per cent if we ignore the shift coefficient. Thus the precise approach adopted can make a substantial difference to the estimate of discrimination or even change its sign.

Earnings equations differentiated by sex, marital status, and full-time/part-time employment (equations 3a–f)

The fact that marriage contributes approximately 40 per cent to the overall difference (14.2/37.1 per cent) emphasizes the importance of treating each sex/marital status group separately, if one wishes to isolate the effect of gender from marital status discrimination. The same can be said for full- and part-time women's work. A series of separate versions of equation (3) were fitted in order to make comparisons between the earnings of married men and married women, married men and single men, single men and single women, single women and married women, and full-time women and part-time women.

Married men and women (equations 3a and 3b)

Married men earn 46.5 per cent more on average than married women. The earnings functions in Table 5.9 enable us to pinpoint some of the reasons for this difference. The intercept term in the male equation (3a) lies substantially above that for women (3b). Married women obtain a higher return to qualifications than do married men, but less to experience, which is consistent with an atrophy of human capital due to time spent out of the labour market. Yet, when regressions were run including a break in service variable (i.e. time spent out of the labour market in quadratic form) this variable was never statistically significant for women, though it was for men, for whom it would in the main represent unemployment rather than time spent in the household. This result for women contrasts with that for many other studies and may be explained by the fact that our experience variable captures true experience rather than imputed experience. Married men obtain a slightly higher return to on-the-job training.

TABLE 5.9 *OLS hourly earnings functions for married men and women (3a and 3b)*

Variable	Full-time married men			Full-time married women		
	Mean	Coefficient	t-stat.	Mean	Coefficient	t-stat.
Basic hourly earnings	4.464			3.047		
CONSTANT	—	1.123**	(12.69)	—	0.702**	(6.58)
OTHQUAL	0.143	0.071	(1.59)	0.172	0.160**	(2.75)
APPQUAL	0.209	0.054	(1.40)	0.124	0.097	(1.55)
OLVQUAL	0.203	0.214**	(5.08)	0.215	0.274**	(5.16)
ALVQUAL	0.048	0.126	(1.84)	0.036	0.222*	(2.10)
PROFQUAL	0.121	0.218**	(4.13)	0.144	0.342**	(5.27)
EXPER (months)	289.636	0.002*	(5.08)	209.165	0.000002**	(2.63)
EXPER^2	100,872.078	-0.000004**	(-4.89)	55,607.131	-0.000003*	(-2.27)
TRAIN	0.581	0.110**	(3.97)	0.481	0.090*	(-2.45)
FRSEG80	7.483	-0.004	(-1.24)	7.483	-0.007	(-1.64)
COLLAR (1 = manual)	0.510	-0.288**	(-9.53)	0.247	-0.085	(-1.79)
SHIFT	0.234	-0.013	(-0.41)	0.131	-0.116*	(-2.15)
MERIT	0.312	0.096**	(3.45)	0.204	0.060	(1.35)
UNION	0.581	0.017	(0.57)	0.500	0.176**	(4.22)

OTHQUAL, APPQUAL, OLVQUAL, ALVQUAL, PROFQUAL } educational dummies

JOB SEC		1.674	-0.007	(-0.46)	1.624	-0.020	(-0.90)
PUBLIC		0.348	-0.023	(-0.77)	0.416	0.052	(1.15)
MEDEST	size of	0.217	0.084*	(2.20)	0.230	0.070	(1.46)
LARGEST	establishment	0.250	0.123**	(3.26)	0.273	0.092*	(1.99)
VLARGEST	dummies	0.312	0.179**	(4.82)	0.187	0.104	(1.95)
COV		0.173	-0.040	(-0.92)	0.133	-0.077	(-1.18)
KIRK		0.180	-0.007	(-0.15)	0.172	-0.057	(-0.88)
NORTH		0.164	-0.036	(-0.75)	0.176	-0.003	(-0.06)
ROCH		0.150	-0.142**	(-2.98)	0.178	-0.026	(-0.40)
SWIND		0.152	0.010	(0.21)	0.165	-0.027	(-0.41)

N = 937
$R^2 = 0.314$
$\bar{R}^2 = 0.296$
SEE = 0.384
F = 18.130

N = 466
$R^2 = 0.268$
$\bar{R}^2 = 0.230$
SEE = 0.368
F = 7.022

Notes: Significance levels: * = 5%; ** = 1%.
Source: SCELI Six Areas WAWH Survey.

Married men's earnings are considerably lower in blue-collar jobs, whilst there is no statistically significant difference for married women between white- and blue-collar jobs. Shiftworking is significantly associated with lower pay only for married women. Whilst both groups earn more where merit-related pay applies the return is greater and statistically significant for married men. Union membership is associated with 17.6 per cent higher earnings for married women, but does not significantly influence the earnings of married men. The extent to which pay rises with establishment size is stronger for married men than for married women and more statistically significant. Finally, pay of married men is significantly lower in Rochdale than in Aberdeen as previously indicated in Table 5.8.

To conclude, the earnings of married men and married women are determined in distinctive ways with married men obtaining a net advantage in terms of the coefficients on the independent variables even ignoring the intercept term. This means that not only is there a large unexplained discriminatory element in the wage differential for married men and women but that the relevant variables affect earnings in different ways for each group. The difference in the intercept term could represent discrimination, an unmeasured link between marital status and productivity, or differences in preferences or opportunity costs between the sexes.

Single men and women (equations 3c and 3d)

The equations for single men and single women (Table 5.10) show little difference in the constant terms, but a higher return for men on educational qualifications, on-the-job training, presence of merit pay system, union membership, and employment in larger establishments. Single women's pay is depressed relative to that of men by father's socio-economic group, blue-collar employment, and shiftworking. Employment in the public sector, however, raised pay by some 12 per cent.

This suggests that there are substantial differences in the earnings functions of married and single men and of married and single women with married men favoured over single men whether because of commitment or discrimination, and single women favoured over married women possibly because of their greater perceived employment stability or discrimination. It is worth remarking that the extent of measured discrimination against single women, the test case for discrimination, is much smaller than in the case of the other groups.

Full- and part-time women (equations 3e and 3f)

Finally, we can compare the earnings functions of full-time and part-time women (Table 5.11). Here there are differential returns to different educational qualifications, though not in a consistent direction. Part-time women do not obtain a significant return to experience, father's socio-economic group, or presence of merit payment systems. On the other hand, they do receive relatively high returns to on-the-job training and particularly to union membership and employment in very large establishments. It is only full-time women whose pay is depressed by the presence of shiftwork.

Measuring discrimination between groups

As outlined above, it is possible to calculate measures of discrimination on the basis of the earnings functions by fitting the characteristics of one group to the function of the other (e.g. women to men, etc.). However, as noted, the results can differ according to which group is taken as the basis for the estimation. Table 5.12 gives the measures of discrimination for the different comparator groups with both alternatives. Thus the first two columns are based on the earnings of the lower-paid group (e.g. married women) if they were rewarded in the same way as the higher-paid group (in this case married men), and the latter two columns are based on the earnings of the higher-paid group if they were rewarded in the same way as the lower paid. Normally the constant term is included in estimates of discrimination as explained above, but it could equally well include the effects of unmeasured non-discriminatory variables, so that there are arguments for providing estimates both including and excluding the constant term.

For married men and married women these results are consistent with a discrimination coefficient of 37 per cent, rewarding women according to the male earnings function, or 23 per cent ignoring the difference in the intercept terms. For single men and women the results are consistent with a pay disadvantage, given characteristics, of some 15 per cent and in this case inclusion or

TABLE 5.10 *OLS hourly earnings functions for single men and women (3c and 3d)*

Variable		Full-time single men			Full-time single women		
		Mean	Coefficient	t-stat.	Mean	Coefficient	t-stat.
Basic hourly earnings		3.550			3.114		
CONSTANT		—	0.606**	(5.44)	—	0.680**	(5.64)
OTHQUAL	⎫ educational	0.237	0.161*	(2.45)	0.222	0.076	(0.99)
APPQUAL	⎬ dummies	0.147	0.161*	(2.33)	0.084	0.159	(1.68)
OLVQUAL	⎭	0.273	0.236**	(3.71)	0.259	0.143*	(1.98)
ALVQUAL		0.067	0.184	(1.91)	0.084	0.184	(1.63)
PROFQUAL		0.088	0.347**	(3.86)	0.158	0.295**	(3.39)
EXPER (Months)		151.727	0.002**	(3.87)	143.701	0.003**	(4.34)
EXPER^2		38,198.227	-0.000003*	(2.32)	32,492.138	-0.000006**	(-3.75)
TRAIN		0.549	0.147**	(3.60)	0.529	-0.020	(-0.43)
FRSEG80		6.768	-0.003	(-0.68)	6.358	-0.011*	(-2.20)
COLLAR (1 = MANUAL)		0.608	-0.101*	(-2.21)	0.199	-0.233**	(-3.87)
SHIFT		0.211	0.003	(0.05)	0.202	-0.140*	(-2.50)
MERIT		0.294	0.153**	(3.48)	0.229	0.110*	(2.10)
UNION		0.472	0.104*	(2.26)	0.471	0.084	(1.72)

JOB SEC	1.673	0.019	(0.76)	1.613	−0.006	(−0.22)
PUBLIC	0.268	−0.048	(−0.98)	0.448	0.121*	(2.41)
MEDEST	0.216	0.149**	(2.80)	0.212	0.165**	(2.67)
LARGEST	0.235	0.208**	(3.92)	0.232	0.108	(1.80)
VLARGEST	0.245	0.251**	(4.29)	0.293	0.125*	(2.16)
COV	0.168	−0.040	(−0.60)	0.118	0.072	(0.89)
KIRK	0.144	0.051	(0.71)	0.185	−0.030	(−0.38)
NORTH	0.170	0.013	(0.18)	0.141	0.138	(1.60)
ROCH	0.183	−0.034	(−0.49)	0.165	0.067	(0.81)
SWIND	0.149	0.099	(1.35)	0.141	0.047	(0.54)

MEDEST, LARGEST, VLARGEST } size of establishment dummies

N = 388
$R^2 = 0.335$
$\bar{R}^2 = 0.293$
SEE = 0.364
F = 7.958

N = 297
$R^2 = 0.320$
$\bar{R}^2 = 0.263$
SEE = 0.344
F = 5.585

Notes: Significance levels: * = 5%; ** = 1%.
Source: SCELI Six Areas WAWH Survey.

TABLE 5.11 *OLS hourly earnings functions for full-time and part-time women (3e and 3f)*

Variable	Full-time women			Part-time women		
	Mean	Coefficient	t-stat.	Mean	Coefficient	t-stat.
Basic hourly earnings	3.074			2.264		
CONSTANT	—	0.710**	(9.24)	—	0.650*	(5.71)
MARRIAGE	0.611	-0.031	(-1.06)	0.871	-0.028	(-0.51)
OTHQUAL	0.191	0.136**	(3.00)	0.129	-0.033	(-0.53)
APPQUAL	0.109	0.110*	(2.16)	0.121	0.125*	(2.04)
OLVQUAL	0.232	0.224**	(5.35)	0.195	0.138**	(2.61)
ALVQUAL	0.055	0.074**	(2.67)	0.036	0.173	(1.65)
PROFQUAL	0.149	0.318**	(6.21)	0.063	0.397**	(4.62)
EXPER (months)	183.685	0.002**	(4.83)	206.184	0.0007	(1.02)
EXPER^2	46,609.552	-0.000004**	(-4.27)	54,582.914	-0.000002	(-1.20)
TRAIN	0.499	0.052	(1.84)	0.215	0.113*	(2.37)
FRSEG80	7.045	-0.008**	(-2.61)	7.518	0.0002	(0.04)
COLLAR (1 = MANUAL)	0.228	-0.123**	(-3.33)	0.283	-0.083	(-1.91)
SHIFT	0.159	-0.130**	(-3.41)	0.170	0.020	(0.40)

The variables OTHQUAL, APPQUAL, OLVQUAL, ALVQUAL, and PROFQUAL are grouped as educational dummies.

Variable							
MERIT		0.214	0.078*	(2.33)	0.073	0.088	(1.22)
UNION		0.489	0.031**	(4.47)	0.273	0.169**	(3.64)
JOB SEC		1.620	−0.018	(−1.10)	1.725	−0.043	(−1.88)
SECTOR		0.429	0.084*	(2.51)	0.410	0.074	(1.78)
MEDEST	size of	0.223	0.092*	(2.48)	0.205	0.075	(1.55)
LARGEST	establishment	0.257	0.036*	(2.55)	0.145	0.027	(0.48)
VLARGEST	dummies	0.228	0.106**	(2.75)	0.069	0.184*	(2.39)
COV		0.127	−0.015	(−0.31)	0.145	−0.093	(−1.38)
KIRK		0.177	−0.047	(−0.96)	0.170	0.028	(0.44)
NORTH		0.163	0.041	(0.82)	0.189	0.037	(0.56)
ROCH		0.173	0.004	(0.09)	0.153	0.099	(1.44)
SWIND		0.156	−0.001	(−0.02)	0.160	0.072	(1.08)

N = 763
R2 = 0.264
R̄² = 0.240
SEE = 0.359
F = 11.027

N = 619
R2 = 0.171
R̄² = 0.137
SEE = 0.452
F = 5.088

Notes: Significance levels: * = 5%; ** = 1%.
Source: SCELI Six Areas WAWH Survey.

TABLE 5.12 *Estimates of discrimination for all comparator pairs (from equation (4))*

Comparator pair	F_e		M_e	
	MDC	Ignoring constant	MDC	Ignoring constant
Single men/single women	15.27	17.65	30.29	40.22
Married men/married women	37.04	23.21	100.96	31.86
Single women/married women	4.82	5.47	29.04	31.87
Married men/single men	4.14	−37.90	15.75	−30.93
Full-time women/part-time women	10.77	13.36	15.97	9.25

Note: Where F_e is estimated earnings of lower paid group in absence of discrimination; M_e is estimated earnings of higher paid group in absence of discrimination.

Measure of discrimination used: MDC $= ((M/F) - (M/F)^o)/(M/F)^o$, where o refers to ratio in absence of discrimination.

Source: SCELI Six Areas WAWH Survey.

exclusion of the constant term makes only a small difference. The estimate of discrimination against single compared to married men is some 4 per cent, but if the constant term is ignored this changes to nearly 40 per cent in favour of single men. In the female comparison there is an estimated discrimination coefficient of 4.8 per cent in favour of single women and ignoring the constant term makes relatively little difference.

The results also suggest a discrimination coefficient in excess of 10 per cent against part-time relative to full-time women. It is not clear, however, to what extent this reflects the willingness of women part-timers to accept jobs with lower pay for reasons of convenience, or to what extent discrimination by the employer who is able to segment the market between full-time or part-time jobs or who may possibly perceive full-time employees to be more productive than part-time employees. (Some of these questions are explored in the following chapter.)

These results are clearly sensitive to the basis of estimation. However, using the estimates based on functions of the higher-paid groups and comparing single men and single women, the latter would earn slightly more than the former if differences in coefficients were removed. That is differences in characteristics equal 106.5 per cent of the wage gap. In terms of contribution to predicted earnings, the constant term is responsible for 47 per cent, personal characteristics 28 per cent, establishment/industry variables 13 per cent, job variables 11 per cent, and locational variables 1 per cent. Discrimination is equal to approximately one-third of the wage gap. Turning now to the comparison between married men and married women, differences in characteristics are responsible for only 20 per cent of the wage gap between the sexes. The constant term 'explains' 79 per cent of predicted earnings, personal characteristics 19 per cent, job characteristics 4 per cent, while location has a negative overall effect of 2 per cent. Here discrimination is responsible for just over one quarter of the wage gap.

Unequal occupational distributions

It is possible to obtain some idea of the relative importance of different distributions of men and women between occupational groups *vis-à-vis* pay differences within these groups, as follows.

Occupational group is included within the earnings equation (not reported here) and the size of the estimated discrimination coefficient thus obtained is compared with that from the unrestricted equations. Hence eight socio-economic groups were added to the four sex/marital status regressions as dummies. There are clear differences in occupational distribution between the sex/marital status groups (see Table 5.13). For example, married men are over-represented in higher non-manual jobs, single men in skilled manual jobs, married women in junior non-manual and unskilled manual jobs, and single women in intermediate and junior non-manual jobs. However, the estimated discrimination coefficient holding occupational group constant for single women relative to single men was 11.12 compared to 15.27 without including occupation (not shown). Hence for this comparator pair, earnings differentials within occupational group are roughly three times as important as differentials between groups in depressing female pay. When the same exercise was conducted for married men and married women the measured discrimination coefficient was actually greater (43.46 per cent compared with 37.04 per cent). Thus married women's occupational distribution is more favourable to raising pay than that of married men.

The occupational attainment model

When the ordered probit model was run with the eight SEGs as outlined above the maximum likelihood estimates showed considerable deterioration compared to the OLS results, the programme having difficulties in converging with this number of groups. As a consequence it was necessary to collapse the eight SEGs into five by combining junior non-manual with semi-skilled manuals (the earnings for which were relatively close), foremen and supervisors with skilled manuals, and intermediate non-manuals with professionals. This enabled a comparison to be made of the extent to which females were under- or over-represented in SEGs compared to men for given attributes (not shown). Useful comparisons can be made for single women relative to single men and married women in relation to married men. In the former case single women would be actually worse off after the occupational redistribution as fewer of them would be found in the relatively

TABLE 5.13 *Sex/marital status groups by socio-economic group, percentage distributions*

Socio-economic group	Married men	Single men	Married women	Single women
Managers/employers	16.8	10.1	5.7	5.9
Professional	7.9	6.0	1.0	2.1
Intermediate non-manual	15.1	9.3	16.5	25.9
Junior non-manual	9.4	14.1	49.8	45.4
Foremen and supervisors	4.6	2.8	1.1	1.1
Skilled manual	26.5	33.0	4.0	6.4
Semi-skilled manual	16.1	19.9	11.4	8.8
Unskilled manual	3.7	4.8	10.5	4.3
	100.1	100.0	100.0	99.9
N	937	388	466	297

Source: SCELI Six Areas WAWH Survey.

high-paying professional and intermediate group. For married women the estimate of discrimination would be increased by 16.5 per cent. Thus at the socio-economic group level the suggestion that occupational differentiation is less important to women than differences of pay within occupations seems to be confirmed.

Reverse regression

In order to test whether women earning the same amount as men were better qualified reverse regressions with experience and qualifications on the left-hand side were run for each sex marital status group. Table 5.14 presents the coefficients on hourly earnings in these regressions (8a and 8b).[12] As far as experience is concerned, for a given level of pay, married women are found to be more experienced than married men and single women more than single men as indicated by the higher coefficients. However, part-time women have less experience than full-time women, suggestive of discrimination against full-time women and conflicting with the results from the earnings equations which suggest there was discrimination against part-time women (Table 5.7).

Similar results to these are found in relation to qualifications (measured on a five-point scale, as in Appendix 5.2). However, when a single regression including all subgroups was run with interaction terms for sex, the coefficient on sex was insignificant in both the work experience and qualifications equations and was in fact positively signed in the equation for qualifications. This suggests that there is no identifiable discrimination in relation to personal characteristics of workers paid at the same level. These different results appear to be partly explained by marital status. As Table 5.14 indicates, single men appear to require more experience than married women in order to obtain the same rate of pay. The conflicting results in relation to qualifications are more puzzling and serve to re-emphasize the need for caution in interpreting unexplained differences in pay as discrimination. These results suggest that we cannot assume that a group suffering apparently from earnings discrimination will necessarily have higher qualifications for a given level of pay.

TABLE 5.14 *Reverse regressions on work experience and qualifications, coefficient on basic hourly earnings*

	(8a) Work experience (months)		(8b) Qualifications (five-point scale)	
Full-time married men	0.632	(0.49)	0.032*	(2.35)
Full-time married women	4.787	(1.42)	0.253**	(5.57)
Full-time single men	6.726**	(3.35)	0.048*	(2.19)
Full-time single women	9.075**	(2.83)	0.125**	(2.73)
Full-time women	6.420**	(2.73)	0.180**	(5.58)
Part-time women	−0.607	(−1.42)	0.003	(0.49)

Notes: Significance levels: * = 5%; ** = 1%.
t-statistics in parentheses.
A full complement of independent variables was included in these regressions.

Source: SCELI Six Areas WAWH Survey.

Sample selection bias

As already indicated sample selection bias can be regarded as a problem where there is a systematic bias in patterns of labour-force participation (e.g. married women). However, it should be remembered that our earnings functions relate only to employed persons and exclude, for example, the self-employed and unemployed as well as those out of the labour-force for one reason or another. In fact, the employee participation rate of married women appears to be higher than that for single women in four of the six local labour markets and in the other two (Aberdeen and Kirkcaldy) the rates are very similar for the two groups. Separate probit participation equations, not shown here, were used for each of the six local labour markets and the resulting λ coefficient added to the earnings equations in each market (see Appendix 5.2).[13] λ was significant at the 5 per cent level for single women in Kirkcaldy, for married women in Rochdale, and for single women and all women together in Swindon, suggesting that these groups are not a random subset of all potential labour-force participants. However, there was no evidence of significant sample selection bias in Aberdeen, Coventry, or Northampton. Because of these mixed results estimates of discrimination using selectivity-corrected estimates are not provided here. Indeed, in view of the fact that substantial numbers of men are also excluded from our employee population, it may be necessary to correct the male earnings functions for sample selection bias before providing revised estimates, which requires the systematic modelling of self-employment and unemployment. Certainly the above results suggest that it is dangerous to infer that employed workers are a random subset of the total population.

CONCLUSIONS

Considerable care must be taken before attributing unexplained differences in earnings to discrimination. This is particularly so when, as in this chapter, a major part of the difference in earnings results from differences in the intercept term, which indicates that earnings differences are explained by variables other than those included in the model. Further there are substantial differences in the estimates according to whether the male or the female earnings function is used as the basis of comparison. However, we can say that there is a systematic wage advantage to men. This is partly a function of sex and partly of marital status. Thus married men earn 14 per cent more than single workers, holding other things constant, but women suffer a substantial earnings disadvantage from marriage. Perhaps the most relevant comparison for purposes of estimating sex discrimination is that between single men and single women, and here the ordinary least squares estimate of discrimination is 15 per cent if the male earnings function is used as the basis of comparison. However, the reverse regression results did not point unambiguously to discrimination against single women and there was also evidence of sample selection bias in some localities when appropriate tests were conducted. One reason for the significant differential in favour of men is that the earnings differential is narrower for manual workers, but the majority of women are located in non-manual occupations, though occupational differences do not seem important when narrower occupational categories than these are used. Further, married women in particular are less likely to be found in larger establishments which offer higher rates of pay. It is not clear to what extent this disparity in employment by size of firm represents hiring discrimination and to what extent restricted job search on the part of married women, constrained as they often are by family considerations. The fact that part-time women earn 10 per cent less than full-time women for given characteristics is also consistent with the job search argument. It does seem, however, that women fare better in the public sector (by 11.3 per cent) and that union membership improves the relative position of women (by 9.3 per cent).

It appears that the major part of the earnings difference is to be explained by differences in pay within occupational groups rather than between them, as supported by the occupational attainment model, suggesting that the importance of occupational segregation or the effect of the crowding hypothesis has been exaggerated by proponents of equal value and comparable worth.[14]

Further, there appears to be no support from these results for the hypothesis that tighter labour markets help to reduce the degree of discrimination. The wage differential is significantly narrower in Rochdale (by 15 per cent) despite the fact that both before and during the period of the survey Rochdale suffered from relatively high unemployment. Elsewhere there were no significant differences in the extent to which women's pay was below that of men.

Apart from the ability to measure discrimination within particular labour market localities, the major novelty of the SCELI data set lies in the ability to employ precise estimates of experience and to incorporate both size of establishment and the degree of sex segregation by establishment. Each of these turn out to be highly significant but produce a wage gap not very different from that found in some other recent studies (e.g. Ermish *et al.* 1990). The findings of a significant impact of establishment size and sex segregation are also consistent with earlier studies of wage determination in general. It should be emphasized, however, that discrimination only accounts for between one-quarter and one-third of the wage gap. We can divide the explanatory variables for the remaining differences into four groups—personal characteristics (education, experience, father's socio-economic group), job variables (training, shiftwork, merit payments, and job security), establishment and industry variables (whether union member, white-collar employee, engaged in the public sector and size of establishment), and location. Of these, personal characteristics are much more important than the rest. The reasons then for the lower pay of women relative to men are multifarious; its elimination will be a slow process and one not susceptible to substantial modification by narrowly defined policies such as equal pay and opportunities legislation.

APPENDIX 5.1: VARIABLE DEFINITIONS

LEARN	log of gross hourly earnings (excluding overtime)
SEX	dummy variable (male = 1)
MARRIED	dummy variable (married = 1)
FT/PT	employment status dummy (full-time = 1)

QUALIFICATIONS DUMMIES

OTHQUAL	Other qualifications
APPQUAL	Apprentice/commercial qualifications

OLVQUAL   GCE O-level qualifications
ALVQUAL   GCE A-level qualifications
PROFQUAL   Higher education/professional qualification

EXPER   Actual work experience (months)—all jobs in work history
COLLAR   Manual/non-manual dummy (1 = manual)
FRSEG   Father's socio-economic group in 1980 (16 groups)
JOBSEC   Job security   1 = very secure
                        2 = fairly secure
                        3 = fairly insecure
                        4 = very insecure

ESTABLISHMENT SIZE DUMMIES

MEDEST   Medium establishment dummy, 25–99 employees
LARGEST   Large establishment dummy, 100–499 employees
VLARGEST Very large establishment dummy, 500 or more employees.

PUBLIC   Public or private sector (1 = public)
UNION   Whether currently member of trade union or similar body
           (1 = member)
SHIFT   Whether job involves shiftwork (1 = yes)
MERIT   Whether job involves merit related payment systems (1 =
           yes)
TRAIN   Whether any training for the current job (1 = yes)
MOSTLYWM   Whether job done mainly or almost exclusively by women,
           informant's definition (1 = yes)
EXCLUSWM   Whether job done almost exclusively by women, infor-
           mant's definition (1 = yes)

LABOUR MARKET LOCALITY DUMMIES

COV   Coventry
KIRK   Kirkcaldy
NORTH   Northampton
ROCH   Rochdale
SWIND   Swindon

SOCIO-ECONOMIC GROUP

7   Managers
6   Professionals
5   Intermediate non-manual
4   Junior non-manual
3   Foreman and supervisors

2   Skilled manual
1   Semi-skilled manual
0   Unskilled manual

QUALIFICATIONS (5-POINT SCALE)

1   Other (basic) qualifications
2   Apprentice level qualifications
3   GCE Ordinary level qualifications
4   GCE Advanced level qualifications
5   Degree/professional qualificationsj

JOB SEGREGATION (5-POINT SCALE)

Perceived job segregation in current job
1   Almost exclusively by women
2   Mainly by women
3   By a fairly equal mixture of men and women
4   Mainly by men
5   Almost exclusively by men

APPENDIX 5.2: THE HECKMAN CORRECTION FOR SAMPLE SELECTION BIAS

Different estimates of discrimination will be obtained according to whether the Heckman adjustment is made, occupational attainment is modelled, or reverse regressions are run, as these are essentially measuring different things.

Correction for sample selection bias requires the estimation of the labour-force participation decision of women by probit analysis. Thus

$$L_F = Z'f\ \delta f + V_F \tag{5}$$

where Z is a column vector of a subset of variables included in the female earnings equation in (3). The error terms ε_{2i} and V_F have the properties: $E(\varepsilon_{2i}) = E(V_F) = 0$, $E(\varepsilon_{2i}^2) = \sigma_1^2$, $E(V_F^2) = \sigma_2^2$ and covariance $(\varepsilon_{2i}, V_F) = \sigma_{12} = \rho\sigma_1\sigma_2$.

If $E(\varepsilon_{2i} \mid L_F > 0)$ is not zero, OLS estimates in the female earnings equation will be biased and inconsistent. The Heckman procedure creates the variable λ in equation (5), defined as

$$\lambda = \frac{\phi(Q)}{1 - \Phi(Q)}$$

where $Q = (-Z'_F \delta_F)/\sigma_2$ and ϕ and Φ are respectively the density and the cumulative distribution functions of the normal distribution. If λ is then added to the list of independent variables in the female earnings equation ordinary least squares will provide consistent estimates of the coefficients on these variables.

MODELLING OCCUPATIONAL ATTAINMENT

If occupational segregation derives in part from discriminatory factors it is necessary to model occupational attainment explicitly. The conditional probability that individual i ends up in occupation j can be written as

$$P_{ij} \mid Z_i = F(Z_i) \tag{6}$$

where Z is a vector of personal and labour market characteristics for individual i. This can be estimated by an ordered probit model in which the predicted conditional probability that an individual will be observed in occupation j is given by

$$\hat{P}_{ij} = \Phi(\hat{\mu}_j - a\hat{Z}_i) - \Phi(\hat{\mu}_{j-1} - a\hat{Z}_i) \tag{7}$$

where $\hat{a} =$ estimated coefficients and μ's are estimated separation points.

REVERSE REGRESSION

In the reverse regression approach personal characteristics become in turn the dependent variable and earnings an explanatory variable. Hence

$$X_i = a_i + b_i E_i + c_i Z_i + \varepsilon_3 \tag{8}$$

where $Z_i =$ a vector of other personal characteristics when X_i is the personal characteristic under investigation. A higher coefficient on E_i for females is consistent with discrimination against women in so far as females are required to have greater personal characteristics for a similarly paid job than are males.

NOTES

1. In principle the same could be done for education, which is conventionally measured in terms of years of education. However, in this chapter we have relied on educational *levels* (as dummies) in order to capture the discontinuous element in qualifications.
2. Using New Earnings Survey data the latter found that this result appeared to be insensitive to the degree of disaggregation. This data set enabled one to distinguish each occupation in the list of Key

Occupations for Statistics (KOS) separately for each industrial division providing potentially over 4,000 cells. In 1992 sex segregation could only explain between 20 and 27% of the difference in earnings, depending on the procedure adopted, with the remainder being explained by differences in pay given occupation.

3. The male unemployment rate, respondents and partners, was 8% in Aberdeen, 6% Northampton, 8% Swindon, 16% Kirkcaldy, 13% Coventry, and 14% Rochdale. The corresponding figures for women were 4%, 5%, 3%, 8%, 5%, and 7% respectively.

4. An important question is to what extent does this reflect hiring discrimination by employers and to what extent restricted job search on the part of married women on account of household and family duties?

5. The self-employed, unemployed, and those engaged in household work are excluded from the analysis.

6. There were relatively few problems from missing data which generally arose from a failure to specify hours.

7. An alternative correction should have been to include an hours worked variable on the right-hand side of the earnings function. The two methods produce in fact similar results.

8. This is known as the index number problem.

9. If one runs the regression excluding the job segregation variables, the coefficient on sex rises to 0.333. That is, males receive a third more pay than females, given characteristics.

10. This result is robust. For instance, substituting ten industry division dummies for the SECTOR variable has no effect on this result.

11. This is not explained by differences in industrial structure. When ten industry division dummies were substituted for SECTOR the Rochdale/sex interaction dummy remained significant with little change in the size of the coefficient. The marital status equation suggests that the explanation is not that women do relatively better in Rochdale, but that men (and particularly if married) do significantly worse than in Aberdeen.

12. The MOSTLYWM variable was included in these regressions.

13. The probit participation equations (not reported here) themselves provided some interesting results. Other than in Swindon marriage did not have any significant depressing effect on the participation of women, but in all cases the number of dependent children had a highly significant and negative effect on participation. Age was also generally significant with participation increasing in the middle years (age being included in quadratic form). The expressed need to obtain more money either for necessities including mortgage payments or for extras results in significant higher probabilities of par-

ticipation. Of the other variables having a husband in a job had a significant and positive effect on participation in all labour markets other than in Aberdeen. This could be associated with the selective mating hypothesis. Additionally education was generally significantly and positively related to the probability of participation. Other family income was generally insignificant other than in Rochdale and Swindon, where it was positively and significantly related to probability of participation for all women combined. Only in Rochdale was there an association between race and participation, with coloured workers less likely to be found in paid employment.

14. It is argued under the crowding hypothesis that women, being excluded from the male-dominated jobs, crowd into largely female jobs, and the additional labour supply depresses wage rates there. While the job segregation variable produces results in the regression analysis which are consistent with this hypothesis, the major difference in earnings by gender is the result of other factors.

REFERENCES

BROWN, C., and MEDOFF, J. (1989), 'The Employer Size–Wage Effect', *Journal of Political Economy*, 97/5: 1027–59.

CHIPLIN, B., and SLOANE, P. J. (1976), 'Personal Characteristics and Sex Differentials in Professional Employment', *Economic Journal*, 86: 729–45.

—— —— (1982), *Tackling Discrimination at the Workplace*. Cambridge, Cambridge University Press.

COTTON, J. (1988), 'On the Decomposition of Wage Differentials', *Review of Economics and Statistics*, 70/2, May: 236–43.

DOLTON, P. J., and MAKEPEACE, G. H. (1986), 'Sample Selection and the Male–Female Earnings Differential in the Graduate Labour Market', *Oxford Economic Papers*, 38: 317–41.

—— —— (1987), 'Marital Status, Child Rearing and Earnings Differentials in the Graduate Labour Market', *Economic Journal*, 97, Dec.: 897–922.

ERMISCH, J. F., JOSHI, H., and WRIGHT, R. E. (1990), 'Women's Wages in Great Britain', Birkbeck College Discussion Paper in Economics 8/90.

GREENHALGH, C. (1980), 'Male–Female Differentials in Great Britain: Is Marriage an Equal Opportunity?', *Economic Journal*, 90: 751–75.

GREGORY, M. B., and THOMSON, A. W. J. (1990) (eds.), *A Portrait of Pay 1970–82*. Oxford, Clarendon Press.

HASHIMOTO, M., and KOCHIN, L. (1980), 'A Bias in the Statistical

Estimation of the Effects of Discrimination', *Economic Inquiry*, 18: 478–86.

JOSHI, H., and NEWELL, M. L. (1987), 'Pay Differences between Men and Women: Longitudinal Evidence from the 1946 Birth Cohort', Centre for Economic Policy Research, Discussion Paper Series, No. 156, Mar.

KIDD, M. P., and VINEY, R. (1989), 'Sex Discrimination and Non-random Sampling in the Australian Labour Market', University of Tasmania Department of Economics Discussion Paper 1989–03, June.

LLOYD, C. B., and NIEMI, B. T. (1979), *The Economics of Sex Differentials*. New York, Columbia University Press.

MASTERS, S. H. (1975), *Black–White Income Differences: Empirical Studies and Policy Implications*. New York, Academic Press.

MILLER, P. W. (1987), 'The Wage Effect of the Occupational Segregation of Women in Britain', *Economic Journal*, 97, Dec.: 885–96.

MINCER, J. (1974), *Schooling, Experience and Earnings*. New York, Columbia University Press.

SIEBERT, W. S., and SLOANE, P. J. (1981), 'The Measurement of Sex and Marital Status Discrimination at the Workplace', *Economica*, 48: 125–41.

—— and YOUNG, A. (1983), 'Sex and Family Status Differentials and Professional Earnings', *Political Economy*, 30: 18–41.

SLOANE, P. J. (1990), 'Sex Differentials: Structure, Stability and Change', in M. B. Gregory and A. W. J. Thompson (eds.), *A Portrait of Pay, 1970–82*. Oxford, Oxford University Press.

TURNBULL, P., and WILLIAMS, G. (1974), 'Sex Differentials in Teachers' Pay', *Journal of the Royal Statistical Society*, ser. A, 137/2: 245–58.

WRIGHT, R. E., and ERMISH, J. F. (1991), 'Gender Discrimination in the British Labour Market: A Re-assessment', *Economic Journal*, 101/406, May: 508–22.

ZABALZA, A., and TZANNATOS, Z. (1985), 'The Effects of Britain's Anti-discrimination Legislation on Relative Pay and Employment', *Economic Journal*, 95: 679–99.

6

Part-time Work and Gender Inequality in the Labour Market

JILL RUBERY, SARA HORRELL,
AND BRENDAN BURCHELL

INTRODUCTION

Women's fortunes in the labour market have been increasingly linked to the seemingly inexorable growth of part-time employment. This type of work now accounts for over 42 per cent of women's jobs and over 23 per cent of the total stock of jobs in the economy. Moreover, part-time work is the fastest growing sector of employment: between 1984 and 1987 female part-time jobs increased by 6.8 per cent compared to a growth of 5.7 per cent in female full time. Male full-time jobs actually declined by over 2 per cent while male part-time jobs grew by no less than 14 per cent. However, the latter still stand at a low level, accounting for only 17.5 per cent of the total stock of part-time jobs. The importance and significance of part-time working for women thus cannot be denied; nor indeed the importance of gender in structuring job content and rewards within the part-time sector. However, there has been relatively little research which has attempted to disentangle the relative importance of gender or working-time patterns on the nature of jobs. To some extent the Women and Employment survey (Martin and Roberts 1984, Ballard 1984) did try to plug this gap by comparing the characteristics of women's full-time and part-time jobs. However, this comparison left unanswered the question of how wide are the differences in women's full-time and part-time jobs compared to those between men's jobs and women's jobs; that is, on what scale is the difference between full- and part-time jobs compared to differences by gender independent of working hours, or are gender differences largely related to differences in working time? These issues are important not only for understanding the pattern and trends in gender inequality but also to shed light on the potential impact of current changes in the employment structure, towards both more feminized jobs and more part-time jobs.

Part-time employment has been growing consistently at the aggregate level over the past two decades, but there is as yet no evidence to suggest that it is becoming a standard alternative to full-time employment in all types of occupations. Instead, part-time work appears to be highly segregated, confined mainly to feminized occupations in the service sector (Rubery and Tarling 1988, Mallier and Rosser 1980, Robinson and Wallace 1985, Beechey and Perkins 1987). Part-time work has been declining in the shrinking manufacturing sector while expanding its share of total employment in the growing service sectors. However, even within services its use is still restricted to more feminized occupations. Part-time jobs are often distinct from full-time jobs in the sense of involving different tasks and responsibilities and do not therefore constitute simply a form of job sharing. They therefore constitute a distinct and very specific segment of the labour market.

This segmentation of the job structure into full- and part-time jobs appears at first to be matched by a segmentation of the labour supply. Most part-time jobs are filled by women. Where men are employed they tend to have other main areas of activity or other main sources of income, for example students, moonlighters, or pensioners. The characteristics of the female labour supply for part-time jobs are more related to stages in the life cycle than to specific labour qualities or credentials. Most women will hold both full-time and part-time jobs during their working lives, and often switch more than once between the two states (Main 1988). Thus women are not permanently segmented into full-time or part-time labour supply groups according to static characteristics such as qualifications or class, but instead move between these supply categories according to their life-cycle stage and responsibility for children. However, many women remain confined to the part-time sector long after the children are grown so that over time a more enduring segmentation of the labour supply develops that is not explicable in terms of women's actual current domestic commitments. Instead, women become restricted to this segment because of limited opportunities for older employees to transfer to full-time and/or higher-status jobs. Thus only relatively few women will escape spending at least part of their lives in part-time work. Moreover, for many this entry into part-time work leads to long-term disadvantage in the labour market (Dex and Shaw 1986, Dex and Walters 1989). The significance of part-time work for women's employment opportunities is thus even greater than its current share of the stock of jobs would imply as the majority of women will move into these jobs, not simply as a transitory phase but often permanently or with permanent effects on their employment status and pay.

The implications of periods of part-time work for subsequent careers is beyond the scope of this study, although the existence of such effects increases the significance of looking at part-time jobs. Instead the focus here is on the quality and characteristics of part-time jobs themselves, in comparison with women's full-time jobs and men's full-time jobs. Much of the research on part-time work has focused on the characteristics of the people employed on a part-time basis, and used their own characteristics in terms of qualifications and work experience as a measure of skill (Main 1988). The approach adopted here is to investigate the actual content of part-time work and not to make inferences about the characteristics of jobs from the characteristics of the job encumbents.

METHODOLOGY

This analysis is based on the Social Change and Economic Life Initiative (SCELI) Northampton Work Attitudes and Work Histories survey including both core data and team-specific questions on skill, job content, and labour market perceptions. The sample of 600 employees[1] was divided into full-time and part-time workers according to the respondent's self-definition.[2]

In this analysis only female part-time jobs were included on the grounds that the sample of male part-time jobs was too small to permit separate analysis by gender. It did not seem reasonable to assume that male and female part-time jobs were sufficiently similar that they should be analysed together; when men and women are employed on similar jobs it is often in young people's jobs, but our sample excluded the under-20s. Most of the analysis thus concentrates on three comparison groups, male full-time jobs (MFT), female full-time jobs (FFT), and female part-time jobs (FPT). Where the main differences in jobs are between full-time jobs (MFT and FFT) and part-time jobs (FPT) we can say the working-time effect is predominant, and where the main differences are between male full-time jobs (MFT) and both types of female jobs (FFT and FPT) we can say the gender effect is predominant.

The Work Attitudes and Work Histories survey collected a range of information on job content, job entry requirements, work organization, promotion prospects, pay and benefits provision, and working-time patterns. These data enable us to look at the quality of part-time jobs from three different angles; differences in jobs (content, skill, and promotion opportunities); differences in pay and benefits; and differences in working-time patterns and requirements. We used some of these data to construct an index of skill (see Horrell *et al.* 1989 and 1990 for full details) in order to compare the job content of part-time with the job content of full-time jobs. We only include in the index information related to the skill content of the job and not to the skill characteristics of the employees. It thus provides another measure of the occupational distribution of part-time and full-time jobs. Further details on the construction of the skills index are given in Appendix 6.1.

To explore the differences in working-time arrangements for part-time and full-time employees we supplement the data available from the WAWH survey with information collected in a follow-up survey of the same 300 respondents who were reinterviewed for the second stage of the core survey programme, the Household and Community survey. This follow up survey, called the Cambridge Team Welfare Survey, took place in May 1988, some fourteen months after the HC survey. All the respondents who were willing to be reinterviewed were followed up but the achieved sample was around two-thirds of the original HC sample.

In the final section we again draw on material from the core WAWH survey to look briefly at the characteristics and attitudes of the employees in the part-time jobs.

DIFFERENCES IN PART-TIME AND FULL-TIME JOBS

Occupational distribution

Part-time and full-time jobs differ in their position within the occupational grading structure, here classified by Registrar-General's social class. Table 6.1 shows that 36 per cent of female part-time jobs were found in the partly and unskilled social classes compared to only 13 per cent of female full-time jobs and 19 per cent of male full-time jobs. However, there is clear evidence of both a gender and a working-time effect in determining occupational distribution; 38 per cent of female part-time jobs were in the routine non-manual worker category, a similar percentage as for female full-time jobs. However, a much smaller percentage were in the top classes and much larger ones in the lower classes. The distribution of female full-time jobs is very similar to that of male full-time jobs in both the higher and lower parts of the occupational structure. The main differences occur around the middle of the scale where nearly one-third of female full-time jobs are in routine non-manual occupations and around one-third of male full-time jobs are in skilled manual ones. Therefore, trends towards increasing part-time work thus seem likely to depress the share of women's jobs found in higher categories and to increase it in lower categories, while maintaining the over-representation in middle level clerical and similar work. Increasing part-time work also seems likely to increase the already strong tendency towards occupational segregation; 72 per cent of women in part-time jobs considered that they were working in mainly or exclusively female jobs compared to 58 per cent of women in full-time jobs. Thus on these basic measures the increasing trend towards part-time work is likely to exacerbate both gender inequality and segmentation. These issues are now investigated in more detail using our richer information on job content, skills, and employment prospects.

Job content and skills

Respondents to the Work Attitudes and Work Histories survey were asked a range of questions relating to the content of their current job and their perceptions of requirements to perform the

TABLE 6.1 *Part-time and full-time jobs by Registrar-General's social class*
(percentage of group in each class)

Registrar-General's Social Class	MFT	FFT	FPT
Professional, managerial, and intermediate			
(I and II)	36	39	21
Skilled non-manual (clerical etc.) (IIIn.m.)	11	39	38
Skilled manual (IIIm)	35	8	6
Partly and unskilled manual (IV and V)	19	13	36
Total	101	99	101
N	334	145	121

Note: MFT = male full-time; FFT = female full-time; FPT = female part-time.
Source: SCELI Northampton Work Attitudes and Work Histories Survey.

job in terms of education, training, and experience. Almost all
these data support the view that part-time jobs differ significantly
from full-time jobs and in practice constitute a less skilled stra-
tum of the job market. Part-time workers were much less likely
to consider that their jobs required further education, involved
extensive training, or had required a lengthy learning time in
order to perform it well. Moreover, when asked whether they
saw their job as skilled only 43 per cent answered positively,
compared to 72 per cent of women in full-time jobs and 82 per
cent of men in full-time jobs. These differences can be seen in
Table 6.2. Although in most cases men in full-time jobs score
somewhat higher than women in full-time jobs in terms of their
perceptions of job requirements and skill, these differences
between full-timers are relatively small compared to the much
larger ones between full-timers (male and female taken together)
and female part-timers.

Part-time jobs also score less well than full-time jobs when the
range and complexity of job requirements are taken into account.
Out of a range of six factors[3] which could be important in doing
a job well, only 14 per cent of female part-timers considered at
least five of these factors to be very important or essential, compared to a quarter of all full-timers. Only in the case of two factors—having good relations with people at work and having
good contacts with clients and customers—were the differences in

TABLE 6.2 *Part-time and full-time jobs by job content and skill*

	MFT	FFT	FPT
Percentage of jobs described as:			
Requiring further education			
(or A-levels plus training)	26	26	9
Training lasts over 2 years	33	16	12
Taking over 2 years to learn to			
do job well	31	16	8
Considered to be 'skilled'	82	72	43
5 or 6 factors considered essential			
or very important to do the			
job well[a]	26	24	14
Involving at least 6 out of 8			
responsibilities[a]	43	41	20

Note: N = 600.

[a] See Appendix 6.1 for listings of factors and responsibilities.

Source: SCELI Northampton WAWH Survey.

scores more related to gender than to working-time. Part-timers are also less likely to see their jobs as involving responsibilities; only 20 per cent considered that their job involved at least six of the eight possible categories of responsibilities compared to over 40 per cent of full-timers.[4] Part-timers were particularly unlikely to say their job involved any of the supervisory type responsibilities, such as supervising others, checking work, maintaining output or services and meeting professional or official standards for quality and reliability.

Range of discretion or autonomy in a job is often taken as both a measure of skill (Braverman 1974) and as a measure of job quality, in the sense of providing opportunities for self-fulfilment and satisfaction in work. However, in contrast to the findings on job content, only relatively small and usually statistically non-significant differences were found between full-timers and part-timers in their perceptions of choice and discretion at work.

Respondents were asked how much choice they felt they had over how they did their job. Well over half of both male and female full-timers and 50 per cent of part-timers felt they had a great deal of choice and around a quarter of all three groups felt they had some choice (Table 6.3). Although only a small group, marginally more part-timers felt they had no choice at all compared to full-timers. When asked how closely they were supervised in their job, men were more likely than women in both full- and part-time jobs to say that they were not supervised at all in their jobs, but within the female work-force it was in fact part-timers who were less likely to be supervised (Table 6.3). Only a very small percentage of employees, between 8 and 11 per cent in each category, considered that they were very closely supervised. Divisions between low- and high-discretion jobs may not be as clearly related to divisions between good and bad jobs or to full- and part-time jobs as the literature on segmented labour markets has tended to suggest (Friedman 1977, Berger and Piore 1980). Such conclusions would, however, fit with previous findings by one of the authors that employees in low-status jobs may still be expected to exercise discretion and to work without close supervision (Craig *et al.* 1982, 1985).

TABLE 6.3 *Part-time and full-time jobs by discretion at work*
(a) *Amount of choice over the way the job is done*

	A great deal of choice	Some choice	Hardly any choice	No choice at all	Total	N
MFT	55	27	9	10	101	334
FFT	57	30	4	8	99	145
FPT	50	25	11	15	101	121

(b) *Closeness of supervision*

	Not supervised at all	Not supervised at all closely	Quite closely supervised	Very closely supervised	Total	N
MFT	34	37	21	8	100	334
FFT	23	37	29	11	100	145
FPT	32	38	22	9	101	121

Source: SCELI Northampton WAWH Survey.

Even though some differences in job content and skills appear to be more associated with gender than working time, the cumulative evidence taken from all these different measures suggests that the greatest divide is between full- and part-time jobs. This conclusion is confirmed through the construction of an index of skill which combines the information on job content and skills requirements outlined above.[5] No less than 69 per cent of part-time jobs fall into the lowest skill band compared to 42 per cent of female full-time jobs and 26 per cent of male full-time jobs (see Table 6.4). The shares of female full-time and male full-time jobs in the middle category are relatively similar, but there is again a markedly higher share of male full-time jobs in the highest category (25 per cent compared to 15 per cent of female full-time jobs).

TABLE 6.4 *Part-time and full-time jobs by 'index of skill'*[a]

	Percentage of respondents in:			Total	N
	Low-skill jobs (<5 points)	Medium-skill jobs (5–8 points)	High-skill jobs (9–12 points)		
MFT	26	49	25	100	334
FFT	42	43	15	100	145
FPT	69	21	9	99	121

[a] Index of skill defined in Appendix 6.1.

Source: SCELI Northampton WAWH Survey.

Employment prospects

Job quality includes not only the current conditions of work but also the prospects for the job continuing and, indeed, leading on to better jobs. Part-time jobs are often categorized as insecure and lacking promotion prospects. Data from the work attitudes and work histories survey provide strong support for the second hypothesis but only rather weak support for the first. On the whole, the majority of the work-force thought their jobs were fairly or very secure and there were only small differences between the three groups in terms of perceptions of security.

Only 9 per cent of part-timers considered their job to be very insecure and only 16 per cent to be either very or fairly insecure (see Table 6.5). These percentages were admittedly higher than male and female full-timers but the differences are hardly startling. However, only 29 per cent of part-timers considered their job offered promotion prospects compared to 52 per cent of female full-timers and 63 per cent of male full-timers. Here there is a major and significant difference between full- and part-time jobs, with the difference between male and female full-timers being, if anything, surprisingly small. Part-time jobs may thus be better classified as reasonably secure but with very limited prospects for upward promotion.

TABLE 6.5   *Part-time and full-time jobs by job security and promotion prospects*

	MFT	FFT	FPT
Percentage of jobs which were:			
Very secure	55	63	48
Fairly secure	38	27	37
Fairly insecure	5	7	7
Very insecure	3	4	9
Percentage of jobs offering promotion prospects	63	52	29

Source: SCELI Northampton WAWH Survey.

PAY AND REWARDS

The 'skill index' enables us to compare the pay for full- and part-time jobs after adjusting for differences in job content measured in this way. Table 6.6 shows that even within skill bands part-timers receive lower gross hourly wages than full-timers, especially male full-timers. Even in the lowest skill category part-timers only earn 93 per cent of female full-time and 71 per cent of male full-time gross hourly pay. These are higher ratios than the overall differential between female part-timers and female full-timers (80 per cent) and between female part-timers

TABLE 6.6 *Pay differentials between part-time and full-time jobs, controlling for index of skill*[a] (gross hourly pay, excluding overtime)

	FPT pay as % MFT pay	FPT pay as % FFT pay
Low-skill jobs (<5 points)	71	93
Medium-skill jobs (5–8 points)	69	84
High-skill jobs (9–12 points)	69	77
All jobs	61	80

Note: N = 536.

[a] Index of skill defined in Appendix 6.1.

Source: SCELI Northampton WAWH Survey.

and male full-timers (61 per cent), as a large part of the differences in overall average pay are accounted for by the higher share of part-timers in the lower-paid low-skill occupations.

What is more remarkable is the size of the pay differential which does not appear to be explained by the skill level of the job. Women's average hourly pay is clearly depressed by the presence of part-time jobs, for the figure for average pay for all women was £3.19 per hour compared to £3.53 for female full-timers. However, only about half of this gap appears to be due to the lower skill level jobs occupied by female part-timers; if women had the same job distribution as female full-timers but were paid the combined average wage of female full- and part-timers for that skill level, average hourly pay for women would only rise by 16 pence to £3.35, leaving 18 pence still unaccounted for. Differences in pay between full- and part-time women for jobs of the same skill level appear to account for 17 pence of this 18 pence gap.[6] If part-timers retained their current skill distribution but were paid at women full-timers' rates for the appropriate skill level the average pay for women would rise to £3.37. Clearly if women part-timers had the same skill distribution and the same pay as women full-timers, average pay for all women would be the same as that of full-timers at £3.53. Thus even if it were possible to remove all the disadvantage, in terms of pay and skill distribution, that accrues to women because of their concentration in part-time jobs, and all were treated as if they were female full-timers, the result would only be an increase in their average hourly wage of 34 pence, still leaving a differential of some £1.06 between women's average hourly pay and that of male full-timers (£4.59).

When it comes to explaining the differential between men's and women's hourly pay, the share of the gap accounted for by differences in skill distribution is only around one-quarter, while over two-thirds of the differential is explained by women receiving unequal pay for jobs of similar skill level. Figure 6.1 illustrates how the gap between men's and women's earnings can be accounted for. The first column shows the gap between average female pay, full- and part-time, and average male full-time pay. If women had the same skill distribution as men but were paid at women's wage rates the gap would close by 36 pence, which is 26 per cent of the gap between £3.19 and £4.59. However, if women retained their current skill distribution but were paid at the appropriate male rate of pay for the skill level, the gap would narrow by 99 pence, that is by around 71 per cent. Clearly part-timers' job distributions differ most markedly from male full-timers and we might therefore expect the share of the gap between part-timers' pay and male full-timers' pay accounted for by unequal jobs to be greater. However, the right-hand column shows that if women part-timers had the same skill distribution as men but were paid at part-timers' rates for the still level the gap would only have narrowed by 42 pence, some 24 per cent of the gap. Again, paying women part-timers on men's rates with no change in skill distribution would have a much bigger effect, closing the gap by some 118 pence per hour, 67 per cent of the total gap between the average pay of female part-timers and male full-timers.

What we have uncovered here is a structuring of pay that is primarily related to differences in gender and not differences between full- and part-time jobs. Thus the increasing confinement of women to low-skill jobs because of the growth of part-time jobs cannot be the main explanation of gender differences in pay, as we have found that despite the narrower differences in skill between male and female full-time jobs, women in full-time jobs do not fare that much better in terms of pay than those confined to part-time jobs. Of course other factors, such as industry differentials, may be invoked to explain the pattern of wages here

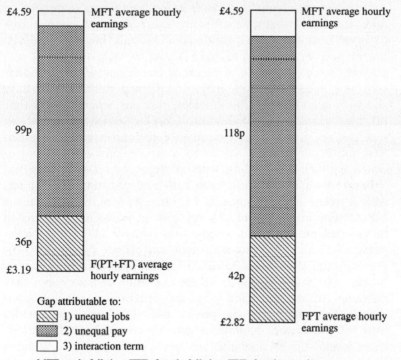

£4.59 — MFT average hourly earnings

£4.59 — MFT average hourly earnings

99p

118p

36p

£3.19 — F(PT+FT) average hourly earnings

42p

Gap attributable to:
1) unequal jobs
2) unequal pay
3) interaction term

£2.82 — FPT average hourly earnings

MFT=male full-time FFT=female full-time FPT=female part-time

Fig 6.1 Unequal pay or unequal jobs? The shares of the earnings gap attributable to differences in jobs or differences in pay for similar jobs

described, but what is interesting about these data is that in so far as we have only looked at differences in job content or skill as an explanation of pay, these have been found wanting. Thus general explanations of women's low pay along the lines of their confinement to low-skilled, part-time jobs are inadequate. Further research is needed to understand the differential impact on pay of job content and skill, industrial and firm characteristics, gender and working time, but what is clear is that differences in skill or in working time do not fully explain the still large disparities in pay between men and women workers.

However, differentials in rewards for part-timers compared to male and female full-timers become more significant once access to benefits at work are considered. The only benefit that part-timers were more likely to have access to than full-timers was unpaid time off for domestic reasons (see Table 6.7). Part-timers were less likely than both male and female full-timers to have access to employer pension schemes, sick pay schemes, paid time off, meal subsidies, accommodation, life insurance, private health schemes, subsidized transport, finance or loans, recreation facilities, and maternity pay. Access to company cars was more associated with male jobs than with all types of full-time jobs and childcare with female jobs, both full- and part-time. Part-timers were also less likely to say that they had personally taken up the benefit. For example, only 16 per cent of part-timers appear to be covered by a pension scheme and to have taken it up compared to 62 and 56 per cent of male and female full-timers. Low take-up rates should not be taken to imply necessarily that part-timers are uninterested in these benefits. Some may have answered in the affirmative to the question whether pension schemes were available for people like them when in practice only full-timers were eligible to take up the scheme. The differences in part-timers' access to benefits is summarized by an index of benefits[7] shown in Table 6.8: 60 per cent of part-timers score 3 or less out of a potential total of 18 compared to 13 and 21 per cent of male and female full-timers.

This analysis of the pay and rewards associated with full- and part-time jobs and with men's and women's jobs clearly hinges on the reliability of the skill index. However, the evidence suggests that women, and especially those in part-time jobs, are more likely to underrate the skill and content of their jobs. For example, women in jobs requiring significant formal qualifications for entry gave lower scores for skill and job content than men in jobs with similar entry requirements. In jobs where entry is restricted to those with A-levels or O-levels plus some vocational training, 97 per cent of men considered themselves to be in a skilled job, but only 84 per cent of women full-timers and 68 per cent of women part-timers considered their jobs to be skilled.[8] Thus it is probable that in some cases, particularly at the bottom end of the distribution, we are comparing more skilled female jobs with less skilled male jobs and thereby

TABLE 6.7 *Access to and take-up of benefits*

	Percentage of jobs where employer provides benefits			Percentage of those eligible who take up benefits			Implied percentage of labour-force who have taken up benefits		
	MFT	FFT	FPT	MFT	FFT	FPT	MFT	FFT	FPT
Pensions[a]	73	68	31	85	82	51	62	56	16
Sick pay[a]	66	58	27	62	59	51	41	34	14
Paid time off for domestic reasons	64	48	30	46	34	28	29	16	8
Unpaid time off for domestic reasons	54	54	57	18	17	29	10	9	17
Company car	30	10	5	84	50	67	25	5	3
Transport subsidies	31	24	17	87	74	86	27	18	15
Goods at a discount	47	40	31	72	65	73	34	26	23
Meal subsidies	39	47	25	71	85	85	28	40	21
Finance or loans	21	20	12	43	41	25	9	9	3
Accommodation	14	17	5	38	30	43	5	5	2
Life assurance	39	19	5	86	79	17	34	15	1
Private health scheme	31	22	9	57	29	42	18	6	4
Recreation facilities	40	36	24	56	63	41	22	23	10
Maternity pay[a]	—	31	16	—	15	10	—	5	2
Childcare facilities	1	13	10	20	15	31	—	2	3

Note: N = 600.

[a] Above the basic government scheme.

Source: SCELI Northampton WAWH Survey.

TABLE 6.8 Part-time and full-time jobs by index of benefits[a]

	Index of benefits score				
	0–3	4–8	9–13	14–18	Total
MFT	13	44	32	10	99
FFT	21	51	25	3	100
FPT	60	31	8	2	101

Note: N = 600
[a] Index of benefits defined in Appendix 6.1.
Source: SCELI Northampton WAWH Survey.

underestimating the gender differential in pay after adjusting for skill content.

WORKING-TIME REQUIREMENTS

The growth of part-time work is often explained by reference to employers' needs for more flexible working-time arrangements and not simply by women's domestic constraints. Working-time requirements for a job extend beyond the simple issue of numbers of hours worked per week. They include the timing of hours of work, the variability of working hours, the degree of choice over work time, and the predictability of working-time requirements. Part-time jobs may differ from full-time in all these dimensions. The differences between part-time and full-time jobs in terms of working-time requirements were only investigated to a limited extent in the Work Attitudes and Work Histories survey, but the Cambridge team conducted a special follow-up survey of a limited but fairly representative sample of the original respondents where these issues were explored in greater depth. This survey (the Cambridge Team Welfare Survey) had around 150 respondents in employment, including sixty-three women workers, twenty-seven of whom were part-timers. The results from this survey should thus be taken as indicative of issues to be taken up in further research rather than as definitive findings on differences in full-time and part-time working-time regimes.

Within the Work Attitudes and Work Histories survey respondents were asked about basic hours and overtime hours, and about whether their job involved shiftwork, frequent nightwork, flexitime, clocking in, being on call, and frequent overtime. On average part-timers worked nineteen hours a week basic hours, and less than half an hour overtime a week (see Table 6.9). However, the main difference in overtime working was by gender and not by working time; male full-timers worked over three and a half hours extra per week in addition to a standard working week of almost forty-one hours, in comparison to female full-timers who worked less than one hour extra on an average standard working week of just under thirty-six hours. There are differences in basic working-time regimes between and within job categories, whether defined by gender or by working time. Table 6.9 shows that some of the main differences are by gender rather than by working time. Men are much more likely to be on call, to have to clock in, and to work frequent overtime, although female full-timers are also much more likely to work frequent overtime than female part-timers. In other areas there are less marked differences by gender; all groups report similar proportions working flexitime, and while 19 per cent of male respondents were on shiftwork, the proportions of female full-timers

TABLE 6.9 *Part-time and full-time jobs by working-time patterns*

	MFT	FFT	FPT
Average hours			
Average basic hours	40.6	35.9	19.5
Average overtime hours	3.8	0.7	0.4
Average total hours	44.4	36.6	19.9
Percentage of jobs involving:			
Shiftwork	19	15	13
Frequent nightwork	12	10	16
Flexitime	20	21	22
Clocking in	38	23	19
Being on call	30	14	14
Frequent overtime	52	28	16

Note: N = 600.
Source: SCELI Northampton WAWH Survey.

and female part-timers, at 15 and 13 per cent respectively, were not that much lower. Part-timers were the group most likely to be engaged in frequent nightwork, but the difference with male and female full-timers was small.

The involvement of part-timers in various forms of unsocial hours and flexible working is confirmed by the findings from the Cambridge Team Welfare Survey. However, no straightforward picture emerges of part-timers facing either the most flexible or the most inflexible working-time regimes; instead it appears that part-timers and full-timers face different types of flexibility requirements. Moreover, there are major differences within the part-time segment, between those jobs which require flexibility and those that offer regular working-time arrangements. These conclusions are necessarily tentative because of the small sample size but are illustrated by the following findings (Table 6.10).

Part-time jobs involved more flexibility and more unsocial hours than female full-time jobs, and also in some cases male full-time jobs, in the following respects.

TABLE 6.10 *Flexible working in part-time and full-time jobs*

	MFT	FFT	FPT
Percentage of jobs involving:			
Frequent variations in days worked	13	13	27
At least one weekend day worked in previous week	42	26	39
More than 5 days worked in previous week	37	10	20
Evening work required	4	7	14
Sometimes work late at short notice	86	78	36
Frequently or occasionally take work home	41	47	16
Have some choice over start and finish times	74	56	32
Have some choice over total number of hours worked	81	59	54
Sometimes work weekends	81	64	53
N	82	36	27

Source: SCELI Cambridge Team Welfare Survey.

Part-timers were:

1. more likely to experience frequent variation in the days they worked each week;
2. almost equally likely as male full-timers, and more likely than female full-timers to have worked at least one weekend day in the week preceding the survey;
3. more likely than female full-timers to have worked more than five days in the previous week;
4. more likely to be involved in evening work than either male or female full-timers.

In other respects part-time jobs appeared to involve less flexibility and unsociability.

Part-timers were:

1. less likely to work late at short notice;
2. less likely to take work home;
3. more likely to have no choice over start and finish times;
4. more likely to have no choice over total hours of work, although here the difference with female full-timers is slight;
5. less likely to have to work weekends than full-timers.

The overall picture is thus one where full- and part-time jobs are associated with different types of flexibility. Full-time jobs, both male and female, are associated with working late and taking work home on the one hand, while part-time jobs involve weekend and evening work and variable days, on the other. In some respects part-time jobs resemble male full-time jobs in their working-time patterns; both are strongly associated with weekend working. In others, there are greater similarities between female full- and part-time jobs, and differences between all female and all male jobs. For example, men are markedly more likely to have worked more than six days in the previous week and to be able to choose their start and finish times and the total number of hours worked. The apparent flexibility for male employees to exercise choice over hours worked is probably associated with greater opportunities for overtime working. However, what is perhaps more notable is the low level of choice available for female part-timers, where almost half have no choice over the total number of hours worked and over two-thirds have no choice over start and finish times. Such flexibility as part-time jobs provide is thus clearly for the benefit of employers and may not fit employee preferences or domestic commitments. However, part-time jobs also seem to differ markedly in the flexibility required; while part-timers were more likely than female full-timers to have worked the previous weekend, almost half of them never worked weekends. These findings suggest a polarization between part-time jobs which require weekend work and those that do not; full-timers are less likely never to work weekends and this requirement to work weekends at least at some points of the year may derive from employers' expectations of greater work commitment by full-timers. Therefore, simplistic notions that part-time jobs are flexible and full-time inflexible cannot be entertained. The data do provide evidence that part-time work is used to meet requirements for variability and for unsocial hours but not all types of variability appear to be accommodated through the use of part-timers, nor do all part-time jobs involve flexible or unsocial hours.

LABOUR SUPPLY

The quality of the labour supply to part-time jobs also has a bearing on the assessment of how far the growth of part-time jobs is responsible for a deterioration in women's employment position, both in terms of job content and rewards. If part-timers were less able workers than full-timers then comparisons with full-timers may not be relevant. The main argument against this view is that most part-timers have previously been full-timers, and many full-timers have also at some stage been part-timers. The main differences between full- and part-timers are in age and domestic responsibilities. Arguments that part-timers constitute a less able work-force therefore must hinge on the ways in which domestic responsibilities and interrupted work histories transform them into less productive workers. It is not possible here to disentangle the question of whether workers with interrupted work histories find themselves in low-skilled jobs because they have lost the capacity to labour or, alternatively, because they have been dislodged from their position within a structured labour market because of recruitment policies. Employers' hiring practices which discriminate on grounds of age and lack of continuous work experience undoubtedly contribute to the tendency for women returners to be confined to jobs which employ them below their full potential (Dex and Shaw 1986, Dex and Walters 1989). These effects have even begun to be recognized recently by employers as they seek to develop 'career-break' schemes to overcome their skill shortages, and have begun to see women labour market returners as an 'underutilized resource'. Studies which attempt to explain gender differentials in terms of differences in work experience often conflate the effects of so-called deterioration of human capital with those of exclusionary hiring policies. However, careful studies of women's work histories under different employment systems indicate the importance of access to good jobs after childbirth in overcoming disadvantage resulting from the career break itself (Dex and Shaw 1986, Dex and Walters 1989).

On average, part-time workers are less well qualified than full-timers; for example, only 13 per cent have post A-level education or training compared to around a quarter of both male and female full-timers. However, *relative to the jobs they do*, female part-timers are overqualified, compared with male and female full-timers. Thus there is a mismatch between job requirements and worker characteristics in terms of formal qualifications. Table 6.11 shows the extent of this mismatch in the survey sample. Respondents were asked to give both their own qualifications and the qualifications that someone would need to get their types of job today using the same listing of types of qualifications. We were thus able to compare directly employee characteristics and job requirements. These show that 40 per cent of part-timers were overqualified for the jobs they were employed in compared to only 28 per cent of female and 27 per cent of male full-timers. These results are all the more significant when it is recognized that more of the part-timers are older workers and could therefore be expected to have lower levels of formal qualifications on average. The tendency towards overqualification for their jobs is again indicated by the second part of Table 6.11 where average educational qualification levels by skill level of job are compared. Female full-timers are the highest educated within each skill band, followed by female part-timers, with male full-timers the least well qualified by skill band. The low quality and rewards associated with part-time jobs do not therefore seem to be adequately explained by the supposed employment of workers with low potential or ability.

TABLE 6.11 *Qualifications of part-time and full-time employees by skill level and qualification requirements of jobs*

	MFT	FFT	FPT
Percentage of respondents who have:			
Higher qualifications than job requires	27	28	40
Same qualifications as job requires	51	56	49
Lower qualifications than job requires	22	16	11
Average qualification levels of employees by skill level of jobs[a]			
Low-skill jobs (<5 points)	1.53	1.94	1.76
Medium-skill jobs (5–8 points)	2.40	2.71	2.64
High-skill jobs (9–12 points)	3.20	3.46	3.30

Note: N = 600.

[a] Based on index of qualification: 4 points were given to those with either further education or A-levels plus training, 3 to those with A-levels or O-levels plus training, 2 to those with O-levels *or* training, and 1 to those with no qualifications. Skill as defined in the index of skill (Appendix 6.1).

Source: SCELI Northampton WAWH Survey.

Any evaluation of whether the growth of low-quality part-time jobs has reduced the overall quality of women's employment position must bear in mind that without this growth many women would be outside the labour market. In some respects the relevant comparison might be between part-time jobs and non-employment. Evidence in favour of this proposition could include the fact that very few women in part-time jobs (23 per cent) would have been willing to consider a full-time job if looking for another job (Table 6.12). Moreover, there is more evidence that full-timers would be willing to make the switch to part-time work than there is of desire for change in the opposite direction; over half of the female full-timers in the sample would be willing to consider a part-time job if looking for another job.

Direct measures of job satisfaction, where the respondent is asked on a scale 0 to 10 to say how satisfied they are with their job, have been found in numerous surveys not only to give rise to high average scores of job satisfaction, but also to give higher scores for women, particularly those in part-time jobs (Agassi 1983). The data from the SCELI survey conformed to this pat-

TABLE 6.12 *Part-timers' and full-timers' desires to change current hours or type of job*

	MFT	FFT	FPT
Percentage of respondents who, if looking for another job, would consider:[a]			
A full-time job	97	80	23
A part-time job	19	55	94
Percentage who would be keen to change jobs if there were plenty available:[a]	40	38	33
Of these, percentage who would like to change:[b]			
Their employer	83	82	66
Their occupation	67	64	91

[a] N = 600.
[b] N = 206.
Source: SCELI Northampton WAWH Survey.

tern, with an average job satisfaction score for female part-timers of 8.6 compared to average scores for female full-timers of 8.3 and for male full-timers of 7.4. These results might suggest that as these jobs appear to generate satisfaction and represent the only viable alternative to non-employment for many women then criticism of the quality of these jobs by reference to full-time jobs is inappropriate.

However, detailed investigation reveals a more complex picture. Evidence is accumulating that the entry of women into part-time jobs in Britain has a permanent downgrading effect on women's employment position, and so part-time work cannot be considered simply as a transitional phase to accommodate problems of childcare which women can choose to enter or to leave as they please (Dex and Shaw 1986, Dex and Walter 1989). Moreover, the generally high satisfaction scores generated by direct questions about satisfaction have led researchers to examine how robust these findings are when issues of satisfaction are addressed in a more complex way. The SCELI survey provided opportunities to explore more indirect measures of attitudinal differences within gender groups according to differences in experience and characteristics. In a separate chapter in this volume

(Chapter 3) we show that the high average levels of satisfaction among part-timers mask considerable differences in attitudes and expectations within the part-time work-force once a more sophisticated analysis is deployed. Other data also suggest a potentially significant level of discontent amongst part-time workers. For example, only 36 per cent of part-timers said that their current job was the one they liked best when asked to choose from all the jobs they had been in during their working life, compared to 50 per cent of both male and female full-timers. Moreover, when asked whether they thought, given their qualifications and experience that they could reasonably expect to be in a better, a similar, or a worse job than their own, 53 per cent of part-timers said they could expect to be in a better job compared to 33 per cent of female full-timers and 37 per cent of male full-timers.

Part-timers are certainly aware of their underemployment. High scores of satisfaction may reflect nothing more than relief that they are not confined to the home and cannot be taken as evidence of unconcern about their downgraded job position. It is notable that although somewhat fewer part-timers expressed a desire to change their jobs if there were plenty available than did full-timers (see Table 6.12), of those who did wish to change jobs more were keen to change occupation than their employer. Those in full-time jobs were primarily anxious to change employers. Dissatisfaction with the nature of the job itself is thus apparent amongst this significant minority of part-time employees.

CONCLUSIONS

Part-time jobs are differentiated from full-time jobs along a range of different dimensions. This differentiation cannot be explained solely in terms of gender as often the differences are more between full- and part-time jobs than between female jobs and male jobs, especially when male and female full-timers are compared. The main areas where there are strong differences by working time are in job content and skills, in promotion prospects, access to benefits, and in types of working-time flexibility required. Thus part-time jobs appear to require less training, experience, and fewer qualifications, to involve relatively few responsibilities (especially those associated with supervisory duties), and to require relatively few attributes or talents for the job to be performed well. Part-timers are very unlikely to consider themselves to be in a job with promotion prospects and they have limited access to a wide range of employment benefits. Part-timers are also used extensively to provide unsocial and flexible working hours, involving weekend working, variable days, and evening and some nightwork. These working-time patterns are distinct from those of full-timers who are more likely to provide flexibility through working late, taking work home, and working occasional weekends. All these characteristics taken together provide strong evidence for the view that part-time jobs constitute a distinct segment of the labour market and that any analysis of the emerging pattern of women's employment needs to separate out full-time and part-time work and to recognize the likelihood of increasing polarization within the female job structure.

Nevertheless, it is important to remember the areas where there was greater similarity between female full- and part-time jobs than between male and female full-time jobs. One area, which is arguably the most important of all, was pay. Differentials between full- and part-time female rates of pay were relatively minor compared to the wide gender differences even after adjusting for level of skill. Women in part-time and full-time jobs also shared some similar skills requirements, particularly the more personal and social skills associated with service type occupations where good relations with clients and customers were important both for doing the job well and in determining how hard women work. Women in full-time jobs are also likely to work shorter basic hours than male full-timers and not to work significant amounts of overtime. These findings might suggest that the distinction between full- and part-time jobs is somewhat arbitrary and that it might be more appropriate to consider women's jobs along a spectrum in terms of basic hours. However, other differences detected in women's working-time regimes suggest that there may be differences between full- and part-time jobs that are not strictly dependent on numbers of hours worked; for example, full-timers may be expected to work late at short notice while part-timers might be used more regularly for unsocial hours working or be expected to change their days of working from week to week.

There are thus both strong differences between female full- and part-time jobs and areas of close similarity; it is not that analyses should now concentrate on distinctions between full- and part-time jobs instead of distinctions by gender but that both categorizations will need to be used and often simultaneously so that it is clear which factors are related to gender and which to working time. Moreover, it must also be recognized that differences between full- and part-time jobs are still differences by gender, since part-time work is mainly women's work. Indeed, further research is required to investigate how the characteristics of part-time jobs are constructed, and the influence of gender on their construction. Are part-time jobs in fact organized as low-skilled jobs because they are designed to employ women or are they primarily concentrated in areas most conducive to the development of deskilled work? If the latter is the case, is the policy issue primarily one of extending part-time work to higher skilled areas or would part-time jobs within those areas also become relatively deskilled? One issue that has not yet been fully explored is the extent to which part-time work becomes a problem or an issue because the hours worked differ from the main core of other employees, so they become marginalized within organizations and organizational cultures. Research needs to locate the analysis of part-time jobs within organizations, and to compare the effect of organizing jobs on a part-time basis in areas where employees are relatively autonomous, or have very differing work-time patterns, compared to organizations where there is both co-ordination of work and the notion of a 'normal working day'.

Part-time jobs also need to be studied for their role in the process of occupational downgrading for women in the later stages of their life cycle. The evidence that part-time jobs are both low quality, as illustrated here, and are associated with long-term career downgrading suggests the need to develop and promote new forms of part-time working which will enhance the quality of part-time jobs and integrate them better into career ladders and promotion chains. Without such a development it is likely that the female labour market will become increasingly polarized between those pursuing a continuous career in full-time jobs, and those who suffer permanent downgrading after leaving the labour market for childbirth and re-entering via part-time employment. Part-time work needs to be transformed into good quality work, with proper access to employment benefits and greater scope for utilizing the skills and capacities of the work-force. Women might then face a genuine choice between full-time and part-time work at particular phases of their life cycle, instead of the current choice which is not simply an issue of working time but one of job quality and life-time employment opportunities.

APPENDIX 6.1

THE INDEX OF SKILL

The index of skill was constructed as a summary measure of a wide range of factors representing both different aspects of skill and any differences in the nature of skills between men's and women's jobs. These included the more conventional measures of skill, such as training, qualifications, and experience; specific job requirements which necessitate skills from the job holders, that is, a range of factors that might be important in doing a job well and a range of responsibilities the job may involve; and the degree of discretion or autonomy.

To examine the requirements of the job respondents were asked how essential the following were for doing the job: having lengthy experience of the type of work, knowing their way around the organization, having good relations with people at work, having good contacts with clients or customers, having a particular talent or knack for the type of work, and having professional, scientific, or business knowledge. Respondents were also asked whether their job involved the following responsibilities: supervising others; safety or health of others; checking work; machines, materials, or goods; confidential information; money; maintaining output or services; and meeting official or professional standards for quality and reliability.

The index was constructed by awarding 2 points for higher education and 1 point for some educational and formal training qualifications; 2 points for at least 2 years' training for the job and 1 point for 6 months to 2 years; 2 points for at least 2 years' experience being necessary to do the job well and 1 point for 6 months to 2 years; 2 points for 5 or 6 factors being essential or very important for doing the job and 1 point for 3 or 4 factors; 2 points for having 6 to 8 of the responsibilities listed and 1 point for 3 to 5 responsibilities; and 1 point each for having a great deal of choice over the way the job is done and being either not supervised or not at all closely supervised. This gives an index with a maximum score of 12. For full details of the construction of the index and responses for the individual components see Horrell *et al.* (1990).

THE INDEX OF BENEFITS

The index of benefits is based on whether the respondent said their employer provided these benefits for people in their type of work, not on whether the person had personally taken up the benefit. Accommodation is an exception; this was only scored if the respondent had personally benefited. The scores awarded for each benefit were as follows:

Employer provides pension, 2; sick pay, 2; paid time off, 2 or unpaid time off, 1; company car, 2 or transport subsidies, 1; goods at a discount, 1; meal subsidies, 1; finance or loans, 1; accommodation (if taken up), 2; life assurance, 2; private health care, 2; recreation facilities, 1. The maximum score for the index is 18. For full details of construction of the index and discussion of how access to benefits exacerbates pay differentials see Horrell *et al.* (1989).

NOTES

1. The self-employed were excluded as a few of the questions used in the construction of the index of skill (see later) were only asked of employees.

2. The 600 employees interviewed were divided roughly equally between men and women. However, these numbers reflect two areas of bias which have been corrected through weighting. First, there is a need to correct for under-representation which occurs through the use of the Kish-grid procedure for selecting respondents. Secondly, women were found to be over-represented in the sample. The weighted sample of employees corrected for these biases gave 346 men and 266 women; 334 men were in full-time employment, 145 women in full-time, and 121 women in part-time work. Sample numbers for the analyses using pay are smaller because of missing values.

3. See Appendix 6.1 for a list of the factors considered.

4. See Appendix 6.1 for the responsibilities covered.

5. See Appendix 6.1 for details on the construction of the index of skill.

6. The remaining 1p is explained by the interaction between differences in skill distribution and differences in pay levels.

7. See Appendix 6.1 for details on the construction of the index of benefits.

8. The respondent's perception of whether or not his or her job was skilled was not included in the skill index as we wished to construct the index on more 'objective' measures of job content. The results suggest that perceptions of skill correlate with the more objective

measures for all groups, but that there are still differences in perceptions between men and women and full-timers and part-timers at
each level of the skill index.

REFERENCES

AGASSI, J. B. (1983), *Comparing the Work Attitudes of Women and Men.*
Lexington, Mass., D. C. Heath.

BALLARD, B. (1984), 'Women Part-Time Workers: Evidence from the
1980 Women and Employment Survey', *Employment Gazette*, 92/6:
409–16.

BEECHEY, V., and PERKINS, T. (1987), *A Matter of Hours: Women, Part-
Time Work and the Labour Market.* Cambridge, Polity.

BERGER, S., and PIORE, M. (1980), *Dualism and Discontinuity in
Industrial Societies.* Cambridge, Cambridge University Press.

BRAVERMAN, H. (1974), *Labour and Monopoly Capital.* New York,
Monthly Review Press.

CRAIG, C., GARNSEY, E., and RUBERY, J. (1985), *Payment Structures and
Smaller Firms: Women's Employment in Segmented Labour Markets.*
Research Paper No. 48. Department of Employment, London,
HMSO.

—— RUBERY, J., TARLING, R., and WILKINSON, F. (1982), *Labour Market
Structure, Industrial Organisation and Low Pay.* Cambridge,
Cambridge University Press.

DEX, S., and SHAW, L. (1986), *British and American Women at Work.*
London, Macmillan.

—— and WALTERS, P. (1989), 'Women's Occupational Status in Britain,
France and USA: Explaining the Difference', *Industrial Relations
Journal*, 20/3, Autumn: 203–12.

FRIEDMAN, A. (1977), *Industry and Labour.* London, Macmillan.

HORRELL, S., RUBERY, J., and BURCHELL, B. (1989), 'Unequal Jobs or
Unequal Pay?', *Industrial Relations Journal*, 20/3, Autumn: 176–91.

—— —— —— (1990), 'Gender and Skills', *Work, Employment and
Society*, 4/2, June: 189–216.

MAIN, B. (1988), 'The Lifetime Attachment of Women to the Labour
Market', in A. Hunt (ed.), *Women and Paid Work.* London,
Macmillan.

MALLIER, A. T., and ROSSER, M. (1980), 'Part-Time Workers and the
Economy', *International Journal of Manpower*, 1/2: 1–7.

MARTIN, J., and ROBERTS, C. (1984), *Women and Employment: A
Lifetime Perspective.* London, HMSO.

ROBINSON, O., and WALLACE, J. (1984), *Part-Time Employment and Sex Discrimination Legislation in Great Britain*. Research Paper No. 43. Department of Employment, London, HMSO.

RUBERY, J., and TARLING, R. (1988), 'Women's Employment in Declining Britain', in J. Rubery (ed.), *Women and Recession*. London, Routledge & Kegan Paul.

7

Gender Segregation in the Retail Industry

ALISON MacEWEN SCOTT

INTRODUCTION

The retail industry is an important case for the study of gender segregation for several reasons. First, until the recent recession, retailing was a modern, dynamic industry, a significant contributor to the ever growing service sector. This was manifested in the development of out-of-town hypermarkets and remodelled shopping precincts in city centres. Such centres have become the symbols of the post-modern age, the focus of a major leisure activity as well as a source of employment. Second, the retail industry is a significant employer of women and has a predominantly female work-force. In 1980, 9 per cent of working women were employed in retailing (Martin and Roberts 1984: 23) and almost two-thirds of the total retail work-force were women, many of them part-timers (NIESR 1986). Retailing also has marked patterns of horizontal and vertical gender segregation. Despite the large numbers of women in sales assistant and cashier jobs, there are very few in management; and at the level of sales assistant men and women tend to sell very different things.

The retail industry has been substantially restructured in recent times, with a high degree of technological and organizational change. It has seen many of the processes traditionally associated with manufacturing: increases in scale, automation, and deskilling have turned the old-fashioned department store into a sales factory. The retail work-force has been described as the 'new

This research is part of a comparative study of gender segregation in retailing and computer services conducted within the Social Change and Economic Initiative. The data on retailing, including the interviews, were collected by Heather Rolfe. I am grateful for her assistance in this project.

proletariat' of modern times. Despite its modern and glamorous image, it has poor employment conditions—low pay, low status, and little protection in terms of social security and fringe benefits.

The questions that arise in this context have to do with the conditions that lead to such large concentrations of women in low grade sales work, e.g. why would women *want* to do it, and why would *women* do it, rather than other groups of cheap labour? Why should there be such marked segregation between men and women within the same type of work? and if women are such a majority at the lower levels, why do so few reach higher levels of management?

One interesting aspect of retailing is that it lacks many of the institutionalized structures that have promoted gender segregation in other industries, e.g. large bureaucracies, highly qualified professions or strong unions. Access to retail employment is relatively open and there is little internal segmentation. Neither formal qualifications requirements nor other restrictive barriers to entry present obstacles to women, or men for that matter. With this relatively low degree of institutional intervention in the labour market, we might expect the retail work-force to be more heterogeneous than it is.

The two most influential theses which have been drawn on to explain gender segregation in retailing are the 'deskilling' and the 'job-gendering' theses. The deskilling thesis is basically a Bravermanian adaptation of Marxist labour process theory (Braverman 1974). It argues that the organization of work under capitalism involves a struggle between management and labour over the distribution of profits, which leads to technological innovation, fragmentation of the labour process and the search for cheap, unskilled labour. This process is often accompanied by a feminization of the work-force, since women provide the best supply of low-cost labour because of their position in the family. The retail industry presents us with aspects of this process since shopworkers have largely lost their trade skills and their jobs have become automated and depersonalized by the adoption of self-service and computerized checkouts (see e.g. Game and Pringle 1984). In the course of this century, the retail industry has changed from a largely male full-time work-force to a female one with large numbers of part-time workers (see e.g. Hoffman 1947, McClelland 1966, Corina 1978, Winstanley 1983).

Several criticisms have been made of the deskilling thesis, particularly that it is based on a crude definition of skill and underestimates the degree of upskilling or enskilling which is brought about by technical change (Wood 1982, Thompson 1989). It also underplays the role of other factors that affect the demand for labour, such as the nature of the product market, the type of technology, and problems of labour supply. It ignores the fact that employers have a range of strategies for maintaining profitability besides cutting labour costs (Rubery 1988). In sum, there is an overemphasis on the deskilling trend and a neglect of other processes that structure employment. The deskilling thesis has been particularly problematic in recent years, with the rise of flexible specialization, subcontracting, and niche marketing. Many employers have looked to increase the quality of labour in order to give them a competitive edge.[1]

The job-gendering thesis has a less developed theoretical structure than the deskilling one; it calls attention to the fact that jobs are not empty positions which may be filled by a man or a woman depending on individual abilities, but have gender assumptions built into them which bias the recruitment process towards men or women (Cockburn 1983, 1987, Knights and Wilmott 1986, Curran 1988, Bradley 1989). Different types of work which are dominated by one sex or the other come to be known as 'men's work' or 'women's work', and this affects the recruitment process in so far as men and women are considered suitable or unsuitable for a job on grounds of gender rather than individual endowments or ability (Scott 1986, Curran 1988). It can also limit the supply of labour to particular jobs by deterring men from applying for 'women's' jobs and vice versa. There is a long history of job-gendering in retailing, as has been described by many authors (Rees 1969, Corina 1978, Craig and Wilkinson 1982, USDAW 1982, Winstanley 1983, Game and Pringle 1984, Webb 1984, Broadbridge 1991).

The job-gendering thesis places less emphasis on the recruitment process than on the way in which gender is built into the structure of work and work organizations (e.g. Cockburn 1983, Knights and Wilmott 1986, Pringle 1989, Hearn *et al.* 1989, Acker 1990). It is argued that work-place relations are not just about relations between capital and labour, but between men and women. This involves elements of power and sexuality which affect men's and women's relations with each other at work and permeates their work identities. Gender identities themselves are constructed within the work-place, as well as outside it. The labels 'men's work', 'women's work', and so on act as symbolic markers of these identities.

An important assumption in this literature is that job-gendering is a social rather than a natural construction, and is potentially variable between different contexts and liable to change. This is exemplified in the case of retailing by the fact that at the beginning of this century only men were considered appropriate for serving the public in shops, but nowadays this is considered a peculiarly 'female' characteristic (Winstanley 1983). However, despite the assertion of variability and contingency, there is a latent essentialism in much of this literature. Job-gendering is often analysed in a very stereotypical way, i.e. prone to generalizing about men and women as unitary categories, with little attention to differences *amongst* women and men. Moreover, it is often offered as a reason for resistance to labour market changes, producing inertia and stasis over time (e.g. Murgatroyd 1982).

Despite the recent growth of interest in the relationship between work, gender, and sexuality, we still lack an adequate explanatory theory for job-gendering. Most of the research has been descriptive in emphasis—unpacking the hidden gender significations in work organizations and practices. This is important in order to attack the assumptions of gender neutrality which still permeate much social science thinking about work and labour markets. However, we still do not know how job gendering interacts with other economic processes, why it should take one form rather than another, why it should be more resistant to change in one case rather than another, or even why it should matter. Why *should* personal identities affect or be affected by the supposed masculinity or femininity of a job?

Studies of retailing have drawn on both the deskilling and job-gendering theses in order to explain gender segregation (see e.g. Game and Pringle 1984). Yet these two theories are potentially contradictory. The major emphasis in the deskilling thesis is on economic factors, i.e. profitability, efficiency, and control over labour, while the job-gendering thesis contends that gender segregation is a product of social factors associated with the way gender is incorporated into the the structure of work and skill itself.[2]

This means that recruitment is structured by social categories and the values associated with them, rather than individual characteristics. Theoretically, the deskilling thesis assumes that relations of production are gender neutral, since capitalist employers will seek to extract the maximum surplus value from all labour, whichever gender. Therefore at the most deskilled level we would expect to find workers with a variety of social characteristics, not just women (e.g. old men, youths, immigrants, handicapped people).

The job-gendering approach, on the other hand, considers that gender attributes are a central aspect of the recruitment process, and that recruitment is based on social pressure which may conflict with market forces. For example, men will not apply for 'female' jobs even if it means risking unemployment and women will not be considered for 'male' jobs, even if they are cheaper than men. Therefore job-gendering can potentially protect women from competition with other groups in the labour market[3] and hence, by implication, from some of the effects of deskilling. Finally, the deskilling thesis is based on the Marxist premiss that work structures are inherently unstable, with a constant pressure from management to change ways of doing things to make them more efficient and workers constantly finding ways to resist this pressure. In contrast, the job-gendering approach sees work structures and recruitment practices to be inherently stable—at least as far as the gender component is concerned.

Nowadays, few sociologists would support an extreme version of either approach, and most would argue for some combination of the two. However, the theoretical basis for this combination is unclear since the most basic assumptions in both positions are in contradiction.

This chapter presents a study of gender segregation in thirteen retail stores in Colchester, carried out in 1986 as part of the SCELI Initiative. It argues that there was evidence of both deskilling and job-gendering in these stores but neither thesis could fully explain the pattern of gender segregation on its own or in combination. Moreover, there was much more variation in employment patterns than is usually allowed for in studies of retailing, perhaps because they have tended to focus on a single firm or work-place. The chapter argues that gender segregation in these stores was a product of *both* economic and social factors. Firms were actively pursuing efficiency and profitability, and deskilling and cutting labour costs played a major role in this. However, they had other reasons for employing women which limited the degree of casualization of employment and the hiring of the very cheapest labour. Some firms had rejected the female/part-time option altogether and had chosen to preserve a stable *male* work-force. However, while firms may have had a more complex set of employment strategies, these strategies were themselves deeply gendered. The analysis of management career structures and promotion systems shows the same combination of economic and social factors in the creation of gender inequalities.

GENERAL CHARACTERISTICS OF THE RETAILING INDUSTRY

Before presenting the detailed research results, it is necessary to review some general features of retail employment in Britain, in order to correct some popular stereotypes about the industry. These have to do with the view that retailing has been a significant source of new service sector jobs, that it has become increasingly feminized and casualized in recent years, and that modernization has improved its status and working conditions and has increased career prospects for women.

The pattern of employment in retailing has to be set within the context of its market conditions and internal restructuring. In terms of growth in investment, volume of trade and levels of profitability, retailing is among the largest and most successful industries in Britain. It is also one of the most fiercely competitive—a factor that has encouraged mergers and take-overs, technical change, and a restructuring of the labour process. The national trend in retailing has been one of increasing concentration of ownership and increasing size and capitalization of stores (Brown 1982, Craig and Wilkinson 1982, Crine 1982, Loveridge *et al.* 1985). The number of large stores, supermarkets, and hypermarkets has increased dramatically while small stores have declined (Craig and Wilkinson 1982). In 1980, large multiple retailers were less than 1 per cent of retail businesses, but had 21 per cent of retail outlets, employed 48 per cent of the industry work-force, and accounted for 55 per cent of turnover (Craig and Wilkinson 1982: 9). The large multiples are associated with the most modern changes in the labour process, such as depersonalization of the sales function, computerization of money transactions and stock control, and part-time work. However, these trends are present to some extent even in small stores.

There has been considerable debate as to whether these changes have generated an increase in employment. Work at the Stirling Institute for Retail Studies argues that superstores are net job creators (Dawson *et al.* 1986); however, most analysts have concluded that there has been relatively little net increase in employment in retailing. Most of the rise in the absolute number of jobs was accounted for by part-time work and was generated at the cost of full-time jobs (Craig and Wilkinson 1982: 10; NIESR 1986: 48–9). Moreover, the increasing level of automation in the superstores and the fine adjustment of part-time workers to the volume of trade means that there has been a net reduction in total hours worked during the 1980s (Craig and Wilkinson 1982: 11). This contradicts the popular perception that the opening of new hyperstores with relatively large work-forces generates new jobs.

Another common view is that retailing has become increasingly feminized and casualized. In fact, the feminization process took place in a much earlier period (the 1950s) and the female-to-male proportion remained relatively stable during the 1970s and 1980s (Craig and Wilkinson: 10; NIESR 1986: 49). There has been a rise in part-time jobs, particularly during the mid-1980s. However, this trend should not be exaggerated; they were still the minority of jobs in the industry in 1985 (about 40 per cent). Moreover, the substitution of part-time for full-time jobs has largely taken place within the female work-force so most male jobs are still full time.

Retailing has contradictory images in terms of status. Historically, shop work was a genteel occupation, to be distinguished from manual work. It was considered appropriate for middle-class wives and upwardly mobile working-class girls. Today, the image of gentility has been replaced by glamour and it is still seen as superior to factory work by the women who work there. However, the pay and conditions are much worse. At the time of our research the pay of shopworkers was covered by the minimum rates set by the Retail Trades Wages Council and the Retail Food Council. In the early 1980s the Low Pay Unit found that most women in retailing earned little above the minimum rate and many were below it. Retail wages were low compared with the average for all industries, and sales staff and shelf-fillers were the lowest paid. In 1981 the average pay of women employed in shop work was £20 per week less than women elsewhere. Moreover, women shopworkers earned on average two-thirds of the pay of male shopworkers (Crine 1982; see also Craig and Wilkinson 1982). Part-time workers are not entitled to fringe benefits and bonuses and, since they do not pay national insurance contributions if they are below the gross earnings threshold, they have less access to social security. If they work less than sixteen hours they also have less employment protection. The unions are not in a good position to improve this situation since levels of unionization in the industry are generally low.[4]

Managerial careers in retailing never acquired the status of their counterparts in other industries. In recent years, the large retail companies have tried to correct this by professionalizing management and modernizing its image. Much of the publicity material conveys a message of increased career opportunities for graduates, especially women. However, the evidence shows only limited increases in the numbers of women in high-level management (Ognjenovic 1979). According to one study less than 40 per cent of the women were in management, and most of these were in staff manager or supervisory positions (USDAW 1986). The percentage of women in store management was less than 4 per cent.

In summary then, there has been more continuity than change in retail employment. The picture of increasing numbers of jobs, and high rates of feminization and casualization has been exaggerated, and the image of modernization, glamour, and expanding opportunities for career women belies continuing patterns of low pay and segregation.

METHODOLOGY

The research on which this chapter is based has an industry and locality focus. We were particularly keen to interview a range of retail firms in order to investigate differences in the structure of employment and patterns of segregation between them. Most of the interviews were carried out in Colchester,[5] partly for convenience and in order to control for any specific local variations in labour market structure, such as the level of unemployment and turnover. We decided to focus on the large stores because they had often been excluded from other studies, and because they were the most significant employers of labour. Time and resource constraints meant that we had to exclude the very small shops. The stores that participated in the study were: Sainsbury's, Presto, Debenhams, the Co-op, Keddies, Williams and Griffin, Marks and Spencer, British Home Stores, Boots, W. H. Smith, MFI, Currys, and Hatfields. At their request, I have protected the anonymity of Debenhams, Marks and Spencer, and BHS by using pseudonyms when citing interview material.

RETAILING IN COLCHESTER

Colchester is a small, relatively prosperous town in the south-east of England, about an hour from London. In 1981 it had a population of around 132,000 and a labour-force of some 61,000. Women were 38 per cent of this labour-force, two-thirds of them being married. Part-time work was an important feature of the Colchester labour market, accounting for 44 per cent of female employment and 58 per cent of married working women (1981 Census, unpublished). Thus the pattern of female employment in this town was very similar to the national pattern reported by Martin and Roberts at around the same time (Martin and Roberts 1984: 17).

Colchester is a garrison town, with approximately 5,000 troops stationed there; there are some important light engineering firms and several large commercial and service institutions such as the University, the Colchester Institute, and the Royal London Mutual Insurance Society. It has also become a base for small companies serving a London market and has increasingly become a dormitory town for commuters.

Like many towns in the south-east, Colchester was cushioned from the recession of the early 1980s by strong regional growth, particularly during the 1984–7 period, when our research was carried out. Between 1981 and 1988 the population grew by 8.6 per cent, well above the average for Essex, much of this being due to immigration from the East End of London. It had the

fastest rate of new housebuilding and one of the lowest unemployment rates in Essex (Central Statistical Office 1990).

In Colchester as elsewhere, there was major growth in retail
commerce during the 1980s, with the development of both out-
of-town hypermarkets and down-town shopping precincts. There
was a variety of different types of retail store, with large
branches of most national chain stores, a range of large and
small independent stores, and a sprinkling of boutiques and specialist shops. Most of these stores exhibited the characteristic pattern of retail employment outlined above, namely, a simple
division of labour, low pay, low unionization, open access, and
high levels of female employment and part-time work.

In most stores, women were the predominant work-force, ranging from 66 to 90 per cent of all employees, although in the specialist furniture and electrical stores, such as MFI, Currys, and
Hatfields, men were the majority. The use of part-timers was
variable—in some stores they were around a third of the work-
force, in others nearly three-quarters. The division of labour
comprised a narrow range of jobs, the vast majority of the work-
force (and most women) being concentrated in sales and shelf-
filling jobs. A few jobs were also in warehousing, transport,
cleaning, and canteen work. There was a small tier of supervisory
employees and only a few managers per store, most of them men.
Levels of pay were generally low, with very little variation
between stores. In most cases, the lowest levels of pay were set at
or around Wage Council rates (about £80.00 per week). The
grading structure was extremely narrow with differentials of only
£5–6 per week. In some cases, pay was increased by sales commissions, overtime rates, or bonuses, but this was not common.

Despite these general similarities, we found that there were
important variations between stores in terms of the organization
of the labour process, the structure of management, the style of
management–labour relations and the use of female and part-
time labour. These variations were linked to the type of retail
outlet, the size of the store, and whether or not it was independent or part of a national chain.[6] They also affected employers'
strategies in response to competition, particularly regarding the
use of labour.

The stores varied enormously in size, the largest ones having
nearly 300 employees (e.g. Sainsbury's, Debenhams, Williams and

Griffin) and the smallest, less than thirty (Currys, MFI). They also varied according to the type and range of products sold. The major differences were between food supermarkets (Sainsbury's, Presto), variety stores (Marks and Spencers, BHS, Boots, W. H. Smith), department stores (Williams and Griffin, Keddies, Co-op, Debenhams) and specialist furniture and electrical stores (MFI, Currys, Hatfields). These different types of store faced slightly different market conditions in terms of the volume and regularity of trade. For example, out-of-town food supermarkets had pronounced short-term fluctuations in trade, with shopping particularly concentrated at the end of the week and month. Stores in the town centre had particular peaks on Saturdays and on the evenings of late-night shopping. The market for food and variety goods was one of high volume and small profit margins, while that of furniture and electrical goods had lower volume and larger margins. These differences in trading patterns affected strategies of employment and pay. The food supermarkets and the variety stores had the greatest reliance on self-service and centralized checkout systems, whereas the department and specialist stores made some attempt to preserve a service element in the sales work, often incorporating a commission into the pay structure.

Another major distinction was whether or not the store was part of a national chain or independent. The former had a more centralized management structure and greater separation between management and sales functions, whereas decision-making in the independent stores was more determined by the management of that particular store. They were less technologically sophisticated, had more internal promotion and tended to be rather paternalistic towards their employees (and more influenced by gender stereotypes). These variations between stores had implications for the pattern of female and part-time employment and the scope for women's entry into supervisory and management levels.

Response to competition and strategies of labour use

The pressure of competition and the small profit margins in the industry were stressed in most interviews. Responses to this included longer shopping hours, refurbishment, closer monitoring of sales peaks and troughs, more efficient stock control, better quality of service, and more aggressive sales activity. Since labour costs were the most significant variable cost in retailing, most employers were looking for ways of reducing their work-force or enhancing its productivity.

Most stores had an element of self-service and had introduced computerized technologies for monitoring sales transactions. However, the extent of deskilling and depersonalization of sales work was variable. Boots, for example, was running a closely supervised staff of checkout cashiers who knew little about the products sold, whereas their main rival, W. H. Smith, invested considerable resources in staff training, encouraging their employees to familiarize themselves with a particular department and its goods, thus providing a better quality of service. MFI's strategy was to 'get the money through the tills', paying a good commission over and above the basic wage and promoting an aggressive mode of selling, whereas Hatfields, the local 'up-market' furniture store, was more concerned to encourage loyalty amongst customers and rejected commissions because it encouraged employees to achieve sales rather than service. In some stores there was a policy of substituting part-time for full-time labour but in others, particularly the specialist stores, there was more interest in maintaining a full-time and dedicated sales force.

Within an overall objective of employing low cost, flexible labour, retailers thus had a variety of different employment strategies; women were usually the target work-force, but there were different reasons for this. In what follows, I will argue that the demand for female labour in retailing was influenced not just by low wages and availability for part-time work, but by notions of *quality* labour. However, these notions were deeply permeated by gender stereotypes.

Recruitment: qualifications, skills, and training

Although the recruitment process did not rely on formal credentials and sales work had become automated and depersonalized, shop managers did not consider sales work to be unskilled. They stressed the importance of *quality* of labour, distinguishing between skilled and unskilled sales workers and contrasting married women with YTS school-leavers as an example of this distinction. The emphasis on sales skills was reflected in their

recruitment practices, their investment in training, their cultiva-
tion of a stable work-force, even amongst part-time workers, and
their practice of promoting internally from the lowest grades of
sales work.

Employers recruited externally only at the lowest levels, i.e.
sales assistants or shelf-fillers. They did not generally advertise
vacancies, but relied upon word of mouth to obtain new staff or
recruited from the regular pool of unsolicited applications. If
pressed, they would advertise jobs in the local paper; many preferred not to take people from the Jobcentre because 'they were
the dregs'.

Few formal credentials were required for entry at this level.
Only W. H. Smith and Boots mentioned that they required
CSEs, but this was not for cashier jobs and the requirement
could be waived if someone had the right personality. The manager at Boots mentioned that they sometimes selected people
with good school qualifications for grooming into management.
Qualifications were also used as a sifting device if they got a lot
of applicants (W. H. Smith), or were used as a talking point in
interviews (Co-op). In the actual selection process, however, personality and experience were the main factors. These qualities
were not defined precisely, but they appeared to involve social[7]
rather than technical skills.

What is important is initiative, confidence, common-sense, and an ability
to talk to customers. ('Greens')

The qualities we look for are an ability to give service, politeness, and
common sense. (Keddies)

We look for people with maturity, a good standard of education, and
common sense. (Currys)

Being a good communicator is the most important, we look for
resourcefulness and a positive approach. (W. H. Smith)

Cheerfulness is more important than qualifications on the tills. (Boots)

Experience is crucial, it counts more than anything else, especially at
higher levels. (Williams and Griffin)

In the absence of objective measures of these skills, hiring decisions clearly rested on employers' subjective perceptions of applicants' suitability, leaving plenty of scope for sex and age
stereotyping (cf. Curran 1988).

When we are recruiting for a job we have a picture of the person we are looking for in mind—young or mature, male or female—you know the sort of person you would like in that job. (Co-op)

Although women were not said to possess such qualities exclusively, managers did seem to be predisposed to consider women for most sales jobs. Moreover, they often targeted particular types of women, especially middle-aged and married women.

Women are better on the tills within a certain age range, for example between 30 and 40 years. Young men are OK for till work but not middle-aged men. We would have strong reservations about employing a 30 to 40-year-old man on cashier duties. (Sainsbury's)

Some managers suggested that such women had the desired qualities because they were themselves shoppers. Others attributed it to 'maturity' or 'background'. The selection process often involved probing into applicants' family backgrounds and it is difficult not to imagine that this information would have affected employers' perceptions as to their suitability.

We always ask about the person's family background in the interviews, for example, what the husband does, what the father does, how many children they have etc., but it's just a way of getting people to talk really. (Co-op)

I try not to employ anyone with school-age children, by which I mean under 14; by then you're out of the measles, mumps, and little Johnny fell off the chair at school . . . (Hatfields)

As we shall see below, managers usually recruited for a specific job within the store, so these perceptions of suitability were strongly influenced by the existing pattern of gender segregation there; for instance, you would put a young girl in fashions, an older woman in the china department, and a man in carpets.

We try to get a lady to suit the department. (Keddies)

These social skills were complemented with in-store training, which was provided by most stores. The type of training varied according to the degree of emphasis on the service element in sales work. Generally speaking, there was less for checkout staff than for other types of salespersons, and there was most where the merchandise involved was valuable (e.g. furniture). Training included basic technical knowledge on how to work the tills,

information about the merchandise, and specific courses on sales-
manship and personal development (leadership and motivational
skills). Presto's staff had a week's induction course on starting
employment there, others had regular training sessions each week
(these seemed to be mainly occasions for dispensing information
about recent company performance, new lines, sales targets, etc.).
Boots had specialized 'trainers' who travelled round the branches,
giving training sessions. MFI and Currys ran special training
establishments in London to which they sent their staff. At
Hatfields, there was an emphasis on product knowledge and staff
would be sent off to visit manufacturers' premises. In other cases,
such as the supermarkets, training simply meant rotating staff
around the store. Training for supervisors was more formal and
often involved doing special short courses at the local Institute or
ones run by the firm. For many firms, training involved developing a distinctive 'brand' style of saleswork, which reflected the
firm's policies and management style. Many managers prided
themselves on training their staff differently from their competitors: 'We like to train the staff to do things our way' (Co-op).

Thus, despite the low level of formal qualifications on entry,
retailers perceived their work-force as having both general social
skills and firm-specific skills. They were predisposed to recruit
women, not just because they were cheap and available but
because of gendered assumptions about their possession of the
right social skills, and these women were then well placed to
receive firm-specific training. The value placed on these skills was
reflected in their reluctance to casualize the workforce fully by
hiring cheaper school-leavers[8] and their preference for recruiting
supervisors internally.

Part-time work

Part-time work presented the same combination of economic and
social factors as those outlined above. It was a source of both
cheap and flexible labour and of quality sales staff. Gender was
an important aspect of the demand for this type of labour, not
only because most applicants were women, but because of stereotyped assumptions about the skills these women had.

Almost all stores used part-time workers, but in varying
amounts. Sainsbury's and Marks and Spencer had the highest

proportions, where they were around three-quarters of the work-force, followed by the Co-op and BHS where they were two-thirds. At Debenhams and Boots they were about half. In the rest of the stores, part-timers were around a third or less of the work-force. Part-time work seems to have been used most in shops which had a pronounced use of checkout cashiers, such as food supermarkets or shops with a food department within the store. The ones with the lowest use of part-time work were the specialist furniture and electrical shops, and these were also the ones with the highest percentage of men.

Stores used part-time workers for a variety of reasons. Many used them as a cost-cutting device, in order to avoid paying national insurance contributions.[9] For most employers, it was the flexibility that was crucial: being able to fine tune their labour hours to variations in the volume of sales.[10] Thus the shifts would be arranged to coincide with peak shopping hours, such as late-night shopping times, lunchtimes, or Saturdays. However, part-time women were also targeted, not just because they were available for shorter hours, but because they were considered good quality labour. They were more responsible, had a better manner with the clientele, were more committed, knew more about the products, and so on.

When I first came here there were a number of men employed part-time. Now what sort of men want to work part time? They were all between 65 and 70. I was horrified. Anyway, I've gradually replaced them with ladies . . . My philosophy of life as far as this is concerned is that the ideal sales consultant is intelligent, articulate, attractive, extrovert, pleasant, and outgoing and is highly committed to the company image and its projection for three days a week. The reason I have ladies is that men with all those qualities don't want to work three days a week and if you have one with those qualities, he wants my job [laughs]. Women who have got homes give four days of intense commitment to their homes but they want something more than domestic bliss for three days. During those three days they give all their commitment to us and they stay on for ten to fifteen years. (Hatfields manager)

Part-time work is popularly seen as casual work, but as the above quote indicates, employers did not consider part-time workers to be casual staff. They usually had a core of stable part-time workers and could call on them to work extra hours when it was necessary, rather than take on casual staff. The most casual workers were Saturday staff or extras taken on during the summer holidays or during sales—but even here the shops tended to have a stable reserve of such workers who were called on year after year. Saturday staff were different from the 'normal' part-timers in that they were usually 16–18-year-olds as opposed to married women. Most stores disliked employing them since they were considered inefficient, inexperienced, and unreliable.

Almost all part-time workers were women and most were married and over 30 years of age. Was this a reflection of their preferences or a lack of alternatives? Almost all the managers reported high levels of job stability amongst part-time workers and a constant level of applications for these jobs. There was plenty of evidence to corroborate the well-known association between part-time work and the domestic cycle. Some women with young children said they were only available for a few hours in the day. Others stated that they could not afford to go full-time because of the extra cost of childminding and national insurance contributions. The full-time salary would have to be significantly higher to make it worth their while. Employers mentioned that part-time workers would often transfer to full-time jobs when their children grew up. Some women stated that they would find a full-time job too tiring or boring. On the other hand, we found cases of women who had wanted to transfer to full-time work who had been prevented from doing so.

Although the shorter working day may have suited women with young families, employers did not arrange the shifts to suit them. One manager said that this used to be the case, but not any longer ('Browns'). They were given little choice about what hours they would work, and often it was made clear in the interview that there would be compulsory overtime. Staff would comply with these requirements out of fear of losing the job. They were told 'if you don't want to work these hours, we can get someone who does' ('Whites'). At Hatfields one member of staff complained about the management taking advantage of women's good nature in constantly asking them to do overtime.

There was a clear segmentation between full- and part-time jobs in terms of pay, fringe benefits, and working conditions. Part-time workers were usually employed in the most routine jobs, especially checkout duties, and they were given less training than full-time staff. In one store, part-time workers were entitled to less breaks than full-timers. They were not eligible for promotion to supervisory status and were excluded from the training that channelled people to such positions. Yet part-time work was a stepping stone into full-time employment; such workers were given the first option on temporary full-time work during the summer holidays and the sales period, and ultimately on permanent full-time work. Thus although many part-timers might have preferred full-time work, they would accept a part-time job because it was a way of getting their foot in the door.

Many managers reported an increasing tendency to substitute part-time for full-time workers and this substitution was largely taking place *within* the female work-force. However, most employers thought it was necessary to retain a balance between full and part-time work for reasons of continuity and control, and in order to maintain the system of internal recruitment and promotion. It is also interesting to note that some stores favoured a much larger full-time work-force than others. In the main, these were stores that sold high-value products and had a smaller overall work-force and one that was mainly male (MFI, Currys). Within department stores, the staff in the sections that sold similar products also had these characteristics.

Job-gendering of sales work

The tendency found in other studies to allocate men and women to different sections within the store according to the type of activity and merchandise sold was confirmed in this research. The common pattern was that women sold women's clothing, home furnishings, kitchen goods, and cosmetics while men sold furniture, carpets, audio and TV equipment, and electrical goods. In the supermarkets, women were mainly on the tills and men were mainly shelf-fillers. Women were also employed in staff canteens and in clerical work and men in warehousing and transport. This allocation was justified by employers on both economic and social grounds, i.e. it was 'appropriate' and economically efficient.

Most managers and many employees we interviewed held definite views on the appropriate pattern of gender segregation within their store. However, there were some discrepancies between stores on specific details of this pattern, which shows that it was a social rather than natural construction. For example, we found cases where women were involved in loading and unloading, in selling furniture and electrical goods and in shelf-filling in supermarkets.

A major factor promoting job-gendering in sales work seems to be the intimate connection between the salesperson, the customer, and the product sold. One manager of a department store stated that the sex of the sales assistant should depend on three factors—the type of goods sold, the sex of the customer, and the sex of the existing staff in that area of the store. The sex of the customer was felt to be of particular importance and should ideally be matched by the sex of the sales assistant, i.e. female customers should be served by women and male customers by men. Female and male customers tended to shop for different things, the women bought food, clothing, and small items for the children and the home, whereas men shopped for leisure goods, TV and audio equipment, cars, and garden equipment. It was thought that men and women would expect to be served by the people who were most knowledgeable about these products, i.e. persons of the same sex: 'The woman in the family is more likely to be the customer so it follows that the woman should serve them' (Co-op).

It is worth pausing for a moment to think why this should be so. Apparently, in the mind of the public and of retail staff, male and female gender roles are associated with specific products, and this association implies a 'natural' interest in and knowledge about such products. Thus, women are assumed to have an interest in and knowledge of fashions and home furnishings and men to have a similar interest in/knowledge of DIY goods and machinery (e.g. computers, hi-fi equipment, etc.). This 'natural' association between gender roles and specific goods is superimposed on to the sales relationship, so that women sales assistants are thought to serve women customers better than men and find selling 'female' goods more interesting. Thus norms of 'suitability' are economically efficient.

We like to rotate the staff around the department according to their interests and needs but the girls are more interested in working on fashions and cosmetics and the boys are more interested in electrical goods. (Williams and Griffin)

For sound and vision we like to have staff who are technically minded. There is new equipment coming out all the time and we need someone who is alert and aware and who can grasp new developments. They are usually the men. (Boots)

Women are just as able to deal with high-tech products as men, but the women tend to go for white goods and the men for video and TV . . . and with repairs and enquiries men take the brunt. (Currys)

The job-gendering process is partly produced by the interests of sales staff themselves, and partly by what employers perceive to be the expectations of members of the public. Sometimes these normative expectations conflict with actual individual expertise and interest. For example, a Co-op employee related the experience of selling a lawnmower to a female customer. The employee knew a lot about these machines and regularly took them apart to do small repairs. She explained all the features of the machine to the customer but the latter was not satisfied until she had been able to talk to a man about it.

Normative controls over who sold what were considered particularly important where the goods were 'personal', such as underwear, or where public decency was involved. For example, it would not be proper to have men near women's changing rooms and it would not be desirable to have women selling men's suits, since they might be called upon to measure an inside leg. Apparently male underwear is less contentious than female underwear; since it is largely bought by men's wives or mothers, it is all right for women to sell it; but women's underwear is surrounded by much stronger sexual taboos and it is definitely not all right for men to sell it to women! 'A few years ago a woman got very upset at being served by a man when she was buying a bra' ('Whites').

The correct association of men and women with the appropriate merchandise is important not just for the customer but for the sales employee. To be identified with the 'wrong' products is to call into question the sexual identity of the person involved. For some reason, this seems to be more important for men than for women. In general, sales work appears to threaten men's masculinity and status: 'years ago there was the idea that if a man went into sales work he was a bit poofy' ('Whites'). To be associated with 'female' goods, however, greatly exacerbates this threat:

We're very limited as to where we can put the men. I suppose you *could* put them on cosmetics, if they want to stand there selling smellies [laughs], but most won't be happy selling those kinds of things. (Boots staff manager)

A man would have to be a bit odd to work on, say wool or selling handbags, he would have to be a bit like that [limp wrist movement]. (Co-op employee)

A man selling women's fashions is low status. ('Greens')

You have to put the men where they would be happy and where the customer would be happy being served by them. A man wouldn't stay very long if he was put in an area like toiletries. (Boots)

The employment of men was considered appropriate in departments that had to do with furniture, carpets, domestic machinery, and electrical goods. Interestingly, this was justified in terms of the heavy lifting involved rather than men's special interest or knowledge. As some employees pointed out, the machines were actually used by women in the home, rather than by men (e.g. washing machines), and women often had to move heavy furniture in order to clean their homes. One cynical employee mentioned that the men in the furniture department never actually did any of the heavy shifting around, they always got the warehouseman to do it. Some stores did employ a few women in these departments, but they were the minority, and even there the department was still considered a male preserve. One notable exception to this is a furniture store in Colchester (not included in the study), where the entire sales staff are women (Multiyork).

The fact that goods with similar gender attributes were clustered together in the same location within the store and had a predominantly male or female sales staff meant that areas of the store were effectively gendered territories, and were referred to as a 'men's world' or a 'women's world'.

Men are put in menswear, furniture, carpets etc. . . . there are one or two ladies there, but it's a man's world . . . obviously it's better to employ a man there. (Keddies)

Behind the scenes, the main gendered territories were the canteen and the warehouse. Work in the canteen was considered 'women's work'. In 'Whites' it was reported that a YTS boy had been employed in the canteen as part of his training and he was keen to continue working there. A vacancy came up but he did not get the job; he was later employed as a cleaner. As far as the warehouse was concerned, most employers said that the reason for women not being able to work there was because of their lack of physical strength. (However, we were interested to discover that in one of the supermarkets (Presto) the women helped with loading and unloading the lorries, alongside the men.)

I couldn't envisage taking on a female warehouseman. No way could a woman cope with the physical aspects of a warehouse job full time. (Sainsbury's)

The warehouse was also described as a male territory that was potentially threatening to women. However, some women employees at 'Whites' mentioned that they would like to do warehouse work for a while, to have a change from sales work— but they did not think management would consider it.

The warehouse is a very male dominated environment, with a lot of shifting of furniture on to lorries. Some YTS girls were put in the warehouse and enjoyed being chatted up by the warehousemen, but that was only temporary. We wanted to put a clerk [female] in the warehouse some years ago, but no one wanted to go. Its not an attractive environment for a woman. (Hatfields).

It might be thought that stores with more depersonalized sales work would be less prone to this normative gendering of work. However, this was not the case. Checkout work was seen as 'feminized' and just as threatening to men's masculinity as selling women's underwear.

It's not the done thing to have men on the tills . . . they only do these things as part of a training for promotion. ('Whites')

Young men are generally OK with the customers but some of the younger ones hate it because they think it's poofy and don't want their mates to see them. (Sainsbury's)

Shelf-filling jobs were considered all right for these men, although ironically, some stores ran a night shift to fill shelves after the store had closed and these shifts were usually staffed by women. It appears then, that the job-gendering process was a product of wider gender oppositions, not just the nature of the work or the types of goods sold. Both men and women felt threatened by working with large concentrations of the other sex, and men's masculinity in particular was undermined by being associated with women's work, whatever form it took.

Managers played a direct role in promoting the job-gendering process. They were responsible for the allocation of men and women to the different departments, so their own perceptions and stereotypes about gender roles and notions of propriety were influential. The fact that many of them were middle-aged men may have meant that their perceptions were biased towards traditional views on these issues. This was particularly the case in the independent stores which had a paternalist ideology towards their work-force in any case. Many women commented that these managers held stereotyped ideas about what work was appropriate for them and which departments they would want to work in.

Management has a definite idea of where male and female staff should be allocated in the store. (Co-op employee)

Employees cited various instances of cases where women had wanted to work in a more 'male' department (furniture), or men in a 'female' one (fashions), but their applications had been refused. To the extent that shops are gendered territories, bounded by joking relationships and sexual taboos, managers clearly played an important role in policing these boundaries.

The job-gendering of work within stores had a direct effect on the recruitment process. Often the same managers who allocated staff to particular jobs and monitored their work on a daily basis, were also responsible for recruitment. They would select staff for a particular vacancy, bearing in mind the type of department, the type of customer and the existing pattern of gender segregation there. Thus the gendered images of these salespersons were confirmed by actual recruitment practices and became self-perpetuating.

Promotion and entry into management

In the Introduction I referred to the small numbers of women in top management in retailing. The few women who reach this level tend to be in staff management and this has the least status of all managerial positions. This national pattern was replicated in the Colchester stores. Most of the store managers were men, and where women had got into management, it was largely at the lower supervisory levels or as staff managers. I shall argue below that this was the result of economic and social factors; the first has to do with the increasing separation between management and sales labour markets, the de-localization of recruitment into management, and the low turnover at local management level. The second refers to the continuing influence of sex-role stereotypes which excluded women from promotion.

One of the major effects of concentration in the large national retail chains has been the centralization of management, the expansion of management positions at Head Office, and the development of specialized management careers. The larger the chain, the more the central management functions have expanded. Marketing, computing, buying, training, layout and design, and so on have all become specialized departments at Head Office. Entry into these jobs is usually direct from formal education institutions rather than through upward mobility from the shop-floor. Whereas previously, independent retail firms had an internal hierarchy of positions through which employees passed as they were promoted, the large retail firms now have special management training schemes for which they recruit nationally at Head Office. Entrants are expected to have quite high levels of formal education, A-levels in some cases and university degrees in others. Management trainees are selected at a relatively young age and are given a combination of specialized courses and in-house training lasting up to two years. Promotion within the management hierarchy is rapid and depends heavily on geographical movement around different branches of the company, from small ones to large ones and then to regional offices or Head Office. Whereas the typical manager of the traditional independent store would have been elderly, male, and would have had years of experience in the store, the modern managers of the large chain stores are young, male, and highly mobile.

The emergence of professional management career structures bifurcated the promotion system in retailing into a low-level hierarchy of supervisory positions and an upper-level hierarchy of management. Below management level, promotion went through various sales assistant grades to supervisor and in some cases to departmental manager. These jobs were usually filled locally, largely by internal promotion, and the people who reached the top positions were usually older and had worked with the firm for a long time. Many of them were women.

The 'decapitation' of the old internal career structure was a source of some resentment amongst many of the sales staff, especially since they often had to work alongside management trainees:

In past years there was much more movement from the shop floor into management. Now, assistants with long years of service are likely to have someone younger step over them into a higher post. It takes the incentive away from the staff. The right people are not getting promotion. It's not being given to those with proven ability or the next in line. ('Whites')

Graduates are taking over more floor responsibility and some supervisory positions are being phased out—but these graduates are not in touch with the customers, they don't know what is required. ('Whites')

Working your way up is better, you become indoctrinated. Those who come in from the outside have no period of acclimatization and find the pressure too much. (Presto)

Some firms recruited internally on to their management trainee programmes. At Boots, for example, they would look out for management potential amongst new young recruits and groom them for promotion.[11] At Presto, management trainees came up through the ranks or were poached from other stores. At MFI, it was said that all jobs were career orientated, no job was a dead-end, even in the warehouse. Most managers started at the bottom and once they had proved their ability were put on to trainee courses. There was some external recruitment onto these courses, but it was small. The same was true of Currys. As we shall see in a moment these internal promotion systems tended to discriminate against women at the higher management levels, and this, together with the fact that many of the stores involved sold 'male' merchandise, meant that most of the managers were men.

Within the independent department stores, the old-style internal career structures were still in place. Promotion from sales assistant to departmental manager could potentially lead to higher managerial positions, such as assistant manager or even store manager. In theory, internal promotion systems should have favoured women since they were such a large proportion of the lower-level sales staff. However, in practice this was the case only up to supervisory level. One reason for this was the low turnover in the top positions and the direct control exercised by the company owners over recruitment and promotion. Promotion depended very much on the discretion of individual managers and sex-stereotyping tended to colour their decisions: it favoured women for lower rather than higher levels of responsibility.

Managerial decision-making in the independent stores was localized and personalistic. Managers would often refer to their work-force as 'one big happy family', and made a point of taking a personal interest in the welfare of their employees. In one store there was a tendency to employ members of the same family. They were directly involved in decisions over recruitment training and promotion and had detailed knowledge of the family circumstances of their employees. Clearly there was ample scope for patronage here, and sex-stereotyping played a role in determining whose careers were to be promoted most. Low turnover in some of these top managerial posts and the fact that they were held by older men meant that the views of those in charge were often out of step with younger women's aspirations—and there were few opportunities for promotion in any case.

In the lower-level hierarchy, promotion ostensibly depended on sales ability and performance. However, the assessment of 'performance' was rarely measured objectively. Only in Currys and MFI was it measured by sales targets. In Boots and BHS there were yearly appraisals of sales assistants' work which looked for evidence of hard work, commitment, and good appearance. In other stores, the criteria were vaguer and appeared to depend on managers' perceptions of 'potential'. Since the initiative for promotion lay with management rather than the staff, it depended in large measure on being 'spotted' and 'sponsored' by managers. In many stores, eligibility for promotion also depended on going on training courses; but again these courses were in the gift of management and women often did not hear about them or were not encouraged to go on them. Employees said you had to make it clear that you wanted promotion, you had to push yourself to get noticed, and men were more prepared to do this than women.

Many managers stated that women tended not to want promotion—although we got a different story from the employees. Several women thought they were discriminated against by managers through not being seen as suitable for promotion.

More women are working now, but most are not ambitious—they are just happy to have a job. (Presto manager)

Women do have an equal chance now, but it depends on your superiors. You have to wait for promotion, you can't ask for it. Managers here are very traditional in their views and approach—men are encouraged more than women for promotion, they rise up more quickly through the ranks, the men favour promoting men. (Co-op)

The personal knowledge that managers had of their employees' domestic circumstances could work against women. We met one woman who had been refused promotion because her family life was 'unstable' (she was a single parent), even though she had being doing the job in question ever since it had become vacant six months earlier.

Higher up the ladder, it was not just a question of women not wanting promotion, they were not 'suitable' for it. Women were not thought able to cope with the responsibility and stress of top management jobs, nor were they able to deal with the problems of security and handling of large sums of money.

Women can't cope with high-pressure management. It's a quick reaction job . . . not that women aren't capable of this, but they are not motivated to do such a high-pressure job. (MFI)

Women were only considered suitable for positions of authority when they were being responsible for other women. This applied to supervisory positions and also to personnel posts. Staff management was considered appropriate for women but not men, and was in fact dominated by women.

Until recently men wouldn't consider applying for the job of staff manager because it was low status, and in part the low status was a consequence of the large numbers of women employed in the job. Men don't want to go into retailing much and they certainly don't want to work in personnel within retailing. ('Whites')

Men were considered to be much more suitable for management posts; they were said to be more forceful, they pushed themselves more, and they were better at handling the responsibility, the authority, and the physical demands of the job. 'Suitability' also depended on sharing some of the interests of the management: 'You only get a chance for promotion if your face fits—you have to be liked by management, the same sort of person' ('Whites'). This coincidence of interests could be cultivated in informal interaction out of hours. Some employees commented that the top managers were like a men's club—they met together out of hours, playing golf and cricket and going sailing together. It was difficult for women to participate in this scene. Thus despite the fact that internal promotion theoretically allowed for people to rise from the shop-floor into management, informal discrimination associated with sex-stereotyping prevented women from getting as far as men.

In the larger national chain stores, the bifurcation of career structures into a lower tier of supervisory positions filled by internal promotion and an upper one of managerial positions recruited externally had positive and negative consequences for women. The criteria for entry into traineeships were more formal and women were more able to use the 'qualifications lever' to obtain access. Employers were also beginning to monitor their employment policies from the point of view of the Sex Discrimination Act, and some had established schemes designed to encourage women into management (Ognjenovic 1979). Their in-house newsletters were full of special features about successful female employees. Although gender stereotypes continued to prevail about women's suitability for staff management and men's superior ability to handle the responsibility and pressure of managing large stores,[12] the existence of formal procedures for handling promoting made it easier for women to challenge these stereotypes. Therefore access to top jobs should have become easier for women, and undoubtedly did so for a few of them.

However, a major problem was the mobility requirement. Most of the large companies had integrated geographical movement into their career hierarchies in order to diversify the experience of their managers and increase their adaptability to different market conditions. A normal career progression would be from assistant manager of a small store to assistant manager of a large one, then to manager of a small store and to manager of a large one. This requirement presented difficulties for married women with schoolchildren or husbands whose jobs did not permit similar mobility.

To be eligible for a job in store management you have to be fully mobile; although there are a few limited mobility posts these are not usually very good ones (because they are smaller and in more remote areas). You have to be able to manage any type of store, and flexibility is very important. They like to fit the management team to the store. ('Whites')

There are two categories of manager, mobile and permanent; in 'Browns' they like to have a mixture in each store, but the mobility requirement works against women. ('Browns')

In order to qualify for a more senior position, applicants have to have management potential and be geographically mobile. All applicants are asked if they were willing to be mobile at the interview stage. (W. H. Smith)

The departmental manager and branch manager have to be mobile throughout the country. The departmental manager only has to be mobile within the area (these areas can span 200 miles). All managers have to be prepared to travel up to twenty five miles to work. (Sainsbury's)

The girls don't want to move around the country, spending nights in hotels. The men are more prepared to move. Management trainees have to move to a different store from the one where they worked as a sales assistant, and having done the training must move to anywhere where the company has a vacancy. The company doesn't like to move people around more than necessary, but the needs of business are changing all the time, new stores are opening up, etc. Another reason for moving managers is to get the right mix of people in a store, for example, they'll move a good manager to a store where there are staff problems. The company likes flexibility. (MFI)

Low turnover can be a problem, you've got to be geographically mobile if you want promotion. ('Whites')

Another problem was the long hours involved in management and the pressure to do work and training out of hours. The larger national chains were usually the ones with more aggressive and demanding styles of management, encouraged by the high competitiveness of the industry. Many managers reported working twelve hours or more per day, travelling long distances by car and working weekends. This was difficult for married women with children. Ironically, therefore, although the larger firms offered more opportunities for women to enter high-level management, it was under conditions that conflicted with their domestic responsibilities. Women's flexibility was strictly limited; they were not available for longer hours and greater mobility. For this reason the proportions of women in management in these firms has remained low.

CONCLUSION

Despite the absence of complex organizational hierarchies and institutional intervention by professional associations and unions, the work-force in retailing was highly differentiated. The differentiation cut three ways: between the types of goods outlets and goods sold; between managerial, sales, and support jobs; and between full-time and part-time contracts. Gender was implied in each of these divisions.

In analysing the pattern of gender segregation in retailing, this chapter has looked particularly at the deskilling and the job-gendering approaches. There was evidence to support both approaches; however, neither was able to provide a sufficient explanation of gender segregation on its own. Moreover, despite their contradictory assumptions, they were strongly linked. The structures associated with deskilling were permeated by gender biases and job-gendering was strongly linked to economic efficiency. This casts doubt on the gender neutrality assumed by the deskilling thesis and the resistance to market forces assumed by the job-gendering thesis. Gender segregation was a product of both economic and social factors.

The deskilling thesis

Most of the elements of deskilling were relevant to the structure of employment in this industry: high street competition had produced concentration, increases in scale, technological innovation, and rationalization of labour use. The automation and depersonalization of sales work had produced deskilling; the fragmentation of working time into shifts that closely matched the volume of trade had produced an increase in part-time work, and the demand for labour was largely predicated upon cheap female labour. The concentration of women in these low-paid sales jobs was partly because there was a ready supply of women who wanted this type of work and partly because the wages were too low to attract men. However, this was not the whole story.

The feminization of sales work was not just the result of deskilling, casualization, and the use of cheap labour. It was also the product of a demand for female-specific skills. The discussion of this issue in relation to retailing shows up the narrow conception of skill in Bravermanian analysis, which is very much based on a manufacturing model. The skills required for retailing were not craft skills nor formal educational skills; they involved social skills and industry-specific experience. Employers could draw on a variety of low-cost labour, some of which was marginally cheaper than women (such as school-leavers); but they preferred married women because they had the desired skills. However, these skills were deeply gendered—they involved special aptitudes and interests that were associated with male and female roles. This shows that the deskilling process is more complex and less gender neutral than is implied in much of the theoretical literature.

There were some limits to the power of the deskilling thesis for explaining gender segregation in retailing. First, there were variations in the degree to which firms had adopted the deskilling strategy. Some employers did not go for the lowest-cost labour, they did not widely adopt part-time working and they did not have a preference for women. Employment strategies varied according to the type of goods sold, the pattern of trading, and whether or not the firm was independent or part of a national chain. Each of these variations had consequences for gender segregation, and even where the outcome was the same, that is the work-force were women, it was often the result of different strategies of labour use. Second, the deskilling thesis cannot explain patterns of gender segregation higher up the organization, particularly in supervisory and management positions. For this we have to look at other explanations.

The job-gendering thesis

Job-gendering was widespread in all the stores studied and clearly affected recruitment and promotion. The main reason for this was the close association between goods sold, the salesperson, and the customer. However, job-gendering also occurred behind the scenes in the warehouse and the canteen, even where the personal element in saleswork had been largely removed (e.g. checkout jobs). Job-gendering meant that the recruitment of men and women was legitimized on a normative basis, that is in terms of what was 'suitable' or 'appropriate', and these norms invoked general gender roles rather than individual abilities.

However, job-gendering was not indifferent to market forces; it was often justified in terms of economic efficiency. Putting men and women into different types of saleswork on the basis of their gender produced more efficient outcomes because customers expected it and the salespersons themselves were happier. Job gendering did not necessarily imply the unitary categories, 'female' and 'male'. There was some differentiation between different groups of men and women (e.g. by age, marital status, class) and between the different qualities associated with gender (strength, aggression, femininity). Yet employers also placed some weight on individual skills, hence the stress on internal training and promotion. Job-gendering appears to define the outer limits of what is acceptable in the recruitment process, and within these limits applicants are selected according to their individual qualities. What we have here, then, is a combination of social categorization and individual selection.

Comparisons between stores showed that although there were broad similarities in the way jobs were gendered, there were also slight differences. Different norms would be invoked in order to justify these patterns. For example, in the case of furniture sales, physical strength would be mentioned to justify men working there, but skills in colour matching and an interest in interior decoration to justify the presence of women. These patterns were also sensitive to economic change. For example, the fragmentation of sales assistants' jobs into checkout cashiers and shelf-fillers was accompanied by a new pattern of gender segregation and job-gendering. Similarly, the changing structure of management had disadvantaged women in new ways. The development of management trainee schemes meant that women had more formal access to management but they were excluded on new grounds. Thus the degree of fixity in patterns of job-gendering assumed in much of the literature may have been exaggerated.

This study has shown that employers have a range of strategies for rationalizing their use of labour, and gender considerations enter into them in a variety of ways. Moreover, these strategies are liable to change and this can alter the pattern of segregation. Explanations of gender segregation therefore need to address the diversity of employment structures and the precise ways in which economic and social factors interact within these structures to produce segregation.

NOTES

1. The flexible specialization literature does relate to the deskilling thesis in so far as part of the subcontracted work-force is considered to be unskilled. For this reason it is also assumed to consist of women workers. The point here, however, is that the *core* work-force is increasingly specialized and skilled.

2. Conceptually, the distinction between economic and social factors is not easy to make. Here I have suggested that it consists in a distinction between economic rationality (profit maximization, individualistic decision-making) and social categorization. In early work, I used a distinction between 'economic' forces (the market) and 'normative' ones (politics and ideology) (Scott 1986: 154–5). However, this assumes a notion of 'pure' economic–market relations, uncontaminated by ideology, which is precisely the notion to be criticized. The argument is that the market itself is imbued with normative elements.

3. See Milkman 1976, for an analysis of how gender segregation protected women from unemployment during the Great Depression in the USA.

4. Union membership in the mid-1980s was estimated at 10% of all shopworkers, and most of these were in USDAW (Union of Shop, Distributive, and Allied Workers). About 75% of the union members were women although there were very few female full-time officials (USDAW interview). Retail employers were not generally sympathetic to unions, and preferred to use a local store-based machinery for dealing with grievances.

5. Interviews were carried out with managers in thirteen stores, four of whom were branch managers, seven were staff managers, and two were training managers. In three of the stores, informal discussions were held with employees, mostly during their tea or dinner breaks. The area organizer from USDAW was also interviewed. The interviews were unstructured, lasting from half an hour to two hours in some cases. A standard *aide-mémoire* was used as the basis for each interview, covering the following topics: the division of labour within the firm, the pattern of gender segregation, the management structure and promotion system, the grading structure and levels of pay, recruitment, the types of qualifications and skills required on entry, training, and unionization.

6. These variations within retailing are similar to those described by Craig and Wilkinson 1982.

7. These skills were 'social' in that they had to do with social interaction and communication, e.g. 'being good with people', helpful,

268 A. M. Scott

friendly, sensitive to people's needs, etc. Although these skills were not confined to women, they were strongly associated with them (cf. Curran 1988).

8. The adult wage rate set by the Wages Council was only applicable for 19-year-olds and over. The wages for 16–18-year-olds were substantially lower.

9. In 1985–6, employers' national insurance contributions were 9% of gross wages and the threshold above which contributions were payable was £35.

10. Some electronically controlled tills record the time of the purchase as well as the amount, so employers can measure precisely the peaks and troughs in shopping patterns and adjust shifts accordingly.

11. These internal promotion schemes did not, however, reach the very top in Boots. Top management posts were in pharmacy.

12. Interestingly, the ability to cope with this kind of pressure was seen as a form of physical strength; compare this with a statement from one female board member of Tesco that 'running a big store is a physically demanding job for which women do not have the stamina' (*Supermarketing*, 10 Sept. 1982).

REFERENCES

ACKER, J. (1990), 'Hierarchies, Jobs, Bodies: A Theory of Gendered Organizations', *Gender and Society*, 4/2: 139–58.

BRADLEY, H. (1989), *Men's Work, Women's Work*. Cambridge, Polity Press.

BRAVERMAN, H. (1974), *Labour and Monopoly Capital: The Degradation of Work in the Twentieth Century*. London, Monthly Review Press.

BROADBRIDGE, A. (1991), 'Images and Goods: Women in Retailing', in N. Redclift and M. T. Sinclair (eds.), *Working Women*. London, Routledge.

BROWN, L. (1982), *Careers in Retailing*. London, Kogan Page.

Central Statistical Office (1990), *Regional Trends* 25. London, HMSO.

COCKBURN, C. (1983), *Brothers: Male Dominance and Technological Change*. London, Pluto.

—— (1987), *Two Track Training: Sex Inequalities and the YTS*, Basingstoke, Macmillan.

CORINA, M. (1978), *Fine Silks and Oak Counters: Debenhams 1778–1978*. London, Hutchinson Benham.

CRAIG, C., and WILKINSON, F. (1982), *Pay and Employment in Four Retail Trades*. Research Paper No. 51. Department of Employment, London, HMSO.

CRINE, S. (1982), *Shopworkers' Low Wages*. Low Pay Report No. 10, London, Low Pay Unit.

CURRAN, M. M. (1988), 'Gender and Recruitment: People and Places in the Labour Market', *Work, Employment and Society*, 2/3: 335–51.

DAWSON, J. A., FINDLAY, A. M., and SPARKS, L. (1986), 'Anatomy of Job Growth: Employment in British Superstores', Working Paper 8601, Institute for Retail Studies.

GAME, A., and PRINGLE, R. (1984), *Gender at Work*. London, Pluto Press.

HEARN, J., SHEPPARD, D. L., TANCRED-SHERIFF, P., and BURRELL, G. (1989) (eds.), *The Sexuality of Organization*. London, Sage.

HOFFMAN, P. C. (1947), *They also Serve: The Story of the Shopworker*. London, Porcupine Press.

KNIGHTS, D., and WILMOTT, H. (1986) (eds), *Gender and the Labour Process*. Aldershot, Gower.

LOVERIDGE, R., CHILD, J., and HARVEY, J. (1985), *New Technologies in Banking, Retailing and Health Services: The British Case*. ESRC Work Organisation Centre, University of Aston.

MCCLELLAND, W. G. (1966), *Costs and Competition in Retailing*. London, Macmillan.

MARTIN, J., and ROBERTS, C. (1984), *Women and Employment: A Lifetime Perspective*. London, HMSO.

MILKMAN, R. (1976), 'Women's Work and the Economic Crisis', *Review of Radical Political Economics*, 8/1: 73–97.

MURGATROYD, L. (1982), 'Gender and Occupational Stratification', *Sociological Review*, 30/4: 574–602.

NIESR (National Institute for Economic and Social Research) (1986), *Young People's Employment in Retailing*. A report prepared by NIESR for NEDO and the Distributive Trades Economic Development Committee. London, National Economic Development Office.

OGNJENOVIC, D. (1979), 'Women in Retailing', *Retail and Distribution Management (UK)*, July–Aug.: 29–35.

PRINGLE, R. (1989), *Secretaries Talk*. London, Verso.

REES, G. (1969), *St. Michael: A History of Marks and Spencer*. London, Weidenfeld & Nicolson.

RUBERY, J. (1988), 'Employers and the Labour Market', in D. Gallie (ed.), *Employment in Britain*. Oxford, Blackwell.

SCOTT, A. MACEWEN (1986), 'Industrialisation, Gender Segregation and Stratification Theory', in R. Crompton and M. Mann (eds.), *Gender and Stratification*. Cambridge, Polity.

THOMPSON, P. (1989), *The Nature of Work*. 2nd edn., London, Macmillan.

USDAW (1982), *Women in USDAW*. First Report of the Working

Party. Submitted by the Executive Council to the 1983 Annual Delegate Meeting.

—— (1986), *Women in USDAW: The Task Ahead*. Submitted by the Executive Council to the 1986 Annual Delegate Meeting.

WEBB, S. (1984), *Counter Arguments: An Ethnographic Look at 'Women and Class'*. Studies in Sexual Politics, Department of Sociology, University of Manchester.

WINSTANLEY, M. J. (1983), *The Shopkeepers World, 1830–1914*. Manchester, Manchester University Press.

WOOD, S. (1982) (ed.), *The Degradation of Work?* London, Hutchinson.

8

The Gendered Restructuring of Employment in the Finance Sector

ROSEMARY CROMPTON AND KAY SANDERSON

INTRODUCTION

Since the Second World War, the finance sector has been a major element in service sector employment growth, particularly for women. It has a high proportion of clerical employees; as is well known, this occupation has become progressively feminized since the beginning of the century. In 1961, women were 48 per cent of clerks, cashiers, and office machine operators in the finance industries, but by 1981 they were 68 per cent (Crompton 1988). By the same time, employees in both banks and building societies—the industry case-studies upon which the empirical discussion of this chapter is focused—were predominantly women. However, women were under-represented in the upper levels of management within the finance sector (Crompton and Jones 1984).

Much of our empirical knowledge of these patterns of gender segregation has been based on the banking industry, especially during the initial phase of women's entry there (i.e. the 1960s and 1970s), when they were mainly concentrated in low-grade clerical jobs and to a lesser extent in deskilled computer-related jobs (Blackburn 1967, Llewellyn 1981; Heritage 1983). However, women's employment within banking has changed somewhat since the 1970s, as a result of a variety of organizational, techno-logical, and social changes, and in any case the situation of women in other parts of the finance sector, such as building soci-eties, developed somewhat differently from that in banking. Any analysis of patterns of gender segregation within the finance sector therefore needs to bear in mind industry specificities within the sector as well as the historical changes in these industries over time. This chapter presents a comparison of patterns of segregation within banks and building societies in the context of both general and industry-specific change. Research on the building society industry was carried out as part of a related study on gender segregation for the Social Change and Economic Life Initiative. Data on the banking industry draws on other research conducted by one of the authors (Crompton and Jones 1984), which was supplemented and updated during the related study.

In the long run, the pattern of female employment in the finance sector has reflected the profound changes affecting women's position in British society since the Second World War—although it is also important to stress the *continuities* of the female experience. During the 1950s and 1960s, women were mainly recruited as low-skilled, young, unmarried employees who were assumed to withdraw from the sector, and the labour market generally, on marriage or at the birth of their first child. Nowadays, following more general trends in female labour supply, they have become an increasingly permanent part of the labour-force in finance, remaining within employment after marriage and often rejoining shortly after childbirth. Indeed many banks and building societies actively encourage women to rejoin their staff after a break for full-time domestic work. By the end of the 1980s, for example, the clearing banks were in the forefront of the development of career breaks, occupational childcare schemes, and so on.

Women have also become an increasingly qualified part of the financial work-force, not only in terms of school and higher degree qualifications, but also in terms of industry-specific ones offered by the Institute of Bankers and Chartered Building Societies' Institute. Legal changes such as the Equal Pay Act 1970 and the Sex Discrimination Act of 1975 have made direct discrimination against women in terms of pay, recruitment, and promotion illegal, and this has led to a number of complaints against certain banks and building societies, causing a ripple effect in terms of altered employment practices within the sector generally.

Notwithstanding these social changes, in both industries the majority of women remain concentrated in the lower levels of the occupational hierarchy. However, this general structure obscures a number of important factors which have affected women's employment: (1) the *content* of lower-level jobs has changed, thus even though women are still employed in low-level positions they are not the same jobs as in the 1960s; (2) following changes in patterns of recruitment and promotion, the structure of internal labour market segmentation has changed; and (3) there has been a small but significant increase of women in middle-level management. Thus within an apparent continuity in the general structure of women's employment in finance, there have been a number of important micro-level changes.

The comparison between banks and building societies reveals both similarities and differences. In particular, the situation in building societies facilitated the earlier entry of women into higher-level supervisory jobs than the banks. Analysis of the reasons for this difference points to the importance of institutional factors, namely the structure of branch networks within the industry, the computerization of financial decision-making, and internal labour market segmentation. These institutional differences are in turn related to the timing of the growth and development of the two industries.

This chapter presents a historical case-study approach towards the analysis of changing patterns of gender segregation in two finance industries. The analysis involves looking at the interrelationships between broad changes in female labour supply, changes in industrial structure, and institutional factors such as the grading system, recruitment, and internal career structures. We shall begin with a brief account of the major differences in the institutional development of the banks and the building societies.

INSTITUTIONAL DEVELOPMENT OF BANKS AND BUILDING SOCIETIES

The organization of the financial market in England prior to recent legislation (the Finance Act 1986) has been described as a system of self-regulating clubs. The various financial services were separated into distinct compartments, each of which oversaw the character and behaviour of their members:

the clubs served to restrict entry, to limit membership to those who played the game by the accepted rules and often to control competition, especially the rates of interest that could be offered and charged, in an oligopolistic fashion. The specialised compartmentalisation ensured that management was expert in its own narrow field of business. (Goodhart 1987)

The London clearing banks and the building societies were each separate clubs within the system. However, the history and development of the two sets of institutions is very different, and this has had different implications for the employment and entry of women.

Building societies originated as mutual institutions, and remained as such until the enabling legislation of the 1986 Building Societies Act. They have not (historically) been part of the City of London and still have strong regional links. For most of the post-war period, their activities have been confined by law to collecting retail savings and making mortgage loans. However, the restrictive legislation governing building societies has protected them from competition from other financial institutions and their favoured situation in this respect has allowed the building societies to grow at a very rapid rate. In 1950, building societies held only 10 per cent of retail savings, and 'although they were significant in the mortgage market, that market itself was small, with owner-occupation accounting for no more than a quarter of all households. Between 1950 and 1980 building societies grew massively, to take over 50% of the retail savings market, and some 75% of a huge and growing mortgage market' (Boléat 1987). The London clearing banks, in contrast, have always been major national profit-making financial institutions. As high-profile, prestige institutions they have from the first been regarded as high-status employers, and bank clerks, as Lockwood (1958) argued, were the 'aristocracy' of clerical labour.

At the time that Lockwood was writing, building societies contributed only a small fraction to employment in the financial sector. In 1969 (the first year for which separate figures are available) only 24,000 people were employed by building societies, whereas the clearing banks employed 177,000. By 1979, however, employment in building societies had increased by 87 per cent to 45,000; bank employment by 42 per cent to 252,000. This more rapid rate of growth in building societies has been maintained, to a total of over 65,000 (73 per cent over the decade) in 1985, although more detailed breakdowns show some slowing down of underlying trends. Employment in banking has increased to 286,000, a 20 per cent increase over the decade. Since the Second World War, the banking sector has been highly concentrated and centralized. In contrast, the structure of the building society industry is more fragmented and regionally diverse (although some mergers and consolidations have occurred as a consequence of recent legislation, for example, the Alliance and Leicester in 1985, the Nationwide Anglia in 1987).

The amalgamations which produced the 'big four' of the banking world had been competed by the 1970s, but in 1985 there were still 167 building societies, ranging from the 'big five' with assets of over £7,000m down to small local societies. The expansion in building society employment was in large part a result of branching, which was itself a consequence of competition for investors. Between 1970 and 1980, employment in building society branch offices grew by a staggering 272 per cent, whereas employment in the chief offices increased by only 35 per cent. At the same time as building societies were expanding their branch network, the major clearing banks were undergoing a period of rationalization and branch closure. It has been suggested that the building societies were, in a sense, simply repeating a 'natural history' in the growth and development of financial institutions which was largely accomplished by banks in the nineteenth century (Davies 1981: 71). However, this comparison is inappropriate. The expansion of branch banking occurred before computerization. Each bank branch represented a 'microcosm' of banking, with a full range of staff including bank managers empowered to negotiate loans and investments (Crompton and Jones 1984). The structure of branch banking established in the first half of this century, was expensive to create and maintain in respect of both staff and facilities, and it was this structure which was undergoing an occasionally painful process of rationalization in the 1970s and 1980s following the introduction of electronic data processing.

In contrast, the expansion of the building society branch network occurred at a time when computing technology was readily available. During the 1970s, efficient terminals linked to a mainframe at regional and/or head office were developed, and the further development of mini- and micro-computers meant that advice on financial matters such as underwriting and mortgage quotes could be given by an efficient machine operator. These technical innovations have made possible the development of what are variously called 'satellite', 'feeder', or 'retail' branches and much branching activity has been of this kind. Satellite branches are effectively shop-fronts, often run by an all-female staff, and controlled from the processing centre or regional office. It is difficult to gather accurate data on the extent to which the creation of the building society branch network has depended upon satellite branches. Figures on the number of staff per branch, however, suggest that well over half the branch network is composed of satellite branches and amongst the smaller societies branching may have been entirely achieved via the creation of satellites (Boléat 1982: 10). As we shall see below, the greater heterogeneity amongst building societies, together with the system of computer-centralized branching, has produced more open employment policies than in banking. These factors have also contributed to the earlier creation of feminized clerical supervisory positions than in banking.

Recent legislation (Finance Act 1986, Building Societies Act 1986) has been designed to break down functional specialization between different financial institutions with the aim of increasing competition within the sector as a whole. However, although the clearing banks and the building societies have very different origins, rates of growth, and historic roles in the financial sector, there were nevertheless important similarities between the two industries even in advance of recent legislation. By the 1980s, a majority of both bank and building society employees were women, although the proportion in building societies (70 per cent) was higher than that in banking (60 per cent). They were (and are) both organized as white-collar bureaucracies with extensive branch structures which offered career opportunities. Each industry has encouraged the development of 'professional' standards, supporting the Institute of Bankers (IOB) and Chartered Building Society (CBSI) qualifications. Both are characterized by the use of extremely sophisticated technology in the conduct of their operations. These broad similarities, however, follow on very different traditions of labour management in the two industries.

EMPLOYMENT POLICIES IN THE CLEARING BANKS

Until the 1980s the banks' employment policies were characterized by tight personalistic control over their career employees and
inter-bank collusion in promoting loyalty to the firm and industry. Most banks were also opposed to trade unionism. The dominant employment model until the 1960s was an internal, lifetime
career structure, entry to which was at school-leaver level.
Thereafter, promotion and pay were partly age related and partly
determined by individual performance. However, technological
changes produced the need for a relatively unskilled and cheap
labour-force, composed mainly of women, which resulted in the
classic dual labour market segmentation pattern.

During the 1960s, the banks still provided a 'clerical career';
the occupation of 'bank clerk' contained a hierarchy of positions
from junior new entrants to senior counter clerks, along which
individuals progressed over time. In most banks, age-related
scales were automatic up to age 31 but, even before this, merit
loadings and special increases could be achieved on an individual
basis. After the age of 31, individual salaries still increased but to
no set pattern. In the case of the Midland Bank, for example,
formalized 'overscales' existed but the details were not published.
Merit increases, and promotion to 'appointed' staff (posts of
responsibility) were explicitly awarded to the individual, rather
than given on the basis of the job he was doing. The criteria for
grading stressed the ability, initiative, energy, and willingness of
the person, rather than the nature of the job (NBPI 1965: 4).
Where an individual's fate rested so clearly on the evaluation of
his employer (or his employer's representatives), it is not surprising that he should act in accordance with his employer's wishes—
even to the extent of collective representation. Thus in-house
staff associations were the favoured channel of collective representation. These were sponsored by the banks in opposition to
trade unions.[1] The banks' hold over their individual employees
was further enhanced by the (unofficial) 'no-poaching' rules that
prevailed between the major clearers, who would not accept each
others' 'career' staff. Such 'career' staff, as far as the banks were
concerned, included all those individuals considered eligible for a
lifetime's employment by the bank; in practice, this meant men.

Not all men would be equally successful in their bureaucratic careers but a senior clerk would be considered a promoted position. The 'no-poaching' agreement, however, meant that an individual dissatisfied at his lack of progress in one bank had scant hope of improving his prospects by attempting to move to another bank. Perhaps in anticipation of the potential difficulties and resentments which might be engendered by these policies of trade union resistance and individual career controls, however, employment conditions have been on the whole favourable, and relatively standardized, as between the major banks.

In the 1960s, the banks' career and salary structure was therefore justified as follows (taken from a contemporary report of the National Board for Prices and Incomes, 1965): 'The structure is related to the tradition that to obtain the type of staff required the banks should offer a safe and steady career for life' (NBPI 1965: 15). However, as the argument continued, economic and technological changes had, relatively speaking, reduced the proportion (if not the number) of career staff required by the banks. The introduction of computers meant that there was a need for less well-qualified non-career staff to carry out routine duties, and the NBPI recommended a substantial restructuring of bank employment.

From the second half of the 1960s onwards, the single clerical pay scale combined with individual merit awards was superseded in the major clearing banks by a system of clerical grades, usually from 1 to 4. These grades were tied to the level of the job, not the individual. Beyond them were Appointed Officer, the managerial grades. In setting the grades, job content had to be specified, and thus routine job evaluation was involved. There was therefore a decisive shift in focus from the individual to the job—in other words, employment in banking was becoming further systematized and bureaucratized. These and other changes contributed to a substantial increase in NUBE's (National Union of Bank Employees) membership and recognition by the late 1960s. However, even after the abolition of the 'clerical career', the banks still relied upon a policy of school-leaver recruitment, followed by steady progress through the clerical grades, in order to generate their managerial cadre. The extensive network of branches found in all of the clearers was the training ground through which managers were developed.

It is not difficult to understand why the clearing banks should have favoured the development of this qualified, captive labour-force. As a strategy, it is a good example of what Kreckel (1980) has described as a process of 'encirclement', which is the employers' most effective counter-strategy against the claims of skilled workers' (p. 541); that is, 'confin[ing] them to tight internal labour markets under their own control' (ibid.). The banks were assured of a stable and loyal labour-force—and for much of the period after the Second World War this was in relatively short supply given the expansion of the financial sector and the wider demand for clerical labour. Although not officially acknowledged, the banks still largely refrain from any exchange of their mainstream career staff, although there is interchange of non-career staff (these will usually be female counter clerks) and the poaching of specialists is not unheard of.

WOMEN WORKERS IN THE CLEARING BANKS

It is a well-established fact that the expansion of women's paid employment since the 1960s has been largely an increase in the employment of married women, often returning to the labour-force after time spent rearing young children. Until comparatively recently, however, most of the clearing banks have tended to make use of relatively young female labour. The historic situation in banking is described by a report of the NBPI in 1965:

Nearly 50% of the bank's [i.e. Midland] staff are women. For the most part they are employed in straightforward jobs, often using machines. Most of them leave the bank on marriage; many of them probably never intend to follow banking as a life-long career and they do not study for the bank examinations. Although the annual wastage rate for women of approximately 20% may seem high against a tradition of entrants staying for life, the figure does not appear to be out of line with that for comparable occupations. Moreover, the banks have been able to recruit sufficient young women not only to make up the wastage, but also to increase the number employed year by year . . . (NBPI 1965: 15)

Women were brought into the banks as short-term, temporary labour, on lower rates of pay, and often to do specific jobs—particularly those associated with the mechanization of clerical work such as the use of electric adding machines in the 'back offices'.

In many banks, the marriage bar—that is a formal requirement that a woman should resign on marriage—was not removed until late in the 1950s. On the whole, women were simply not considered as far as promotion was concerned, which tended to be an entirely male affair (Blackburn 1967). It is apparent, therefore, that in the 1950s and 1960s, women were recruited initially by the banks as cheap, disposable labour.

The introduction of the differentiated structure of clerical grades at the end of the 1960s and early 1970s, which replaced the 'clerical career' has to be understood against this previous history of women's employment. The new grade structures were introduced in recognition of the fact that many employees of the banks would not have lifetime careers, and in the expectation that these non-career staff would be women. Ironically, the fact that most women left employment at a relatively young age, meant that the banks could introduce the new grade structures under the banner of equal opportunities, given that the same *job* would henceforth receive the same rate of pay regardless of who was doing it. (Equal pay had been adopted as a policy by NUBE 1967; the Equal Pay Act was passed in 1970, coming into force in 1975.)

Throughout the 1970s, despite this formal equality of opportunity, women in banking continued to be concentrated overwhelmingly in the lowest clerical grades. There was supposedly equality of opportunity, and men and women were recruited at the same grade level, but as women were not prepared to be geographically mobile, did not gain further qualifications, and broke their employment for child-rearing, they did not get promoted. This prophecy was further fulfilled by recruiting women with lower entrance qualifications than men, and actively dissuading them from taking the Institute of Bankers' examinations (Llewellyn 1981, Crompton and Jones 1984). Thus a feminized office proletariat was being consolidated at the same time as opportunities for women were—in theory—improved. Research in the late 1970s and early 1980s suggested that many women were becoming increasingly resentful of the fact that they were being passed over for younger, 'career track' men. The bank's promotion rules (qualifications, length of service, unbroken work experience), meant that many women did not qualify for promotion, but nevertheless they were aware of their superior technical competences as compared to the young men who would shortly be promoted and become their hierarchical superiors. That is, they were well aware of the fact that the bank's internal promotion system worked against them, despite the fact that it was supposedly gender neutral (Crompton and Jones 1984). In contrast, the same research suggested that women in other finance sector jobs, in relatively *segregated*, albeit low-level, occupations were not particularly worried as far as promotion opportunities were concerned; it was the inequitable opportunities for advancement following uniportal entry that caused resentment in the banks.

As we shall see presently, this resentment was to lead to a case being brought against one bank under the Sex Discrimination Act, which ultimately produced a switch by all banks away from the uniportal system of recruitment towards multi-level or tiered entry in the late 1980s. However, this latter system was already in place within the building societies, as will now be described.

EMPLOYMENT POLICIES AND THE POSITION OF WOMEN IN BUILDING SOCIETIES

The relatively large number of individual building societies, together with the regional spread of the industry, means that co-ordinated employment policies have not been a feature of this industry. Unlike the situation in banking, recruitment has always been multiportal rather than uniportal and personnel movement between different societies is common at all levels. The smaller societies tend to recruit their trained managers from the larger societies who, as will be discussed in a later section of this chapter, have for many years recruited and trained management trainees. There is also a considerable heterogeneity in wage rates both within and between different societies. This more open situation has had both advantages and disadvantages as far as the employment of women is concerned.

Although detailed empirical research is lacking, we can be confident that employment practices in building societies were not standardized to the same extent as in the clearing banks. Regional differences, variations in size, and type of business transacted, have all contributed to diversity (Ashburner 1987). A lack of systematic data makes a straightforward comparison between the employment practices of banks and building societies as a whole problematic. Nevertheless, some general comparisons may be made relating to management, recruitment, and promotion.

The centralization of financial decision-making and the early computer linkage of building society branches has promoted shorter and less complex occupational hierarchies than in banking, with more technological deskilling at all levels. Labour has not been recruited at a single entry point, i.e. school-leavers, but occurs at all levels of the occupational hierarchy. As previously noted, the smaller societies have tended to recruit their management staff from those trained by the larger—a practice which is apparent from even the most cursory skim through the job advertisements in the 'trade journal' (*Building Societies Gazette*). Since the building societies' branch network, in contrast to that of the banks, was built up rapidly from small beginnings from the 1970s (Davies 1981), the senior managers in building societies would not usually have passed through the clerical grades, as in the banks, but would have been recruited as management trainees. Women in building societies are concentrated in the lowest clerical grades, but unlike the situation in the banks, most of them would not have had experience of being passed over by men who had started at the same grade level. Rather they were recruited directly, as cashier-clerks, into the expanding branch network. Thus the gender segregation of women's employment in building societies has largely been achieved at entry—'only women', as one review of the situation commented, 'seem to apply for clerical jobs' (IRRR 1985). Thus, although there will no doubt have been internal exclusion within the building society industry, the segregation of the labour-force by sex has been largely achieved at the point of recruitment.

In the case of the Abbey National, for example, a recent report revealed that, after some years of overtly 'affirmative' action, women had penetrated only as far as the assistant branch manager level in the Abbey job hierarchy. At this level, however, the change had been considerable. In 1975 there were 520 assistant branch managers (ABMs), of whom 20 (4 per cent) were women; by 1985, out of 723 ABMs, 432 (60 per cent) were women (IRRR 1985). However, this penetration of the lower managerial grades to some extent masks a major technological transformation and deskilling of building society work throughout the 1960s and 1970s exemplified by the creation of the 'woman's' job of cashier-clerking. The development of the building society branch network was heavily dependent upon the application of advanced technological systems, and as a consequence mass, feminized clerical-cashiering was introduced. Women have not replaced men as cashier-clerks, rather, they have been directly recruited into technologically deskilled clerical work, albeit with a new emphasis on service to the public. This interpretation lends a particular twist to the penetration of the lower managerial grades by women in building societies, as it has been accompanied by the deskilling of 'management' functions.

In all three societies investigated during empirical research, the job of assistant branch manager (or equivalent) was very different from that of branch manager, and it would have been unusual for an assistant branch manager to be promoted to branch manager unless the assistant branch manager was also a management trainee, who would have been recruited directly as such. The job of the assistant branch manager in the Abbey National was described by the Regional Personnel Officer as involving 'some responsibility for figures, day-to-day running of the branch, organizing staff if you've got people off. Spending a lot of time dealing with the customers'. The branch manager's job, it was emphasized, was quite different. 'Overall responsibility for the branch—costs and budget. Outside contacts—with builders, solicitors, companies. They are expected to bring business in. They will have quotas to lend on properties.' Managers do not get paid commission. In contrast, they will be expected to fulfil a business target. The job of an assistant branch manager, by comparison, was described by the same informant as 'cosy' and undemanding. Most women in assistant branch manager posts, it was stressed, would not want to take on a branch manager's job with the outside contacts involved. In this account of the two jobs, the comparison between the gender division of labour within the building societies and that between women and men more generally was quite suggestive. Women stay in the branch office/'home' ensuring that everything runs smoothly in the comfortable base, men go into the outside world/public sphere to bring in the business. This characterization and comparison places a lower relative value on the 'feminine' contribution in the branch offices, and is entirely congruent with gender stereotypes.

A similar situation prevailed in both the 'Regional Plus' and the 'Holyoake Permanent' (pseudonyms for the other two medium to large societies for which data was also gathered[2]). In the Regional Plus, the 'branch managers' of the satellite offices had neither cars nor expense accounts, outside contacts were made by area managers with both. In the Holyoake Permanent, the assistant branch manager ('I used to be called Chief Clerk but Assistant Manager sounds better)' 'couldn't see herself' as a branch manager. 'I might have to move out of the area, it would mean taking exams—I think I'm too old' (she was 28). 'Now the Management Trainee—*he'll* be a Branch Manager.' The presence of women in lower-level management in the building societies, therefore, is as female supervisors of an all-female labour force of cashier-clerks. Such positions are final destinations, rather than staging posts on a career trajectory.

In summary, although the entry of women into building societies has taken a similar form to that in banking, i.e. concentration in lower clerical grades, the job content at these levels and the way they integrate into internal career hierarchies has historically been different. Throughout the period of expansion from the late 1970s, career structures have been shorter, more truncated, and segmented in terms of function and recruitment. In addition, gender roles have penetrated these occupational structures in new ways as new feminized jobs, such as cashier-clerk, have been created, and the content of assistant branch manager jobs has become progressively feminized.

MULTI-LEVEL RECRUITMENT AND THE ROLE OF FORMAL QUALIFICATIONS

During the 1980s there was an increasing convergence in the two industries in terms of diversification of internal career hierarchies with multi-level recruitment and explicit reliance on formal qualifications as a condition for entry. This implied increased mobility of labour at all levels and a greater role for supposedly gender-neutral criteria in processes of selection. We shall now examine the implications of this trend for patterns of gender segregation in the two industries.

Mention has been made above of the emergent practice in the

clearing banks during the 1970s of gender differences in terms of qualifications at the point of recruitment. Boys, as likely managers of the future, were recruited at A-level; girls, as short-term routine workers, at O-level—although both were recruited at the same grade. In 1983 a complaint was made to the Equal Opportunities Commission that Barclays Bank were operating 'an informal two-tier recruitment system which appeared to be based more upon sex than on ability. Of the applicants with GCE 'A' levels a higher proportion of males were successful than females, and the situation was the reverse for applicants at 'O' level' (EOC 1987).

Thus, although the Bank's recruitment was officially 'uniportal' in that every employee was recruited at the same level, to what was usually their first job, and into the same grade structure—it was in practice multi-level and, moreover, stratified by gender.[3] Barclays' response has been to adopt a system of multi-level or tiered entry to clerical grades, in addition to the graduate admissions programme. Applicants for the Accelerated Training Programme (ATP) are expected to have at least two A-levels, and will move more quickly through the lower clerical grades. 'Standard Entry' clerical applicants are divided into two categories, A and B, according to the number of their O-level passes. Only those recruited at or above A-level standard will in the future be given automatic leave to study for the Institute of Bankers' examinations. (O-level entrants will be given study leave if they manage to pass the first stage on their own account.)

The EOC investigation of Barclays was a source of considerable unease within the industry—as a manager in another bank commented: 'I think every bank thought "there but for the grace of God go all of us"—it was just that they got caught', and the other major clearers, too, have switched to tiered entry. It could be suggested that the move to tiered entry in the clearing banks, although representing a break with established formal practices, merely regularized a structure of internal labour market segmentation which had already been established informally. However, the really important change which seems to have been brought about by the EOC investigation is that the formal rationality now imposed upon recruitment practices means that discrimination by sex at the point of recruitment is extremely difficult. It is also possible that internal exclusionary practices, centring on promotion, are becoming less important as far as women are concerned.

The transition to a multi-level system of recruitment explicitly differentiated in terms of formal qualifications should potentially reduce vertical gender segregation because of the sharp reduction in educational inequality between men and women in recent years. In general, young women have considerably enhanced their levels of formal academic qualifications to virtual parity with those of young men (Crompton and Sanderson 1987). Important variations by subject still remain, but these are not particularly relevant as far as careers in the finance sector are concerned. This increase in the level of academic qualifications has been followed by a substantial increase in levels of formal occupation-related qualifications amongst women, such as the Institute of Bankers, the Chartered Building Societies' Institute, and all of the major accountancy qualifications. The proportion of women finalists in the Institute of Bankers' examinations, for example, has risen from 2 per cent in 1970 to 27 per cent in 1988.

However, the explicit segmentation of the work-force between career and non-career groups has had an effect on the gender distribution of applications at the different entry points. The initial monitoring of tiered entry in Barclays demonstrated that there was little evidence of systematic gender discrimination within the different entry categories, that is, women and men are admitted in due proportion according to the categories they apply for. However, variations in the proportions of sexes making applications within different categories have resulted in a systematic gender imbalance between different grades. Thus women predominate at all levels, but, in terms of job offers, comprise just over half (54 per cent) of the ATP category, but over two-thirds (68 per cent) of Standard A and three-quarters (75 per cent) of Standard B (Crompton 1989). It is reasonable to conclude, therefore, that women will continue to constitute a majority of the 'office proletariat' in banking—although the fact that between a quarter and a third of those directly recruited into the lower grades are men is of some significance. A real change, however, seems to be in progress at the higher (ATP) recruitment levels, which has also been reflected in the proportion of women qualifying for the Institute of Bankers' examinations (Crompton and Sanderson 1986; EOC 1987). The continued recruitment of women to low-level clerical work reproduces the framework established when women were first brought into clerical work. The direct recruitment of women into higher-level, career-track positions, however, represents a clear break with the past.

The entry of women into lower-level supervision and management within the finance sector has had interesting consequences for the industry-specific qualifications offered by bodies such as the Chartered Building Societies' Institute and the Institute of Bankers. The Associateship of the CBSI is a qualification pitched at a level similar to the qualifications offered by other financial institutes—that is, it is a full 'professional' qualification. Most management trainee schemes within the industry require that the trainee should register for the CBSI examinations. The number of women registered for and taking the CBSI examinations has been increasing, but by 1983 had only reached 14 per cent of the Final pass rate—reflecting the relatively slow progress of women in the higher echelons of building societies at this time. In 1983, the CBSI launched a Certificate in Building Society Practice. No academic or age restrictions are placed on staff wishing to sit the certificate, and 'It was recognised that many students will not have studied for some time'. Four subjects must be passed during a two-year registration period. As we have seen, women are still a relatively small minority of those passing the Associateship examinations. In the case of the certificate, however, the situation is almost exactly reversed. Of 187 gaining the final certificate in June 1986, only 30 (16 per cent) were men. The certificate, it would appear, is a 'woman's qualification'.

From discussions with the Institute, it became apparent that the certificate is viewed as an ideal qualification for a clerical supervisor. It is not surprising, therefore, that it should be predominantly women who take it. Indeed, it was suggested that many women were taking the qualification in anticipation of a career-break; it would render re-entry into building society clerical work much easier. The Institute of Bankers have also recently developed a similar, lower-level qualification, the Banking Certificate (1986). Although the qualification is too recently established for long-term trends to be predicted, of the first twenty completions in 1988, fifteen were women. These developments in the area of formal qualifications, therefore, are moulded to the contours of the gender/occupational structure which has emerged within the financial sector over the last two decades. The large, complex white-collar bureaucracies, pyramidal in structure and strongly associated with an official universalist career ideology, have been replaced by segmented structures associated with multi-level recruitment and short career hierarchies (Rajan 1987). The rise of intermediate qualifications reflects this new pattern of career segmentation.

Further evidence in support of this argument can be derived from a comparison of gender, age, and grade structures in one area of 'Southbank' between 1981 and 1988. Southbank had been the subject of an intensive case-study conducted by Crompton in 1981, and aggregate data for the same region was made available in 1988.[4]

As can be seen from Table 8.1, in 1988 a majority of women are still located in the lowest clerical grades, but the increase in the proportion of women on senior clerical grades is quite striking—from 8 to 26 per cent. Indeed, because of the predominance of women within the industry as a whole, there are now more women (174) on senior clerical grades than men (117). Table 8.1, however, does not enable us to distinguish between two rather different processes. These are, first, the consolidation of largely female clerical hierarchies, with senior clerical female supervisors (i.e. a situation similar to that prevailing within the Building Society industry), and second, the penetration of the managerial grades by women (i.e. Appointed Officer and above). It is of

TABLE 8.1 *Gender and grade structures 'Southbank', 1981 and 1988* (%)

	1981 (sample of employees)			1988 (all employees)		
	Men	Women	Total	Men	Women	Total
Appointed officer and above	43	0	19	43	3	19
Clerical 3 and 4	26	8	16	26	26	26
Clerical 1 and 2	31	92	65	31	71	55
Total	100	100	100	100	100	100
N	90	113	203	460	674	1,134

Source: see n. 4.

some interest to note that whereas the proportion of women in senior clerical jobs has increased between 1981 and 1988, the proportion in managerial grades appears to have barely changed. The question is, therefore, how many of the women on clerical grades 3 and 4 have reached the limit of their careers, and how many may yet move into Appointed Officer grades?

Some insights may be gained from more detailed age and grade breakdowns. Census data for 1981 suggests that the banking and finance industries were still relying mainly on young female labour in the early 1980s; 57 per cent of female clerks in banking and finance were under 25 years of age, as compared to 33 per cent of all female clerks (Crompton 1988). The data for 'Southbank' suggested an even greater concentration of young women, as 74 per cent were under 25 in 1981 (Crompton and Jones 1984). The 1988 regional figures show that the age structure has shifted upwards (to 63 per cent of women aged under 25 in 1988). A comparison of age/grade data for 1981 and 1988 suggests earlier promotion to senior clerical grades (26 per cent of men on grades 3 and 4 were aged 20–5 in 1981, but 34 per cent in 1988), and the 'make or break' age as far as promotion is concerned seems to have fallen to 30. It seems reasonable to suppose, therefore, that women over 35 on clerical grades 3 and 4 (14 per cent) will be unlikely to progress much further. It is probable that many of the women on grades 3 and 4 (16 per cent) in the 30–5 age group have also reached their peak, but it is as yet too early to be certain.

THE ROLE OF EQUAL OPPORTUNITIES LEGISLATION

The extended participation of women in paid employment has been recognized and developed by bank employers. The knowledge and experience of female clerks is no longer entirely trapped in frustrating, dead-end jobs; rather, women can now aspire realistically to middle-level supervisory positions without having to follow through the prerequisites of a career modelled on linear, male, 'breadwinner' experience. It may also be suggested that the policies of the Conservative government, which have sought to establish a 'people's capitalism', directed at the small and often first-time investor, has further enhanced the employment opportunities of experienced female clerks. Such women will reassure, rather than threaten, the inexperienced investor. Sales campaigns emphasize the helpful and non-aggressive (in short, feminine) qualities of these women. In the 1950s, 1960s, and even into the 1970s, the emphasis was on women as skilled machine operators, or more generally as routine clerical labour. Their profile has now shifted to that of an intelligent resource—although this should not be allowed to obscure the fact that the majority of clerical drudges will still be women.

However, it would be misleading to suggest that employers have simply adapted their practices to take advantage of the changing nature of the female labour-force. This would obscure the fact that considerable pressure has been brought to bear on them to change their employment policies. The most striking evidence of this pressure is to be found in the higher levels of employment within the finance sector, occupations which were once entirely the preserve of men. Even after a notional equality of opportunity had been achieved (and it should be remembered that even formal legislation did not reach the statute book until 1970 and 1976), women were still kept out of higher-level occupations by a variety of strategies including direct male exclusionary practices (Collinson and Knights 1986), as well as indirect mechanisms such as requirements for unbroken work experience, or formal, work-related qualifications, which women found difficult to achieve. Although sex equality legislation has many flaws and has only been weakly supported by government, it nevertheless renders both direct and indirect exclusionary strategies problematic. It has also contributed to what may be described as an 'opportunity climate' as far as younger women are concerned, encouraging them to acquire the appropriate levels of qualification for a career in banking and finance. Although it cannot be automatically assumed that qualifications will be matched to jobs, nevertheless, the 'qualifications lever' is a central element in the liberal feminist strategy of gaining equality of treatment and opportunity for individual women. It is significant that the two major EOC investigations in the finance sector (into the Leeds Permanent Building Society and Barclays Bank) have both used comparative levels of academic and professional qualifications as major points of reference.

All of the clearing banks are now concerned to emphasize equal

opportunities: 'We all take equal opportunities very seriously . . .
I bang the drum for equal opportunities in all my school talks.
We still have to live down the "Captain Mainwaring" days when
the banks were very stuffy institutions. In my last office, I think
you would have found that 50 per cent of those getting
Appointed Officer grades were women' (Personnel Manager,
'Southbank'). Part of the explanation of the banks' conversion to
equal opportunities, it may be argued, lies in the fact that the
looming shortage of school-leavers—the banks' traditional recruitment pool—has led to a renewed emphasis on the need to attract
women, including 'job changers'—i.e. older women. It is felt that
an equal opportunities policy will enhance the banks' attraction as
an employer. Nevertheless, tiered entry was not actually introduced by the major clearers until 1986–7; that is, around the time
of the Barclays referral. EOC pressure, therefore, has been very
important.

A decade earlier, the EOC investigation of the Leeds
Permanent Building Society was also instrumental in increasing
the direct entry of women into higher-level positions within the
finance sector. As with the EOC investigation of Barclays, it
focused on overtly rational, academic selection criteria. In April
1977, a woman who had been interviewed for a post as a management trainee with the Society complained that she had been
discriminated against on the grounds of her sex during the course
of the interview. The case was taken up by the Equal Opportunities Commission, who undertook a thoroughgoing investigation of the process of recruitment in the Leeds in 1978. They
found that, of the 412 women and 1,382 men who applied for
management traineeships, 58 per cent of the men who applied,
but only 39 per cent of the women were called for interview; 30
per cent of the men interviewed were offered a second interview, as
compared to 4 per cent of the women. No women were offered
jobs as management trainees as compared to 145 of the men.

The evidence gathered by the EOC provides a rich and fasci-
nating account of the processes of male exclusionary practice. In
1978, nearly 1,800 people applied for 145 management traineeships with the Leeds Permanent. Direct discrimination on the
basis of sex was illegal and universalistic criteria had to be
employed in order to sift applicants. In the case of the Leeds,
three criteria were laid down in the job advertisements: (1) age

(precise specifications varied between the 20–30 age range); (2) educational requirements (a minimum of 4 O-levels including Maths and English); and (3) a sound financial or commercial background. In respect of these characteristics there were no differences between the men and women who applied. However, women who possessed all three of the characteristics specified stood *less* chance of being offered an interview than men who had none of them. In the words of the Commission, 'since the singular lack of success of female candidates in gaining interviews and jobs could not be explained by any lack of the relevant criteria sought by the Society its Managers directly discriminated against women applicants because of their sex' (EOC 1985: 26).

The EOC investigation of the Leeds caused a considerable *frisson* within the building society industry. The case was discussed in the industry's journal, and a confidential six-page memorandum was circulated to all members of the Building Societies' Association giving advice on the consequences of the investigation—advice which included the recommendation that societies carry out their own internal investigations to ensure that direct and indirect discrimination was not taking place. These pressures towards change, however, have been comparatively recent and it would be unwise to assume that results will be immediate. Nevertheless, there have been some changes—between 1980 and 1985, for example, 65 per cent of the management trainees recruited by the Abbey National were women.

Pressure from equal opportunities legislation has thus had a general impact on the structure of employment in the finance sector and hence on the position of women in it. It drew attention to the fact that the uniportal recruitment system was discriminatory since it informally drew in two different pools of labour in terms of qualifications and subsequently sifted them into career- and non-career-track positions. This led to changes in the grading system, increasing the number of layers and in the process of recruitment—differentiated career tracks—as well as a more explicit dependence on formal qualifications as the mechanism for entry into different career structures. As we have seen in the case of the EOC investigation of the Leeds Permanent, the increased formalization of recruitment cannot prevent discrimination entirely, but it does create a lever that can be used by many women to obtain entry to higher-level positions.

CONCLUSION

Both the clearing banks and the building societies have relied upon the recruitment of specifically female labour in the conduct of their operations. However, the patterns of female labour-use characteristic of the two industries have been shaped by both the level of technology, and the characteristics of the female labour available at the historic point of recruitment, as well as the past employment practices in the two industries. In the 1960s, when the 'feminization' of banking was proceeding very rapidly, the banks were focusing on the recruitment of primarily young women as short-term employees to work first as machine operators, then as counter clerks as well. The computer batch systems prevailing at the time required a lot of routine machine work.

Indeed up to the 1960s the composition of the female labour-force in Britain as a whole was skewed in the direction of young women. The massive increase in building society employment for women, as we have seen, occurred rather later than in the banks and was closely associated with the expansion of the branch network. Given the technology available at the time of expansion as well as the nature of building society business, there would have been less emphasis upon the recruitment of machine operators, and more on the sales and public relations function. Building societies, as we have seen, owe much of their success to the growth of personal savings, and much of their business lies with the previously 'under-banked' working classes. The role of the soothing, competent, and female building society clerk is, in the late 1980s, widely featured in advertisements for the 'product'. Multi-level recruitment means that the building societies have recruited older, as well as younger, women—indeed, the presence of these older women may well have facilitated the relatively rapid consolidation of the feminized clerical hierarchy revealed in the Abbey National data cited earlier. The clearing banks too, have adapted to changes in both technology and the nature of the female labour supply, and have developed middle-level, career clerical grades in which women predominate. However, it is interesting that, although these grades reflect a rational use of female labour in that they better utilize the experience of older women clerks, it was pressure for equal opportunities which was effective in bringing them about, as is demonstrated by the consequences attendant upon the Equal Opportunities Commission's monitoring of Barclays Bank recruitment procedures.

The gendered restructuring of clerical employment in the finance sector, therefore, has been accompanied by liberal feminist pressure which has brought about real changes in women's opportunities. The predominantly female, segmented, short career clerical hierarchies which have been developed as a consequence of technical and labour market changes do not represent the taking over of 'men's jobs' by women, rather, they are new jobs. However, the penetration by women of the career managerial grades, even if so far relatively limited, does represent a feminine encroachment into what were once exclusively male preserves.

Many different factors have contributed to the restructuring of employment in the finance sector, and it would be difficult to attach causal primacy to any of them. One of the most important, however, has been technological innovation. The most immediate impact of 'computerization' was on the labour process, as clerical work at the lower levels was routinized and fragmented. It is not too fanciful to compare the impact of electronic data processing on clerical work with that of the machine revolution on skilled manual work—but the pace of change is much the greater in the twentieth century. New technology, however, has had an impact reaching far beyond that of the labour process. The 'information revolution' has facilitated the development of truly global financial markets; 'The information standard' states a leading financier, 'has replaced the gold standard as the basis of world finance; (Wriston cited in Hamilton 1986). It may be argued that the deregulation of the finance sector and the 'Big Bang' were inevitable, given these technological developments, but the political ideas of the 'new right' were not unfavourable to a strategy which broke up cartels, removed barriers to competition, and so on. The introduction of competitive market or quasi-market forces has permeated to all levels—in 'Southbank', for example, bank managers are now paid (in part) by results, on a performance-related bonus related to the level of branch profits.[5]

These changes in both the nature and extent of labour required within the finance sector have been taking place during a period in which, it may be argued, gender relations were also in the process of a profound restructuring. The increase in the proportion of married women going 'out to work' and the growth of 'second wave' feminism were almost simultaneous. Thus whereas a young woman starting work in a bank at the beginning of the 1960s would have encountered the remnants of the marriage bar, separate pay scales for men and women after the age of 23, as well as separate grades for men and women, her daughter would have entered into a very different employment situation in the 1980s and with a different set of expectations.

Management's use of female labour has, to a considerable extent, changed in accordance with these expectations. Although it may be argued that employers often create employment opportunities which serve to reproduce the subordinate position of women in society—this has been forcefully argued, for example, in respect of part-time work in Britain by Beechey and Perkins (1987) and Walby (1986)—employers also respond actively to changes in the nature of gender relations, as well as to more overt constraints such as equality legislation. Thus the jobs offered to the first generation of married 'returners' in the 1950s and 1960s tended to reflect the characteristics of the then returning female white-collar labour-force. Such women had little in the way of formal academic or job-related qualifications (excepting secretarial qualifications) and extended breaks in formal employment. These women joined their younger sisters in the clerical jobs then available which, in the early stages of mechanization and computerization, were often in routine, deskilled clerical tasks (this element is caught, in a somewhat extreme fashion, by the rise and fall of the data preparation operator or 'punch room girl'; an occupation that bloomed and died in approximately fifteen years).

However, education and employment statistics suggest that, particularly since the mid-1970s, the 'human capital' of the female labour-force has been improving rapidly. Women are gaining more relevant qualifications, staying in paid employment for longer, and so on. In the preceding discussion, it has been suggested that the 'late development' of the building society industry in the 1970s (i.e. expansion/branching in a protected market position, with the capacity to take advantage of the most recent technological innovations) meant that they were able to adapt very quickly to these changes in the nature of the female labour-force. Thus segmented, relatively short, feminized 'career clerical' hierarchies developed earlier in building societies than in the banks, the latter being hampered by a history of employment practices relating to the male clerical 'career'.

Changes in the employers' use of female labour, therefore, have reflected adjustments to the nature of the female labour supply. Women still perform deskilled clerical work, but the increased emphasis on marketing which is characteristic of the finance sector at all levels has led to an emphasis on selling and customer care—and women are considered particularly appropriate as far as the latter activity is concerned. Together with these shifts in the nature of clerical work, the enhanced work experience and qualification levels of the female clerk have resulted in the creation of segmented, largely female clerical hierarchies, within which supervision is also carried out by women. Such supervisory positions correspond to the lower- to middle-level 'management' positions which in the past were more usually occupied by men working their way up through the bureaucratic hierarchy.

The fact that this relative upgrading of the structure of 'women's clerical employment in the finance sector was occurring at a time when equality of opportunities for the sexes had a high social and political profile is not irrelevant.[6] However, the most visible impact of equality legislation has been in respect of higher-level managerial positions. The fact that women have historically been excluded from such positions has been well established (Dohrn 1988). As we have seen from our discussion of EOC investigations in the Leeds Permanent and Barclays, direct male exclusionary practices at the point of recruitment were obviously crucial in keeping women out of the higher levels of internal labour markets in the finance sector up until the end of the 1970s and into the 1980s, and conversely, liberal feminist pressures have been very important in breaking them down. (Although it can be argued that the ideology of bourgeois liberalism has from the first included elements which contained a threat to male hegemony (Connell 1987), it would be unwise to assume that a 'natural' withering of patriarchal structures would inevitably follow in the absence of feminist pressure.)

This chapter has shown that patterns of gender segregation are not as stable and immutable as aggregated data might suggest.

The continued feminization of employment within these two industries, and the persisting concentration of women in the lower clerical grades within them belies a number of industry-specific differences in employment and changes over time. The challenge of any analysis of gender segregation is to detect the changes within continuity, and to disentangle the interplay of sociological and economic as well as micro- and macro-level factors. We have seen in this chapter that micro-level differences between the clearing banks and the building society industry were in part the product of specific patterns of recruitment and promotion within organizations, but they also reflected wider processes such as the changing female labour supply, equal opportunities legislation, and differing market conditions. Cultural/ideological factors such as gender stereotypes, service ideologies, and the prevailing economic ethos (free market competition) also played a role. Recent changes in the position of women in society, and in the corresponding structures of gender relations, have served to enhance their legal status, heighten perceptions of unequal opportunities, and change attitudes—particularly amongst younger women. These are reflected in the increase in the level of formal qualifications amongst women, their greater participation in paid employment, and their enhanced aspirations. Thus increased numbers of women are now occupying promoted positions within the financial sector. Nevertheless, the recent history of patriarchal exclusionary practices, together with the persistence of traditional or customary socio-cultural differences also serve to reproduce the lower-level participation of women within the occupational structure. This chapter has shown that in the finance sector this is in part a consequence of the feminization of newly created occupations (i.e. the reproduction of a modified form of occupational sex-typing). It also arises because for many women, their entry into the labour market continues to be shaped by assumptions about the likely future balance between home and employment—thus women apply for lower-level clerical jobs, men for higher level. However, writing in 1991, we may be cautiously optimistic that one of the most significant elements contributing to gender segregation within the finance sector—the systematic exclusion of women by men from access to the better jobs within the industry—has become more difficult to carry out.

NOTES

1. The particular nature of collective representation in banking was the major focus of sociological interest in the industry through the 1960s and 1970s. The Bank Officers' Guild—which became the National Union of Bank Employees (NUBE), then the Banking, Insurance, and Finance Union (BIFU)—although a moderate institution in trade union terms, was from its foundation in 1917–18 registered as a trade union. Trade unionism in banking faced immediate competition from the Staff Associations created in the individual clearing banks. These internal bodies were supported and recognized by the employers, and the system of collective representation which emerged has been described by Blackburn (1967: 148): 'the banks were opposed to the union, refusing recognition and supporting internal Staff Associations. The Staff Associations were subsidised by the banks, three in the major banks having no subscriptions and the other three charging only nominal subscriptions, and they were largely under the bank's control. They opposed the BOG on behalf of the employers, so that a relationship of hostile competition between Staff Associations and the Union developed.'

2. Three different Building Societies provided information. The Abbey National allowed access to aggregate-level data, and some interviews with management. The 'Holyoake Permanent' allowed interviews at branch level, but aggregate data was not available. The 'Regional Plus' allowed interviews at branch and managerial level. All quotes in this chapter are taken from interview transcripts and/or notes. We would like to thank all three Building Societies for their co-operation. (The 'Regional Plus' and the 'Holyoake Permanent' preferred not to be identified.)

3. In 1985 the Equal Opportunities Commission signed an agreement with Barclays Bank plc 'to ensure that there were no practices or arrangements in the recruitment procedures employed by the Bank which would contravene the employment provisions of the Sex Discrimination Act 1975 and to thereby promote equal opportunities within the Bank' (EOC, 1987). Following this agreement, the Commission deferred its proposal to conduct a formal investigation into the Bank. Monitoring since the agreement has revealed that there is no longer any statistical evidence of sex discrimination at recruitment within the Bank.

4. We would like to thank 'Southbank' for making this information available. During the research in 1981, we were not given access to aggregate-level data (Crompton and Jones 1984). The 1981 data, therefore, was gathered from self-completion questionnaires which

were sent to all employees in thirteen different branches, which had been selected as providing examples of the whole range of branches in the region. (The response rate was 75%.) The 1988 data gives information for the region as a whole. The geographical boundaries of the region have been extended, but in the main they remain as they were in 1981. Table 8.1, therefore, compares a sample of bank employees in 1981 with the data for the whole region in 1988. Besides information on gender and grade, information was also provided on age structure and numbers qualifying for the IOB examinations.

5. It may be suggested that the enhanced capacity for monitoring such employees is an important factor changing the nature of their employment relationship. This aspect is relevant to the continuing debate on the 'service class' (Savage *et al.* 1988).

6. It should be noted that the upgrading of the *structure* of clerical opportunities for women is compatible with an actual increase in the number of routine clerical positions. It should also be noted that many women in white-collar jobs deemed to be 'unskilled' in fact carry out complex and demanding tasks. See Crompton and Jones 1984, ch. 4.

REFERENCES

ASHBURNER, L. (1987), 'The Effects of New Technology on Employment Structures in the Service Sector'. Ph.D., University of Aston, Birmingham.

BEECHEY, V., and PERKINS, T. (1987), *A Matter of Hours: Women, Part-Time Work and the Labour Market*. Cambridge, Polity.

BLACKBURN, R. M. (1967), *Union Character and Social Class*. London, Batsford.

BOLÉAT, M. (1982), *The Building Society Industry*. London, George Allen & Unwin.

—— (1987), 'Building Societies: The New Supervisory Framework', *National Westminster Bank Quarterly Review*, Aug.: 116–25.

COLLINSON, D., and KNIGHTS, D. (1986), '"Men Only": Theories and Practices of Job Segregation in Insurance', in D. Knights and D. Collinson (eds.), *Gender and the Labour Process*. London, Macmillan.

CONNELL, R. W. (1987), *Gender and Power*. Cambridge, Polity.

CROMPTON, R. (1988), 'The Feminisation of Clerical Work Since the Second World War', in G. Anderson (ed.), *The White Blouse Revolution*. Manchester, Manchester University Press.

—— (1989), 'Women in Banking', *Work, Employment and Society*, 3/2: 141–56.

300   R. Crompton and K. Sanderson

CROMPTON, R. and JONES, G. (1984), *White-Collar Proletariat*. London, Macmillan.

—— and SANDERSON, K. (1986), 'Credentials and Careers: Some Implications of the Increase in Professional Qualifications amongst Women', *Sociology*, 20/1, Feb.: 25–42.

—— —— (1987), 'Where Did All the Bright Girls Go?', *Quarterly Journal of Social Affairs*, Apr.: 135–47.

DAVIES, G. (1981), *Building Societies and their Branches: A Regional Economic Survey*. London, Franey.

DOHRN, S. (1988), 'Pioneers in a Dead-End Profession: The First Women Clerks in Banks and Insurance Companies', in G. Anderson (ed.), *The White Blouse Revolution*. Manchester, Manchester University Press.

EOC (1985), *Formal Investigation Report: Leeds Permanent Building Society*. Manchester, Equal Opportunities Commission.

—— (1987), 'Interim Report of the Commission's Agreement with Barclays Bank plc'. Manchester, Equal Opportunities Commission.

GOODHART, C. A. E. (1987), 'The Economies of the "Big Bang"', *Midland Bank Review*, Summer: 63–75.

HAMILTON, A. (1986), *The Financial Revolution*. Harmondsworth, Penguin.

HERITAGE, J. (1983), 'Feminisation and Unionisation: A Case Study from Banking', in E. Gamarnikow (ed.), *Gender, Class and Work*. London, Heinemann.

Industrial Relations Review and Report (IRRR) (1985), 356, Nov.: 9–11.

KRECKEL, R. (1980), 'Unequal Opportunity Structure and Labour Market Segmentation', *Sociology*, 14: 525–50.

LLEWELLYN, C. (1981), 'Occupational Mobility and the Use of the Comparative Method', in H. Roberts (ed.), *Doing Feminist Research*. London, Routledge.

LOCKWOOD, D. (1958), *The Blackcoated Worker*. London, George Allen & Unwin.

National Board for Prices and Incomes (NBPI) (1965), Report No. 6, 'Salaries of Midland Bank Staff', Cmnd. 2839, Nov.

RAJAN, A. (1987), *Services: The Second Industrial Revolution?* London, Butterworth.

SAVAGE, M., DICKENS, P., and FIELDING, T. (1988), 'Some Social and Political Implications of the Contemporary Fragmentation of the "Service Class" in Britain', *International Journal of Urban and Regional Research*, 12/3: 455–75.

WALBY, S. (1986), *Patriarchy at Work*. Cambridge, Polity.

9

Gender, Technology, and Employment Change in Textiles

ROGER PENN, ANN MARTIN,
AND HILDA SCATTERGOOD

The textile industry is of particular interest for the debate about gender and employment since historically it was the engine of British industrialization in the period between 1780 and 1914 and has long been a major employer of female labour (Turner 1962, Penn 1985). Indeed, in many ways the textile industry represents the classic example of the relationship between industrialization and female employment (Hartmann 1976, Lown 1983, Lewis 1984, Rose 1986).

This chapter focuses upon the relationship between employment change and gender relations in the British textile industry since 1971. The empirical data are based upon Rochdale, a town in south-eastern Lancashire which has been a major textile-producing centre since the 1830s. Rochdale developed in the early nineteenth century as both a woollen and cotton manufacturing town, but after the mid-nineteenth century the woollen industry collapsed and by 1901 it had become one of the largest cotton manufacturing centres in the world. (For an extended analysis of this period see Penn 1985.) The manufacture of cotton provided large numbers of jobs for women in Rochdale throughout the period between 1881 and 1961. In fact for most of this period the textile work-force was around two-thirds female. The dominance of textile employment in Rochdale has produced a particular kind of local economy and a distinctive local social structure.

An earlier version of this chapter appeared in *Sociology*, 25/4: 569–87. We would like to thank Richard Davies and Alison Scott for their comments, and Brian Francis and David Dawkins for their help with the graphical representations in the chapter.

Economic activity rates for women in Rochdale have long been disproportionately high when compared with other towns in the north-west of England and with towns in other regions of Britain (Warde 1986: 57). The 'modern' pattern of women in paid employment has been a 'traditional' feature of economic and social life in the town. Indeed, there has been a long-standing expectation, amongst both women and men, that women will engage in paid employment, on both a full-time and a part-time basis.

The effects of these economic and cultural structures can be seen in a variety of contexts. Rochdale has been a centre of the fast-food industry for at least a century. Indeed, the industry was invented in the Lancashire cotton towns. Fish and chips predate McDonald's and Pizzahut by a century or more. Home ownership has also been a marked feature of local life since the latter part of the nineteenth century (see Clarke 1971 for the putative political effects of this feature of the Lancashire textile towns). Similarly, Rochdale has long been the centre of a dynamic holiday transport industry, catering for the high family incomes that derived from dual-earner and multi-earner households in the town. The 'Yelloway' bus company was headquartered in Rochdale and provided an extensive network of holiday transport to Torquay, Clacton, and, of course, to the popular holiday resort—Blackpool.

Since 1961, however, there has been a massive restructuring of employment in textiles. This has involved a dramatic reduction in the total numbers employed in the industry, the virtual abolition of part-time employment, and a progressive 'masculinization' of the remaining work-force. In 1961 67 per cent of textile employees in Rochdale were women, but by 1987 the proportion had fallen to almost 30 per cent. This chapter involves an examination of recent developments in female employment in the textile industry in Rochdale since 1971 and an analysis of the major changes in these patterns over the period.

PATTERNS OF EMPLOYMENT CHANGE IN THE TEXTILE INDUSTRY

It is clear from Figure 9.1 that textile employment in Great Britain has fallen sharply over the last twenty years. The data are

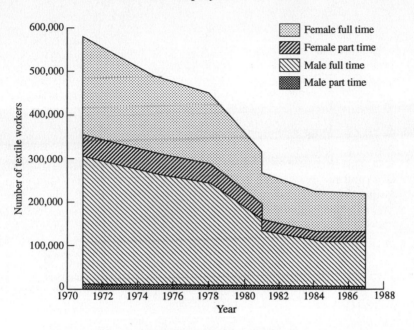

Source: Censuses of Employment 1971, 1975, 1978, 1981, 1984, 1987.

Fig. 9.1 Textile employment in Great Britain 1971–1987

taken from the Department of Employment's Censuses of Employment between 1971 and 1987.[1] Two figures were entered for 1981 to allow for a revision to the Standard Industrial Classification introduced in 1980.[2] Overall, the number of textile employees in Britain fell by almost 50 per cent between 1971 and 1987. The pattern of employment decline is similar in north-west England, which has been the historic centre of cotton textiles in Britain. The degree of fall was somewhat sharper than the national average and there is some evidence of a small resurgence in textile employment within the region between 1984 and 1987. Nevertheless, the contours of employment decline are broadly the same in the north-west region as within Britain as a whole. Figure 9.2 reveals a similar story for Rochdale. The decline in overall textile employment is, nevertheless, sharper in the town, involving a loss of around 75 per cent of total textile employment between 1971 and 1987. It is also clear that, unlike the regional

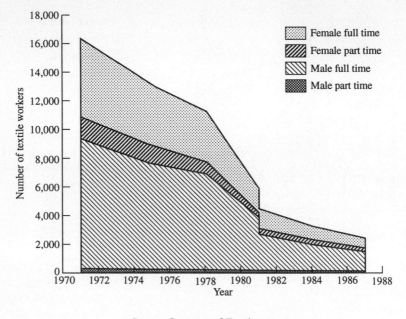

Source: Censuses of Employment

Fig. 9.2 Textile employment in Rochdale 1971–1987

data, there has been no reversal of this trend during the 1980s, merely a reduction in the rate of decline.

The data for Great Britain include the cotton, woollen, and hosiery industries, whereas the Rochdale data are overwhelmingly based on cotton manufacture and, latterly, on the production of those man-made fibres that have increasingly come to be mixed with cotton in much contemporary manufacturing. The Rochdale data, therefore, can be taken as representative of changes in the cotton industry in north-west England but not of the entire range of textile activities in Britain.

The reduction in Rochdale's textile employment has been dramatic. In 1971 there were around 16,000 men and women in the industry, but by 1987 the figure was less than 3,000. Whereas in 1971 textiles were 38 per cent of total employment in the town, by 1987 they comprised only 7 per cent. Although textile employment has been contracting throughout the twentieth century, the post-1970s fall was unprecedented. Neither the Great Depression of the 1930s nor the post-Second World War slump after 1952 witnessed such a dramatic transformation in the pattern of employment in the town. Between 1978 and 1982 43 per cent of employees in textiles were made redundant.[3] This involved the closure of thirty-eight plants in Rochdale, including such historic firms as Courtaulds and John Bright. In the period between 1981 and 1987 textile employment fell by a further 42 per cent and in 1986 one of Rochdale's two largest remaining textile-related employers made one-third of its work-force redundant.

Changes in the composition of textile employment in terms of gender and the balance between full- and part-time work have to be seen against this background of falling employment in the industry. Figure 9.2 shows that textile work was always primarily full time, but part-time work has now virtually disappeared. It also shows that the reduction in female employment has been sharper than that for male employment. This trend had already begun prior to the 1970s, so that by 1971 women were no longer a majority of the work-force, and their more than proportionate fall in employment was particularly marked during the rest of the 1970s. In the period between 1981 and 1987 women's full-time employment fell by 51 per cent while men's fell by 39 per cent. In addition, women's already small amount of part-time work fell by 49 per cent.

As a result of these differential rates of employment decline, men's share of textile employment has gradually increased. Figures 9.3 and 9.4 show that this process of 'masculinization' has been more pronounced in Rochdale than elsewhere. Thus Rochdale has undergone a more dramatic shift in the gender composition of employment in recent years and, as such, constitutes an ideal locality within which to examine these processes in detail.

These developments within the textile industry are in marked contrast to the general pattern of employment in the town during the 1970s and 1980s, which has seen an increase in part-time work and a rise in the female share of total employment. Between 1981 and 1987 overall employment rose by 2.5 per cent, but most of this growth consisted of increases in female full-time employment, since male full-time and female part-time employment fell during this period. It is thus a paradox that, whilst

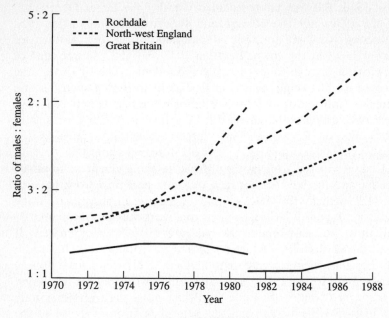

Source: Censuses of Employment.
Fig. 9.3 The changing gender ratio of textile employment 1971–1987
(all employees)

employment in Rochdale has generally become more feminized
and part-time since 1971, the major industry that traditionally
provided large amounts of female full-time and part-time work
has progressively ceased to do so. This conundrum forms the
basis of the subsequent analysis reported here.

HYPOTHESES CONCERNING RECENT CHANGES IN THE GENDER COMPOSITION OF TEXTILE EMPLOYMENT

Four sets of factors have been identified as significant in the
changing pattern of gendered employment in the British textile
industry. These are technology and skill, subsectors of textile
employment, hours of work, and competition from emergent

industries. In addition, it has been suggested that there is a traditional pattern of gender differentiation within textile employment
that has interacted with these factors. These hypotheses are outlined below and subsequently examined in relation to the
Rochdale data.

Technological change, skill, and gender

It has been argued, both in the United States and in Great
Britain, that technological change in the modern textile industry
has produced increasingly skilled jobs (Bureau of Labor Statistics
1974, Harwood 1985, Penn and Leiter 1991). This can be seen as
an elaboration of the traditional skilling thesis associated with
human capital theory (Penn and Scattergood 1985). Skilled manual jobs in textiles have traditionally been the preserve of male
workers as a result of their exclusive access to the 'ports of entry'
into such work (Kerr 1954, Penn 1985).

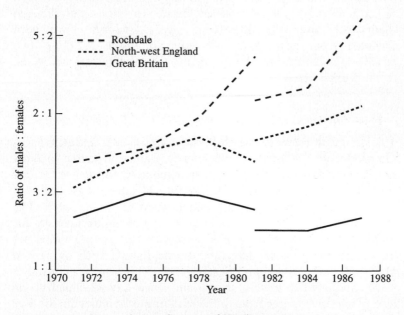

Source: Censuses of Employment.

Fig. 9.4 The changing gender ratio of textile employment 1971–1987
(full-time employees only)

There are three types of skilled manual work in textiles. These are general machine maintenance crafts like electricians and fitters, specialist production workers like mule spinners, tapesizers, and beamers, and specialist maintenance workers such as overlookers and strippers-and-grinders. Access to general machine and specialist machine skilled work is via apprenticeships which have been restricted traditionally to men, whereas entry into specialist production skills is conditional upon movement up a lengthy internal career ladder. These latter kinds of work have also been dominated by male workers historically (Turner 1962, Penn 1985).

The technological argument as it pertains to changes in the contemporary gender balance of textile employment hinges on two sets of interrelated processes. First, it is claimed that there is a general tendency for existing skilled work to become more skilled with the introduction of new technologies, particularly those associated with micro-electronics. Secondly, it is contended that, since traditional patterns of gender segregation between skilled male work and non-skilled female work have not changed significantly over the last twenty years, women have been excluded from new skills. The overall effect of these two processes is, therefore, the progressive 'masculinization' of the textile work-force.

Subsectoral change: consumer versus industrial textiles

This argument refers to the shift from consumer to industrial textile production[4] in Britain. Historically, industrial textile production has been far more 'male' proportionately and hence, as this subsectoral, industrial shift has occurred, there has been an increasing tendency for textile employment to favour men. The reasons for this shift are a function of the changing markets for textile products in Britain. The aerospace and vehicle industries increasingly require sophisticated textile imputs such as carbon fibres and kevlar (Penn and Scattergood 1987), whereas consumer textile markets like towels, sheets, and shirts have declined in the face of cheap imports from industrializing economies in the Far East (Lloyd and Shutt 1983). In the context of Rochdale, this would suggest that since industrial textile production has survived better than the consumer textile sector, *ceteris paribus*, overall employment within textiles in the town will have become proportionately more male. Rochdale has long been a centre for the manufacture of industrial textiles (Penn and Scattergood 1987) and is, therefore, an excellent locality within which to examine these hypotheses in detail.

A further argument suggests that there is an interaction between the asymmetries of subsectoral survival and the rate of technical change. In other words, it is more likely that technical change will have occurred in the industrial textile sector since it has been more buoyant economically and, all things being equal, this will compound the overall 'masculinization' of textile employment.

Hours of work: the demise of flexibility

It has been suggested that hours of employment in textiles have become increasingly inflexible and hence decreasingly attractive to women workers who have domestic commitments that preclude certain forms of shiftwork. This is in marked contrast to traditional forms of textile employment, which involved a range of flexible shifts that could accommodate women workers' domestic and familial ties. The argument runs counter to the currently fashionable theories of 'flexibility' (Atkinson and Meager 1986), which suggest that there is a universal and economically rational process of increasing flexibility in the hours of paid work in contemporary Britain.

Competition from new industries: the rise of the service sector

The argument here is that women increasingly prefer paid work in shops or offices rather than in factories. Such service sector jobs have expanded rapidly in Rochdale since the mid-1960s. This is partly due to the expansion of employment in health, education, and welfare, but is also related to the rapid rise of Rochdale as a major distributional centre with its central position on the motorway network built in the 1960s. This argument suggests both that older women left textiles for these other forms of employment during the 1970s and that younger women entering the labour market tend to enter the service sector rather than textiles. The combination of these two patterns has generated an increasing tendency for overall textile employment to become male. This hypothesis also relates closely to the previous one in that a reason for the attraction of service work is the presence of more flexible hours, especially part-time work, compared with textile employment.

SOURCES OF DATA

Traditional patterns of gender differentiation in textiles can be assessed using a variety of data. As we have seen, recent Censuses of Employment provide evidence on aggregate patterns of gender employment within textiles. Questions about technological change and sectors of textile employment, on the other hand, can only be assessed by intensive case-studies since there are no aggregate data available in Britain on either of these topics. The SCELI data can illuminate these processes in a variety of ways. As part of a related study on textile and engineering firms, the Lancaster team administered a postal questionnaire to textile employers in Rochdale in 1986 which ascertained changing numbers in employment since 1980 and rates of technical change within such establishments. This was supplemented by intensive interviews at selected firms between 1986 and 1989 with managers, work-force representatives, and employees about changing forms of employment and the factors that have influenced these developments. Our temporal frame of reference in the postal survey was changes in employment between 1980 and 1986 since, in our judgement, to go further back in time would have greatly reduced both the reliability and validity of the data. In our employer case-studies we were able to adopt a rather longer chronology (Penn and Scattergood 1987). The textile questionnaires were sent out in the summer of 1986. The twenty-two textile firms that responded included all textile firms with fifty or more people in 1980 and covered approximately 85 per cent of all textile employment in Rochdale at the time of the survey.[5]

Finally, the data collected on the work histories of 987 adults as part of the SCELI Work Attitudes and Work Histories Survey provide information on how individuals have moved through the changing economic structure, thus helping to assess the validity of the various hypotheses concerning competition from new industries and changes in the patterns of hours worked outlined above.

ASSESSMENT OF HYPOTHESES ABOUT THE
CHANGING GENDER COMPOSITION OF TEXTILE
EMPLOYMENT IN ROCHDALE 1980–1986

Technological change, skill, and gender

We have data on twenty-two textile firms in Rochdale. These data cover 4,768 employees in 1980 and 3,273 in 1986. This involves a fall in employment within the textile plants in our survey of 31.4 per cent. Clearly these data are broadly similar to those from the Census of Employment portrayed in Figure 9.2.

The postal survey did indicate a tendency for employment to become proportionately more male (Table 9.1). In only one firm did the proportion of female workers increase by more than 10 per cent, whereas the proportion of men increased by more than 10 per cent in nine out of the twenty-two firms. However, it should be noted that the intermediate category where gender composition was constant was actually the largest, in terms of both the number of firms and the proportion of the work-force. This suggests that part of the decline in female employment in textiles may have been due to plant closures, rather than to changes within firms.

TABLE 9.1 *The changing gender composition of textile work between 1980 and 1986 and the implementation of micro-electronic technologies*

Change in the proportion of men in the work-force 1980–6	New technology implemented 1980–6		
	Present	Absent	Total
Decreasing	0 (0)	1 (87)	1 (87)
Constant	2 (1,246)	10 (764)	12 (2,010)
Increasing	5 (830)	4 (346)	9 (1,176)
Total	7 (2,076)	15 (1,197)	22 (3,273)

Note: Numbers refer to plants, numbers in brackets refer to employees in these plants in 1986. 'Increasing' and 'Decreasing' refer to changes in the proportion of men greater than 10% between 1980 and 1986.

Source: Social Change and Economic Life Initiative (SCELI) Rochdale Textile and Engineering Survey.

As far as technological change is concerned, the fact that this had been introduced in only a third of the firms during the period is of some note. In these firms there was increased masculinization, while, on the other hand, amongst the firms that had had no new technology there was an overwhelming tendency for the gender balance to remain constant. (We should also note that there were a minority of firms whose male–female ratios were increasing despite a lack of technological change. Clearly other factors were also at play in these changes.) Nevertheless there was considerable evidence of a positive association between masculinization and technical change. This relationship was more marked in terms of numbers of employees than the number of plants, suggesting that gender changes in employment were concentrated in larger-sized textile plants in Rochdale.

The changing gender composition of employment was neither associated with whether the firm was a subsidiary of a larger firm nor with whether overall employment in the firm had contracted or expanded. Nor was it related to whether or not a firm recognized trade unions within its plant.

There are various ways of assessing whether textile employment has become more skilled. One measure is based on the proportion of skilled workers within the manual work-force, another is based on the proportion of skilled workers within the total work-force. A third measure refers to changes in job content within existing skill categories. From Table 9.2 it is evident that there was no marked increase in the skill levels of the total textile labour-force between 1980 and 1986.

However, there was evidence that skilled workers were an increasing proportion of the manual work-force. This may have been because non-skilled (i.e. semi- and unskilled) manual employment—the traditional area of female labour—experienced the sharpest reduction in employment during this period. These changes were independent of the introduction of new forms of technology over this period. Seven of the firms had introduced micro-electronic technologies,[6] but there was no evidence to suggest a significant relationship between technical change and the changing proportion of skilled manual workers in the industry.

Nevertheless, it is still possible that textile jobs have become more skilled independently of changes in occupational structure. There was considerable evidence from both the postal survey and

TABLE 9.2 *The changing proportion of skilled textile workers 1980–1986*

Change in the proportion of skilled workers	Within the manual work-force		Within total work-force	
	Firms	Employees[a]	Firms	Employees[a]
Decreasing	4	300	5	285
Constant	8	1,086	10	2,460
Increasing	7	1,749	4	390
Total	19	3,135	19	3,135

[a] The subtotals of employees differ between the manual and total work-forces because it was not possible to calculate the skilled ratios in several plants which had either no skilled or no non-skilled workers.

Source: SCELI Rochdale Textile and Engineering Survey.

the case-studies that skilled textile work was becoming *more* skilled in its content. One-third of the firms in the postal survey thought that the skills of overlookers, technicians, and maintenance electricians had increased. None felt that they had decreased. This corresponded with the views expressed to us by trade union officials and employees. Indeed, there had been considerable retraining of skilled workers within the Rochdale textile plants surveyed, mostly provided by machinery suppliers in the plants themselves or on specialist training courses conducted away from the plants. However, there was no evidence that non-skilled work was becoming more skilled. Rather, there was evidence of an increasing bifurcation of the manual work-force around the traditional axis of skill.

The hypothesis concerning the relationship between technology and skill outlined earlier suggested two propositions about the relationship of these factors to gender. First, it was argued that work was becoming more skilled in content, and secondly that women fail to gain access to skilled occupations. There was no strong evidence to support the view that the proportion of skilled workers in total employment was increasing dramatically, but there was evidence that existing skilled occupations, particularly those requiring apprenticeships, were becoming more skilled. There is no doubt that women continue to be excluded from apprenticeship programmes and therefore from entry into much skilled work in Rochdale. Our research into the provision of apprentice training in Rochdale has revealed a persistent and marked absence of female apprentices (Scattergood 1986, Bragg 1987). This is in line with the wider pattern in Britain and compares unfavourably with the United States of America (Penn 1990).

The reasons for this pattern are complex, but centre around two features of industrial life. Few 16-year-old girls are attracted to apprenticeships in Rochdale (see Penn and Scattergood 1991). Apprenticeships fail to conform to their ideals of paid work. In a separate survey of 15- and 16-year-olds in Rochdale we encountered a strongly negative view of traditional manual labour, particularly in factories. These images contain stereotypes of dirt, lewd humour, and hard physical effort. Such orientations interact with very powerful traditions of exclusion, particularly amongst the male textile crafts. Occupations like overlookers, tapesizers, and twisters and drawers all decide collectively on the suitability of managerial candidates for apprenticeships (Penn 1985, 1990). These groups are deeply conservative and have a strong predisposition to accept male members (Penn 1988). Management are not greatly interested in the problem, preferring rather to 'let sleeping dogs lie' in order to avoid major confrontations on the shopfloor.

Nevertheless, whilst there is a strong relationship between technology, skill, and the preservation of male domination of these areas of work, such factors can only explain the continuity of male skilled employment. Given that this has not expanded dramatically as a type of work within textile plants, this argument cannot explain why textile work in general is becoming less female in composition.

Subsectoral change: consumer versus industrial textiles

The argument concerning subsectoral change was that there had been a relative shift from consumer to industrial textile employment in Rochdale. Given that industrial textiles traditionally have been proportionately more 'male' in composition,[7] this is held to have generated an increasing masculinization of overall textile employment.

There was some evidence of a positive relationship between the subsector of textile production and the changing gender balance (Table 9.3). However, the relationship was not as suggested by the above hypothesis. Rather, the evidence suggested a stronger tendency for employment to become more male within *consumer* textile plants. Of the twelve firms that can be identified as either consumer or industrial textiles manufacturers, there is a far greater likelihood for consumer textile firms to become more male. The same holds true for the relationship between subsectoral employment and the increase in full-time work. This has expanded more in consumer textiles than in industrial textiles plants. We can conclude, therefore, that the specific subsector of textile production is not a critical factor in the growing masculinization of textile employment in contemporary Rochdale. Indeed, the evidence was of an increasing similarity of patterns of gender and employment in all kinds of textile plants in Rochdale. Consumer textile employment has converged with the traditional pattern of male dominance in industrial textiles.

TABLE 9.3 *Changing gender composition of work between 1980 and 1986 and the subsector of textile production in 1986*

Change in the proportion of men in the work-force 1980–6	Subsector of textile production (1986)			
	Consumer	Industrial	Both	Total
Decreasing	0 (0)	0 (0)	1 (87)	1 (87)
Constant	2 (71)	4 (1,357)	5 (512)	11 (1,940)
Increasing	4 (661)	2 (127)	3 (388)	9 (1,176)
Total	6 (732)	6 (1,484)	9 (987)	21 (3,203)

Note: This table excludes one firm (a specialist carpet manufacturer). Numbers refer to plants; numbers in brackets refer to employees in these plants in 1986. 'Increasing' and 'Decreasing' refer to changes in the proportion of males greater than 10% between 1980 and 1986.

Source: SCELI Rochdale Textile and Engineering Survey.

Hours of work

There was a tendency for textile employment to become even more full time after 1980, although this was not pronounced. In eighteen firms there were neither increases nor decreases of more than 10 per cent in full-time employment between 1980 and 1986. Three firms experienced an increase, whereas only one witnessed a decline of more than 10 per cent in full-time employees. These changes were neither associated with whether the firm was a subsidiary nor with whether it had been expanding or contracting. Neither were they associated with the relative size of the firm, either in 1980 or 1986, nor with the recognition of trade unions by employers.

However, there was a powerful association between the changing balance of full-time employment and the implementation of new micro-electronic technologies. Full-time employment increased by more than 10 per cent in three plants, all of which had implemented some micro-electronic technologies between 1980 and 1986. Full-time employment had not increased by more than 10 per cent in any of the plants where there had been no such technological change. Furthermore, in the eighteen plants where full-time employment had neither increased nor decreased by more than 10 per cent, fourteen of them had no micro-electronically based systems of production. Whilst there was no significant relationship between textile sector and full-time employment, it was the case that all six purely industrial textile producers were approximately constant in their employment of full-time workers, whilst two of the six purely consumer textile firms had increased their proportion of full-time workers. Therefore, there does appear, prima facie, to be a significant relationship between the trend towards more male and more full-time work and the introduction of new micro-electronic technologies and the specific subsector of textile employment.

The case-study data show that textile firms in Rochdale have increasingly adopted less flexible hours of work. Many firms have eliminated the 'swing shift' where women could work for three or four hours in the evening, and there is an increasing tendency for firms to offer two eight-hour shifts per day—either 6.00 a.m. until 2.00 p.m. or 2.00 p.m. to 10.00 p.m. Such hours of work are distinctly unattractive to many female workers, as was cor-

roborated by all our interviews with employers, trade union officials, and textile workers. This orientation towards new forms of
textile shiftwork is partly because of the continued performance
by women of domestic work, but it is also connected with changing patterns of male work. Rochdale is now a major distribution
centre and is also the headquarters of a national private bus
company. Various changes, some legislative and others economic,
have meant that lorry and coach drivers are away when children
have to be delivered to school and when they return home and
during the early evening. These considerations weigh heavily with
many women and have a significant impact on their strategies for
seeking paid work. Similar factors have been illuminated at great
length by Pyke (1987) in his analysis of household structures and
paid work in Macclesfield. He has shown that service sector
employers are increasingly adopting flexible hours of working to
suit their economic needs and to attract various forms of part-
time and full-time labour. Our research in Rochdale confirmed
these tendencies. Indeed, Rochdale's largest employer (Rochdale
Metropolitan Borough Council), with one-sixth of the employed
population, is formally committed to the development of job
sharing and this has grown within almost all of its thirteen sub-
departments. Similar patterns of flexible hours can also be seen in
the major retailing and distribution centres in Rochdale.

Why have textile firms moved over to increasingly inflexible
and conventional forms of shiftwork? Various factors interact in
this process. First, the textile industry has become increasingly
capital-intensive and sophisticated in its techniques of production. Much of this investment has been in advanced machinery
during the 1970s and 1980s. The rationale for such investment is
generally an attempt to improve the quality of output. Such
machinery requires maximum working time to be economic.
However, the persistent economic uncertainties in textiles during
the 1980s, coupled with an increasing lumpiness of demand, have
often meant that firms cannot work continuously twenty-four
hours a day. The upshot is the two eight-hour shift pattern outlined above. This has led to the elimination of part-time workers
in general, particularly the evening shifts traditionally worked by
part-time female workers. It has also led to the elimination of
night shifts traditionally worked by Asian full-time male employees (Penn, Scattergood, and Martin 1990).

Whilst such factors can explain the reduction of part-time female labour, they remain silent about the relative decline of full-time female labour in textiles. There is no evidence from our research to suggest a significant decline in demand for full-time work by women in Rochdale other than in textiles. Both our interviews with local employers and successive Censuses of Employment in the 1980s have indicated that large numbers of women still undertake full-time paid employment. However, the expansion of service sector industries and the increasing rigidity of the forms of full-time employment in textile plants interact to generate a decreasing tendency for women to seek such work in textiles, as we shall see below.

Nor is it the case that the relative elimination of women is a function of changes in payment structures or of the power of male-dominated unions as suggested by writers like Walby (1986). Women's decline within textile employment has been as strong in plants where there was no trade union recognition as in those where unions were recognized. Likewise, the proportionate decrease of women was as likely in firms that had been expanding as in those that had been contracting. Certainly, equal pay legislation has eliminated any specific cost advantage to the employment of women, but the central factor appears to be the increasing perception by women in Rochdale that textile employment is undesirable when compared with new types of paid employment in the town. Such a view has been confirmed by all our intensive case-studies of textile employers. All such firms reported increasing difficulties in recruiting women into textile occupations traditionally undertaken by women and increasing difficulty in retaining women within these categories of employment. We now turn to the issue of alternative opportunities for women.

Competition from new industries

This hypothesis suggests that women are increasingly moving from textile employment into retailing and various forms of office work within the service sector. There is no doubt that there has been a strong association between the rise of female employment in such areas and a concomitant decline in textiles. The vast bulk of the loss of manufacturing employment over this

period is accounted for by the losses in textiles, which traditionally dominated employment in the town (Penn 1985: ch. 5).
Similarly, three industries—public administration and defence,
distributive trades, and insurance and banking—accounted for
most of the increases in service employment (Table 9.4).

Clearly, female employment in Rochdale witnessed some dramatic changes between 1971 and 1987. Employment in textiles
became less female overall and less part-time female as the industry
contracted. The converse was true in most of the service industries
(Table 9.5). The critical question becomes, therefore, whether the
rise of these new forms of employment has had an effect on the
gender composition of textile employment.

The work history analysis presented in Figures 9.5 and 9.6
reveals that there has been a marked shift in the destination of
females upon first entry into paid employment in Rochdale.[8] In

TABLE 9.4 *The changing balance of employment in various industries in
Rochdale 1971–1987*

Industries	1971		1987	
	N	% women in industry	N	% women in industry
Textiles	16,100	42.7	2,700	31.4
Metalworking	8,900	18.1	7,800	19.6
Transport and communication	1,500	14.5	3,100	18.6
Distributive trades	4,500	61.3	8,300	51.1
Professional and scientific services	5,900	73.0	3,300	82.6
Public administration and defence	1,800	27.9	9,400	57.0
Insurance and banking	800	59.9	2,900	57.8
Miscellaneous services	2,500	53.3	2,000	78.4

Source: Censuses of Employment, 1971 and 1987. Numbers given to the nearest
hundred.

TABLE 9.5 *Changes in part-time female employment in selected industries in Rochdale 1971–1987*

	% change 1971–87
Textiles	−90.4
Metalworking	−1.4
Transport and communication	+70.7
Distributive trades	+77.9
Professional and scientific services; public administration and defence	+39.3
Insurance and banking	+266.4
Miscellaneous services	+15.2
Overall work-force	+11.0
Overall female work-force	+18.7
Overall female part time work-force	+33.9

Source: Censuses of Employment, 1971 and 1987.

the 1950s and 1960s almost half of women's first jobs were in textiles whereas by the 1980s virtually no females entered textiles upon initial entry into the labour market (see Figure 9.6). By the mid-1980s around 80 per cent of women entered service sector employment when they first started work in Rochdale. On the other hand, 40 per cent of men's first jobs were in textiles in 1986, which represents a significant reversal of the trend over previous decades (see Figure 9.5). Such findings reveal a major change in the initial transition from non-employment (usually full-time education) to the labour market in Rochdale in the post-war period. Women are far less likely to enter the textile industry today than at any time since the establishment of factory production in the town in the early nineteenth century.

Nevertheless, women within the textile industry remain highly likely to obtain another job in textiles after they have left textile employment (for whatever reasons). Figures 9.7 and 9.8 show that throughout the post-war period there has been a general tendency for female textile workers to remain within the industry despite redundancies or other factors that have prompted them to leave employment in specific textile plants. A similar pattern is evident for male textile workers. However, Figures 9.9 and 9.10

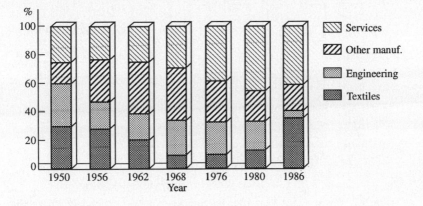

Source: SCELI Rochdale Work Attitudes and Work Histories Survey (Rochdale events only).

Fig. 9.5 Men's first job, Rochdale 1950–1986

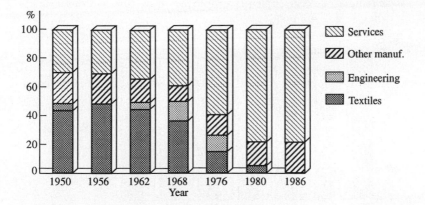

Source: SCELI Rochdale Work Attitudes and Work Histories Survey (Rochdale events only).

Fig. 9.6 Women's first job, Rochdale 1950–1986

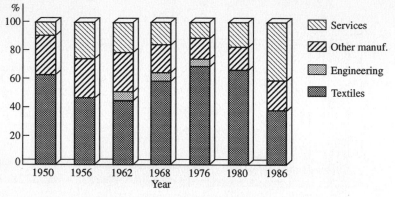

Source: SCELI Rochdale WAWH Survey (Rochdale events only).
Fig. 9.7 New jobs for men after leaving a textile job, Rochdale 1950–1986

demonstrate that few men or women move into textiles after initial entry into the labour market in sectors other than textiles. In
the period since the mid-1970s very few men or women indeed
have moved into textiles from other sectors of employment in
Rochdale.

These longitudinal results from the work history data reveal that
textiles are decreasingly the source of new female employment.
The female workers currently employed in textiles are increasingly

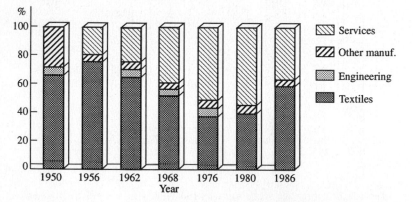

Source: SCELI Rochdale WAWH Survey (Rochdale events only).
Fig. 9.8 New jobs for women after leaving a textile job, Rochdale 1950–1986

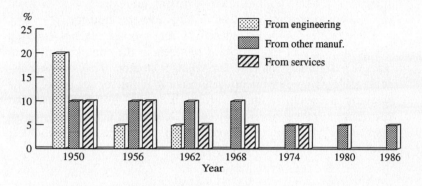

Source: SCELI Rochdale WAWH Survey (Rochdale events only).

Fig. 9.9 Percentage of men moving out of specified sectors into a new job in textiles, Rochdale 1950–1986

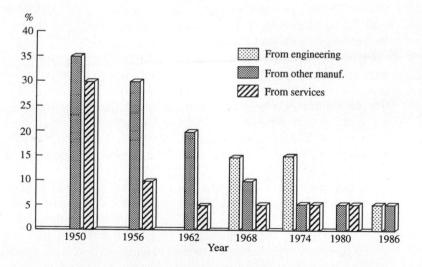

Source: SCELI Rochdale WAWH Survey (Rochdale events only).

Fig. 9.10 Percentage of women moving out of specified sectors into a new job in textiles, Rochdale 1950–1986

middle-aged and likely to have long periods of continuous or interrupted employment within the industry. Male workers are increasingly likely to begin employment in textiles, but decreasingly likely to return to textiles if they leave the industry.

There is clear evidence, therefore, that women are not entering textile employment in significant numbers in the contemporary era. This is particularly the case for younger women. They are increasingly taking employment in certain parts of the service sector, particularly in public administration, insurance and banking, and distributive trades. Such a situation represents a major historical shift in the relation between gender and employment in Rochdale.

CONCLUSIONS

The national trend towards increasingly female, part-time, and service sector employment has also occurred in Rochdale over the last twenty years. However, although Rochdale historically has been a centre for female employment as a result of the presence of widespread textile production in the town, employment in textiles has become increasingly male and decreasingly part time over the same period. This represents a major structural shift in the pattern of local employment.

One possible explanation of this development centred upon the increasing dominance of industrial textiles within overall textile employment. Whilst it is the case that traditionally industrial textile employment has been far more masculine than consumer textiles and that it remains predominantly male, this explanation was rejected. The evidence suggested rather that consumer textile employment was converging upon the traditional pattern in industrial textiles.

Another possible explanation suggested that technical change was producing an overall skilling of the work-force within textiles. Given that skilled work had traditionally been reserved for male workers and that this pattern of gender exclusion has not changed, it was hypothesized that this skilling process would produce an increasingly male work-force. However, despite the continued existence of gender exclusion around the axis of skill, there was little evidence to indicate a general expansion of skilled workers. Rather, the existing skilled categories of workers were becoming even more skilled as a result of technical change. Consequently this explanation was also rejected.

There was evidence of a significant relationship between technological change in the 1980s and increasing proportions of male and full-time employees. This is in stark contrast to the popular notion that technological change is producing an increase in the proportion of employees who are both female and part time. This was shown to be associated with major transformations in the pattern of hours provided by many textile plants. These changes involve the elimination of many traditional shifts that employed part-time workers. Such a trend, which is in complete reverse to the much-vaunted 'logic' of flexibility, is the result of the increasing capital intensity of the industry and the drive towards longer shifts on all equipment. This change in the pattern of hours is a major factor in the elimination of both female part-time and female full-time employment within textiles.

These changes are also affected by the concomitant rise of flexible patterns of hours and more attractive working conditions in other industrial sectors, especially within the service sector. It is a paradox that these 'modern' industries attract female labour in Rochdale by providing 'traditional' patterns of hours. Clearly the changing structure of employment opportunities within and without textiles interact to a considerable degree. The longitudinal analysis of the work history data revealed that almost no women work in the textile industry upon first entry into the labour market today. This is not because of a general lack of demand by local textile firms but rather because very few women in contemporary Rochdale seek employment in the textile industry. However, there has not been a massive outflow of women from textiles once they have been recruited, rather there has been a decrease in the likelihood of women entering the industry to replace those who have left.

In summary, then, the increasing masculinization of textile employment in Rochdale is partly explained by internal transformations within the industry related to technological and organizational changes and partly by the alternative opportunities provided by the burgeoning service sector. A large amount of 'women's work' has no doubt been reduced by the modernization of the textile industry, but women have also voted with their feet and are increasingly likely to opt for paid work outside textiles.

NOTES

1. The data were collected for the years 1971, 1975, 1978, 1981, 1984, and 1987.
2. The difference in classifications centres upon the reallocation of various textile-related activities to the chemical or rubber industries after 1980. The data for later years, therefore, are based upon a tighter, more restrictive definition of 'textiles'.
3. Information supplied by the Planning Department of Rochdale Metropolitan Borough Council.
4. Consumer textiles refer to the manufacture of such fabrics as cotton and man-made fibres like polyester, rayon, and acrylic, which are produced for the clothing and related sectors of consumption. Industrial textiles refer to the manufacture of such fabrics as asbestos, glass fibres, carbon fibres, and kevlar, which are produced for the automotive or aerospace sectors of industry.
5. In all, 374 questionnaires were sent to textile and engineering firms based on a list compiled by Rochdale Metropolitan Borough Council in 1984. Seventy-one questionnaires were returned, of which twenty-two were textile firms. A very high proportion of non-response was due to firms having closed down or moved away from Rochdale since 1984, and most of the rest were very small firms who did not have the time or inclination to reply.
6. These micro-electronic technologies included: micro-electronic machine control systems, machine monitoring systems, handling systems, robotics, CADCAM, and computer-based testing or inspection.
7. In 1980, industrial textiles were 73.3% male, whilst consumer textiles were 56.7% male. By 1986 the percentages were 75.9% and 62.6% respectively.
8. The work history data reported here pertain to events taking place within Rochdale.

REFERENCES

ATKINSON, J., and MEAGER, N. (1986), *Changing Working Patterns*. London, National Economic Development Office.
BRAGG, C. (1987), 'The Development of Apprentice Training in the Contemporary Rochdale Engineering Industry', Lancaster University Social Change and Economic Life Research, Working Paper No. 29.
Bureau of Labor Statistics (1974), 'Technological Change and

Manpower Trends in Six Industries', *Bulletin 1817*. Washington, DC, US Department of Labor, Bureau of Labor Statistics.

CLARKE, P. F., (1971), *Lancashire and the New Liberalism*. Cambridge, Cambridge University Press.

HARTMANN, H. (1976), 'Capitalist Patriarchy and Job Segregation by Sex', in M. Blaxall and B. Reagan (eds.), *Women and the Workplace*. Chicago, University of Chicago Press.

HARWOOD, G. (1985), *A Survey of Textile and Related Education in Britain*. London, Association of Livery Companies.

KERR, C. (1954), 'The Balkanisation of Labour Markets', in E. Wight Bakke *et al.* (eds.), *Labour Mobility and Economic Opportunity*. Cambridge, Mass., MIT Press.

LEWIS, J. (1984), *Women in England 1870–1950*. London, Routledge.

LLOYD, P. E., and SHUTT, J. (1983), *Industrial Change in the Greater Manchester Textiles-Clothing Complex*, North West Industry Research Unit, Manchester University.

LOWN, J. (1983), 'Not so much a Factory, more a Form of Patriarchy: Gender and Class during Industrialization', in E. Gamarnikow *et al.* (eds.), *The Public and the Private*. London, Heinemann.

PENN, R. D. (1985), *Skilled Workers in the Class Structure*. Cambridge, Cambridge University.

—— (1988), 'Changing Patterns of Employment in Rochdale', Lancaster University Social Change and Economic Life Research, Working Paper No. 51.

PENN, R. D. (1990), *Class, Power and Technology: Skilled Workers in Britain and America*. Oxford, Polity.

—— and LEITER, J. (1991), 'Employment Patterns in the British and US Textile Industries: A Comparative Analysis of Recent Gender Changes', in J. Leiter, M. Schulman, and R. Zingraff (eds.), *Hanging by a Thread: Social Change in Southern Textiles*. Ithaca, NY, ILR Press.

—— and SCATTERGOOD, H. (1985), 'Deskilling or Enskilling? An Empirical Investigation of Recent Theories of the Labour Process', *British Journal of Sociology*, 36/4: 611–30.

PENN, R. D. and SCATTERGOOD, H. (1987), 'Corporate Strategy and Textile Employment: A Comparison of Two British Multinationals', paper presented to the Southern Sociological Association Meeting, Atlanta, 11 Apr. Available as Lancaster University Social Change and Economic Life Research, Working Paper No. 12.

—— —— (1991), *Career Aspirations of Fifth Formers in Rochdale*. Sheffield, Department of Employment.

—— —— and MARTIN, A. (1990), 'The Dialectics of Ethnic Incorporation and Exclusion: Employment Trajectories of Asian Migrants in Rochdale', *New Community*, 16/2: 175–98.

328   R. Penn, A. Martin, and H. Scattergood

PYKE, F. (1987), 'Labour Organization and the Use of Time', Mimeo, Department of Sociology, Manchester University.

ROSE, S. (1986), 'Gender at Work: Sex, Class and Industrial Capitalism', *History Workshop,* 2/1, Spring: 113–31.

SCATTERGOOD, H. (1986), 'The Contradictions of Training Provision in Contemporary Rochdale', Lancaster University Social Change and Economic Life Research, Working Paper No. 14.

TURNER, H. A. (1962), *Trade Union Growth, Structure and Policy.* London, George Allen & Unwin.

WALBY, S. (1986), *Patriarchy at Work.* Oxford, Polity.

WARDE, A. (1986), 'The Homogenisation of Space? Trends in the Spatial Division of Labour in Twentieth Century Britain', in H. Newby (ed.), *Restructuring Capital: Recession and Reorganisation in Industrial Society.* London, Macmillan.

10

Employers, the Sex-Typing of Jobs, and Economic Restructuring

JOHN LOVERING

INTRODUCTION

According to some writers, the pervasive segregation of jobs by sex is the 'central feature' of the inequality between men and women in the world of paid work (Walby 1990: 37; Collinson *et al.* 1990: 16). Occupational sex-typing involves a dual process whereby the characteristics of employees are defined in terms of their gender (rather than individual abilities or qualifications) and jobs become known as 'men's work' or 'women's work' (Murgatroyd 1982, Bradley 1989). Sex-typing has been described as a cultural or ideological process influenced by gender roles outside the market which interacts with the market processes shaping the demand for and supply of labour at a given level of pay. Recently, research on gender segregation has focused on the nature of this interaction.

This chapter examines the recruitment practices of employers in relation to the sex-typing of jobs. Employers play a central role in occupational sex-typing because they are responsible for defining what 'jobs' entail, and how labour is allocated to them. Yet much of the work on sex-typing has been based on *inferences* about employers' practices (often drawn from interviews with employees), rather than researching them directly (for a notable exception see Collinson *et al.* 1990). We need to know more about how the sex-typing of jobs is related to the general employment strategy adopted by a company, and how this relationship is influenced by other economic factors such as their competitive position in product and labour markets, or changing technologies, as well as by aspects such as 'corporate culture'.

The 'subjective dimension' is important here, that is, how employers understand their own actions and explain or rationalize the results. It is not enough to point out that employers consistently recruit men or women to a particular job—this is well known. What is less clear is whether this outcome is something employers choose, or whether it is one with which they have to make do, and whether they are striving to consolidate or change it. It takes only a few interviews with employers to discover that, for some, the sex of the applicant is clearly a salient characteristic when recruiting, training, or promoting employees, while for others it is not an issue at all. The latter may be indifferent as to whether a particular vacancy is filled by a woman or a man, and they are likely to see the gendered patterns of recruitment within their work-force as the result of extra-market rather than intra-market influences. To ask about the subjective perceptions of recruiters is to place the 'agency' of employers at the centre of the picture. As we shall see below, this approach reveals the coexistence of powerful gender ideologies alongside 'economic rationality' in employers' decision-making.

ECONOMIC RESTRUCTURING

This chapter sets employers' practices in the context of economic restructuring. According to many observers, the 1980s saw not only fluctuations in the level of activity as the economy moved from recession to boom and back to recession, but more profound changes in the structure of economic organization and in managerial ideology (Green 1989). A major debate over the nature of contemporary economic change has centred on whether these changes amount to the demise of 'Fordism' and the passage to 'post-Fordism' (Piore and Sabel 1984, Lipietz 1987, Harrison and Bluestone 1988, Jessop *et al.* 1988, Lovering 1990*a*, Pollert 1987). The term Fordism has a number of meanings. In the sociological literature it is associated with mass production, a routinized labour process, career hierarchies in which labour is recruited from internal promotion (referred to as internal labour markets), and institutionalized collective bargaining. Post-Fordism designates the break-up of each of these, as companies seek increased flexibility in production and employment of labour, or in order to compete in volatile and fragmenting markets.

Despite the proliferating literature on this subject, the implications of a transition away from Fordism for gender segregation have received relatively little systematic attention. One hypothesis might be that a shift to flexible employment would favour women, particularly part-timers, because they are usually a more casual work-force than men. Another is that a movement away from rigidly structured internal labour markets, which have tended to favour men in upper positions, would free up recruitment at this level for suitably qualified women (Walby 1990, Crompton and Sanderson 1990: 71). At the level of managerial ideology, the adoption of a 'market forces' policy could imply more meritocratic criteria for recruitment and promotion, and the destruction of many male privileges. In theory at least, the shift to post-Fordism might be expected to produce a progressive weakening of traditional patterns of gender segregation.

However, different commentators have drawn different conclusions about the usefulness of the 'post-Fordism' model and about the extensiveness of the alleged transition in the UK (Pollert 1987, Green 1989, Lovering 1990*b*). In Britain in the 1980s many long-established employers did indeed restructure their market focus, production technology, and employment practices. But the emergence or expansion of many of the newer industries, especially in services, seems to have been based on quite conventional employment practices (see Elger 1989, Green 1989, Lovering 1990*a*). The British reality cannot be described in terms of a straightforward transition from Fordism to post-Fordism, and the gender implications of economic restructuring remain open. The lesson here is that an empirical study of occupational sex-typing should recognize both the continuities and the changes involved in the current restructuring.

METHODOLOGY

The Social Change and Economic Life Initiative provided the opportunity to examine these issues through the thirty employer case-studies. Face-to-face interviews provided a quantitatively modest but qualitatively rich data set on firm and work-force characteristics and employers' perceptions on a range of issues.[1] This chapter draws on some of this material to examine the employers' role in perpetuating, modifying, and resisting gender inequalities in employment. A set of case-studies will be described focusing on four main types of employer chosen to reflect differences between manufacturing and service establishments and continuities and changes in employment patterns. Since both of the latter processes are to be found in manufacturing and services, we have a fourfold typology of employers as follows (all names are pseudonyms):

Case-studies by company type

1. Manufacturing; continuity in employment patterns:
   'Bakers' (confectionery);
   'Bishops Engineering' (mechanical engineering).
2. Manufacturing; innovations in employment patterns:
   'Mandex' (pharmaceuticals);
   'Computrol' (computer equipment).
3. Services; continuity in employment patterns:
   'Ministry' (departmental office);
   'Cottage Hospital' (health).
4. Services; innovations in employment patterns:
   'Motormeals' (catering);
   'Winco' (retail);
   'Stanford Research' (research and development).

In the analysis below, each group of case-studies begins by describing the company and its main pattern of gender segregation. This is followed by observations on recruitment and promotion, selection criteria, and employers' perceived reasons for the pattern of gender segregation, with particular reference to gender stereotypes. Pressure for change from the product and labour markets and employers' strategies for implementing change are then discussed.

THE SWINDON LABOUR MARKET

Swindon is a particularly interesting location in which to study the connections between job sex-typing and economic restructuring. Situated on the border of the prosperous outer south-east and the expanding south-west, Swindon has been a beneficiary of the concentration of economic activity in the South of England in the last decade. New manufacturing and service employers opened, although some large industries and service sectors left over from earlier periods remained important.

In the nineteenth century Swindon was a 'company town' dominated by the huge workshops of the Great Western Railway, established in 1941 (Hudson 1967). There were few industrial jobs for women. As late as the 1940s, the labour market participation of women was only two-thirds the UK average. In the 1950s a series of companies moved to the town, in parallel with massive immigration of London 'overspill'. Typically, men moved to prearranged jobs in local engineering factories, bringing their spouses with them. The number of jobs for women grew slowly until the 1970s, then female employment expanded by 27 per cent, nine times the national rate. The transformation continued, less dramatically, into the 1980s. Between 1981 and 1984 female employment grew more than twice as fast as nationally (5 per cent and 2 per cent respectively).

Swindon is now part of Britain's relatively prosperous 'Sunbelt' (Bassett *et al.* 1989). In the mid-1980s employment was biased towards motor vehicles and railway engineering, but also towards finance and insurance. High-technology industries and producer and consumer service industries were well represented, but the largest single industry was wholesale and retail distribution, accounting for a fifth of jobs in the travel-to-work area. Table 10.1 shows the main sectors of employment in Swindon by the period of their arrival in the town.

Women are concentrated in the same set of service industries as in Britain as a whole (Webb 1989, EOC 1988). In manufacturing there are three men to every woman. In services the ratio falls to around one, and in hotels and catering, or banking and finance, women just outnumber men. In the education and health sectors, there are two and four women respectively to every man.

TYPE 1: MANUFACTURING; WITH CONTINUITY IN EMPLOYMENT PATTERNS ('BAKERS LTD.' AND 'BISHOPS ENGINEERING')

These two companies arrived with the first wave of manufacturing investment in Swindon. Both still occupy factory premises built in the 1940s, and much of the plant and equipment is of similar vintage. 'Bakers' is a family-owned food manufacturer. In

TABLE 10.1 *Summary of Swindon labour market: industrial sectors representing different waves of investment*

	Employees	Location quotient[a]
Large-scale 'traditional' manufacturing *(main employers since 1950s)*		
Motor vehicles	2,400	2.2
Rail engineering	2,400	2.1
Mechanical engineering	2,700	0.9
Public sector (main employers *since 1940s/1950s)*		
Health	4,300	0.9
Education	5,600	0.9
'High-technology' industries and *'modern' services (main employers* *since 1970s)*		
Finance	5,000	2.1
Electronics/pharmaceutical	2,200	1.6
Wholesale distribution	6,500	1.8
Retail distribution	10,200	1.3
Insurance	2,300	2.5
Research and development	1,000	2.2
Total	44,600	
Total Swindon employment	72,702	

[a] Industrial specialization in the local labour market as compared to the national labour market. A location quotient of 2, for example, would indicate that the proportion of local employment in the industry in question is twice the national average.

Source: Annual Census of Employment 1984, travel-to-work area data.

the 1960s most employees were the wives of men who worked at Pressed Steel, a large motor plant less than a mile away. The company now sells over three-quarters of its output to a major national retail chain, which sells the products under its brand name. Demand is seasonal, employment peaking at 500 in December, and falling to 300 in January. 'Bishops' is all that is left of the local plant of a leading British engineering company which set up in Swindon in 1945 and was one of its largest post-war employers. It makes handling equipment for the nuclear industry. Employment at the time of interview was about 120 and was expected to remain roughly constant.

In both factories women and men are almost completely separated into different jobs and locations. Three-quarters of 'Bakers'' work-force are women, confined almost entirely to shop-floor production work. Men are concentrated in dispatch, mixing ingredients, and loading and unloading the ovens. Two men tip trays of cooked cakes and tarts on to a conveyor belt, and then the women take over. About twenty women sit along the belt adding fillings and decorations by hand, tidying and finishing the product, and loading the packing machines. All the bakery assistants (the basic grade) are women. All the mixers, the next highest job category, are men. The mixers work in an open room, handling ingredients which arrive in a range of sacks and containers. The bakery assistants work in a production hall adjacent to, but separated from, the mixing room. There is a marked contrast between the internal labour markets open to women and men. Men are expected to advance to mixer chargehand, while women have the chance to become quality controllers. They are responsible for meeting the pace of the machine, overcoming bottlenecks, and checking quality. The ratio of mixer chargehand to mixer is about 1 : 6, and that of quality controller to bakery assistant about 1 : 20. A couple of women have entered management, one from outside and another from the owning family, none from the shop-floor. The remaining 80 per cent of management are men.

The production process in 'Bishops Engineering' entails manual assembly of batches of equipment in a workshop. All forty-two fitters and machinists in the shopfloor, thirty engineers, draftsmen, inspectors, managers, and directors are men. The ten women work exclusively in the office as clerks and typists.

Gender and recruitment practices

In both companies recruitment for most of the year is limited to replacement of staff lost through turnover, although in 'Bakers' there is seasonal recruitment near Christmas. This means that both employers are looking for staff who will fit into well-defined jobs and get on with existing employees. The major reason given for the predominance of women or men in particular jobs in

'Bakers' was that only one sex usually applies for vacancies. Since virtually all shop-floor recruitment is via word of mouth, applicants tend to assume in advance that vacancies are for either 'men's' or 'women's' jobs. Similarly, gender segregation in 'Bishops Engineering' was seen as an effect of the pattern of labour supply. In the rare event of a vacancy the usual channel of recruitment is word of mouth, and the supply of applicants is invariably gendered in accordance with tradition. No women have applied for other than clerical and typing jobs in recent years.

Selection criteria and gender stereotypes

For both managements the rationale for the sex-typing of jobs lay in the allegedly inherent characteristics of men and women. In 'Bakers' it was said that 'the work suits women', 'it's fast and fiddly, and needs dexterity', 'the product can be easily damaged, and men simply do not have a sufficiently delicate touch'. On the other hand, 'men get bored and want more masculine jobs'. Gender is also perceived to influence work-place interactions; since the work-force is already predominantly female, new recruits should ideally be biased towards women to maintain the smooth running of the plant. Single-sex teams 'co-operate better'.

The female bias in employment was said to influence the length of shifts; the plant runs on three shifts: 8.00 a.m.–12.15 p.m., 1.15–5.00 p.m., and 5.00–9.00 p.m. The employer's experience was that 'women will work a morning shift but not all day, they need to get home to cook a meal for their husbands or collect the children'. Although wages are modest, there is no shortage of demand for jobs on the morning shift and the evening shift, because 'they leave the rest of the day free'.

The management of 'Bishops Engineering' said that the sex-typing of jobs was a legacy of traditional patterns in the engineering industry, buttressed by the conservative attitudes of existing staff; 'a woman in the design office would be a disturbance', while on the shop-floor 'the foreman wouldn't hear of it'. The low level of turnover and recruitment meant that the institutionalization of these attitudes had not been challenged.

Pressures for change

Both companies occupied old-fashioned premises and there was little evidence of major recent investment in plant and equipment.

Over the previous five years 'Bakers' had recovered from stagnation, but at the cost of dependence on one customer (described as 'the real boss here'). This customer had given advice and a loan to help 'Bakers' meet its requirements by becoming more flexible. Production runs had shortened, and the firm took on responsibility for a higher share of costs, and sourced packaging itself to the customer's specification. After almost a decade of minimal investment, a modest rate of technical change was evident. Two new production line machines had been installed in the last two years, employing six (female) assistants each in place of the previous twenty. Further technical change of this kind was expected. There was no intention to alter the sex-typing of jobs, but, given the reduced demand for bakery assistants, this implied a fall in the demand for women, but not men. Speeding up output, the company was thus preserving the gendered pattern of jobs while reducing female employment.

'Bishops Engineering' was surviving in an unusual niche market in which little had changed for two decades. Management said the company was 'living in the past', and was likely to continue so to do for some time. The new parent company showed no intention of making any major investment, or significantly changing the product range, labour process, technology, or style of management. It was content to maintain the unit as a source of regular if modest income, through sales to long-established public sector customers in the defence and energy sector. So long as the existing cohort of senior staff was still in place, some having worked at that plant for thirty years, little was likely to change, including the gender pattern of employment.

Summary

These two companies offer examples of the traditional pattern of occupational segregation by sex in manufacturing industry (Bradley 1989). A rigid sexual division of labour was sustained on the demand side by low turnover to established posts, and on the supply side by a widely recognized gender-labelling of vacancies.

The informal nature of recruitment and selection perpetuated this situation. Neither employer was under pressure to change selection practices, although they operated in very different markets. The outcomes of recruitment were felt to be acceptable not only to themselves, but also to most employees, and to the somewhat insignificant trade unions present in both plants. 'Bishops' encountered little to disturb the sex-typing of jobs, and was able to act in accordance with the conventional stereotyping of gender characteristics in terms of both technical and social skills. 'Bakers' found that the sex-typing of jobs and stereotyping of employee characteristics was no barrier to adapting to changing market circumstances, although technical change was altering the sex ratio of the work-force. Gender differentiation was associated with the exclusion of women from one factory, and their decline in the other.

TYPE 2: MANUFACTURING, WITH INNOVATIONS IN EMPLOYMENT PATTERNS ('MANDEX' AND 'COMPUTROL')

These companies opened in Swindon during the wave of industrial modernization in the late 1960s. Both are hailed in local promotional literature and the media as 'high-technology' industries. They are particularly interesting because they offer examples of a tendency towards change in employment patterns.

'Mandex', a subsidiary of a European corporation, employs 550 people in the design and manufacture of prescription pharmaceuticals. Research and development takes place in laboratories adjacent to the factory, built in 1971. Production is mechanized in batches in a clean-room environment. The main customers are in the public health sector (general practitioners and hospital pharmacists) in the UK and abroad. Since it produces potentially dangerous drugs, there is a greater than usual emphasis on security.

'Computrol' is owned by a UK subsidiary of a US multinational and assembles electronic equipment for the computer industry. Identical machinery is manufactured for the American market in a sister US company. 'Computrol' occupies a ten-year-old one-storey unit on an industrial estate. Assembly is in batches, using bought-in components. The unit employed 330 workers at the time of interview and this was expected to rise to about 500 over the following five years.

Gender and recruitment practices

In both firms men and women can be found in most job categories, but each one is predominantly male or female, and some are one sex only. In both companies all the secretarial staff are female. No men have ever applied. Some of the senior 'Mandex' staff, such as accountants, sales staff, and scientists, are female (although the two women scientists are outnumbered by nineteen men). The proportion of women drops with each step up the management hierarchy, the top management being all male. All fifty-six senior packaging staff are women, while all twenty-seven craft grades are men. All the part-time workers at Mandex are women, including six laboratory assistants. A 'twilight shift', recently introduced to increase the utilization of equipment, employs thirty-six women from 4.30 to 9.30 p.m. Twenty-six technicians load, set, and 'mind' the large machines, and all but one is a man. In the tablet department, however, the machine minders are all women.

At 'Computrol' all the seventy craftspeople and fifteen technologists and scientists are men, but a printed circuit board (PCB) unit is staffed entirely by women. The latter fall in a job category of their own, and earn the lowest shop-floor wage (£140 p.w.). Men making sub-assemblies earn £148 p.w., and skilled wiremen earn £154 a week basic. There are two women in this third group, both promoted from the PCB unit.

Selection criteria and gender stereotypes

Both employers felt that the 'social aspects of work', rather than the technical skills required, were the critical influence on the sex-typing of jobs. In both plants work is done largely in teams. Employers said that on the shop-floor single-sex teams have been found to be more efficient. The presence of a member of the minority sex is disruptive; 'a young man in a mainly female team will be mothered by them, while older men always try to assert their authority'. Supervision is also easier with a single-sex team. Line supervisors of female teams at 'Mandex' are women, 'because female staff will work for them'. In the few cases where teams are mixed (as for example in the 'Mandex' laboratories) staff are engaged on 'individual jobs' rather than 'line jobs'. In both establishments production jobs are primarily filled through word of mouth. Applications come exclusively from one sex, because 'people round here know what the jobs are and who does them'.

A further influence shaping the sexual distribution of shop-floor jobs was the alleged natural or social characteristics of men and women. 'An experienced middle-aged mum' was a recognized ideal as a quality controller in one plant. In 'Mandex' packaging is done by women because of 'the inherent femininity of the job' (the packaging of tablets by hand was traditionally done by women, and this tradition has continued even though it is now done mechanically). 'Computrol's' PCB unit is exclusively female because 'women are more nimble fingered . . . ladies tend to do it better than men'. Although dexterity is measured by a test given to all applicants before they are taken on, no men have ever applied.

All the 'Mandex' part-timers are women because 'on the whole women are more interested', 'men prefer to be the full-time breadwinner'. The few men who had been taken on part-time in the past had 'usually been moonlighting, or had other part-time jobs'. 'Computrol' employs no part-timers, because of a strategy to nurture a stable full-time skilled work-force. The employer recognized that one unintended consequence of this was to exclude women almost entirely from the shop-floor apart from the PCB unit.

In both establishments the occupations of scientist, engineer, and technician were overwhelmingly male. Graduate vacancies are filled by men, because few women apply. This was regretted by both employers, who perceived a national lack of appropriately qualified women. The greater sex equality amongst pharmacists was similarly explained by supply; more women choose pharmacy. 'Mandex's' laboratory technicians were almost equally balanced between men and women, mostly recruited direct from local schools.

Both employers were striving to recruit women to 'non-traditional jobs' such as engineering and scientific grades; but the result had not been very significant. 'Computrol' had taken on a female apprentice toolmaker who 'could strip an engine as fast as any of the boys'. But she left after only two years. The only female draftsperson had moved sideways into sales. The employer explained both cases as the result of the pressures of being an isolated woman in a male-dominated environment. The managers of 'Mandex' told similar stories concerning shop-floor jobs. One employer commented that gender divisions at that level tended to be self-fulfilling because 'few women want to do something different . . . it's especially hard for women round here from a working-class background to stand out and do an isolated job amongst men'.

Pressures for change

In recent years the markets for both these companies have become much more competitive, more 'bespoke', and more unpredictable. For 'Mandex' the market has also become more seasonal, mirroring the cycles of public expenditure in the UK and overseas. Stock levels have fallen from an average of twelve weeks' supply to eight weeks'. Part-time work is growing in importance because it allows management to meet peak demands by extending the morning shift into the afternoon, or, more rarely, vice versa: 17 per cent of employees are part time, and the share is rising slightly. 'Computrol's' strategy for adapting to changing market conditions is to maintain the competitiveness of product design and the technical quality of the product. Stock levels were already minimal. Remaining 'up-market' depended above all on securing and retaining the necessary skilled staff and, unlike 'Mandex', on decasualizing the work-force.

Both employers were anxious to increase and retain qualified staff, and both expected and hoped to increase the number of women employed, but the uneven supply meant that they expected to fill the bulk of new vacancies with men. 'Mandex' had sponsored graduate pharmacy students for some years, and the last two were women. 'Computrol' sponsored students on undergraduate electronics sandwich courses, but all were male.

Summary

As prominent members of Swindon's much-publicized high-technology community, these establishments offer some clues to future trends in growing sectors of the local and national economy. Faced with shortages of labour in key manual grades, both aimed to be leaders amongst local employers (a local joke had it that the subsidized 'Mandex' staff canteen was the best restaurant in Swindon). But the attempt to attract labour was only associated with modest innovations in job sex-typing.

In both plants, gender segregation was prominent and highly conventional. From the employers' point of view, this was fundamentally the result of external factors over which they had little influence. Despite the 'high-technology' image, many traditional jobs survived complete with their gender-labels. Company efforts were shifting the balance of the sexes in some higher-level grades, where labour shortages were critical. However, the modest trend towards reduced gender inequality at this level coexisted with the continuation of gender imbalance in 'lower' grades where prospects for women were largely determined by the expansion or contraction of part-time work. The overall pattern of job sex-typing reflected the coexistence of national shortages of qualified women applicants, and plentiful supplies of unqualified local women looking for part-time jobs.

In summary, then, despite many differences between the two stable traditional firms ('Bakers' and 'Bishops') and the two high-technology restructuring firms ('Mandex' and 'Computrol') the patterns of gender segregation were very similar. Gender stereotypes were profound and there were few signs of change.

TYPE 3: SERVICES; CONTINUITY IN EMPLOYMENT PATTERNS ('THE MINISTRY' AND 'THE COTTAGE HOSPITAL')

These organizations are representatives of the public service sector which has been one of the major employers of women since the 1950s. The 'Ministry' is an office and customer service unit of a major government department, employing 190. The 'Cottage Hospital' employs around 150.

Gender and recruitment practices

In both establishments there is marked 'vertical segregation' by gender. The manager and two deputy managers at the 'Ministry' are all men, but women predominate at the 'coal-face' clerical grades. This employer felt himself to be constantly struggling to retain female staff who wish to leave for domestic reasons or to move to better paid and more attractive office jobs in Swindon's growing finance sector. It was said that 'most women come in at age 16 and leave at around 25'.

Women's employment in the 'Cottage Hospital' closely reflects the pattern of part-time work: 94 per cent of nursing grades are women. All the five full-time nursing assistants are men, while all the thirteen part-timers are women. Three of the kitchen staff are part-time women workers, alongside two men full-timers. All secretarial and typing staff are women; 95 per cent of the female staff are married. Male nurses, who are appreciably older than the female nurses, are concentrated in mental care. Mental nurses received £210 a year on top of the basic nurse's rate of £7,300 to £8,600. The supply of nursing, administrative, and domestic staff is good because 'there are a lot of companies moving into the area which employ men who bring their spouses with them'.

Selection criteria and gender stereotypes

Both employers saw core tasks as inherently gendered: 'something women are good at.' Both required employees to perform a 'caring' role and this was seen as a definite influence in favour of women. In the work of the 'Ministry', the conscientiousness of employees directly affects the quality of the service given to clients. Young women (16–18) were perceived to be better in this respect than boys of the same age, 'they are more mature, and more confident and have no delusions of grandeur'. A few jobs are deemed unsuitable for women, such as home visits to difficult and possibly dangerous clients.

The female bias amongst nurses was also explained with reference to the distinctive abilities of women and men. Hospital work is 'messy, with lots of dirt, grot and muck'. This deters men, who are 'less able to put up with it'. Young girls are said to be especially good with geriatric cases. But another factor cited was linked to women's position in the home. Asked why nursing has been almost a female monopoly, with the exception of psychiatric nursing, our informant (a woman) was forthright: 'it's traditional and it's low paid, it would be impossible for a man to support a family on a nurse's wage'. About 15 per cent of staff (mostly young nurses, married with mortgages) worked other jobs in their 'spare time', through nursing agencies. This was a new development reflecting the decline in real pay; five years previously none of the staff had second jobs.

Pressures for change

The changing local labour market posed new problems for the 'Ministry'. Most of the new jobs in Swindon were designed for the kind of women it traditionally employed. The employer felt that the training in office work provided in the 'Ministry' made his staff highly marketable, but governmental limits on pay meant that he was unable to counter the attractions of other local employers. He had adopted a defensive strategy to reduce losses by promoting as many young women into executive officer grades as soon as possible; 'bringing them on ensures we get five years' good service out of them before they leave to have families'.

The number of men applying for entry grades had increased in both establishments. This was thought to be partly because local employment prospects for men, in contrast to women, had become more difficult. Some of the men in basic grades were there because they 'hadn't been successful getting into the finance sector'. However, these men have a good chance of rising to higher ranks, which can compensate for the relatively unattractive early stages. In the 'Cottage Hospital' male nurses were said to be much more likely to want to climb the ladder, and less likely to stay as long in basic grades or in one hospital. In the longer term, however, the supply of young nurses to the Hospital is threatened by the declining flow of school-leavers.

The future of employment in both establishments was intimately dependent on government policy. The lack of autonomy at establishment level meant that the scope for responding to a tightening local labour market by changing employment practices was limited. There were few signs of any tendency to change the gender composition of jobs. Both employers had begun to look favourably on women applying to return after child-rearing. At the 'Ministry', applications for reappointment from former employees are encouraged. Recruitment of returners is likely to increase in the future, but they will mostly return to established gendered jobs.

Summary

Gender segregation in these two organizations was deep-rooted historically and rationalized by gender stereotypes. These patterns were being sustained against a background of high turnover rates. Changing market pressures were not leading to any radical restructuring of tasks or of employment patterns in these establishments. The absence of major innovations in employment practices was attributable partly to the lack of local management autonomy, the result of direct control by central government. However, both employers were anxious about the future, and the wastage of young female labour was leading to new efforts to recruit older women. The main adjustment therefore consisted in focusing on women at a different stage in their life cycle.

TYPE 4: SERVICES, INNOVATIONS IN EMPLOYMENT PATTERNS ('MOTORMEALS', 'WINCO', AND 'STANFORD RESEARCH')

The establishments in this group fall within the most rapidly expanding sectors in the local and the national economy. 'Motormeals' is a large motorway service station, employing 286 full-time staff, thirty-nine part-timers, and up to a few dozen casuals. 'Winco' is the Swindon outlet of a well-known national high-street retailer. This is the biggest store of the thirty-five in the district, and employers forty full-timers and sixty part-timers. 'Stanford Research' is a prestigious quasi-governmental establishment engaged in teaching and research and development serving high-technology industry. It occupies a large country estate and employs 380 staff, of whom nine are part time (mostly clerical staff). Formerly controlled by the Ministry of Defence, it is now an autonomous campus of a major technological institute. In the 1980s it expanded dramatically, student numbers doubling and the value of research contracts increasing five times in three years. Employment increased by fifty in the year before interview.

Gender and recruitment practices

Most of 'Motormeals' kitchen staff are men (twenty-three out of twenty-six) but cooks are equally balanced between men and women. Front-of-house workers (in the shops) are mostly women and virtually all office staff are female. Many are part time, nearly all of these being women. All the 'Winco' stockroom staff are men, although their supervisor is a woman. Most sales assistants are female. There are thirteen full-time female sales assistants and three males, and forty-four part-time female sales assistants, including 'Saturday girls' (and two Saturday boys). The store manager is a man but the section manager is a woman. Nationally, 'Winco' employs three male and seventy female personnel managers. At 'Stanford Research' all but fourteen of the 200 teaching and research staff are men, but all the routine and almost all the senior clerical grades are filled by women.

Selection criteria and gender stereotypes

In each case the main reason for the pattern of gender segregation was that applications for vacancies usually came from one
sex. Men in general do not apply for shop work or (to a lesser
degree) catering. Very few women apply for research and development vacancies. Each employer maintained that social attitudes beyond the work-place played the major role in the gender
distribution of jobs. The experience of management of 'Motormeals' was that 'boys don't like their mates to see them clearing
tables . . . boys seem more happy in back-of-house jobs, behind
the scenes'. The work was described by the employer as like
much of the catering industry, 'hot, sticky, mucky and low-paid',
and this is why it is performed mainly by women. The only jobs
that were exclusively male were on the forecourt nightshift, and
this was for reasons of personal safety.

'Winco's' management found that 'women are usually better
on the tills than men', 'men don't like to be seen at the tills, the
Saturday boys don't like to be seen by their mates. They prefer
to be shelf-fillers.' The one exception was the audio section. This
reflected the tendency for boys to associate with the 'mechanical
aspect' of these goods. 'Stanford Research' offered another
aspect of social stereotyping; one reason given for the bias
towards men was the military environment; 'the subject-matter is
one that women tend not to get involved in'. This was seen as a
factor further limiting the supply of female graduates in the relevant disciplines (i.e. physics, mathematics, electronics, etc.).
However, the Professor of Ballistics was a young woman.

Pressures for change

One of the most interesting features of this group was that each
employer was making conscious efforts to change employment
patterns. 'Motormeals' and 'Winco', both consumer service
industries, felt that their competitive position depended on the
quality of the interaction between front-line staff and customers.
Both adopted a strategy of moving 'up-market' by establishing a
new customer identity, and distancing themselves from the popular image inherited from the past. In 'Motormeals' this entailed
increasing the range and quality of services and goods provided,
and above all improving the quality of service. In 'Winco' on the

other hand the number of product lines was being reduced, but, like 'Motormeals', the new strategy required a new emphasis on the 'calibre' of staff.

Both 'Motormeals' and 'Winco' had introduced new recruitment and promotion policies nationally to attract and retain good quality staff. It was said that in the past many of the staff were people who could not get better jobs, but this would not be the case in future. A central aspect of the new employment policy is increased internal recruitment to all grades above entry points. Internal recruitment ladders are being created where there were none before 'to give people something to aim for'. Branch managements are required to upskill the work-force, to encourage staff to recognize that success 'is all about sales'. All 'Winco' staff (full-time, part-time and Saturday staff) will be trained in customer care and buying and product policy. The 'dead-end jobs' in the previous employment structure are now seen as inhibiting flexibility and efficiency. 'Winco' staff identified as having potential may be taken on to a Rapid Development Programme.

Recruitment criteria and methods are also changing: one company decided to stop recruiting through the Jobcentre altogether, as the quality of applicants is now thought to be unsuitable. 'Winco' prefers applicants with O-levels for sales assistants vacancies, and A-levels for sales supervisors. Graduates are to be sought for section managers. In 'Winco' and 'Motormeals' social skills, such as the ability to work in teams and leadership qualities, have risen to the top of the selection criteria, well above formal qualifications.

'Stanford Research' operates in a very different industry, yet some of its labour market problems and responses are similar. The deregulation of research in defence and high-technology industry has exposed it to new competitors, and the solution is seen in securing high-quality staff. The traditional civil servant style of management has been abandoned and a more entrepreneurial approach adopted towards both markets and employees. Staff are encouraged to set up consultancies and spin-off independent companies, and salary levels vary widely as a result. The employer has an explicit commitment to staff development, designed to maximize the potential of staff at all grades and engender flexibility and efficiency. This implies increased use of external labour markets for recruitment to higher research posts, where informal academic and business contacts are important. At the same time, internal recruitment for higher clerical and support-staff positions is increasing. In these grades the employer is hoping to overcome deepening local labour shortages by 'growing its own' staff.

Summary

The pattern of gender segregation in these establishments is highly orthodox; high-level jobs are overwhelmingly held by men, and low-paid and part-time jobs by women. This can be attributed partly to a conventional sex-labelling of jobs, partly to differences in the supply of men and women for low-paid and part-time work, and the uneven acquisition of qualifications and experience. However, this 'snapshot' misses out some possibly important developments in the employers' strategies. These are especially interesting because establishments of this type are likely to play an increasingly important role in the labour market nationally.

In each case it had been decided at the highest corporate level that competitiveness depended on the 'quality' of staff. The definition of quality varied according to case (skills in presentation of products to customers, efficiency of service, ability to generate research funding, etc.). The quality imperative was being translated into changes in recruitment and promotion practices. Each firm was investing in staff acquisition of social skills, company-specific knowledge, and technical qualifications. In some cases they were creating what were in effect new jobs, broadening the bundle of tasks entailed (e.g. by adding sales functions) and upskilling the staff performing them. This was associated with the provision of new career structures, which implicitly, and sometimes explicitly, challenged the existing sexual distribution in employment. The potential improvement in the opportunities for women to advance to positions above entry grades ran alongside some increase in the proportion of men in basic grades formerly dominated by women. But the scope of these equalizing tendencies was limited by the partial and modest character of the new career structures.

CONCLUSION

The case-studies confirm that sex-typed jobs are to be found in new and old companies, expanding and contracting industries. They also show that gendered employment patterns are associated with a variety of employment practices. Sometimes they are linked to the fact that recruitment is targeted on one sex, but often they reflect asymmetries in the supply of male and female workers. Both these mechanisms of gendering may operate simultaneously within the same establishment.

Sex-typing was most marked and least challenged in long-established companies in older industries, especially manufacturing assembly (Type 1) and public sector services (Type 3). It was somewhat less sharply defined in the 'restructuring' manufacturing companies (Type 2), and in the emergent service sectors (Type 4). The employers varied in the degree to which the existing pattern was regarded as desirable. Some were content to carry on as before, others perceived a need for change, and, of the latter, some were actively attempting to bring about change through new employment strategies.

The introduction made reference to the debate over the extent to which Fordism is giving way to post-Fordism. In the terms of this scenario our first group of companies ('Bakers' and 'Bishops Engineering') correspond most closely to Fordism. Traditional selection criteria and recruitment practices, combined with low turnover, sustained the sex-typing of jobs. The third group (the 'Ministry', the 'Cottage Hospital') represent a public sector variant of Fordism. Jobs here were also highly sex-typed, and routinized recruitment and promotion practices sustained the gender bias. The second and fourth groups correspond to companies breaking away from Fordism to some degree, but this was not universally associated with radical innovations in employment practices.

If 'Mandex' and 'Computrol' represent companies which are moving away from Fordism, they also represent overwhelming continuity in the pattern of gender segregation. But the fourth group ('Motormeals', 'Winco', and 'Stanford Research') revealed more complex and ambivalent tendencies. These are new and expanding companies in the most rapidly expanding industries, moving towards flexible product strategies and some new employment practices. As such they appear to come closest to the post-Fordist stereotype. In terms of tasks and status some new jobs were being created, and this was associated with attempts to reduce or modify the sex-typing of employment. In particular, the creation of new internal career structures implied an increase in the proportion of jobs filled by sex-neutral meritocratic selection criteria, opening up the prospect of some weakening in gender segregation.

On this evidence, contemporary economic restructuring in Britain is characterized by considerable diversity in employment practices. Although it does not imply a systematic trend towards sexual equality (or 'post-Fordism') in the labour market as a whole, this diversity *is* opening up some fields of employment where sexual inequality is less sharply defined. However, the significance of these 'liberated zones' is limited. First, the new meritocratic career paths appear to be confined to a limited range of jobs and industries. The emergent new internal labour markets are relatively short or 'truncated', covering jobs characterized by modest pay and status, as illustrated in the 'Ministry', 'Motormeals', or 'Winco' (see also Crompton and Sanderson 1990). Secondly, new jobs may still incorporate some degree of sex-typing. In service industries where competitiveness depends on presentation to the customer the product market offers an incentive for sex-typing. Employers find it profitable to allow, or encourage, the 'appropriate' gendering of jobs (e.g. preferring women as waitresses, customer counter staff, care workers, etc.).

Thirdly, changes in the pattern of demand create a potential for greater equality that is realizable only to the extent that women can take advantage of it. Labour supply differences limit the equalizing impact of new career structures at the intermediate level and of the expanding external labour markets at the élite end of the occupational scale. Moreover, historical experience suggests that a persistent employment bias tends to crystallize into a recognized sex-typing of jobs (Bradley 1989, Scott 1986). Finally, employer intentions are one thing, outcomes may be another. In the case-studies the immediate impact of employers' stated policies on gender segregation had been extremely modest.

THEORETICAL IMPLICATIONS

Different theories of occupational segregation offer different interpretations of employers' practices (Dex 1985, Hakim 1988). In the mainstream 'women's dual role' perspective employers are regarded as rational economic agents whose practices are gendered only to the extent that they are forced to adapt to social pressures beyond their control, rooted in the given 'preferences' of men and women and manifested in the supply side of the labour market (Chiplin and Sloane 1976).[2] The feminist 'patriarchy-at-work' perspective attributes to employers a more active role in generating and reproducing gendered outcomes, either through their own autonomous sexist preferences or in collusion with male employees (Walby 1986, 1990). Some of the case-study material could be used to support either of these positions. However, an explanation which focused on either the supply or demand side exclusively would only account for some sex-typing processes, and fail to come to grips with others. So much is familiar (Dex 1985, Collinson *et al.* 1990). The contribution of this study has been to show the salience of both these dimensions in the current economic restructuring.

JOB SPECIFICATIONS AND GENDER CHARACTERISTICS

The case-studies show that, when they recruit to recognizably sex-typed jobs, employers attempt to match some features of the job with the alleged characteristics of one of the sexes. The case-studies show that a range of job features may be selected as the basis for this 'matching'. Perhaps the most familiar is the *tasks* entailed in the job. Here sex-typing is based on alleged differences between men and women in terms of physical abilities (e.g. nimble-fingered women and clumsy men), or psychological and social characteristics (women's tolerance for unpleasant or boring work versus men's resistance or sullen resentment). If tasks fail to provide a basis for sex-typing, the *social relations* within which they are performed may still provide such a rationale (e.g. the belief that single-sex teams are more efficient). The *hours of work* form a third basis for sex-typing (women's preference for part-time work). Other job features such as pay, status, and prospects may also serve this purpose (e.g. the view that low-paid and 'dead-end' jobs are more suitable for or acceptable to women).

These job features can function as bases for sex-typing only because recruiters can connect them to some widely shared characterization of men and women as possessing distinctive technical and social skills. Economic theory suggests that screening job-seekers on the basis of group characteristics is rational for a recruiter wishing to minimize costs (Chiplin and Sloane 1976). However, it says nothing about where employers get their ideas about which group an individual belongs to, and what the groups' characteristics are. These are products of 'culture' or 'ideology'.

In other words, job features work as segregation devices because they allow employers to mobilize gender stereotypes. Stereotypes are one aspect of gender ideologies, which Cockburn has defined as the prevailing systems of belief and power which define 'what a man "is", what a woman "is", what is right and proper, what is possible and impossible' (Cockburn 1986: 85). Gender ideologies designate 'the appropriate meaning of labour for men and women' (Barrett 1980: 98).[3] Putting gender ideologies on the agenda raises three related but logically separate theoretical problems; the historical origins of the particular ideology, the mechanisms through which it is sustained in the present, and the social function it performs (which social relations are sustained, whose interests protected, etc.).

This modest study only begins to address the second question; that of the mechanisms of perpetuation. It shows some ways in which gender ideologies are embedded in, and sustained by, employers' practices. Further research would be necessary to trace the connections between employers' practices and the corroboration, reinforcement, or undermining of these ideologies themselves.

ECONOMIC RESTRUCTURING AND THE MOBILIZATION OF GENDER IDEOLOGIES

The case-studies suggest that some tendencies in the current restructuring conservatively capitalize on and reinforce existing gender ideologies, while others challenge prevailing assumptions and practices. Most jobs continue to be sex-typed in conventional ways, and market forces do not often lead employers to resist this (where they do, as in scarce professional occupations, the quantitative impact is small). Some less gendered spheres of employment can be found, especially in the emergent services and restructuring manufacturing industries, but it should not be assumed that all jobs in 'new' industries are free from sex-typing influences. Many newer industries are not built on new jobs, and older jobs which have become firmly sex-typed continue to predominate in the labour market as a whole. Moreover, even genuinely new jobs are often susceptible to sex-typing. Given the complex and sometimes contradictory nature of gender ideologies (Segal 1991), employers can often find an appropriate stereotype to bring into play to meet new circumstances in the product market. The case-studies suggest a shift from an emphasis on female 'dexterity' to an emphasis on female personal skills (the 'friendly waitress', the 'attractive shop assistant', the 'conscientious' personnel manager), for example.

The current economic restructuring seems likely to bring about a modification in the rationale for sex-typing, and some new gendering patterns in the new jobs, rather than a general decline in sex-typing. This is because market forces are necessarily 'mediated by other factors' (Crompton and Sanderson 1990: 6). Gender ideologies, activated in employers' recruitment practices, play a fundamental role in the social construction of the labour market.

NOTES

1. The School for Advanced Urban Studies (SAUS) team participating in the SCELI Swindon employer survey consisted of Martin Boddy, Gill Court, Kevin Doogan, and John Lovering. The SCELI household interviews generated the names of local employers. A telephone survey provided basic data on this sample, from which a group of thirty were selected for face-to-face interviews. Interviews were sought with personnel managers, but where their functions were performed by production managers these were interviewed instead. Interviews averaged an hour and a half, and transcripts were returned to the interviewees for their comments. Interviews were followed by a tour of the work-place.
2. On women's preferences see Chs. 1, 2, and 6 in this volume.

3. The term ideology has had a number of meanings (Eagleton 1991) and a controversial role in feminist theory (Brenner and Ramas 1984, Segal 1991). Some object that to invoke ideology in an explanation is to 'relegate gender to the superstructure' (Walby 1986: 34). But this is only the case if ideology is used in its implausible and 'vulgar Marxist' sense, as derivative of economic relationships (Eagleton 1991). More usefully, ideology can refer not only to normative values, but to the institutionalized practices (coercive as well as consensual) through which they are embedded in subjectivity and in social relations (Scott 1986: 155). Gender ideologies can be regarded as a particular category of beliefs as to the difference between men and women, which impact on practice with the effect of sustaining male domination (Cockburn 1986: 85; see also Collinson *et al.* 1990: 134).

REFERENCES

BARRETT, M. (1980), *Women's Oppression Today: Problems in Marxist Feminist Analysis*. London, Verso.

BASSETT, K., BODDY, M., HARLOE, M., and LOVERING, J. (1989), 'Living in the Fast Lane: Economic and Social Change in Swindon', in P. Cooke (ed.), *Localities*. London, Unwin Hyman.

BRADLEY, H. (1989), *Men's Work, Women's Work*. Cambridge, Polity.

BRENNER, J., and RAMAS, M. (1984), 'Rethinking Women's Oppression', *New Left Review*, 144: 33–71.

CHIPLIN, B., and SLOANE, P. J. (1976), *Discrimination at the Workplace*. Cambridge, Cambridge University Press.

COCKBURN, C. (1986), 'The Relations of Technology', in R. Crompton and M. Mann (eds.), *Gender and Stratification*. Cambridge, Polity.

COLLINSON, D., KNIGHTS, D., and COLLINSON, M. (1990), *Managing to Discriminate*. London, Routledge.

CROMPTON, R., and SANDERSON, K. (1990), *Gendered Jobs and Social Change*. London, Unwin Hyman.

DEX, S. (1985), *The Sexual Division of Work*. Brighton: Wheatsheaf.

EAGLETON, T. (1991), *Ideology: An Introduction*. London, Verso.

ELGER, T. (1989), 'Flexible Futures? New Technology and the Contemporary Transformation of Work', *Work, Employment and Society*, 1/4: 528–40.

EOC (Equal Opportunities Commission) (1988), *Women and Men in Britain: A Research Profile*. London, HMSO.

GREEN, F. (1989), (ed.), *The Restructuring of the UK Economy*. Hemel Hempstead, Harvester Wheatsheaf.

HAKIM, C. (1988), 'Women at Work: Recent Research on Women's Employment', *Work, Employment and Society*, 2/1: 103–11.
HARRISON, B., and BLUESTONE, B. (1988), *The Great U-turn: Corporate Restructuring and the Polarising of America*. New York, Basic Books.
HUDSON, K. (1967), *An Awkward Size for a Town*. Newton Abbot, David & Charles.
JESSOP, B., BONNETT, K., BROMLEY, S., and LING, T. (1988), *Thatcherism: A Tale of Two Nations*. Oxford, Polity.
LIPIETZ, A. (1987), *Miracles and Mirages*. London, Verso.
LOVERING, J. (1990a), 'A Perfunctory Kind of Post-Fordism: Economic Restructuring, Spatial Change, and Labour Market Segmentation', *Work, Employment and Society*, additional special issue, May: 9–28.
—— (1990b), 'Fordism's Unknown Successor: A Comment on Scott's Theory of Flexible Specialisation', *International Journal of Urban and Regional Research*, 14: 159–74.
MURGATROYD, L. (1982), 'Gender and Occupational Stratification', *Sociological Review*, 30/4: 574–602.
PIORE, M. J., and SABEL, C. (1984), *The Second Industrial Divide*. New York, Basic Books.
POLLERT, A. (1987), *The 'Flexible Firm': A Model in Search of a Reality (or a Policy in Search of a Practice?)*. Warwick Papers in Industrial Relations No. 19.
SCOTT, A. (1986), 'Industrialisation, Gender Segregation and Stratification Theory', in R. Crompton and M. Mann (eds.), *Gender and Stratification*. Cambridge, Polity.
SEGAL, L. (1991), *Slow Motion: Changing Masculinities, Changing Men*. London, Virago Press.
WALBY, S. (1986), *Patriarchy at Work*. Oxford, Polity.
—— (1990), *Theorising Patriarchy*. Oxford, Blackwell.
WEBB, M. (1989), 'Sex and Gender in the Labour Market', in I. Reid and E. Stratta (eds.), *Sex Differences in Britain*. Aldershot, Gower.

METHODOLOGICAL APPENDIX

The Social Change and Economic Life Initiative

DUNCAN GALLIE

1. INTRODUCTION

The Social Change and Economic Life Initiative (SCELI) focused on six local labour markets—Aberdeen, Coventry, Kirkcaldy, Northampton, Rochdale, and Swindon. These were selected to provide contrasting patterns of recent and past economic change. In particular, three of the localities—Coventry, Kirkcaldy, and Rochdale—had relatively high levels of unemployment in the early and mid-1980s, while the other three had experienced relatively low levels of unemployment.

In each locality, four surveys were carried out designed to provide a high level of comparability between localities: the Work Attitudes/ Histories Survey, the Household and Community Survey, the Baseline Employers Survey, and the 30 Establishment Survey. The interview schedules for these surveys were constructed collectively by representatives of the different teams involved in the research programme. In addition a range of studies was carried out that were specific to particular localities. These were concerned to explore in greater depth a number of themes covered in the comparative surveys.

A distinctive feature of the research programme was that it was designed to provide for the possibility of linkage between the different surveys. The pivotal survey (and the first to be conducted) was the Work Attitudes/Histories Survey. This provided the sampling frame for the Household and Community Survey and for the Employers Baseline Survey. The Baseline Survey in turn provided the listings from which organizations were selected for the 30 Establishment Survey.

The field-work for the Work Attitudes/Histories Survey and for the Household and Community Survey was carried out by Public Attitudes Surveys Research Ltd. The Baseline Employers Survey was a telephone survey conducted by Survey and Fieldwork International (SFI). The interviews for the 30 Establishment Survey were carried out by members of the research teams.

TABLE A.1. *The Work Attitudes/Histories Survey 1986: achieved sample*

	Aberdeen	Coventry	Kirkcaldy	Northampton	Rochdale	Swindon	TOTAL
Eligible addresses	1,345	1,312	1,279	1,400	1,350	1,321	8,007
Achieved sample							
Main sample	997	990	1,011	957	987	955	5,897
Booster sample	48	23	—	65	18	60	214
Total interviewed	1,045	1,013	1,011	1,022	1,005	1,015	6,111
Response rate (%)	78	77	79	73	74	77	76

2. THE WORK ATTITUDES/HISTORIES SURVEY

This survey was concerned primarily with people's past work careers, their current experience of employment or unemployment, attitudes to trade unionism, work motivation, broader socio-political values, and the financial position of the household.

Two pilot studies were carried out in the preparation of the Work Attitudes/Histories Survey, testing questionnaire items, the placing of the work history schedule, interview length, and the contact procedure. The main field-work was conducted between June and November 1986. The objective was to secure an achieved sample of 1,000 in each of the six localities. As can be seen in Table A.1, the target was marginally exceeded, providing an overall sample of 6,111.

The sampling areas were defined in terms of the Department of Employment's 1984 Travel to Work areas (TTWA), with the exception of Aberdeen. In Aberdeen, where the TTWA was particularly extensive and included some very sparsely populated areas, the Daily Urban System area was used to provide greater comparability with the other locations.

A random sample was drawn of the non-institutionalized population aged 20–60. The electoral register was used to provide the initial selection of addresses, with probabilities proportional to the number of registered electors at each address. A half open-interval technique was also employed, leading to the identification of a small number of non-registered addresses in each locality. Doorstep enumeration of 20- to 60-year-olds was undertaken at each address followed by a random selection using the Kish procedure of one 20- to 60-year-old at each eligible address.

To provide sufficient numbers for analysis, it was stipulated that there should be a minimum of 150 unemployed respondents in each locality. A booster sample of the unemployed was drawn in the localities where this figure was not achieved through the initial sample. The booster sample was based on a separate random sample of addresses, with a higher sampling fraction in the wards with the highest levels of unemployment. As with the main sample, addresses were selected from the electoral register. But, for the selection of individuals, only the unemployed were eligible for inclusion. This booster sample was implemented in five of the six localities, producing a total of 214 respondents. Response rates for the combined main and booster sample were approximately 75 per cent in each of the localities, ranging from 73 per cent in Northampton to 79 per cent in Kirkcaldy (see Table A.1).

Where appropriate, weights have been used to take account of the booster sample, using the estimates of the proportion of unemployed available from the initial sample. There are also weights to provide a Kish adjustment for household size and to correct for an over-representation of women in the achieved sample (3,415 women compared with 2,696 men). The sex weight assumes equal numbers of men and women in the relevant population, as is shown to be almost exactly the case by examination of census data.

The interview consisted of two major sections. The first was a life and work history schedule in which information was collected about various aspects of the individuals' labour market, family, and residential history over the entire period since they had first left full-time education. Information about family and residential history was collected on a year grid basis. Information about labour market history—including spells of unemployment and economic inactivity—was collected on a sequential start-to-finish date-of-event basis. In the case of 'employment events' further information was collected about *inter alia* the nature of the job, the employer, hours of work, number of employees, gender segregation, and trade union membership. The second part of the interview schedule was a conventional attitudinal schedule, with a core of common questions combined with separate subschedules designed specifically for employees, for the self-employed, and for the unemployed and economically inactive.

While the greater part of the questions in the schedules provides direct comparability between localities, some scope was given for teams to introduce questions that would be asked only in their own locality (or in a subset of localities). This usually involved teams introducing a broader range of questions for investigating one or more of the themes covered in the common questions.

3. THE HOUSEHOLD AND COMMUNITY SURVEY

In 1987 a follow-up survey was carried out involving approximately one-third of the respondents to the 1986 Work Attitudes/Histories Survey. This focused primarily on household strategies, the domestic division of labour, leisure activities, sociability, the use of welfare provision, and attitudes to the welfare state. The survey was conducted in each of the localities, with the field-work lasting between March and July. The survey produced an achieved sample of 1,816 respondents, of whom 1,218 were living in partnerships and 588 were living on their own. Where applicable a range of questions was asked of partners as well as of the original respondents.

The sampling lists for the survey were generated from computer listings of respondents to the Work Attitudes/Histories Survey who had agreed to being reinterviewed. To ensure that a sufficiently large number of the unemployed respondents from the Work Attitudes/Histories Survey were reinterviewed, it was decided to specify that, in each locality, approximately 75 of the households in the follow-up survey would be from households where the respondent was unemployed at the time of the Work Attitudes/Histories Survey. For sampling, the lists were stratified into four groups, separating the unemployed from others and people who were single from those with partners. The sampling interval was the same for those of different partnership status, but different sampling intervals were used for the unemployed and for others to obtain the target numbers of people who had been unemployed at the time of the first survey.

In the event, 87 per cent of respondents (ranging from 84.8 per cent in Coventry to 89.7 per cent in Aberdeen) had indicated that they were willing to co-operate in a further phase of the research. Since the sampling areas were once more defined in terms of local labour markets, there was a further attrition of the original eligible sample due to people leaving the area (between 7 per cent and 9 per cent, depending on the locality). Response rates (for those that had agreed to be reinterviewed and were still in the area) were 75 per cent or better in each locality, ranging from 75 per cent in Rochdale and Northampton to 77 per cent in Kirkcaldy. The structure of the achieved sample is given in Table A.2. It should be noted that the table describes respondents with respect to their characteristics at the time of the Work Attitudes/Histories Survey, 1986, since this was the relevant factor for the sampling strategy. The economic and partnership status of a number of respondents had changed by the time of the second interview. For instance, while 1,223 of these respondents were classified as having had partners in 1986, the number with partners at the time of interview in 1987 was 1,218.

The questionnaire for this survey consisted of three sections: an interview schedule including questions of both respondents and partners, a respondent's self-completion, and a partner's self-completion. There was a shorter separate schedule for single people. The questionnaires included an update of the life and work histories of the original respondent and a full work history was collected for partners interviewed. The self-completion for respondents and partners was used at different points in the interview to collect independent responses from partners where it was thought that issues might be sensitive or that there was a danger of contamination of responses. The respondents and their partners filled in the relevant sections of the self-completion in the presence of the interviewer, but without reference to each other. The great majority of questions were common to all localities, but, again, a limited number of locality specific questions were allowed.

The *Time Budget Survey*. The data available through the Household and Community Survey interview was extended through a linked time

TABLE A.2. *The Household and Community Survey 1987: achieved sample by characteristics at time of Work Attitudes/Histories Survey*

	Aberdeen	Coventry	Kirkcaldy	Northampton	Rochdale	Swindon	TOTAL
Total issued	390	400	399	404	402	394	2,389
Achieved sample							
Employed/non-active with partner in 1986	153	162	167	163	155	175	975
Employed/non-active, single in 1986	68	54	62	60	68	48	360
Unemployed with partner in 1986	42	42	40	40	45	39	248
Unemployed, single in 1986	41	44	40	38	32	38	233
Total interviewed	304	302	309	301	300	300	1,816
Response rate (%)	78	76	77	75	75	76	76

budget survey. This project was directed by Jonathan Gershuny of the University of Oxford. The final five minutes of the Household and Community Survey were devoted to introducing the time budget diaries to the individual or couple present. The diaries were designed to cover a full week starting from the day following the household interview. They required natural-language descriptions of the diarist's sequences of activities to be kept on a fifteen-minute grid, for the whole week, together with any secondary (i.e. simultaneous) activities and a record of geographical location and whether or not others were present during the activities carried out. Interviewers left behind addressed, reply-paid envelopes for return of the diaries at the end of the diary week.

Forty-four per cent of those eligible (802 of the original 1,816 respondents and 533 of their 1,218 partners) completed usable diaries for the whole week. This low rate of response, though not unexpected from a postal survey, raises the issue of the extent of non-response biases. In anticipation of this problem, a number of questionnaire items were included in the original Household and Community Survey interviews which were intended to 'shadow' or parallel evidence from the diaries (i.e. questions about the frequency of participation in leisure activities and about the distribution of responsibilities for domestic work). An analysis of the two sources of data showed that the distribution of frequencies of the questionnaire responses of those who failed to complete diaries was very similar to the distribution of questionnaire responses for those who did keep diaries. From this we may infer an absence of bias at least with respect to estimates of these leisure and unpaid work activities (for a fuller account, see Gershuny 1990).

4. THE EMPLOYER SURVEYS

The implementation of the Baseline Employers Survey, which was a telephone survey, was the responsibility of Michael White of the Policy Studies Institute. The schedule was drawn up in collaboration with a working party of representatives from the different teams involved in the SCELI programme.

The survey involved a sample of establishments. The major part of the sample was drawn from information provided from the Work Attitudes/Histories Survey about people's employers. Each of the 1,000 individuals interviewed in each locality was asked, if currently employed, to provide the name and address of the employer and the address of the place of work. The sample was confined to establishments located within the travel-to-work areas that formed the basis of the research programme. Approximately 12 per cent of establishments initially listed

TABLE A.3. *The Baseline Employer Survey*

	Aberdeen	Coventry	Kirkcaldy	Northampton	Rochdale	Swindon	TOTAL
Sample from survey	345	280	229	287	233	273	1,647
Booster sample	52	54	32	51	55	39	283
Out of area	1	30	16	27	11	4	89
Eligible	396	304	245	311	277	308	1,841
Interviews	308	203	174	209	177	240	1,311
Response rate (%)	77.7	66.7	71.0	67.2	63.9	77.9	71.2

could not be included in the sample because of insufficient information or closures. The sample covers all types of employer and both the public and the private sectors.

This method of generating a sample differs from a straight random sample drawn from a frame of all establishments. The latter would have resulted in a very large number of small establishments being included, while there was considerable theoretical interest in medium-sized and large establishments as key actors in the local labour market. The method used in SCELI weights the probability of an establishment's being included by its size: the greater the number of employees at an establishment, the greater its chance of having one or more of its employees included in the sample of individuals (and hence itself being selected).

The above method is closely related to sampling with probability proportional to size (p.p.s.); however, there are generally too few medium-sized and large establishments to generate a true p.p.s. sample. To increase the numbers of these medium-sized and large establishments, an additional sample of private sector employers with fifty or more employees was drawn from market research agency lists, supplemented by information from the research teams. The booster consisted of all identifiable establishments in this size range not accounted for by the basic sampling method. The sampling method, then, was designed to be as comprehensive as possible for medium-sized and larger employers. In practice, 70 per cent to 85 per cent of the sample by different localities were provided through the listings from the Work Attitudes/Histories data, while only 15 per cent to 30 per cent were from the booster sample. The structure of the achieved sample is presented in Table A.3. The sample so generated under-represents smaller, and over-represents larger, establishments, but provides adequate numbers in all size groups. It is also approximately representative of employment in each area, but it is possible to use weighting to achieve an even more precise representation of local employment. This was carried out using tables of employment by size group of establishment within industry group within each local labour market, from the 1984 Census of Employment (by courtesy of the Statistics Division, Department of Employment).

There were five stages of piloting over the summer of 1986, particularly concerned to develop the most effective contact procedure. The main field-work period was from October 1986 to February 1987. The overall response rate was 71 per cent, ranging from 64 per cent in Rochdale to 78 per cent in Aberdeen and Swindon.

The interview schedules focused particularly upon occupational structure, the distribution of jobs by gender, the introduction of new technologies, the use of workers with non-standard employment contracts, relations with trade unions, and product market position. Different questionnaires were used for large and small organizations, with fewer questions being asked of small organizations. There were also minor variations in the schedules for public and private organizations, and for different industries. The four industry subschedules were: (1) manufacturing, wholesale, haulage, extractive, agriculture; (2) retail/hotel, catering/personal, and other consumer services; (3) banks, financial and business services, and (4) construction. These were designed to provide functionally equivalent questions with respect to product market position for different types of organization.

In each locality, there were follow-up interviews in at least thirty establishments—the 30 Establishment Survey—designed in particular to explore the motivation behind particular types of employer policy. While steps were taken to ensure that cases were included across a range of different industries, the composition of the follow-up sample was not a random one, but reflected team research interests. In contrast to the other surveys, the data from this survey should not be assumed to be generalizable to the localities.

5. THE RELATED STUDIES

Finally, most teams also undertook at least one smaller-scale further enquiry in their localities, each being designed exclusively by the team itself and funded separately from the three main surveys. These Related Studies sometimes built upon previous fieldwork a team had undertaken in its locality, and upon the resulting network of research contacts. Adopting for the most part documentary, case-study, or open-ended interviewing techniques of enquiry, the Related Studies dealt with special issues ranging from local socio-economic history to present-day industrial relations trends.

In one sense, then, the Related Studies can be thought of as free-standing research projects. At the same time, however, in interpreting the findings from a related study, a team could take advantage of the extensive contextual data provided by the main surveys. What is more, thanks to their use of methodologies permitting enquiry in depth and over time, the Related Studies could throw more light on many of the quantitative (and at times somewhat summary) findings of the main surveys. Several Related Studies were of particular value in validating and extending core-survey findings.

INDEX